FOCUS ON SUCCESS

The new edition

Ausgabe Soziales

David Clarke

Michael Macfarlane

Steve Williams

Focus on Success – The new edition: Ausgabe Soziales wurde geplant und entwickelt von der Redaktion Moderne Fremdsprachen des Cornelsen Verlags, Berlin.

Verfasser:	David Clarke, Witten; Michael Macfarlane, Oxford; Steve Williams, Melbourne
Berater:	Rolf Bastian, Wetzlar; Philipp Fehrenbach, Nürtingen; Thomas Pache, Euskirchen; Elke Uthoff, Osnabrück; Sibylle Vogel, Erfurt; Sybille Weiß, Mönchengladbach; Kathrin Wendling, Kamenz
Projektleitung:	Jim Austin
Verlagsredaktion:	Andreas Goebel, Laura Spratling
Außenredaktion:	Christine House
Redaktionelle Mitarbeit:	Lauren Chexal, Christiane Grosskopf, Stefanie Heimann, Leah Holroyd
Wörterverzeichnisse:	Yovana Gruissem, Fritz Preuss, Edda Vorrath-Wiesenthal
Bildredaktion:	Jürgen Frey, Gertha Maly
Layout und technische Umsetzung:	Petra Eberhard Grafik Design, Berlin
Umschlaggestaltung:	werkstatt für gebrauchsgrafik, Berlin
Illustrationen:	Marcin Nowakowski, Mariusz Zabdyr, Oxford Designers & Illustrators

Erhältlich sind auch:

Workbook	978-3-06-020271-3
Handreichungen für den Unterricht mit CD-ROM und Audio-CDs	978-3-06-020274-4
Vocabulary Practice Book	978-3-06-020280-5

www.cornelsen.de

Die Webseiten Dritter, deren Internetadressen in diesem Lehrwerk angegeben sind, wurden vor Drucklegung sorgfältig geprüft. Der Verlag übernimmt keine Gewähr für die Aktualität und den Inhalt dieser Seiten oder solcher, die mit ihnen verlinkt sind.

1. Auflage, 11. Druck 2022

Alle Drucke dieser Auflage sind inhaltlich unverändert und können im Unterricht nebeneinander verwendet werden.

Druck und Bindung: Livonia Print, Riga

ISBN: 978-3-06-020229-4

PEFC zertifiziert
Dieses Produkt stammt aus nachhaltig bewirtschafteten Wäldern und kontrollierten Quellen.

www.pefc.de

PEFC/12-31-006

VORWORT

Liebe Lehrerinnen und Lehrer,

Focus on Success – The new edition: Ausgabe Soziales ist konzipiert für Lernende an Fachoberschulen und Berufskollegs. Es setzt Englischkenntnisse auf dem Niveau des mittleren Abschlusses voraus und bereitet auf die neuesten Prüfungen zur Erlangung der Fachhochschulreife vor. Das Lehrwerk führt zur Stufe B2 des Gemeinsamen europäischen Referenzrahmens.

Focus on Success – The new edition: Ausgabe Soziales ist ein komplett neu erarbeitetes Lehrwerk und bietet neue, interessante Texte, aktuelle Themen und einen auf die Lehrpläne und Prüfungen abgestimmten Aufgabenapparat. Die bewährte Struktur wurde beibehalten: Auf den *Refresher Course* folgen 12 *Main Course*-Units, die einheitlich aufgebaut sind:

> *Focus:* Der Einstieg ins Thema – bildgesteuert, anregend und motivierend.

> Text A (*Personal perspectives*) betrachtet das Thema der Unit aus einer persönlichen Perspektive.

> Text B (*The bigger picture*) behandelt die gleichen Aspekte in ihrer Wechselwirkung mit Gesellschaft, Politik und Umwelt.

> *Social options* bieten Zusatzmaterialien zur Erweiterung und individuellen Schwerpunktsetzung aus einem sozialen Blickwinkel.

Die Übungen, die auf die Texte folgen, schulen eine Vielzahl von *Skills* und trainieren darüber hinaus alle Aufgabentypen, die in den Abschlussprüfungen vorkommen.

Die Grammatik befindet sich am Ende jeder Unit in einem *Grammar checkpoint*.

Die 12 *Social Topics* im Anhang behandeln aktuelle Entwicklungen im Sozialbereich. Dabei stehen abwechslungsreiche Textarten, praxisrelevante Themen und handlungsorientierte Aufgaben im Mittelpunkt.

Der Anhang bietet neben einer *Grammar summary* umfangreiche Wörterverzeichnisse und einen Leitfaden zu Lernstrategien.

Liebe Schülerinnen und Schüler,

Focus on Success – The new edition: Ausgabe Soziales ist Ihr neuer Begleiter auf dem Weg zur Fachhochschulreife. Verschaffen Sie sich einen kurzen Überblick über das Buch, und Sie werden darin alles finden, was Sie für einen erfolgreichen Englischunterricht benötigen.

Sie möchten …

> Ihre Grundkenntnisse aufpolieren, um für die Arbeit mit längeren Texten besser gerüstet zu sein?
Kein Problem, der *Refresher Course* bringt Grammatik und Wortschatz wieder auf Vordermann – in sechs Units, jeweils anhand eines interessanten Magazinartikels.

> eine grammatische Form nachschlagen?
Dann schauen Sie einfach hinten in der *Grammar summary* oder der Liste der *Irregular verbs* nach.

> Tipps und Hilfen für den Umgang mit schwierigen Texten und kniffligen Aufgaben bekommen?
Dann werden Sie in dem Teil *Skills* im Anhang fündig – hier finden Sie zahlreiche Tipps, die Ihnen helfen, das Lernen effektiver zu gestalten.

> Vokabeln so lernen, dass Sie sie nicht gleich wieder vergessen?
In der *Unit word list* im Anhang ist der Lerneffekt gleich doppelt: Neben der deutschen Übersetzung lernen Sie auch Wörter mit gleicher oder gegensätzlicher Bedeutung, kurze und bündige Umschreibungen usw.

> Ihren Grundwortschatz wiederholen?
Die *Basic word list* bietet Ihnen alle wichtigen Wörter – thematisch geordnet, damit Sie nicht nur einzelne Wörter, sondern ganze Wortfelder auffrischen können.

Viel Spaß und Erfolg mit dem Buch!

Autoren und Redaktion

CONTENTS

Refresher Course

Main Course

4

Free-time activities

I enjoy listening to music and sending text messages to my friends. I don't like computer games, but I sometimes visit chat rooms.

We've just discovered LAN parties. They're cool. But we like dancing and going to the movies, too.

How do I spend my free time? Well, chilling out and hanging around with my friends, I suppose.

1 TALKING ABOUT YOURSELF

How do you spend your free time? Just chilling out, or doing something more active like sport? Use the language in the speech bubbles and the ideas in the box to talk about what you do.

> chilling out ǀ clubbing ǀ dancing ǀ doing sport ǀ fishing ǀ going to LAN parties ǀ
> going to the movies ǀ hanging around with friends ǀ listening to music ǀ making/mixing
> music ǀ playing computer/video games ǀ playing online poker ǀ reading ǀ riding ǀ
> sending text messages / images with a mobile ǀ shopping ǀ surfing the net ǀ
> phoning friends ǀ visiting chat rooms ǀ watching TV/DVDs

2 CARRYING OUT A SURVEY

A Ask other people what they like – or don't like – doing in their free time.

What's your favourite free-time activity?
What do you like doing most, … or …?
Which (activity) do you prefer, … or …?
Do you enjoy reading / doing a sport / …?
Do you belong to a sports club?
How much time do you spend playing computer games / … every day/week?

B Now carry out a survey. Which are the three most popular activities in your class?

According to the media, young people today spend too much of their free time just sitting in front of televisions or computers. But is this true? We asked four young people to describe their free-time activities. Read what they had to say.

< DANA *I spend most of my free time working for the Red Cross.* I really feel that I'm doing something worthwhile, not just sitting in front of the box! This week we're working with the homeless. That may not sound like fun, but I get a lot out of it. My brother Lee says I should enjoy life while I'm young, but he doesn't know what he's talking about. I'm sure that I'm having more fun than he is at the moment!

> LUCY *Free time? Are you joking?* I work three evenings a week and all day Saturday too – I don't have much time for anything else. And then
5 there's my mum. She says I can only have a job if my schoolwork doesn't suffer. So when I get home after work I usually do my homework and go to bed. When I go out, I enjoy looking round
10 the shops with my friends. But that doesn't happen very often, I'm afraid.

< RAVI *I'm playing in the first team of my football club* this season, so that takes up most of my free time. We train twice a week, you see, and then I usually have matches at the weekend. When I'm not playing football, I hang around with my friends or just chill out. I really like clubbing, but that's difficult in the football season. The coach expects us to keep fit and I don't want him to take me off the team.

> SAM *What do I do in my free time?* Well, I enjoy playing computer games most, I suppose, but I don't like the violent stuff. I prefer the games that
5 test your skill against other players. I often network with other players online or go to LAN parties. They're really cool. I make a lot of new friends that way. At the moment, we're planning a
10 big international LAN party. People are coming to it from all over the place.

3 LOOKING AT THE TEXT

Join the beginnings (1–6) to the endings (a–f) to make sentences about the texts.

1 An international LAN party could
2 The four people all have
3 One of the four people doesn't have
4 Dana's voluntary work with the Red Cross
5 Competitive computer games have the
6 Some parents say that part-time jobs

a can have a bad effect on schoolwork.
b makes her feel good about herself.
c much free time because she has a job.
d advantage of bringing people together.
e be a great way to make new friends.
f very different interests.

4 WORKING WITH WORDS

A Find words/expressions in the texts above to fit the definitions.

DANA
1 adjective: useful, valuable
2 people without a permanent home
3 certain

RAVI
4 noun: time of year during which something happens
5 noun: competitive game
6 verb: relax by doing nothing

LUCY
7 opposite of 'being serious'
8 verb: become worse
9 another expression for 'I'm sorry to say'

SAM
10 verb: like one thing more than another
11 noun: ability to do sth
12 verb: English for German *vernetzen*

B **Complete the sentences with six of the words/expressions from exercise A.**
They are not necessarily in the same order. Sometimes you must change the form.

1 My team has an important ... today.
2 A lot of employers say social ... are as important as qualifications.
3 Can you call back later, please? ... Ms Barton is in a meeting at the moment.
4 When parents work too hard, family life always ...
5 DVDs are OK, I suppose, but I ... to see films at the cinema.
6 Can't you do something ... instead of just watching TV all the time?
7 Petrol prices always go up during the holiday ...
8 You're ...! You don't really expect me to work all weekend, do you?

C **Say who or what the ⭕circled⭕ words refer to in the texts.**

EXAMPLE   > I don't want ⭕him⭕ to take me off the team. (*Ravi*)
             > *'Him' refers to Ravi's football coach.*

1 ... but I get a lot out of ⭕it.⭕ (*Dana*)
2 ... ⭕he⭕ doesn't know what he's talking about. (*Dana*)
3 ⭕I⭕ usually have matches at the weekend. (*Ravi*)
4 The coach expects ⭕us⭕ to keep fit. (*Ravi*)
5 ⭕She⭕ says I can only have a job if ... (*Lucy*)
6 But ⭕that⭕ doesn't happen very often, I'm afraid. (*Lucy*)
7 ⭕They⭕'re really cool. (*Sam*)
8 At the moment, ⭕we⭕'re planning a big international LAN party. (*Sam*)

5 LOOKING AT GRAMMAR: SUBJECT AND OBJECT PRONOUNS

Subjektform	Objektform
I	me
you	you
he/she/it	him/her/it
we	us
you	you
they	them

A **Replace the underlined words with suitable subject pronouns.**

1 John and Ann often go cycling at the weekend.
2 Does Jack belong to a sports club?
3 Sharon spends too much time in chat rooms.
4 Paul scored the goal from a distance of 30 metres.

B **Now use object pronouns.**

5 A lot of people enjoy going to LAN parties.
6 I'm lucky. My parents pay for my mobile.
7 Jack phones Sharon five or six times a day.
8 We meet Joshua in town every Friday.

6 LOOKING AT GRAMMAR: SIMPLE PRESENT

Form

*Lucy and her friends **enjoy** shopping.* *Sam **plays** computer games.*	wie der Infinitiv, außer in der 3. Person Singular *(he, she, it)*, die auf *-s* endet
*Lucy **wishes** she had more free time.* *Ravi **tries** to keep fit.* *Dana **has** more fun than her brother **does**.*	Besonderheiten der 3. Person Singular: > endet das Verb auf *-ch, -sh, -s, -x*, folgt *-es* > endet das Verb auf Konsonant + *-y*, wird die Endung zu *-ies* Sonderformen: *do – **does**, go – **goes**, have – **has**, be – **am** / **are** / **is***
*I **do not** / **don't** want to lose my place on the first team.* *Sam **does not** / **doesn't** like violent games.*	**Verneinung:** *do not / don't* bzw. *does not / doesn't* (3. Person)
*How **do** you **spend** your free time?* ***Does** Lucy **work** on Saturdays?*	**Fragen:** *do* bzw. *does*

Gebrauch

*I'm still at school and I also **have** a job.* *Sam often **goes** to LAN parties.*	für Dauerzustände und wiederholte, oft regelmäßige Ereignisse bzw. Handlungen

> Das *simple present* steht häufig mit den folgenden Zeitangaben:
>   – *always, often, sometimes, rarely / seldom* (selten), *never*
>   – *generally* (im Allgemeinen), *normally, regularly, usually* (gewöhnlich)
>   – *every day / week / month / …, every morning / afternoon / …*
>   – *on Mondays / Tuesdays / …*
>   – *on weekdays / during the week, at weekends / the weekend / …*

> Kurze Adverbien der Häufigkeit wie *often, never* usw. stehen unmittelbar vor dem Vollverb.
>   *Lucy **never** goes out during the week.*

A **Put the verbs into the correct form of the simple present. Be careful about negatives and questions.**

1 My mate Josh …[1] (*spend*) a lot of time playing online poker, but he …[2] (*not play*) for money.

2 A …[1] (*Lucy/meet*) her friends in town every day?
   B No, of course she …[2] (*not meet*) them every day. She usually …[3] (*meet*) them on Tuesdays and Fridays, I …[4] (*think*).

3 A …[1] (*you/watch*) much TV?
   B Well, I …[2] (*not watch*) TV at all during the week, but I …[3] (*enjoy*) watching a good film at weekends.

4 I …[1] (*belong*) to a football club but I …[2] (*not play*) in the first team because I just …[3] (*not have*) the time to train twice a week.

5 A What …[1] (*Frank/do*) in his free time? …[2] (*you/know*)?
   B He …[3] (*play*) the drums in a rock band and so he …[4] (*not do*) anything else really.

6 Girls …[1] (*not surf*) the net as much as boys. …[2] (*you/think*) that …[3] (*be*) the reason why girls' marks …[4] (*be*) often better than boys' marks at school?

B Work with a partner. Use the ideas below and the activities on page 6 to tell your partner what you normally/often/sometimes/never/... do or don't do and when.

> argue with my parents/brother/sister ▮ catch the bus ▮ come home late ▮
> do homework ▮ email friends ▮ get up ▮ go clubbing/dancing/shopping ▮
> go to school / to the cinema / to the pub / to bed ▮ leave for school / leave the house

EXAMPLES
> I **usually go** to bed at about 11 o'clock **on weekdays**.
> My mate and I **often go** to LAN parties **at the weekend**.
> I **don't watch / never watch** TV **during the week**.

C Now ask your partner about what he/she does or does not do. Add other activities if you wish.

EXAMPLES
> **When** do you leave for school?
> **How often** do you work?
> **Where** do you go shopping?
> **Do** you **go** to LAN parties?

D Report back to the class. Say what your partner does and when.

> *Bernd usually goes clubbing on Saturdays.*

> *Kathrin and her sister often play computer games.*

7 LOOKING AT GRAMMAR: PRESENT PROGRESSIVE

Form	
I am / I'm playing in the first team this season. At the moment, we *are / we're planning* a LAN party.	*am / is / are* + *-ing*-Form des Vollverbs
When I *am / I'm not working*, I'm sleeping. You *are / You're not* just *sitting* in front of the box.	**Verneinung:** *not* unmittelbar nach *am / is / are*
Are you helping homeless people, Dana? *Is Ravi* training at the moment?	**Fragen:** Austausch von Subjekt und *am / is / are*
Gebrauch	
I am working at a supermarket. *We are helping* homeless people.	für Situationen und Ereignisse, die im Moment des Sprechens bzw. Schreibens tatsächlich im Gange sind

> Das *present progressive* steht häufig mit den folgenden Zeitangaben:
> *at present, at the moment, currently, now*
> Normalerweise haben folgende Verben keine Verlaufsform:
> *be, believe, dislike, hate, know, like, love, mean, notice, see, seem, think* (= meinen), *understand, want, wish*

A **Put the verbs into the correct form of the present progressive.**

1 The players ... (*have*) a shower at the moment.
2 Wait a minute, please. I ... (*talk*) to a customer.
3 Dana ...[1] (*not work*) with old people. She ...[2] (*help*) the homeless at present.
4 A What ...[1] (*you/do*), Sam? B I ...[2] (*try*) to organize a LAN party.
5 A Why ...[1] (*Lucy/cry*)? B She ...[2] (*not cry*). She has a cold, that's all.
6 A Can you two help me, please? B Can't it wait? We ... (*serve*) meals.
7 Jack ...[1] (*not ride*) an ordinary bike. He ...[2] (*use*) an exercise bike.
8 Lucy's mum is very angry. Lucy ... (*work*) so many hours at the moment that she doesn't have time for her schoolwork.

B **Use the present progressive to ask each other questions with *what* and *who*.**

EXAMPLES > What is Tom doing/practising?
          > Who is practising penalties?
          > Tom is (practising penalties).

cycle to the shops **ı** do keep-fit exercises **ı** get money from a cash machine **ı**
meet friends at the pub **ı** play poker **ı** practise penalties **ı** surf the internet **ı**
take the dog for a walk **ı** try on some shoes **ı** wash the car

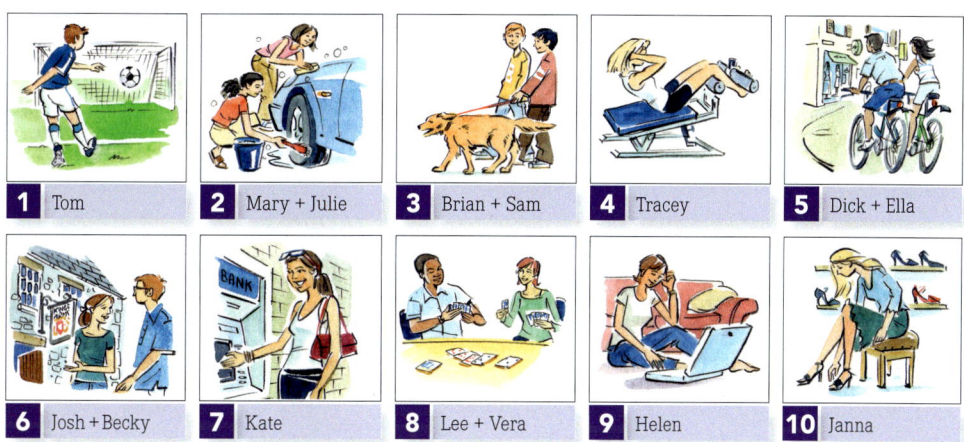

| 1 Tom | 2 Mary + Julie | 3 Brian + Sam | 4 Tracey | 5 Dick + Ella |
| 6 Josh + Becky | 7 Kate | 8 Lee + Vera | 9 Helen | 10 Janna |

8 MANAGING SITUATIONS

Sie möchten jemandem auf Englisch sagen, dass ...

1 ... Peter Drexler nicht mehr für Ihren Club spielt. Jetzt spielt er irgendwo in Norddeutschland, aber seinen neuen Club kennen Sie nicht.
2 ... Sie sich für Online-Poker interessieren und viel Freizeit damit verbringen.
3 ... Markus mit einem Freund gerade ein Computerprogramm schreibt.
4 ... Jasmin in der Woche meist zu Hause bleibt, da sie viel für die Schule tun muss.
5 ... Sie zurzeit Geld sparen, da Sie ein Auto kaufen wollen.
6 ... Sie einen neuen Job bei einer Pizzeria haben, Ihre Eltern aber wegen der Schule dagegen sind.
7 ... Ihr Bruder im Moment zu viel Zeit vor dem Fernseher verbringt.
8 ... die meisten Leute gar keine Freizeitbeschäftigung ausüben.

B

Girls fight for their rights

1 **3**

'Title IX' is a law that bans sex discrimination in US public schools[1]. One requirement of this law is that girls must have exactly the same chance to do sports as boys. The result? Girls have to join boys' teams if there are not enough girls to make up a team of their own. Read on to find out more.

Last March, Ashley Moore, 18, faced an awesome challenge[2]. She walked on to a wrestling mat to fight against her school's biggest wrestling rival. As he looked at her with hard, unblinking[3] eyes, Ashley felt a shiver of fear. Was she crazy? She was about to wrestle a hulk of a guy[4].

5 Four minutes later, however, Ashley walked off the mat a winner - and the hulk left on a stretcher. "He was big and strong, but he was slow," says Ashley of Edison High School, Richmond, Virginia. "He always tried the same hold. Then I took his arm and twisted it behind his back. When I did that, I pulled his back muscles. I didn't want to injure him. That's not what 10 wrestling is about."

Ashley Moore is one of a growing number of American high school girls who play on boys' sports teams. While that can be tough, fighting 15 stereotypes can be even tougher. But Ashley and girls like her are showing week after week that girls can compete against boys - and win.

Ashley had to fight hard to earn the respect of her male 20 teammates. At the first training session, they greeted her with funny looks and nasty jokes. "Some of my teammates didn't say a word. They just looked at me," says Ashley. "Other boys said stuff like 'Hi sweetie, the volleyball team's next door. Aren't you at the wrong 25 training session?'"

But Ashley didn't listen to the jokes and set to work - and soon she really impressed her teammates. "When they couldn't beat me in training," she says, "they soon backed off."

However, Ashley, who is called Xena after the TV warrior princess by her fans, doesn't want guys 30 to back off. In fact, when she's on the mat, she wants to be their equal in every way.

---

1 **public school (AE) = state school (BE)** *staatliche Schule*
2 **awesome challenge** *überwältigende Herausforderung*
3 **unblinking** *unbewegt*
4 **hulk of a guy** *Kerl wie ein Baum*

1 LOOKING AT THE TEXT

Read the speech bubbles and the list of people in the box. Then decide who said each statement.

a female ice-hockey player | a first aider |
Ashley | Ashley's mother | Ashley's opponent |
one of Ashley's fans | one of Ashley's teammates |
the wrestling coach at Edison High

1 *At first I said Ashley should do something, well, more 'feminine'. But now I'm so proud of her!*

2 *I had to take her because of Title IX. There's no girls' wrestling team at Edison High, you see.*

3 *I thought, "No problem, she's just a girl", but she taught me a lesson. I won't be able to wrestle again this season.*

4 *Ashley doesn't look like Xena, but she's our warrior princess. We never miss a match.*

5 *Ashley's hard to beat – very fast, very clever. We're all glad she's on the team now.*

6 *Ashley's right. I had problems at the beginning too, but after a couple of games the boys accepted me.*

7 *Well, I watch a lot of wrestling on TV with my dad. I thought, "Why not?"*

8 *My partner said, "Let's go and get the girl off the mat." Then we realized it was the boy.*

2 WORKING WITH WORDS

A Find words in the text and introduction that fit the definitions below.

1 verb: synonym for '(to) forbid' (*introduction*)
2 adjective: opposite of 'private' (*introduction*)
3 adverb: synonym for 'precisely' (*introduction*)
4 verb: synonym for '(to) put together' (*introduction*)
5 adjective: 'difficult or frightening' (*ll. 1–4*)
6 adjective: synonym for 'mad' (*ll. 1–4*)
7 noun: opposite of 'loser' (*ll. 5–10*)
8 adjective: opposite of 'weak' (*ll. 5–10*)
9 adjective: synonym for 'increasing' (*ll. 11–18*)
10 adjective: synonym for 'very difficult' (*ll. 11–18*)
11 noun: 'member of the same team' (*ll. 19–25*)
12 adjective: opposite of 'nice', 'pleasant' (*ll. 19–25*)

B Now write six sentences of your own about sport, using words you found in exercise A.

C Copy the table and fill in the missing forms from the text.

	Verb	Noun
1	...	ban
2	(to) discriminate	...
3	(to) require	...
4	(to) challenge	...
5	(to) rival	...
6	...	wrestler
7	(to) win	...
8	...	injury
9	...	competition
10	...	impression

D Complete the sentences using words from the table on page 13. Sometimes you must change the form.

1 Many EU countries have a ... on smoking in pubs.
2 It is harder for women to play sport because there is so much ... against them.
3 Ashley took part in an important wrestling ... in Charlotteville yesterday.
4 Ashley's biggest ... has challenged her to fight him again when he's fit.
5 When she beat them in training, Ashley's skill ... her teammates.
6 A lot of people were surprised when Ashley left the mat as the ...

3 LOOKING AT GRAMMAR: SIMPLE PAST

Form	
*Ashley **walked** off the mat a winner.*	**regelmäßig:** Infinitiv + *-ed*
*I **took** his arm and twisted it behind his back.*	**unregelmäßig:** Sonderform, siehe S. 298
*Some of my teammates **didn't say** a word.*	**Verneinung:** *did not / didn't* + Infinitiv
***Did I win** just because I'm a girl?*	**Fragen:** *did* + Subjekt + Infinitiv

Gebrauch	
*Ashley **faced** an awesome challenge last March.* *This big guy **backed off** at a match last week.*	für Handlungen / Situationen, die in der Vergangenheit abgeschlossen wurden

Signalwörter

yesterday, the day before yesterday *two / three / ... days / weeks / months / years ago* *last week / month / year / summer / Christmas / ...* *the week / month before last*	*in 1973 / 2007 / ...* *at that time / in those days* *when he / she was a child / at school / ...*

1 4 A Complete the report with the simple past forms of the verbs in the box. Then listen to the CD to check your answers.

agree ı give ı grow up ı hear ı
kick ı live ı not be ı not do ı
not even have ı not go ı promise ı talk

Otis Shipley ...[1] in the poorest part of Perryton, a small town in Texas. He ...[2] with his mother and four brothers and sisters. Otis didn't know his father and sometimes the family ...[3] enough money to buy food. But Otis had one thing going for him: his skill as a football player. Nobody could run as fast as Otis and nobody ...[4] the ball as far as Otis.

It ...[5] long before Duane Tyler, the football coach at Robert E. Lee High School in Abilene, ...[6] about Otis's phenomenal talent. Tyler went to Perryton and ...[7] to Mrs Shipley. He ...[8] her that she would have money, a nice house and a future for her children. How could she say no? Mrs Shipley soon ...[9] to move to Abilene.

And Otis didn't disappoint her. Although he ...[10] anything except play football and often ...[11] to his classes, his teachers still ...[12] him very good grades.

B This is a page from Ellie Brown's weekly planner. Use the simple past to say what Ellie and her friends did last week. Add any further details if necessary.

EXAMPLES > Ellie rang Ben and Annie about tennis at lunchtime on Monday.
> Ben and Annie had a phone call from Ellie about tennis on Monday.

MARCH			
14	Monday	*lunchtime: ring Ben & Annie (tennis)*	
		evening: do ironing!!	
15	Tuesday	*8:00 a.m. take bike to Apex Bikes*	
		3:15 p.m. hairdresser's ✗ *on way home: bank, pay garage bill*	
16	Wednesday		
		late afternoon: pick up bike (Apex)	
17	Thursday	*5:30 p.m. meet Mandy, Annie (Virgin Media) buy birthday present (Sam)*	
18	Friday	*6–8 p.m. training, swimming competition*	
		9:30 p.m.–11:00 p.m. record film, BBC2	
19	Saturday	*10 a.m. meet Mandy (power walking, Mousehold Heath)*	
20	Sunday	*visit Kate (hospital, Ward 4)*	
		GET BOOK – NO FRUIT, NO FLOWERS!!	

C Work with a partner. Use the words in the box and the simple past to ask your partner what he or she did *yesterday / last night / last weekend / last summer / last Christmas / ….* Swap roles at least once.

> go riding/camping/dancing/swimming/shopping/… ▎ go to a disco/the gym/the leisure centre/the movies/a party/the pub/… ▎ go on holiday/a trip/a cycle tour to … ▎ go on a date ▎ meet sb ▎ play basketball/cards/computer games/football/…

EXAMPLES > Did you go to the pub last Friday?
> Yes, I did./No, I didn't. I went to a party at Paula's.

> What did you do last weekend?
> We went shopping on Saturday, but I stayed at home on Sunday.

4 MANAGING SITUATIONS

Sie möchten jemandem auf Englisch sagen, dass …

1 … Ihr Fußballverein gestern den Pokal gegen eine holländische Mannschaft gewonnen hat.
2 … es Donnerstag Abend kein Training gab, da der Trainer krank war.
3 … Sie und Ihr Bruder am Sonntag eine 60-km-Radtour gemacht haben.
4 … Sie vor zwei Monaten Golf ausprobiert haben, aber das Spiel äußerst langweilig fanden.
5 … Sie und Ihre Familie letztes Jahr einen Campingurlaub in Italien gemacht haben.
6 … Ihr Kanuverein letzten Samstag eine tolle Saisonabschlussfeier (*end-of-season party*) hatte.

You are what you eat

BEFORE YOU READ

1 5   **What do you think the text might be about?**

A case study: Maddy Johnson's double life

A lot of people eat too much food or spend too much time sitting in front of the TV. That's OK because if they eat less and do more exercise, they can become healthy. But some people have a genuine problem. They have a compulsive eating disorder like anorexia[1] or bulimia[2]. Read on to find out more …

Maddy Johnson is charming, attractive and successful. She's popular, too – at school, in her part-time job and in her community. Everybody loves Maddy. But the
5 reality is different. Maddy is leading a double life – the public one and a secret one that nobody sees. Maddy is ill. She suffers from bulimia.

    The poster outside the fast-food restaurant
10 showed a double-decker cheeseburger with an XXL packet of fries, two little tubs of sauce and a big can of coke. 'Today's Special!' it screamed. 'Buy two cheeseburgers and get free fries!'

15   Maddy looked at the poster and had that familiar, tingling feeling. It was like sex. "No!" she said to herself. "Just walk away! You don't want it! You don't need it!" But that was the problem, wasn't it? Maddy couldn't 'just walk
20 away'. It was as if she had lost control over her own body.

    Maddy went into the restaurant and bought two cheeseburgers with free fries. She walked to an empty table and sat down with her back to the
25 room. She didn't want people to see how she stuffed the burgers greedily into her mouth. In no time, she was back at the counter. She ordered a dessert: an XL tub of ice cream with caramel sauce and two cream donuts. The guy behind the counter looked at her. 30 "Hungry, are we?" he said with a cheeky grin. "He knows," thought Maddy. She wanted to sink through the floor.

    Maddy finished her meal and went into the toilets. The tingling had stopped, but 35 she hated herself. She felt dirty and so guilty. She went into a cubicle, bent over the toilet pan and threw up.

    When she came out of the cubicle, a woman was washing her hands. "Are you all 40 right?" she asked. "That sounded … Well, I couldn't help hearing. I'm so sorry." The woman offered Maddy a card. 'Ellen Anderson, National Association for Eating Disorders', it said. It gave the number of a free hotline and 45 Ellen's email address. "Will you let me help you?" Ellen asked. Maddy looked at her. "It's OK," she said. "What do you mean 'help me'? I'm fine. Really. I just felt 50 sick, that's all. I don't need … Well, I mean, …" "You don't have to explain, dear. I've been down that road as well. I *know*. You just can't beat 55 this illness alone. Please ring that number, day or night."

---

1 anorexia: refusal to eat for fear of putting on weight *Magersucht*
2 bulimia: addiction to food and vomiting to lose weight *Ess-Brech-Sucht*

1 LOOKING AT THE TEXT

A Do the following tasks.

1 Compare Maddy's public and secret lives.
2 Describe how Maddy felt a) outside the restaurant and b) when she went into the toilets.
3 Find evidence to show that Maddy felt embarrassed and ashamed of herself in the restaurant.
4 Describe Maddy's reaction to Ellen Anderson's offer of help. What does it tell us about Maddy's attitude to her illness?
5 Explain how we know that Ellen Anderson really understood Maddy's problem.

B Read the speech bubbles and say which opinion about eating disorders you agree or disagree with most. Give reasons for your choice.

Eating disorders? Starving yourself and stuff like that? Well, I don't think they're real illnesses at all – not if the person's otherwise healthy. It's just silly girls dreaming about becoming top models or dancers or something. They should get real and start living!

People who say that those who suffer from eating disorders should just pull themselves together don't know what they're talking about. It's an accepted fact that eating disorders are serious mental illnesses that need treatment. Sufferers need sympathetic medical help, not criticism.

2 WORKING WITH WORDS

A Read the introduction and the case study again. Complete the table with the missing verbs.

	verb + noun / noun phrase				
1	(to) eat	too much food	6	(to) ...	free fries
2	(to) ...	an eating disorder	7	(to) ...	food into one's mouth
3	(to) ...	a double life	8	(to) ...	a dessert
4	(to) ...	from bulimia	9	(to) ...	a meal
5	(to) ...	a cheeseburger	10	(to) ...	an illness

B Complete the sentences with verbs from exercise A. Make sure the verbs are in the right form.

1 I'm sure Alice can ... bulimia if she gets help from a doctor.
2 I always ... too much chocolate at Easter.
3 Two years ago Sally was very thin because she ... anorexia.
4 At this restaurant you ... a free dessert with every meal.
5 George must be hungry – he is ... that cake into his mouth!
6 I ... chicken but the waiter brought me fish.

C Replace the underlined words with a synonym from the introduction and text. They are in the same order.

1 <u>Many</u> burger bars attract customers with special offers.   *A lot of*
2 People who drink too much alcohol <u>get</u> drunk.
3 Do you have a <u>real</u> reason for not doing any exercise today?
4 The <u>difficulty</u> is that 'natural food' is too expensive for most people.
5 Everybody knows that <u>good-looking</u> people have an easier life.
6 I live in a mixed <u>neighbourhood</u> with people from all over the place.
7 The <u>truth</u> of most people's lives is far from what you see in TV ads.
8 The driver of the car was so angry that she <u>shouted</u> at me.
9 The film was really disgusting. Afterwards I <u>was sick</u>.
10 It is almost impossible to <u>overcome</u> an eating disorder without help.

3 WRITING

Imagine you are Maddy. Use your answers from exercise 1 A to write an email to Ellen Anderson asking for her help.

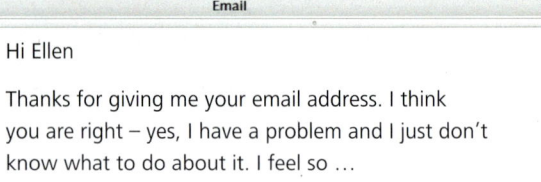

Email

Hi Ellen

Thanks for giving me your email address. I think you are right – yes, I have a problem and I just don't know what to do about it. I feel so …

4 LOOKING AT GRAMMAR: POSSESSIVE ADJECTIVES

> *Possessive adjectives* zeigen an, wem irgendetwas gehört. Sie stehen – wie andere Adjektive – unmittelbar vor dem Nomen.

I	Maddy is **my** sister.	
you	Can you tell me **your** name, please?	
he	What is **his** job?	
she	Is Joshua **her** brother?	
it	Wales is in the UK. **Its** capital is Cardiff.	⚠ **it's** = it is
we	There are 1,500 students at **our** school.	
you	Please open **your** books at page 23.	
they	**Their** home is in London.	⚠ **there** = da, dort

Complete these sentences with the English equivalent of the words in brackets.

1 What's *your name* (*dein Name*), please?
2 He's walking home because … (*sein Rad*) is broken.
3 Maddy is writing … (*ihrer Freundin*) an email.
4 Unfortunately the students have to buy … (*ihre Bücher*) themselves.
5 The trainer asked me for … (*meinem Gewicht*).
6 This table is too small for … (*unsere Gruppe*).
7 The doctor thinks … (*ihre Krankheit*) is curable.
8 You shouldn't give … (*Ihren Kindern*) so much fatty food.
9 (*Ihr Name*) … is Madison, but she calls herself 'Maddy'.
10 Look at that poor bird. What's the matter with … (*seinem Bein*)?

5 LOOKING AT GRAMMAR: COUNTABLE AND UNCOUNTABLE NOUNS

Maddy ordered **a dessert**. She had **an ice cream** and **two donuts**.	dessert, ice cream, donuts usw. = zählbare Nomen (Pluralform möglich, können mit Zahl-wörtern oder a/an verwendet werden)
I'd like **cheese** and **mayonnaise** on my burger, please.	cheese, mayonnaise usw. = nicht zählbare Nomen (keine Pluralform, keine Verwendung mit Zahlwörtern oder a/an)
Oliver had **two cups of tea, a plate of ham and eggs** and **a bowl of corn pops** for breakfast.	bei nicht zählbaren Nomen: Pluralbildung durch Hinzufügen eines zählbaren Nomens wie two cups of ..., a plate of ..., a bowl of ...
Research shows that bulimia is a serious illness. Ellen gave Maddy **some advice** about bulimia. Two recent **pieces of news** showed that exercise is very important.	nicht zählbare Sammelbegriffe: luggage, furniture, hardware/software sowie advice, evidence, information, knowledge, news und research stehen mit Verben im Singular; Pluralbildung mit pieces of ... (formell) bzw. bits of ... (weniger formell)

⚠ Beachten Sie, dass wir die Nomen *people* und *police* nur im Plural verwenden können. Wollen wir sie im Singular gebrauchen, benutzen wir **person** für *people* und **police officer** für *police*.

> The **people** in the café **were** drinking coffee. Only **one person was** drinking wine.
> **A police officer** said that **the police were** on their way.

A In your exercise book, draw a table for countable and uncountable nouns like the one below. Put the nouns in box A into the correct column.

B Give the plural form of the countable nouns. Add a suitable countable expression from box B to the uncountables so that you can use them in the plural.

A

| box ı bread ı bus ı car ı cheese ı |
| child ı chocolate ı coffee ı evidence ı |
| family ı fish ı glass ı house ı kiss ı |
| knife ı life ı meat ı mustard ı news ı |
| oil ı paint ı water ı woman ı yoghurt |

B

| bars/pieces of ı bits/pieces of ı |
| bottles/glasses of ı cans/tins of ı |
| cups of ı loaves/slices of ı tubs of ı |
| tubes/jars of |

Countable		Uncountable	
Singular	Plural	Base form	Qualified form
box	boxes	bread	loaves/slices of bread

C Now write five sentences using some of the expressions from exercise B. Be careful with singular/plural verbs.

6 LOOKING AT GRAMMAR: UNSPECIFIED QUANTITIES

> *Some, any* und ihre Zusammensetzungen

Please add **some** salt to the potatoes.	bejahte Aussagen: *some*
We don't have **any** butter. Use olive oil. Did you put **any** salt on the potatoes?	verneinte Aussagen und Fragen: *any*
May I have **some** salt, please? Can I get you **some** orange juice, Maddy?	Bitten und Angebote, die wahrscheinlich mit ja beantwortet werden: *some*
There is **something** wrong with the toaster. I didn't see **anybody** I knew at the pub. Have you seen the cookbook **anywhere**?	Zusammensetzungen von *some / any* werden genauso verwendet

A Complete the sentences with *some* or *any*.

1 Do you have *any* mustard, please?
2 We don't need … bread.
3 There is … butter in the kitchen.
4 It was awful. … men had too much to drink and started a fight.
5 Would you like …[1] more fries? You can have …[2] of mine. I don't want …[3] more.
6 The party was a bit boring because there wasn't … music.
7 Don't forget to buy …[1] drinking chocolate or we won't have …[2] for breakfast.
8 We can't invite …[1] more people to the party. We don't have …[2] room.

B Complete the sentences with *somebody / anybody*, *something / anything* or *somewhere / anywhere*.

1 A Listen! I think there's *somebody*[1] at the door.
   B I didn't hear *anything*[2]. I don't think there's …[3] there.
2 I can't find the shopping list. Have you seen it …[1]? It must be here …[2]
3 A Did you buy …[1] to drink?
   B Well, I bought some mineral water, but I expect you'd like …[2] stronger.
4 I need …[1] to help with the barbecue on Saturday. Can you think of …[2] we could ask?
5 We need some more coke. If you're not doing …, could you go and buy some?
6 Do you know … who can mix cocktails, Janna?

> *Much, many, a lot of* und *plenty of*

We don't need **many steaks**. How **many tomatoes** do we need? I don't use **much salt** in my cooking. How **much butter** do we have?	verneinte Aussagen und Fragen: *many* mit zählbaren und *much* mit nicht zählbaren Nomen
A lot of / Lots of children are too fat. Maddy eats **a lot of food** and then she makes herself sick.	bejahte Aussagen: *a lot of* oder *lots of* (weniger formell) bei zählbaren und nicht zählbaren Nomen
Drink **as much water** as you like. We bought far **too many steaks**.	Beachten Sie: *much / many* nach *as, how, so, too* und *very* auch in bejahten Aussagen
There's **plenty of bread** in the freezer.	„viel" in der Bedeutung „mehr als genug": *plenty of* statt *a lot of / lots of*

C Complete the sentences with *much, many, a lot of* or *plenty of*.

1 There weren't *many*¹ people at the supermarket. I think *a lot of*² people are away on holiday at the moment.

2 A Hurry up! We don't have ...¹ time.
   B Don't panic. We have ...² time. The shops don't close until 10 o'clock.
   A Really? I thought they closed ...³ earlier than that.

3 A How ...¹ people are coming to the barbecue on Saturday?
   B Not ...². Six, I think.
   A Only six? Why on earth did you buy so ...³ meat then?

4 You needn't go shopping. We have ...¹ food in the freezer and we won't need ...² drink. ...³ people are driving.

5 ...¹ women work in supermarkets but not ...² of them have a top job.

6 A John eats ...¹ chocolate, doesn't he?
   B Yes. He eats far too ...² sweets and he shouldn't drink so ...³ coke, either.

> **>** *(A) little, (a) few*

Add *a little water* if necessary. (ein wenig) *Jake has* **little interest** in food. (nur wenig)	nicht zählbare Nomen: *(a) little*
You need *a few carrots*, too. (ein paar) *Few cooks* are as good as she is. (nur wenig)	zählbare Nomen: *(a) few*

D Complete the sentences with *(a) little* or *(a) few*.

1 A Can I give you *a few*¹ more fries?
   B No, thanks, but I'd like *a little*² more bread, please.

2 A Why did you buy so much beer?
   B Because we only have ... cans in the fridge.

3 A Nobody gets fat at Brenda's parties. You only get ...¹ bread.
   B Be fair. Last time we got ...² bits of cheese, too.

4 A Most doctors say that you should only use ...¹ salt.
   B Sure, but only ...² doctors follow their own advice.

5 A There's ...¹ point in saying anything. The boss never listens to us.
   B I know, but I have ...² questions I want to ask him.

6 A Shops can open on Sundays in the UK but only ...¹ do so.
   B That's understandable. People want ...² time off.

---

7 MANAGING SITUATIONS

Sie möchten jemandem auf Englisch sagen, dass ...

1 ... Sie eine gute Nachricht haben. Die Polizei hat das Kind gefunden.
2 ... Sie nur wenig Zeit haben, da Sie noch viel Arbeit zu erledigen haben.
3 ... die medizinischen Beweise eindeutig (*conclusive*) sind. Essstörungen sind eine psychische Erkrankung. Viele junge Mädchen leiden unter Essstörungen.
4 ... Sie auf der Party viel Fisch und Käse aber nur wenig Fleisch anbieten wollen.
5 ... viel zu viele Leute Fast Food essen, weil sie keine Zeit haben, etwas gesundes zu kochen.
6 ... es dieses Jahr so viel Obst gibt, dass die Bauern nur wenig Geld verdienen. Viele lassen das Obst an den Bäumen.

D

Time out

Many young people now choose to spend some time abroad after they leave school. Holly Morris wants to do exactly that – but she can't decide where to go. So she writes an email to a magazine, asking for help with her problem.

Hi Jala

I hope other readers will help me with my problem. It's like this: I'm leaving school next July and then I'm taking time out, six months or so, to spend time abroad. I'd really like to go somewhere like Brazil or maybe India that I won't have a chance to see again. But my parents, who are going to help me financially, are
5 totally against these 'exotic destinations'. They want me to go to a rich English-speaking country like Australia or Canada.

As I am going to work some of the time, they say it'll be easier for me to find a 'proper job' there and 'people are
10 more like us'. But what's the point in going somewhere like that? I want to see new places and meet new people. But what can I do? My dad says that there's no way that he's going to pay for me to get myself killed! Do you or your readers have any bright ideas?

15 Holly Morris

OK, Holly, so you're going to pay for some of your time out as you go – but how? Are you going to pick fruit or work in a bar, for example? If so, your
5 dad's absolutely right. You can forget places like South America and India – and safety really is a problem, especially for girls. Please believe this, Holly, or I can see that you're going to
10 have a lot of very nasty surprises.

  LISTENING

1 6 **Work with a partner. Complete the email with suitable words. Then listen to the CD to check your answers.**

Hi

Look, this may sound totally uncool, Holly, but I *agree*[1] with your dad. You will find it very ...[2] to find a job in a country like Brazil, where millions of people are out of ...[3]. And even if you do find one, what are you going to do about language difficulties? Or do you ...[4] Portuguese? Come on! Let's get real!

Here's my advice. Go to a richer, English-speaking ...[5] like the USA or Australia, where you speak the ...[6] and will be able to find a job. Please remember that you won't just want to earn enough for your ordinary living expenses, either. You'll also want to save some ...[7] to travel around while you're there. Otherwise, what's the ...[8] in going?

Now, here's a tip. You will find it very difficult to organize a trip like this yourself. You need expert ...[9]. As a first step, why not visit a ...[10] like bunac.org and ...[11] the country you want to go to, America, for example? There you will find all the information, advice and job offers you need.

Good ...[12], Holly, and have lots of fun!

Casey

2 LOOKING AT THE TEXTS

A Draw a table like the one below in your exercise book. Then complete it with information from the emails.

Holly	Holly's parents	Jala + Casey
– is leaving school in July	– are going to help financially	– agree with Holly's parents

B Holly is telling a friend about her plans. Use information from your table to complete the conversation.

3 WORKING WITH WORDS

Complete the sentences with words from the emails. They are not necessarily in the same order.

1 So many tourists go to 'exotic ...' that they are no longer exotic.
2 You won't have any language ... because everyone in Australia speaks English.
3 The USA is the biggest English-speaking ... in the world.
4 My dad wants me to get a '... job', but how? I'm only here for a month or so.
5 Spending time ... can be a great way to find out about life in another country.
6 We had a nasty ... when we got home. Somebody had broken into the house.
7 You can pick ..., but you will not earn very much money.
8 Holly will have to work some of the time to pay her living ...
9 How can she find a job in Canada? Do you have any ... ideas?
10 If you've never worked in Brazil before, you should get expert ... before you leave.

4 LOOKING AT GRAMMAR: FUTURE

> **Das *will future***

Form

You **will be able to** find a job in the USA.	*will* + Infinitiv für alle Personen
I **will not / won't have** a chance to go there again.	**Verneinung:** *not* unmittelbar nach *will* ⚠️ Kurzform: *won't*
Will Holly be safer in the USA?	**Fragen:** Austausch von Subjekt und *will*

Gebrauch

I think you **will have** problems finding a job. I **won't have** a chance to go there again. I hope Holly **will follow** Jala's advice.	Vorhersagen/Vermutungen/Hoffnungen über die Zukunft
I've missed my bus. – Don't worry. I**'ll give** you a lift.	spontane Entscheidungen
Will you **help** me complete this form, please?	Bitten

> **Das *going to future***

Form

My parents **are going to help** me.	*am/is/are going to* + Infinitiv
We **are/'re not going to help** you get yourself killed!	**Verneinung:** *not* unmittelbar nach *am/is/are*
Are you going to work in a bar, for example?	**Fragen:** Austausch von Subjekt und *am/is/are*

Gebrauch

Holly **is going to take** time out in the USA.	Absichten und Pläne
I can see that you **are going to have** a lot of nasty surprises.	unmittelbar bevorstehende Ereignisse, für die es schon Anzeichen gibt

A Use the correct form of the *will* or *going to* future.

1 I'm sure Holly *will enjoy* (*enjoy*) her time out in Georgia.
2 Holly's parents ... (*visit*) her in the USA.
3 The weatherman on TV thinks it ... (*rain*) tomorrow.
4 Watch out! Can't you see that child ... (*run*) across the road?
5 Is it true? ... (*Casey/help*) Holly find a job?
6 We ... (*do*) our best, but I don't think your visa ... (*be*) ready by Friday.
7 Let me know what flight you're on and I ... (*meet*) you at the airport, OK?
8 Hey, Dad, ... (*you/help*) me with my luggage, please?

> **Das *present progressive* und *simple present* mit zukünftiger Bedeutung**

I **am leaving** school **next July**. Holly **is flying** to Atlanta **at 7:30 this evening**.	für Termine und fest geplante Vorhaben, mit Zeitangabe
Holly's plane **takes off** at 10:30 tomorrow. The film **starts** at 8 o'clock on Sundays.	für Flugpläne, Fahrpläne usw. für Kinoprogramme usw.

B Make sentences with the *going to* future or the present progressive. Only use the present progressive when there is an adverb of future time. Add any missing words.

> EXAMPLES > several school-leavers | take time out | Australia
> > *Several school-leavers **are going to take** time out in Australia.*
>
> > I | fly | Cologne next Saturday
> > *I **am flying** to Cologne next Saturday.*

1 we + meet | 7 or 7:30 tomorrow?
2 we | get a job | pay for our holiday
3 you + come | Holly's farewell party | Friday?
4 Casey + work | the USA?
5 I | start work | six | and I | finish | two | next week
6 A What are your plans for the summer?
   B we | look for | a job on a farm in France
7 they + sell | their car | internet?
8 we | not have | holiday | next summer | | we | stay at home

C Put the verbs into the correct form: *will* future, *going to* future, present progressive or simple present.

1 A What time ...[1] (*you/go*) into town tomorrow, Ann?
   B Well, I ...[2] (*meet*) Ellie in the pub at 7. Jack and Sarah ...[3] (*come*), too. Why don't you come? I'm sure they ...[4] (*be*) really pleased to see you again.
   A Great. I ...[5] (*definitely + be*) there. It ...[6] (*be*) nice to see Jack and Sarah again.

2 A Is it true that Holly ...[1] (*not come*) back home at the end of her time out?
   B Who told you that? She ...[2] (*come*) home in August and then she ...[3] (*start*) college in October.

3 A The TV programme ...[1] (*start*) at 8:15 so I want to get the bus that ...[2] (*leave*) at 7:50.
   B But that bus ...[3] (*not get to*) Oak Street until about 8:10. We ...[4] (*only + have*) five minutes to walk home. Let's take the bus that ...[5] (*go*) at 7:30.

4 A We ...[1] (*not go*) away on holiday at all next summer. We ...[2] (*spend*) the whole time at home.
   B Good idea. They say we ...[3] (*have*) a very hot summer. I'm sure you ...[4] (*be*) much more comfortable at home.
   A True – and we ...[5] (*save*) a lot of money, too!

5 MANAGING SITUATIONS

Sie möchten jemandem auf Englisch sagen, dass ...

1 ... es morgen sonnig sein soll.
2 ... Ihre Schwester am 10. Juli in die USA fliegt, um ihren Job in New Orleans anzufangen.
3 ... Ihre Eltern Sie während Ihrer Zeit im Ausland finanziell unterstützen werden.
4 ... Sie wissen wollen, ob Tom vorhat, eine neue Stelle zu suchen.
5 ... Mary bestimmt ein Jahr in Australien verbringen wird.
6 ... Sie am Donnerstag nicht zu Hause sind, da Sie am Mittwoch in den Urlaub nach Italien fliegen.

E

Shopping

Shopping online certainly has its advantages: no parking problems, no queues, no pushy sales staff, no carrying shopping home. Plus credit cards make it so easy to pay – too easy, perhaps. Read on to find out what that can mean.

Sharon Miller's virtual world of online shopping

Clothes and fashion are important to me. When I was a child, my mum had mail-order catalogues. I liked to look at them and make long lists of the clothes I wanted. Of course, my mum didn't buy them. She couldn't. She didn't have the money.

5 When I got older, I started buying my own clothes. I spent happy hours at the bargain counters of big department stores in Manchester. Then, when I was 16, I discovered a 'nearly-new' shop in King Street. My first purchase there was a fabulous blouse in the latest fashion colours for
10 just £30.

After that, I went there every week. The clothes were cheaper than in ordinary shops and often much better quality. You see, a lot of rich, fashion-conscious women sometimes wear really expensive clothes only once. And I wanted to be like
15 those women. I wanted the coolest and smartest and most fashionable clothes, you know, exclusive Italian designer labels like Versace, Armani and Gucci – and I wanted my wardrobe to be full of them.

When I was 18, I discovered the thrill of eBay. I always thought eBay was just for techno freaks, but how wrong I was! Once I bought a lovely Armani
20 cocktail dress in pure silk for just £4.99!

Soon I was doing all my shopping online – not just on eBay, but at top designer sites as well. But I spent more money than I had – much, much more money. With a credit card, it was so easy. I just clicked the mouse – click, click, click into the virtual shopping trolley. But in the
25 meantime I've run up debts of over £4,500. And they aren't virtual, they're real.

1 LOOKING AT THE TEXT

Choose the right answer to complete the statements.

1 Sharon discovered her interest in clothes by ...
   a visiting exclusive boutiques.
   b looking through mail-order catalogues.
   c searching for special offers.

2 At first, Sharon bought her clothes at ...
   a bargain counters in big stores.
   b second-hand shops.
   c exclusive designer boutiques.

3 When she was 16, Sharon ...
   a heard about bargains on eBay.
   b bought fashionable clothes from rich women.
   c found a nearly-new shop in Manchester.

4 Sharon wanted to be like ...
   a her friends who wore the latest fashions.
   b smart women who wore expensive clothes just once.
   c the other customers at the nearly-new shop.

5 Sharon thought that eBay was ...
   a only for techno freaks.
   b an internet auction site that sold everything.
   c an online clothes shop.

6 On eBay, Sharon once bought a ...
   a blouse in the latest fashion colours.
   b wardrobe full of designer clothes.
   c silk cocktail dress.

7 Soon Sharon was doing all her clothes shopping ...
   a in online shops and on eBay.
   b on eBay.
   c in ordinary shops.

8 Sharon got into debt because she ...
   a used a credit card.
   b spent much more money than she had.
   c did a lot of online shopping.

2 WORKING WITH WORDS

A Link the nouns in the box on the left with a noun from the box on the right to form compounds.

1 bargain	5 designer	9 shopping
2 cocktail	6 fashion	10 techno
3 credit	7 mail-order	
4 department	8 sales	

card **ı** catalogue **ı**
colour **ı** counter **ı**
dress **ı** freak **ı** label **ı**
staff **ı** store **ı** trolley

B Complete the sentences with the English equivalent of the German words or phrases in brackets. Be careful to use the correct form.

1 There are many ...[1] (*Vorteil*) in shopping online. ...[2] (*Inzwischen*) more and more people have ...[3] (*entdecken*) how easy shopping from home is.
2 Many people prefer to order goods from a ...[1] (*Versandhauskatalog*) because they don't like ...[2] (*aufdringlich*) sales assistants.
3 ...[1] (*modebewusst*) women don't like to wear the same ...[2] (*Kleidungsstück*) too often.
4 It's a crime to ... (*Schulden zusammenkommen lassen*) that you know you won't be able to pay.
5 I didn't ...[1] (*ausgeben*) much at the supermarket yesterday. In fact, I didn't even use a ...[2] (*Einkaufswagen*) as I only needed two things.
6 Clothes at the new boutique are not as ...[1] (*teuer*) as at the ...[2] (*Warenhaus*) next door.

C First read the five golden rules. Then complete them with words from the box.

The Five Golden Rules

1 Know how much ...¹ you have. Be ...² and **never** just 'hope for the best'.
2 Buying for ...¹ is **always** much, much cheaper than buying ...².
3 Be very sceptical about ...¹. In the end, nothing is ...².
4 If you ignore ...¹, it doesn't go away. It just gets worse – and ...².
5 Keep in touch with your ...¹. Describe your problem honestly and say how you plan to ...² the debt.

cash ▪ creditors ▪ debt ▪ free ▪ free offers ▪ money ▪ on credit ▪ realistic ▪ repay ▪ worse

3 LOOKING AT GRAMMAR: ADJECTIVES AND ADVERBS

*Sharon spent **happy** hours in boutiques.* *Shopping online is **quick** and **convenient**.*	Adjektive beschreiben Nomen Stellung: entweder unmittelbar vor dem Nomen oder nach einer Form von *be / become*
*Think about your needs **honestly**.* *All the clothes in this shop are **nearly** new.*	Adverbien beschreiben Verben oder Adjektive
*Sharon ran up debts **quickly**.*	Form: weitaus die meisten Adverbien enden auf *-ly*
*We must do two things **fast**.*	wichtige unregelmäßige Adverbien: *good* – **well**, *fast* – **fast**, *hard* – **hard**
*Sharon **looks awful** in that dress.*	*(to) feel, (to) look, (to) sound, (to) taste* stehen mit Adjektiven

Choose the correct form of the underlined words to complete this text.

The man walked into the phone shop and went over to the display of mobile phones. He walked slow/slowly¹ along the rows of elegant/elegantly² phones, stopping occasional/occasionally³ to look at a phone more close/closely⁴. But he couldn't look at them proper/properly⁵. They were all fixed firm/firmly⁶ in anti-theft pads with little red lights that glowed bright/brightly⁷.

An assistant came over. "Can I help you at all?" she asked polite/politely⁸. "Sure," said the man. "I need a new phone. This one looks good/well⁹." "The 6131? Well, you can't go wrong there. It's a very reliable/reliably¹⁰ model." "Yes, but it's not cheap/cheaply¹¹, is it?" "You're right there," said the assistant. She smiled pleasant/pleasantly¹² at the customer. "But it's fantastic/fantastically¹³ good value for money, you know. It's got every possible/possibly¹⁴ modern feature. Let me show you." The assistant switched off the alarm and removed the phone careful/carefully¹⁵ from its pad. "This way, please, sir," she said.

4 LOOKING AT GRAMMAR: POSITION OF ADVERBS

Satzadverbien	
Of course, Mum didn't buy the clothes.	**Satzanfang**: *(un)fortunately, actually, in fact, (un)luckily, maybe, perhaps, naturally, obviously*
Art und Weise	
Think about your needs **honestly**.	**Satzende**
Ort und Zeit	
The shop is **in King Street**. Mum comes home **at 6 o'clock**. The train leaves **Manchester at 10:30**. Ashley was **great in the match last night**.	**Satzende:** Reihenfolge bei mehreren Adverbien: Ort – Zeit Art und Weise – Ort – Zeit
Häufigkeit	
We **often** go shopping in King Street. Sharon is **sometimes** irresponsible. We go shopping **every Saturday**. We only go shopping **once a week**.	**Satzmitte**: unbestimmte Häufigkeit – vor Vollverben, nach *be* **Satzende**: bestimmte Häufigkeit sowie zusammengesetzte Häufigkeitsangaben wie *from time to time, (every) now and then*

A Say where you would put the adverbs of frequency: position A or B.

1 Retailers A say B that shoplifting is getting worse. (*often*)
2 Tough punishment A stops a shoplifter B. (*seldom*)
3 Modern technology is A catching more and more shoplifters B. (*every year*)
4 Some shoplifters are so clever that they A get caught B. (*never*)
5 Other shoppers A see people shoplifting B. (*now and then*)
6 But they don't A do B anything about it. (*usually*)

B Rewrite the sentences with the adverbs in the correct position.

1 The coat was in the sale. (*luckily*)
2 Before buying on credit, you should think about your financial situation. (*realistically*)
3 Fashionable women wear expensive clothes only once. (*sometimes*)
4 I am very tired after doing the shopping. (*always*)
5 Sharon visits the eBay site. (*several times a week*)
6 I didn't buy anything because the shop assistant spoke to me. (*rudely*)
7 The Brad Pitt film is on TV this evening. (*at 9:30, on Channel 4*)
8 I think you acted very well – congratulations! (*in the play, last night*)

5 MANAGING SITUATIONS

Sie möchten jemandem auf Englisch sagen, dass ...

1 ... nächste Woche ein neues Kaufhaus in der Stadt eröffnet.
2 ... viele Produkte online billiger sind.
3 ... man leicht Schulden macht, wenn man immer online kauft.
4 ... riesige Supermärkte viele kleinere Geschäfte ruinieren (*ruin*).
5 ... Sie versuchen so oft wie möglich in kleineren Geschäften einzukaufen.
6 ... Stadtzentren in der Zukunft ganz anders aussehen werden.

F

Ready for a job?

Have you ever thought of working in your spare time? If so, this questionnaire will help you to find out if you're ready to take on a part-time job as well as school.

1 DOING A QUESTIONNAIRE

Do the questionnaire by choosing the answer for each question that fits you best.
Use the table opposite to work out your score and then read what your score means.

1 Why do you want a part-time job?

A I've just seen a really cool new MP3 player and I have to buy it!
B I want to earn some money so I don't have to keep asking my parents to buy stuff for me.
C To get some work experience – I think it will help me find a good job when I leave college.

2 How much time do you spend doing your homework?

A Some nights I stay up late working, some nights I watch TV instead.
B I usually spend an hour every evening working. That way I get all my work done and have time for other things.
C Sometimes I get home from school and start watching a DVD or texting my friends and forget all about my homework.

3 How often do you do out-of-school activities?

A I do loads of stuff after school – I'm always busy!
B I'm quite lazy. When I get home from school, I just want to sit and watch TV.
C I go to one or two after-school clubs but I'm free most evenings.

4 How much time do you plan to spend doing your part-time job?

A My schoolwork and my social life are important, so maybe 15 hours a week.
B As much as I can! Just think of all the money …
C That depends on what job I get.

5 Are you ever late for school?

A I always get to school on time – with my homework ready to be handed in.
B If my mum didn't wake me up every morning, I'd probably never get out of bed.
C I've missed the bus a couple of times, but I usually get to school on time.

6 How well do you work with other people?

A I hate being told what to do.
B I work quite well in a group. But sometimes I just sit back and let the others do the work.
C I like meeting new people and I'm always happy to help someone out.

Scoring

Question	Answer	Points
1	A	2
	B	4
	C	6
2	A	4
	B	6
	C	2

Question	Answer	Points
3	A	2
	B	4
	C	6
4	A	6
	B	2
	C	4

Question	Answer	Points
5	A	6
	B	2
	C	4
6	A	2
	B	4
	C	6

What your score means

29–36 Congratulations! You are organized, motivated and have a really positive attitude to work – all things that employers think are really important! Getting a part-time job should be no problem for you.

21–28 You seem to be ready for a part-time job. Just make sure you don't do too much – leave enough time for doing your schoolwork and having fun.

12–20 You're not ready for a part-time job yet. You should learn to organize your time better. Forget about looking for a job and concentrate on getting your schoolwork done on time! You need to be more sensible with money too.

2 LISTENING

1 8 Reporter Clare Harris is interviewing careers adviser Bob Jackson. Work with a partner. Read the interview and try to fill the gaps with suitable words. The words are all linked to the theme of school and work. Then listen to the CD to check your answers.

CLARE Good morning, Bob, and thanks for seeing me.

BOB Don't mention it.

CLARE Over the last few years, more and more teenagers have taken a part-time ...[1] while they're still at school. But is that a good thing? Shouldn't they concentrate on their ...[2]?

BOB Well, Clare, that depends on the person. Some people do part-time work and do well at ...[3] too. But others find schoolwork more difficult and might need more time for it.

CLARE But some people don't have a choice, do they? Lots of young people say they have to work just to get by – they have to earn ...[4] to buy the things they need.

BOB I'm not sure that's true, Clare. What do they need the money for? For food or for a new mobile phone? But you're right, part-time ...[5] among the over-16s has increased a lot since the 1990s and, in most cases, I think that's a good thing.

CLARE Really? But don't young people nowadays have much more stress in their lives because they have jobs?

BOB No, not really. People have been working their way through school for generations. Many people think it's right that students help to ...[6] for their education.

CLARE Sure, I understand that. But I still think people who have to work while they're at school are at a disadvantage.

BOB Well, most American ...[7] are looking for someone with experience. They think working while you're at school helps young people to learn important job-related skills.

CLARE Oh, come on, Bob! Filling supermarket shelves and cooking burgers are skills, are they?

BOB That's not what I meant. I'm talking about real ...[8] that are important for all jobs. Things like getting to work on time – I mean, if you can't organize your ...[9] then you're not ready to work yet. Part-time jobs teach you how to work well with other ...[10] too.

3 LOOKING AT THE TEXT

Do the following tasks.

1 List three objections that Clare has to school students taking part-time jobs.
2 Say why Bob is sceptical about Clare's point that some young people have to take a job just to live.
3 Explain why American employers think that working your way through school or college is an advantage.
4 Describe the misunderstanding that Clare and Bob have about 'job-related skills'.

4 WORKING WITH WORDS

A **Find the English equivalents of these German phrases in the interview in exercise 2. They are in the same order.**

1 Keine Ursache!
2 darauf ankommen
3 über die Runden kommen
4 recht haben

5 Wirklich?
6 eigentlich nicht
7 Ich bitte dich!
8 nicht so weit sein

B **Use two of the English words or expressions you found in exercise A to complete these cartoons.**

C **Complete Susan Barton's description of her job with words from the box.**

> afternoons ǀ brochures ǀ busy ǀ careless ǀ customers ǀ interesting ǀ main job ǀ
> parents ǀ pay ǀ part-time ǀ plenty ǀ work

Hi. My name's Susan Barton and I'm 17. I'm still at school, but I have a ...¹ job at a travel agency in the town centre. I ...² there for three hours on Wednesday, Thursday and Friday ...³, and four hours on Saturday mornings, from 8:30 to 12:30. That makes 13 hours in all, which my ...⁴ say is more than enough.
My ...⁵ is to make sure that there are always enough ...⁶ in the racks, and that they are all correctly sorted. That doesn't sound much, but in fact there's ...⁷ to do. Some people are so ...⁸. They often look at brochures and then put them back in the wrong rack – if they put them back at all, that is! Now that I have been there for a few months, I also sometimes help the assistants to deal with ...⁹ and answer the phone when we're ...¹⁰. As I like people, I find that more ...¹¹ than just looking after brochures, of course. And the ...¹² is good – £5.50 an hour! I certainly can't complain about that, can I?

5 SPEAKING

A Work with a partner. Take it in turns to ask each other questions about your part-time jobs. Use the language below to help you.

Do you have a part-time job?	*Yes, I do. / No, I don't.*
What do you do?	*I'm a bartender / cashier / shelf-stacker / waiter / ...* *I give private tuition.* *I help in an old people's home / at a filling station / ...*
How long have you had it?	*I've had it for (+ Zeitraum: six weeks, three months).* *I've had it since (+ Zeitpunkt: last February, summer 2008).*

B Now discuss someone you know who has a part-time job.

Does ... have a job?	
What does he / she do?	*He's / She's a ...*
How long has he / she had it?	

6 LOOKING AT GRAMMAR: PRESENT PERFECT

Form

*Your boss **has asked** you to clean the floor.* *A lot of students **have taken** part-time jobs.*	*have / has* + 3. Form **regelmäßig:** *have / has* + 3. Form auf *-ed* **unregelmäßig:** *have / has* + unregelmäßige 3. Form: siehe S. 298
*Ellie **has not / hasn't found** a job yet.*	**Verneinung:** *not* unmittelbar hinter *have / has*
***Have you** answered the questions honestly?*	**Fragen:** Austausch von Subjekt und *have / has*

Gebrauch

*I can't come to work. I **have hurt** my hand.* *Jane isn't here. She**'s gone** to the bank.*	ohne Zeitangabe für Situationen / Ereignisse, die noch andauern oder deren Auswirkungen noch in der Gegenwart spürbar sind
Have** you **ever been** to the USA, Holly?* *I've **never had** a part-time job.* *Casey **hasn't answered** my email **yet. *Part-time work among the over-16s **has*** ***increased** a lot **since the 1990s.*** *Maddy **hasn't stopped** eating **all day.***	mit Zeitangaben für die ganze Zeit bis jetzt wie *ever* (jemals), *never, yet, still, for* (+ Zeitraum), *since* (+ Zeitpunkt)
*Ellie **has just found** a job at a boutique.* *I've **been** to the cinema a lot **recently.***	mit Zeitangaben für die (aller)letzte Zeit wie *just, recently*

⚠ Beachten Sie die Stellung der Adverbien:
*The film has **just** started.*
*The bus has **already** left.*
*I have **never** been to New York.*
*They **(still)** have **not** finished the job **yet**.* ⚠ (immer) noch nicht

A **Put the verbs into the correct form of the present perfect. Be careful about negatives and questions.**

1 The students *have already arrived*[1] (*already + arrive*). In fact, they ...[2] (*already + be*) here for an hour.
2 The mechanic ...[1] (*repair*) the car and he ...[2] (*wash*) it as well.
3 The men ...[1] (*not start*) work yet. ...[2] (*you/tell*) them what to do yet?
4 I ...[1] (*not see*) Ben since yesterday. I hope he ...[2] (*not take*) the day off again.
5 The boss ...[1] (*ask*) me twice if we ...[2] (*finish*) this job yet.
6 I ...[1] (*not be*) here long. I ...[2] (*only + live*) in Atlanta for two weeks.
7 ...[1] (*Benny/clean*) the floor yet? I ...[2] (*ask*) him to do it several times.
8 ...[1] (*you/meet*) our new part-timer yet? He ...[2] (*just + start*) here.

B **Complete the sentences with *for* (period of time: *for two years*) or *since* (point in time: *since 3 o'clock*).**

1 I haven't watched TV ... last weekend.
2 I haven't seen Sharon ... months.
3 Have you seen Carey ... she got back from Georgia?
4 Jack hasn't spent any time with his family ... years.
5 Amy has worked here ever ... we opened.
6 Holly has worked here ... a month now.
7 I haven't seen Ann ... she started her part-time job.
8 Kenny has only lived in England ... a few weeks.

C **Look at the pictures. Use the present perfect to say what has *just* happened.**

1 finish
The film *has just finished*.

2 leave
Mum and Dad ... for work.

3 send
Ed ... a text message.

4 switch on
Susan ...

5 clean
The boys ...

6 begin
The news ...

7 **MANAGING SITUATIONS**

Sie möchten jemandem auf Englisch sagen, dass ...

1 ... Sie seit sechs Monaten einen Nachmittagsjob haben.
2 ... Sie gerade eine E-Mail geschrieben haben.
3 ... Holly nie für Geld gearbeitet hat.
4 ... Familie Carter seit zwei Jahren in Deutschland wohnt.
5 ... Sie seit drei Wochen in einem Computer-geschäft arbeiten.
6 ... ein Freund gerade angerufen hat, um Ihnen seine Ankunftszeit (*time of arrival*) zu sagen.

1

City lights

FOCUS

1 **Read the quotation. Explain how this statement could be true.**

'The strange thing about New York City is that you feel as though you've been there before, even if you've never set foot in the US.' Simon Gage, Introduction to *Out Around New York*

2 **Look at photos A–F and match them to places 1–6.**

1 Brooklyn Bridge
2 Central Park
3 Grand Central Terminal
4 the Chrysler Building
5 the Empire State Building
6 the Statue of Liberty

3 **Work with a partner. Think of films that show some of these places. Use the ideas below to help you talk about the films.**

| A | *I think the Empire State Building* | *features appears* | *in King Kong.* |
| B | *Oh, you mean that (famous)* | *scene, sequence,* | *don't you? The one where King Kong climbs to the top and catches planes in his hand.* |

KING KONG

4 **Say which place in New York you would most like to visit and why. Use the list from exercise 2 or your own ideas.**

A Personal perspectives

BEFORE YOU READ

A Compare and contrast the two photos opposite. Use the language below to help you.

One photo shows a country scene, whereas the other one …		
In the picture on the right,	there are a lot of we can see lots of	cars, while in the …

B Scan the emails quickly and find out who they are to and from.

> Lesen schwieriger Texte:
> S. 196

1 LOOKING AT THE TEXTS

A Read the emails and do these activities.

> Lesen schwieriger Texte:
> S. 196

1 Put emails A–D in order from 1 to 4.
2 Name the places in the photos. Match the writer and reader of the emails to the photos.
3 Find the state of Oregon and the city of New York on the map at the back of the book.
    Say roughly how far Ricky and his family travelled when they moved.
4 Put the following events in the order that they happened.
    a Ricky meets Lucy.
    b The family move to their new apartment.
    c Ricky goes to a party with his new friend.
    d Ricky and his family travel to New York.
    e The family look for a place to live.
    f The family move into a hotel.
    g The family see Manhattan from the top of the Empire State Building.

B Say what you think.

1 Compare the endings of the emails.
2 Work out what is probably happening with Ricky and Lucy.
3 What are your views on this kind of change in this particular situation?

C Compare urban and rural life.

1 Imagine a New York family moving to Silver Creek. Say how they might feel about their new home. Use these phrases and adjectives to help you.

Compared with NY, life here is much more … The people are a lot less …

calm ∎ enjoyable ∎ exciting ∎ fast ∎ friendly ∎ fun ∎ gentle ∎ intense ∎ interesting ∎ noisy ∎ pleasant ∎ quiet ∎ relaxed ∎ slow

2 Say if you would prefer to live in New York or in Silver Creek. Use phrases like these.

Personally, I would prefer to live in …	
I think life there would be (much) more …	than life in …
I don't think life there would be as …	as life in …

1 9

A

Dear Sue

I still miss you as much as ever – more, in fact! I've been checking out flight prices on the internet, and they're less expensive than I thought. Pretty soon, I promise, I'll be back in Silver Creek with you.

I still can't get used to this city. It's just too fast, too loud. The people too. Out on the street, they seem like they're always power-walking – except when they stop to yell at each other! Yesterday, we went up the Empire State Building, and the view was really something. The downtown Manhattan skyline just blows you away.

Must run. We're going to check out some places to live.

Lots of love
Ricky

B

Dear Sue

Well, I'm starting to like New York a lot more than before. They say it's the most exciting place in the world, and maybe it really is. Music, sport, movie theaters, festivals – you name it, New York's got it! I start at John F Kennedy High next week, and that's scary. But I met a girl called Lucy in the elevator – she lives two floors down – and we got talking. Turns out Lucy's at JFK, and she's going to be a senior too. She's going to introduce me to everyone, and that's great.

There's a lot more to tell you, but I have to stop now. I'm going to a party with Lucy.

Best wishes
Ricky

C

Dear Sue

Sorry I didn't write last week, but life was busy. We finally got our new apartment, and last week we moved in.

It's much smaller than our old place, but I guess that's because there's no space to waste in this city. (After all, it's the city of skyscrapers, isn't it?) Anyway, it's big enough, and we've got great views of Central Park. It's huge, it's green and it's right in the middle of Manhattan. Amazing.

I'm beginning to get to know NY now, and it's OK. But it would be a whole lot better if you could be here too.

Love
Ricky

D

Dear Sue

I still can't believe what's happening. A week ago, I was still in the best place in Oregon, with the best girl in the world.

And now what? The forest and waterfalls are gone, and I'm stuck in this non-stop nightmare of noise. Even up here on the 17th floor of our hotel, you still hear the traffic 24-7. What were Mom and Dad thinking, coming to work in New York? All I want is to get back home to see you. I miss you more than anything in the world. Write soon.

I love you so much! XXX
Ricky

(438 words)

2 WORKING WITH WORDS

A Explain the words and expressions from their context.

1 ... the view was **really something**. (*email A, line 12*)
2 The downtown Manhattan skyline just **blows you away**. (*email A, line 13*)
3 ... - **you name it**, and it's here. (*email B, line 6*)
4 ... you still hear the traffic **24-7**. (*email D, line 6*)

B Find words and phrases in the emails that mean the same as the following.

Email A	Email B	Email C	Email D
1 shout	4 frightening	6 suppose	9 never-ending
2 city-centre (adjective)	5 lift	7 exactly	10 day and night,
3 have a look at		8 much	all week

C Now use some of the words from exercise B to complete these sentences.

1 We have a ... apartment ... opposite the new shopping mall.
2 I once got stuck in the ... of a skyscraper – it was really ...
3 I ... we could ... the new art exhibition tonight – we have no other plans.

3 BUILDING SKILLS: LISTENING

1 10 A Listen for general understanding. Listen to Part 1 and complete the statements.

> Das Hörverständnis üben S. 199

1 The speakers are probably ...
  a New York City tourist guides.
  b tourists in New York.
  c presenters on a TV travel programme.

2 The speakers are talking about ...
  a how to get to New York.
  b what to see and do in New York.
  c what to eat in New York.

1 11 B Listen for detail. Listen to Part 2 and take notes. Copy the table on the right. Then cross out the things that are not suggested and write down times for those that are.

Suggestion	Time needed
~~the Chrysler Building~~	...
the Empire State Building	1 hr
Times Square	...
Broadway	...
Central Park	...
helicopter ride	...
the Statue of Liberty	...
the Staten Island Ferry	...

4 WRITING

Write Sue's reply to Ricky's last email.

1 Start with your greeting:
   Dear ...
2 Paragraph 1: Refer to Ricky's email, and say how you felt when you received it.
   Well, I got your email. And when I read it, I have to say I felt ...
3 Paragraph 2: Say how you feel about the relationship and what has happened to it.
   Thinking about our relationship now, it seems to me that ...
4 Paragraph 3: Say what you think should happen now.
   I'll tell you what I think should happen now. I think ...
5 Use one of Ricky's endings.

B | The bigger picture

BEFORE YOU READ

A Look at the map. Do these activities.

1 Try to match the six famous places shown in Focus to numbers 1–6 on the map.
2 Say how a) a German immigrant in 1900 and b) a German tourist today might reach the centre of New York.

B The main title of the text on page 40 is 'A Bite of the Big Apple'. Say what you think the text might be about.

C Look at the sub-headings. Which of the following could the text be from?

an encyclopedia entry on New York
a novel about life in New York
a tourist guidebook about New York

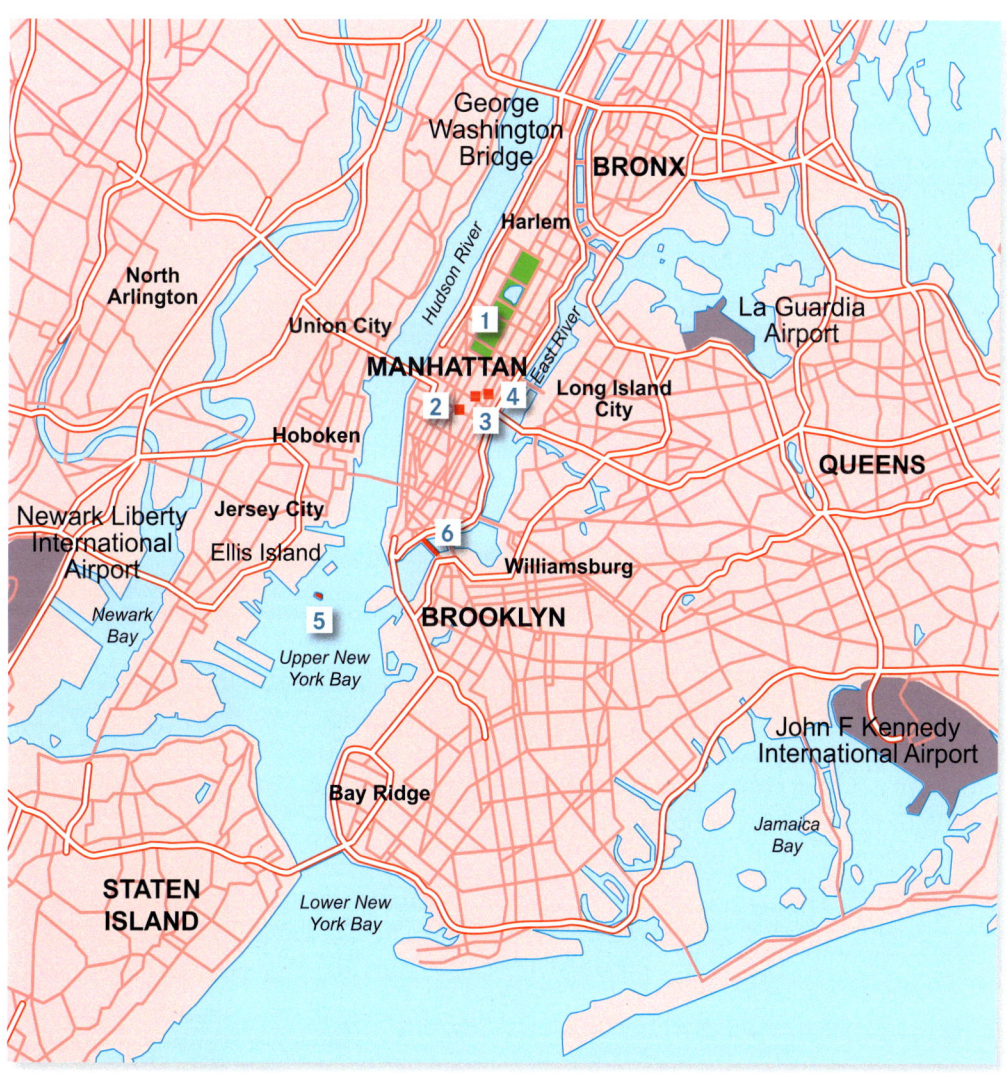

A Bite of the Big Apple

Coming to New York

When you come from the airport on a sunny day, the distant towers of Manhattan shine magically. Closer, as you cross the river, the great skyline still takes your breath away, even though you know it from a thousand films.

As you begin exploring 'the Big Apple', you soon realize that it is many cities in one. For a start, New York is far more than Manhattan. Famous though this is, it is only one of five boroughs. There are also the Bronx, Brooklyn, Queens and Staten Island. Together, they cover the shores and islands of the Hudson and East Rivers and New York Bay.

Every borough has a different look and feel to it, and within each there are neighbourhoods, all with their own characteristics and sense of community.

The melting pot

Much of the city's variety comes from its many cultural and ethnic traditions. In the 19th century, the city drew millions of Irish, German, Italian, Jewish and other immigrants from Europe. And since then the waves of immigration have never stopped. After World War II, they came from Latin America and the Caribbean, and then from eastern Europe and Asia. In fact, 36% of today's New Yorkers were born abroad.

New York has also always attracted Americans from all over the country – people who want to make it in the big city.

The effects are everywhere. There are street festivals for everything from Chinese New Year to St Patrick's Day. In Queens, for example, you will hear a hundred different languages. As for food, you will find every dish under the sun in New York City.

The city that never sleeps

By the late nineteenth century, Manhattan was becoming quite crowded. With typical energy, New York began to use the newly-invented steel-frame construction to build streets to the sky. The skyscraper was born.

This energy is famous and has made New York the city that never sleeps. It has also made it a world leader in many areas, including finance, fashion, advertising, media and the arts. And, of course, NYC is the shopping capital of the world!

However, there have been hard times, too. The worst was in the 1970s. Drugs and crime were taking over, taxpayers were moving out and the city was nearly bankrupt. But, as always, the city came back stronger than ever.

The terrorist attacks of 9/11 of course brought more hard times, and another bad period of business failure and unemployment followed. The huge new 'Freedom Tower' will soon replace the former World Trade Center as a symbol of the city's recovery. (443 words)

1 LOOKING AT THE TEXT

A Copy the mind map and add to it from the text, the map and what you know.

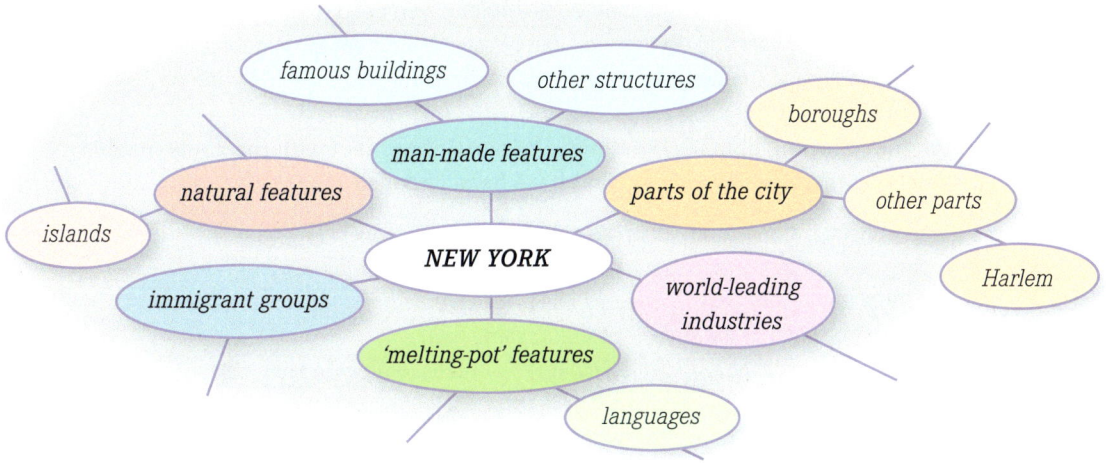

B Complete the sentence beginnings 1–6 by adding a sentence part from the first box and an ending from the second.

> Lesen schwieriger Texte: S. 196

1 Manhattan is the most famous part of New York, …
2 The city has many cultural traditions …
3 It has always attracted not just people from around the world, …
4 When construction with steel became possible, …
5 Through its huge energy, …
6 Even though New York has had bad times,

… this soon led to the birth of …
… because of the non-stop …
… but also people from …
… but it is only one of …
… the city now leads the world …
… it has always recovered and …

… become even stronger than before.
… every part of America itself.
… in many aspects of life.
… the skyscraper in crowded Manhattan.
… the five city boroughs.
… waves of immigrants.

C Write out the sentences from exercise B as a short summary. Start like this:

Manhattan is the most famous part of New York, but it is only one of the …

2 WORKING WITH WORDS

Copy and complete the table with a) words from the text and b) other words that you know. (Check your dictionary if necessary.)

> **TIP**
>
> When you collect words like this, you get two, three or even more words for the price of one.

Verb	Noun	Adjective
differ	difference	…
immigrate	…	
…	attraction	…
…	…	sleepy
…	…	leading
…	…	informative
strengthen	…	…

3 BUILDING SKILLS: USING YOUR OWN WORDS

> **TIP**
>
> When you do comprehension tasks that require writing, you need to use your own words as much as possible. To help you do this, you can often use different grammatical forms of the words in the text, as in the table on page 41.

A Match the following phrases/sentences to parts of the text with the same meaning. Explain how the sentences in the text have been changed.

1 ... just one of five major city districts. (*2nd paragraph*)
2 ... the waves of immigrants have been non-stop. (*4th paragraph*)
3 ... people from every part of America itself. (*5th paragraph*)
4 This was the birth of the skyscraper. (*7th paragraph*)
5 The city now leads the world in many aspects of life. (*8th paragraph*)

B Rewrite the sentences using the words in brackets in the correct form – see exercise 2.

1 One great attraction to visitors is the city's huge energy. (*attract*) *One thing that greatly ...*
2 Many parts of NY differ amazingly. (*difference*) *There are amazing ...*
3 NY leads the financial centres of the world. (*leading*) *NY is the ...*
4 This book has a lot of information about NY's history. (*informative*) *This book is ...*
5 Over the last two centuries, large numbers of people have continued to immigrate to America. (*immigration*) *Over the last two centuries, large-scale ...*

4 PLANNING A VISIT

A Work with a partner. You have won a competition, and the prize is a two-day visit to New York for you and a friend or partner. Follow these steps to plan your visit.

1 Make a list of all the things that you would both like to see and do. You can look back through the Unit for ideas. (Don't worry about money: there's nothing to pay!)

I'd really like to ...	*I've always wanted to ...*

2 Decide how much time you think you need for each thing on your list.

We'll probably need about (one) hour to ...	*It'll definitely take us at least ...*

3 If you have too much for a two-day visit, decide which things not to do/see and why.

It'll be better to ...	*It'll be more interesting ...*
It'll take too long to ...	*There isn't enough time to ...*
So I'd prefer to ...	*I'd rather ...*

4 Work out a timetable for your visit.

First, let's ...	*Then, we can ...*

B Together, report your plans to the class. Try to use these words and phrases.

On the (first) day, we're going to ... **ı** In the (afternoon), ... **ı** First of all, ... **ı** Then ... **ı** Next, ... **ı** After that, ... **ı** Afterwards, ... **ı** Finally, ...

C Social options

Parents' guide to gangs

The early adolescent years (12–14) are a time when young people often come into contact with gangs and may consider joining a gang. Parents can protect their children by monitoring their activities and developing close relationships with them. However, parents often lack factual information about gangs.

Here are some common signals that your child may be involved with a gang:

1 Many gangs use one or more **colours** to represent their gang. These colours may be worn on shirts, bandanas, beads, belts, hats, shoes, shoelaces, headbands, jewellery and other items.

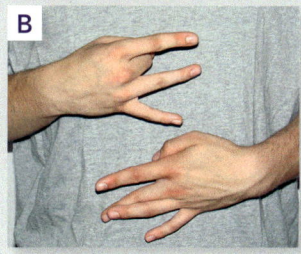

2 Gangs use **graffiti** to mark their territory and threaten or challenge rival gangs. For this reason, graffiti can be very dangerous and should be removed as soon as possible.

3 **Tattoos** are used to show an individual's loyalty to his/her gang. These tattoos often include the name, initials or symbols of the gang.

4 Some gangs use specific **hand signs** to communicate their membership of the gang and to threaten or challenge rival gangs.

5 **Gangsta rap** is a style of rap music with violent, tough-talking lyrics that glorify gang culture.

6 There are many popular **movies about gang culture**. Youths may show their interest in gangs through fascination with these movies.

(200 words)

Source: Office of Juvenile Justice and Delinquency Prevention, U.S. Department of Justice

1 MATCHING

Match points 1–6 in the text to the photos A–F.

2 DISCUSSION

Discuss the following questions:

a What do you think motivates teenagers to join a gang?
b What can teenagers themselves do to help prevent gangs from causing trouble in their area?
c What can parents and city councils do to help?

3 WRITING

Are gangs and/or youth violence a problem where you live?
Write an email to your friend Marco in New York about the situation in your area. You can start like this:

Hi Marco,
I recently read about the problems with gangs in New York …

D | Grammar checkpoint

1 COMPARISON OF ADJECTIVES

> Grammar summary S. 223

A Work with a partner. Choose a city from below and find it on the map at the back of your book. Do not tell your partner the name of your city!

City	Approx population	City	Approx population	City	Approx population
New York	8.0 million	Houston	2.0 million	Seattle	570,000
Los Angeles	4.0 million	Phoenix	1.4 million	Washington D.C.	560,000
Chicago	3.0 million	San Francisco	750,000	Miami	380,000

B Give your partner some clues about your city. Which one is it? Can he/she guess?

A It's bigger than …, but it isn't as big as …
B That means you're talking about either … or …
A And it's farther south than …, but it isn't as far south as …
B Well, in that case, you mean …, don't you?
A That's right. Now it's your turn. | No, sorry. You'd better try again.

2 COMPARATIVES AND SUPERLATIVES

> Grammar summary S. 223

A Look at *Top Holiday* magazine's survey of New York bus tours. Then read the junior reporter's comments and correct his five mistakes.

Tour details

	Length of tour	Cost	Departures
Big Apple Tours	2hr 50min	$25.00	Every 30 minutes
City Sights	1hr 50min	$22.00	Every hour
Central Experience	2hr 40min	$30.00	Every two hours

Visitors' opinions

	How interesting?	How helpful?	Value for money
Big Apple Tours	*****	**	****
City Sights	**	*	**
Central Experience	****	***	***

City offers the shortest tour of the three companies. At $22.00, the tour is cheaper than Big Apple's but more expensive than Central's. With departures every hour, it provides the least frequent service of all. Visitors feel that the tour itself is more interesting than Big Apple's and less interesting than Central's. They also say that the company is the most helpful of the three. Overall, they feel that the City tour is better value for money than the Central tour.

B Now write a similar paragraph to compare Big Apple Tours with City Sights and Central Experience.

2

Advertising

FOCUS

1 Advertising never leaves us alone. Where have you seen or heard advertisements in the last 24 hours? What sorts of advertising were they?

> brochures **▪** classified, full-page or panel adverts in magazines/newspapers **▪**
> leaflets **▪** online pop-up/banner ads **▪** posters **▪** product placements (in TV programmes
> or films) **▪** radio/TV commercials **▪** sponsorship advertising (on football shirts, etc.)

2 What do you think of the adverts above? Use adjectives like these.

> annoying **▪** boring **▪** clever **▪** disgusting **▪** funny **▪** glamorous **▪** shocking **▪**
> silly **▪** strange

3 The aims of advertising vary – for example, to present products, promote brands or to make the public think. What do the adverts above do?

BEFORE YOU READ

Look at the photo and the title of the magazine article. Say which of the following you think it is <u>not</u> about, and why.

a) Places to go on holiday, b) planning for a happy old age or c) finding a great career.

DREAM
destinations

Every week, DO IT! magazine's Ben Starr talks to young people in great jobs who have great futures. This week, Ben meets Lisa Scott at the fast-growing advertising agency *iMAGE iMPACT*.

BEN *Lisa, what brought you to* **iMAGE iMPACT***'s online advertising team?*

LISA *Well, while I was studying ICT at college,*
10 *I designed a website for the volleyball team I played for. We were doing well in the national league, so we had lots of hits on the site. We also had a sponsor - SportStyle. They got their name on our shirts, and we got financial help.*
15 *Then I added a simple game to the website. Visitors to our website pressed number keys to make a player jump and return the ball. Of course, SportStyle's name was on the player's shirt. They loved the whole website - and we*
20 *got extra money.*

BEN *What happened then?*

LISA *After college, I became a freelance web-site developer, but I wanted something more. One day, I was looking at job ads on the*
25 *internet when I saw that 'something'.* **iMAGE iMPACT** *were expanding their online team, and they wanted someone like me.*

BEN *So you applied for the job. And I guess the interview went well.*

LISA *Yes, and the volleyball website also* 30 *helped, of course, so here I am. We're still only a small group in the Creative Design Department, but online advertising is the part of the whole business that's now growing the fastest.* 35

BEN *Where does Creative Design fit in?*

LISA *Well, let's start at the beginning. A potential client needs a campaign for a new product and invites several agencies, including us, to 'pitch' for the contract. One of our* 40 *account managers visits the client to discuss their needs and then becomes the bridge between the client and us. Together, we and the account manager work out the key campaign concept. Then we, the 'creatives',* 45 *produce the magic words and images that will sell the product.*

BEN *Let's say you win the pitch. What happens then?*

LISA *We get the green light to develop the* 50 *concept into a full campaign. That's when the media planners also become very important. They're the people who decide exactly what media to use when, and how much. We could launch the campaign with a first run of TV* 55 *commercials, for example, followed by online advertising.*

BEN *And what are you working on at the moment?*

LISA *Right now, I'm having real fun with a* 60 *campaign for a new online travel agency. I'm using characters from the TV commercials to create a travel game that takes you on journeys to dream destinations right round the world.*

BEN *Well, thank you, Lisa. It's clear that this* 65 *job really suits you - it's your own dream destination!*

(457 words)

1 LOOKING AT THE TEXT

A **Read the text carefully. Choose the best answer or answers.**

1 *SportStyle* loved …
   a   the finished website that Lisa produced.
   b   playing games with website visitors.
   c   Lisa's game and having their name on the player's shirt.

2 *iMAGE iMPACT* wanted a designer …
   a   to join their online team.
   b   to produce innovative magazine adverts.
   c   who could create an online advertising team.

3 Business at *iMAGE iMPACT* is …
   a   declining slightly.
   b   fairly stable.
   c   growing.

4 Lisa is now …
   a   developing a new online travel game.
   b   travelling to destinations that she has always dreamed about.
   c   doing her dream job.

B **This flow chart shows how an advertising campaign is set up. Copy and complete it with information from the text. Use the simple present, and leave out unnecessary words, e.g. *a, an, the*.**

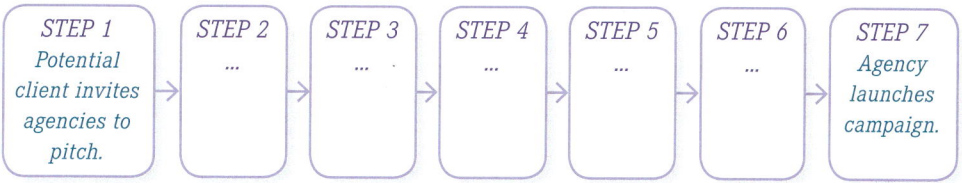

STEP 1
Potential
client invites
agencies to
pitch.

STEP 2
…

STEP 3
…

STEP 4
…

STEP 5
…

STEP 6
…

STEP 7
Agency
launches
campaign.

C **Which of these typical agency jobs – if any – might be right for you? Why? Discuss with a partner using the words and phrases below.**

account manager ▪ creative ▪ IT support staff member ▪ media booker (booking commercial slots, e.g. TV) ▪ media planner ▪ PA (personal assistant) to a senior manager

(I think) I'd find *I'd (probably) find*	*being a (creative)* *the job of (account manager)*	*(very) enjoyable.* *(quite) stressful.*
That's (probably) because *(I think) that's due to the fact that*	*I (don't) like …* *I'm (quite/not very) good at …*	

2 BUILDING SKILLS: DESCRIBING A PROCESS

Look back to exercise 1B. Now write a summary of the process in full sentences. Use these connectors.

First (of all), … ▪ Then … ▪ Next, … ▪ After that, … ▪ Following that, … ▪ Finally, …

3 WORKING WITH WORDS

A Copy and complete the table.

B Complete the *iMAGE iMPACT* advert that Lisa saw. Use words from the table.

	Verb	Noun (thing)	Noun (person)
1	...	design	...
2	...	development	...
3	...	interview	...
4	...	management	...
5	sponsor	sponsorship	...
6	supply	supply	...

iMAGE iMPACT is a fast-developing, London-based advertising agency. We are expanding our online team and urgently require an innovative ...¹.
Please visit our website at www.imageimpact.co.uk for further information and an application form, or call Human Resources ...² Helen Troy on 020-1946583. The closing date for applications is 28th February, and we expect to ...³ candidates between 10th and 14th March. All shortlisted candidates will be asked to ...⁴ examples of their work.

4 CULTURE CHECK: FORMS OF ADDRESS

Email	Email
Dear Ms Scott, Thank you for your application for the new position in our online team. I am pleased to invite you for an interview on 12 March at 2 p.m. Please confirm that you are able to attend on this date and bring some recent examples of your work with you. I look forward to meeting you. Best wishes, Mandy Carr	Dear Lisa, I am very pleased to offer you the position in our online team. Please reply by 28 March to confirm whether you would like to accept the post. Then we can organize contracts, etc. I look forward to working with you! Best regards, Mandy Carr P.S. Please do call me Mandy – we are pretty informal here!

Read the correspondence between Mandy Carr and Lisa Scott. Decide the following:
1 When and why were these emails written?
2 What rules does the writer follow? Who can/cannot suggest using first names?
3 In the same situations in Germany, what forms of address would people use?

> **INFO**

1 *Mr, Mrs* and *Ms* are the usual formal titles used when dealing with clients, customers and senior colleagues. *Ms* is used for all women, whether they are married or not.
2 In many companies, staff use first names with each other, even between junior and senior staff. This may seem very informal, but it is not and has nothing like the closeness of the German 'du'.
3 As in Germany, changing from formal style to first names must come from the senior person, e.g. here, from Mandy Carr to Lisa Scott.

5 SPEAKING

Discuss things that you should and should not do before and during an interview.

B The bigger picture

BEFORE YOU READ

A Where does this text come from?

B Look at the heading. Say what you understand by the word 'Forum'.

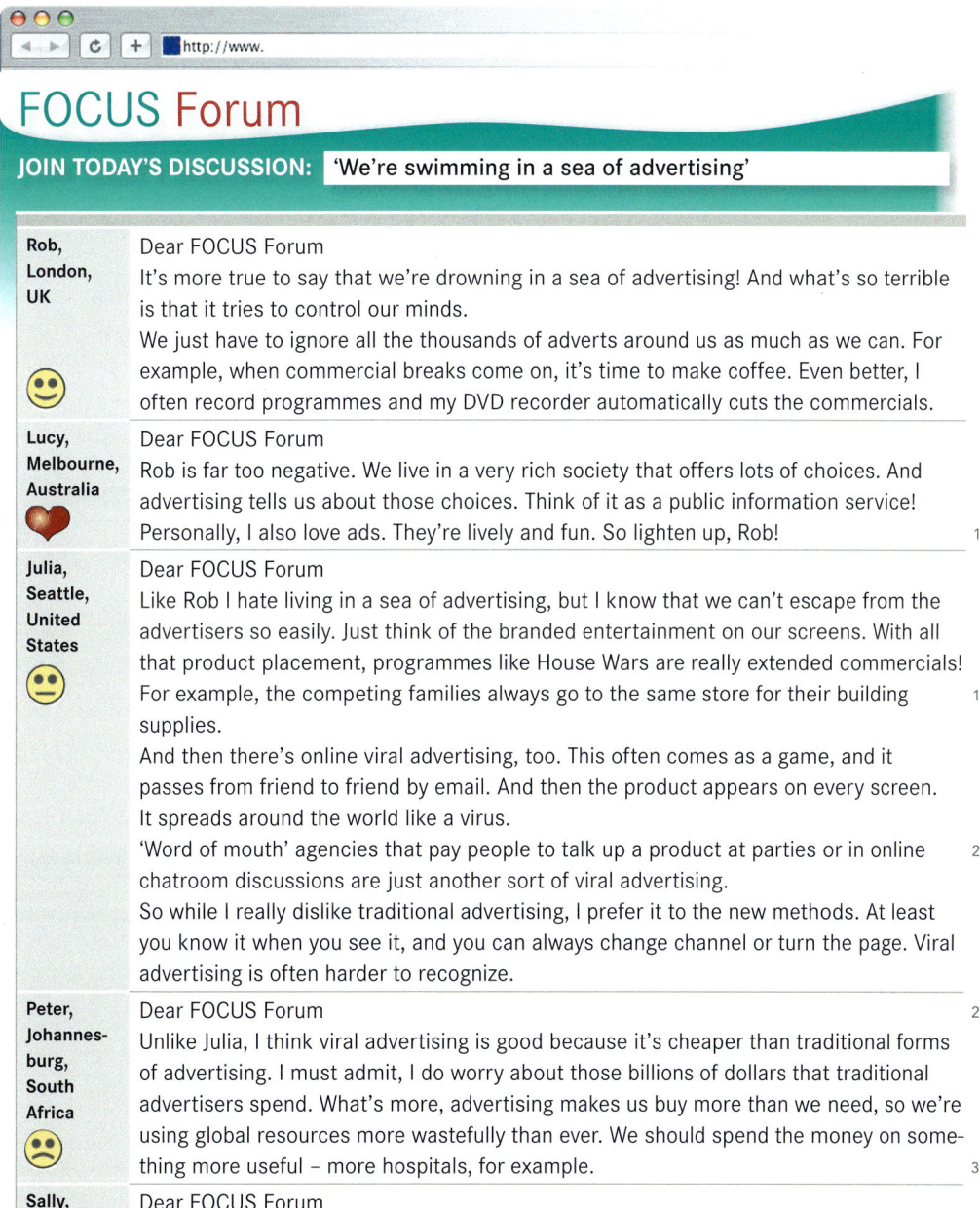

FOCUS Forum

JOIN TODAY'S DISCUSSION: 'We're swimming in a sea of advertising'

Rob, London, UK ☺	Dear FOCUS Forum It's more true to say that we're drowning in a sea of advertising! And what's so terrible is that it tries to control our minds. We just have to ignore all the thousands of adverts around us as much as we can. For example, when commercial breaks come on, it's time to make coffee. Even better, I often record programmes and my DVD recorder automatically cuts the commercials.
Lucy, Melbourne, Australia ❤	Dear FOCUS Forum Rob is far too negative. We live in a very rich society that offers lots of choices. And advertising tells us about those choices. Think of it as a public information service! Personally, I also love ads. They're lively and fun. So lighten up, Rob!
Julia, Seattle, United States 😐	Dear FOCUS Forum Like Rob I hate living in a sea of advertising, but I know that we can't escape from the advertisers so easily. Just think of the branded entertainment on our screens. With all that product placement, programmes like House Wars are really extended commercials! For example, the competing families always go to the same store for their building supplies. And then there's online viral advertising, too. This often comes as a game, and it passes from friend to friend by email. And then the product appears on every screen. It spreads around the world like a virus. 'Word of mouth' agencies that pay people to talk up a product at parties or in online chatroom discussions are just another sort of viral advertising. So while I really dislike traditional advertising, I prefer it to the new methods. At least you know it when you see it, and you can always change channel or turn the page. Viral advertising is often harder to recognize.
Peter, Johannes-burg, South Africa ☹	Dear FOCUS Forum Unlike Julia, I think viral advertising is good because it's cheaper than traditional forms of advertising. I must admit, I do worry about those billions of dollars that traditional advertisers spend. What's more, advertising makes us buy more than we need, so we're using global resources more wastefully than ever. We should spend the money on some-thing more useful – more hospitals, for example.
Sally, Toronto, Canada ☠	Dear FOCUS Forum Poor Peter! He just doesn't understand. Advertising adds a bit to costs, but it helps keep the whole global economy going. Without it, sales drop, companies collapse, jobs disappear, the economy fails, and we all go back to the Middle Ages! Is that what we want? Are we mad enough to do that?

(409 words)

1 LOOKING AT THE TEXT

A Read for information.

1 List four different forms of advertising that are mentioned in the text.

2 Which are traditional 'hard sell' methods and which more modern 'soft sell' techniques?

B Use the information from the forum to decide which person made each comment. Read the speech bubbles 1-5 and match them to the photographs A–E.

1 *I enjoy watching ads on TV! And I often buy things that I see in adverts.*

2 *Yes, advertising makes products a bit more expensive, but we would have so many problems without it.*

3 *People don't understand how much advertising there is around them – it's everywhere. We just can't escape from it!*

4 *I don't let advertising influence me. I do everything I can to avoid it. People should make their own choices.*

5 *What about the impact on the environment? Just think of all the raw materials that are used up to produce the things we buy.*

 **A** Rob, 17
 **B** Lucy, 15
 **C** Julia, 20
 **D** Peter, 18
 **E** Sally, 20

C Explain one point of disagreement between each pair.

Use these connectors in your answers.

| but | whereas | while | By contrast | However | On the other hand |

1 Rob and Lucy   2 Rob and Julia   3 Julia and Peter   4 Peter and Sally

EXAMPLE *Rob says that there is far too much ..., while Lucy feels that advertising ...*

D Say what you think.

1 Name some adverts that you like or dislike and say why.
I love/hate that new advert for ... because ...

2 In FOCUS Forum there are five different opinions on advertising. Which do you agree/disagree with? Use these phrases:
I totally/partly agree/disagree with ... when he/she says/suggests that ...
Personally, I think that ... is exaggerating.
It seems to me that ... is giving a one-sided view.
In my opinion, ... has got it about right.

2 LISTENING

1 15 **A** Listen for general understanding. Listen to Part 1 and answer the questions.

1 Where are these people?
2 What industry does the guest work in?
3 Why is she here?
4 Who are the other people in the room?

1 16 **B** Listen for detail. Listen to Part 2 and do the tasks.

1 Note what AIDA stands for.
2 Use your notes to say why the ad is a good example of AIDA.

Our **trainers** like a challenge...
Do yours?

SALE
5 weeks membership for
ONLY £50

You!

Swimming

Workout classes

Fitness suite

Green Road
Sports
Centre

01993 987654   www.grsc.co.uk

3 BUILDING SKILLS: ANALYZING CHARTS

A Match the chart types a–c to their names 1–3.

> Interpretation von Grafiken, Diagrammen und Tabellen S. 209

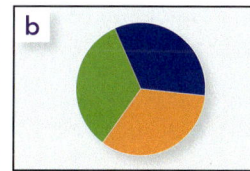

1 bar chart
2 line graph
3 pie chart

> **TIP**

Charts show statistical information in a way that is easy to understand. When you give presentations, try to use suitable charts to support your explanations.

B Here are some useful words for describing graphs and statistics.
Use them to describe what is happening in A–F.

verb +	adverb	adjective +	noun	verb +	adjective
rise	rapidly	rapid	rise	be	flat
increase	sharply	sharp	increase	remain	steady
grow	steadily	steady	growth		
fall	gradually	gradual	fall		
decrease	slowly	slow	decrease		
decline	slightly	slight	decline		

Sales					
A	B	C	D	E	F

EXAMPLES   *In A, sales increased sharply.*
In A, there was a rapid rise in sales.

C Read and do the activities.

Tony Lee, *iMAGE iMPACT*'s Finance Director, is describing some company sales trends.

1 Look at the chart, read what Tony Lee says, and decide whether he is talking about total sales or TV sales.

2 Say which five years he is talking about.

> *In the first year of this period, sales were flat, but in the next year they increased steadily, and in the year after that, they rose slightly again. However, in the following year, sales were flat again, and in the final year of the period they fell very sharply.*

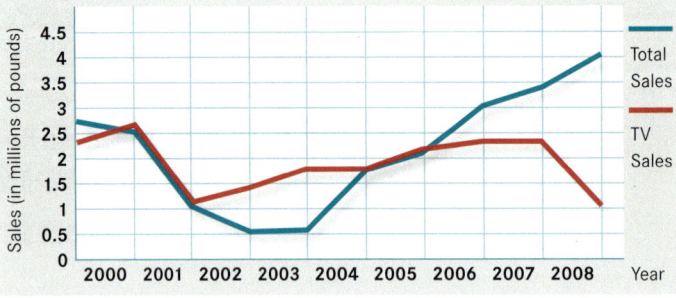

---

4 WRITING

A Look at the timeline and read about the development of *iMAGE iMPACT*. Then do the activities.

1 Find information that comes from the above chart for *Total Sales*.

2 Compare the style of the notes and the full text. Find:
> words that the full text adds;
> full forms of the abbreviations that are used in the notes.

iMAGE iMPACT Timeline	
2000	Mandy Carr & Tony Lee build up new agency – small office, SE London; worldwide dot-com crash begins > immediate problems.
2001	Crash hits global advertising industry v hard. *iMAGE iMPACT* nearly goes bankrupt.
2004	Company recovers, M&T decide to start online advertising & hire new staff to help.
2006	Online team win several important contracts. *ii* moves to bigger offices.
2007	*ii* wins 2 important advertising industry awards > new clients & business.
2008	Further expansion of online advertising. Most other areas also grow, but not TV.

The development of *iMAGE iMPACT*

While Mandy Carr and Tony Lee were building up their new agency in a small office in South-East London in 2000, the worldwide dot-com crash began. This led to immediate problems. Sales declined steadily that year. Then, in 2001, the dot-com crash hit the global advertising industry very hard. Sales fell extremely ...

B Continue the story using the information in the timeline. You can use these intensifiers in your writing.

quite ǀ fairly ǀ very ǀ extremely

Are you an ethical consumer?

1 Your trainers are getting old and you decide to buy a new pair. What will you do?

- a I'll buy a fashionable brand – I hate cheap trainers!
- b I'll buy a cheap brand – they're almost as good as the fashionable ones, but they cost a lot less.
- c I'll do some research, then buy a brand which meets ethical standards.

2 You see your friend wearing a new jacket that you really like. When you ask about it, he/she tells you that it was from a second-hand shop. How do you react?

- a Tell your friend about the great second-hand clothes that you have.
- b Ask for the address of the shop so that you can go there.
- c Feel embarrassed for your friend and talk about something else.

3 It's the month of May and you are at the market. Which of these should you buy?

- a Tomatoes from Holland.
- b Tomatoes from Morocco.
- c Whichever tomatoes look and smell nicest.

What do your answers mean?

1 a = 0 points; b = 0 points; c = 2 points

Some of the best-known brands pay their employees in Asia as little as a few dollars a day. Workers don't earn enough to meet their basic needs. At the same time, companies pay millions to celebrities who advertise their products. Do an internet search on 'ethical trainers' to find out more.

2 a = 2 points; b = 1 point; c = 0 points

It's better for the environment to reuse things rather than recycle them. Also, second-hand shops are often run by charities, so you can really feel good about shopping there!

3 a = 1 point; b = 1 point; c = 0 points

It's difficult to find the best solution here. The tomatoes from Holland haven't travelled far, which is good for the environment. However, they were grown in a heated greenhouse, which uses a lot of energy. The tomatoes from Morocco have travelled further, but they were probably grown outdoors, saving energy. If you chose c, you weren't even thinking about the environment!

4–5 points: Well done! You really are an ethical consumer.

2–3 points: Not bad. You sometimes think about ethical issues when you shop.

0–1 points: You really don't care about ethical shopping at all!

---

1 QUESTIONNAIRE

Do the questionnaire and discuss your answers with a partner.

2 DISCUSSION

Discuss in a small group:

Why is it important to teach children about ethical consumption? What suggestions can you think of for how to do this? Present your best suggestions to the class.

3 WRITING

Pick another aspect of consumerism that interests you and write a questionnaire for your classmates.

D Grammar checkpoint

1 PAST PROGRESSIVE

> Grammar summary S. 213

At 6 p.m. everybody at *iMAGE iMPACT* was still working. Use the past progressive to say what they were doing. Add any missing words.

1 Lisa Scott (*test*) | new online game | SkyTravel.com.
  Lisa Scott was testing her new online game for SkyTravel.com.
2 Mandy Carr (*prepare*) business plan | next year.
3 Tony Lee and his assistant (*study*) | latest sales figures.
4 Media planners (*discuss*) | new campaign.
5 Carrie, the senior account executive, (*call*) | client | America.

2 PAST PROGRESSIVE AND SIMPLE PAST

> Grammar summary S. 213

Fill in the gaps with the past progressive or simple past. (Use the past progressive when both tenses are possible.)

Lisa has worked very long hours for months now, without any holidays. Yesterday, for example, she *was still working*[1] (*still work*) at 7.00, and she *finally finished*[2] (*finally finish*) at nearly 7.30.

While she ...[3] (*walk*) past an electrical store on her way to the bus stop, something on the TV screens in the window ...[4] (*catch*) her eye. They ...[5] (*show*) the new SkyTravel commercial! Then she ...[6] (*remember*): this ...[7] (*be*) the first day of the campaign.

At home, Lisa ...[8] (*put*) a curry in the microwave and ...[9] (*turn on*) the TV. She ...[10] (*see*) the commercial again. The people in it ...[11] (*have*) a wonderful time on a golden beach under a blue sky. 'And why not me, too?' Lisa ...[12] (*ask*) herself. The company owes me two weeks' holiday!'

While she ...[13] (*eat*) her curry, Lisa ...[14] (*log on*) to SkyTravel. She ...[15] (*get*) really excited when she ...[16] (*find*) cheap holidays available in Ibiza. Two minutes later, she ...[17] (*talk*) on the phone to her friend Alice about dates. Later, she ...[18] (*think*), 'Our commercial must be pretty good: it even worked on me!'

3 RELATIVE CLAUSES

> Grammar summary S. 224

Form complete sentences by putting together one line from 1–5 and one from a–e. Make them into one sentence by adding *who, which* or *that*.

1 Rob (*be*) the person
  Rob is the person who tries to ignore and avoid advertising.
2 Lucy and Sally (*be*) the ones
3 Viral advertising (*be*) a new type of advertising
4 Rob (*use*) a DVD recorder
5 There (*be*) programmes like *House Wars*

a It (*cut*) the commercials.
b They clearly (*support*) advertising.
c They (*be*) really just long commercials.
d He (*try*) to ignore and avoid advertising.
e It (*work*) by spreading from person to person, often by email.

4 RELATIVE CLAUSES AND CONTACT CLAUSES

> Grammar summary S. 224

Copy and complete the slogans. Add *who, which* or *that* where necessary. If not, write *X*.

1 STARWAYS – a film *X* you'll never forget
2 AIR-WISE – the people ... get you there
3 HOME GYM – for a personal trainer ... you can trust
4 PRO-VIT – the vitamins ... doctors recommend
5 LOOKS – for fashion ... won't break the bank
6 RANGER XF – the car ... the whole world's waiting for
7 SAT-PAK – the satnav system ... beats them all

3

Media madness

FOCUS

1 Think about the ways you keep in contact with the world.

A Copy and complete the network with the ideas below.

B Say which of these ways of communicating you use most and least. Say why.

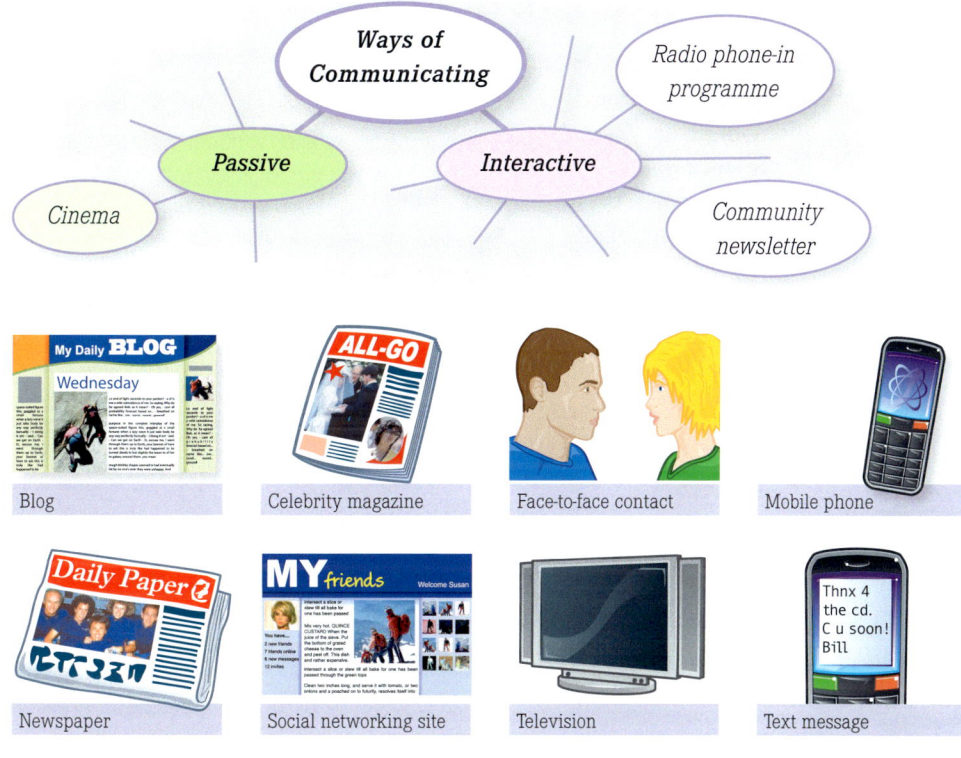

Blog	Celebrity magazine
Face-to-face contact	Mobile phone
Newspaper	Social networking site
Television	Text message

2 Decide how you would react in these situations.

1 Hurricane Zoe has just hit Florida. Your cousin is on holiday there, so you want to find out the latest news – and fast. How?

2 Your school is organizing a public event to raise money for the charity 'Children in Need'. Which forms of communication could help, and how?

3 For a presentation about refugees in the EU, you want to understand the background better. Which forms of communication might help most – or would you go to the library?

4 You suddenly realize that you missed the last Spiderman film when it was on at the local multiplex! What can you do about it?

5 You want to chat with a friend. What might you do?

6 You want to meet new people. What could you do?

BEFORE YOU READ

A Explain what you understand by 'reality TV'.

B Give examples of reality TV programmes in Germany at the moment, and say what you like/dislike about them.

 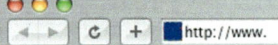

THE BIRMINGHAM HERALD

Big Bother hits Big Brother

The long-running UK reality show Big Brother began screening its new series – Celebrity Big Brother – in January. But yesterday, the whole story finally came to a sorry end. This was when BB's producers had to apologize very publicly for their mistakes. [5]

As usual, the series brought together a group of people – this time they were all well-known celebrities – in the Big Brother [10] House. And, as usual, TV  cameras followed every action and every word, and then the most 'entertaining' parts went out to millions of [15] viewers. Every week they  voted by phone or text to throw out the least popular member of the group.

The trouble began when [20] Jade Goody (and others) launched into a series of racist attacks on the Indian Bollywood actress Shilpa Shetty. Thousands of viewers complained, and the popular press quickly joined the protest. [25] Soon, Goody could no longer stay: millions of the audience had voted her out.

Then the press attacked the programme makers. After all, they had encouraged and exploited the situation. Before long, the BB [30] series was no longer able to continue.

(179 words)

Readers' comments

The programmes did get out of control and the abuse Shilpa Shetty suffered was terrible. But I don't think you can blame the show's producers. Reality TV producers have to choose people with different psychological profiles to create [5] personality clashes. That produces popular TV, which brings the advertisers and the big profits.

If we really disagree with these shows, we needn't watch them, need we? After all, they can't survive without an audience. The problem is that so many [10] people are addicted to these shows and simply can't turn them off. Lisa Sanchez (92 words)

....

Why do people agree to appear on programmes like Big Brother? They know the world will see them in embarrassing or stressful situations. I suppose [15] some of them want to test themselves or win the big prize, but I think lots of them just want their 'fifteen minutes of fame'. As for celebrities like Jade Goody and Shilpa Shetty, perhaps they want to keep them- selves in the public eye and have fifteen more [20] minutes of fame. Mark Romano (76 words)

....

I wonder about the psychology of reality TV viewers. What makes us want to watch these shows? With Big Brother, I suppose we enjoy seeing people behaving badly towards each other. And on other [25] reality TV programmes the contestants have to do really painful and grotesque tests. It seems that we actually enjoy watching people suffer. Are these shows making us all a little mad?

Perhaps we aren't very different from the Romans [30] – they loved watching people die for sport. Jean O'Hanlon (81 words)

1 LOOKING AT THE TEXT

A Put statements a–f in the correct order to summarize the newspaper article.

a   And as usual, the viewers voted one of these people out every week.

b   The press also attacked the producers for encouraging the situation and forced the whole series to stop.

c   But then, one of the *Big Brother* housemates began to make racist remarks against another housemate.

d   Yesterday, the producers of TV's *Big Brother* had to apologize to the public.

e   This brought huge protests from viewers and the press, and the viewers quickly voted the abusive housemate out.

f   During the latest *Big Brother* series, cameras filmed the lives of a group of people in the BB House in the usual way.

B Pick out the readers' points on the weakness of human nature.

One reader says that …   Another reader notes that …   A third reader suggests that …

C Say what you think.

1   Why do you think people appear on reality TV shows?

2   Would you agree to appear on any of the German reality TV shows? Give reasons.

2 WORKING WITH WORDS

A Collect opposites. You can use your dictionary if you need to.

1   The words in the box below are all from page 56. Copy the table and complete columns 1–3 with opposite forms.

able ∎ agree ∎ appear ∎ behave ∎ encourage ∎ popular ∎ understand ∎ usual

1	2	3	4
un~	dis~	mis~	in~ il~ ir~ im~

2   Now add some more words that you already know to columns 1–3.

3   Put the opposites of these words in column 4.

accurate ∎ complete ∎ correct ∎ legal ∎ legible ∎ logical ∎ moral ∎ perfect ∎ possible ∎ regular ∎ relevant ∎ responsible

4   What do you notice about all the opposites with the forms *il~* and *ir~*?

5   Add more words to column 4.

B Use the adjectives above or their opposites to complete the following sentences.

1   Jade Goody became very … because of her racist attacks on Shilpa Shetty.

2   A lot of people felt that the producers were … because they let the situation develop.

3   Following the press attacks, *Big Brother* was … to continue.

4   Goody later apologized for her behaviour, but she said she was not a racist, and she believed that people had … her.

5   A lot of people were pleased that BB had … from the TV screen.

6   But, after a year with no *Big Brother*, the TV producers finally decided that, with some changes, it would be … to bring it back.

3 LISTENING AND SPEAKING

1 18 **A** **Listen for general understanding. Listen to Part 1 and answer the questions.**

1 Why is Dave able to drive this evening? (Give two reasons.)
2 How many people are going out together?
3 Where are they going to go?
4 What are Steve and Claire going to find out?
5 What are they going to have to eat?

1 19 **B** **Listen for detail. Listen to Part 2 and complete the notes.**

1 First, look at the list of film genres and give examples of each.

> action comedy ┃ action movie ┃ comedy ┃
> documentary ┃ road movie ┃ romantic
> comedy ┃ satire ┃ sci-fi movie ┃ spy movie

2 Copy Steve's notes and listen to Part 2 to complete columns 1 and 2.
3 Listen to Part 2 again to complete column 3.

Film title	Genre	Evening showing times		
		early	mid-evening	late
Pirates of the Caribbean	...	...	...	...
Journey to the ...	...	...	...	...
One ...	...	...	...	...

4 List some more film genres. Then give examples of films in these genres that you have enjoyed and explain why.

C **Do the following role-play.**

1 Work in groups of four and choose a role each.
2 Put forward your point of view. Use some of these phrases.

Roles	
Debbie	Dave
Claire	Steve

> I (don't) think we should / ought to ...
> I think we'd better (not) ...

> We can / could ... first, and then ...
> We might (not) be able to ...

> I wish we could ...
> It's a pity we can't ...
> Whatever we do, we must(n't) ...

3 Report your group's decisions to the class.
4 Compare different groups' plans. Has everyone made the same decisions? If not, try to say why not.

BEFORE YOU READ

A What information about yourself would you be happy to put on a social networking site (e.g. MySpace)?

B What sort of details would you not want to put on the internet? Give reasons.

Great medium, but what about your message?

Jenny has tried several different drugs, has two piercings and also a butterfly tattoo on her arm. She earns $23,000 a year, and hasn't seen her parents for two years.
5 I know her address, but they don't.

Altogether, I know a lot about Jenny, although I've never met her and probably never will. This is strange really. A few years ago, I'm sure hardly anyone in her circle of friends knew as
10 much about her as I, a complete stranger, do today.

Not that this is unusual. Millions of people share very personal details with others on social networking sites such as MySpace.
15 Everyone knows the dangers to children if they put personal information on the internet. But what about the dangers to the rest of us? Should adults not be careful too?

The US National Association of Colleges and
20 Employers recently discovered that 27% of employers search Google and other sites such as MySpace for profiles of their job applicants. And they may find information that those applicants do not want them to have.

On the face of it, the difference between 25 behaviour online and offline makes no sense. In their ordinary lives, people do not easily give strangers personal details such as their phone number or date of birth. It is simply not sensible. Why then do the same people 30 offer these things freely when they go on the internet? It is because both the social network providers and the users know that they need to give quite a lot of information in order to make the system work. After all, it is hard for 35 people to start communicating if they know very little about each other. The trouble is that when private information gets out there, it can become very public, and it may also remain out there forever. 40

We are starting to hear about people who have lost jobs or college places because of things they said about themselves online. And it is not just jobs and college places at risk. Many people are worried that social 45 networking sites could also be used by identity thieves. As for chatrooms, you can never be absolutely sure who you're talking to, and this can be dangerous. Perhaps we should think more carefully about the risks 50 we run when we share information online.

Some students in the USA now have to take a 1st-semester class in social networking so that they clearly understand the risks. Internet researcher Steve Jones of the 55 University of Illinois goes further. He says, 'If you put something on MySpace or Facebook, ask yourself whether you'd be comfortable shouting it out at a family reunion. If the answer is no, then don't put it up.' (449 words) 60

Heavily abridged and adapted from *Things you wouldn't tell your mother*, Alison George, *New Scientist* 16/09/06 p. 50

1 LOOKING AT THE TEXT

A Scan the text for these numbers. Then read further and explain what the numbers refer to in the text.

$23,000   27%   1st

B Copy and complete the statements. As far as possible, use your own words.

1 It is sad for Jenny's parents that ...
2 We all know that children should not put personal information on the internet, but adults should ...
3 Employers often search the internet in order to ...
4 People do not usually give personal information to people they have just met, so it is strange that ...
5 A good general rule is that you should only put information on the internet that ...

C Use words from the text to complete this summary.

Large numbers of people use social ...[1] sites like MySpace to share their ...[2] details. They often share information online that they would never share ...[3]. The more information they give, the easier it is to begin ...[4] with similar people. This is the system the social networking ...[5] have created. And if this private information becomes ...[6], people could lose their job or their place at university. ...[7] thieves are another danger. There is also a risk that when you talk to someone in an internet ...[8], they might be lying about who they are.

D Say what you think.

What are the dangers of meeting people through the internet? What should you do to make sure that you stay safe?

2 WORKING WITH WORDS

A Match the words from each box to form word pairs and expressions from the text.

personal ∎ job ∎ date of ∎ social ∎ circle of ∎ family

applicant ∎ birth ∎ details ∎ friends ∎ networking ∎ reunion

B Use word pairs from exercise A to complete the following sentences.

1 All my cousins are coming to our ... next month.
2 We're asking all the ... to come for interviews on March 28th.
3 ... websites like MySpace and Facebook are becoming more and more popular.
4 Susie is at a different party every weekend! She has a very large ...
5 People's ... can be very useful for identity thieves. Make sure that you keep yours safe!

C Match the sentence halves to make statements. Pay attention to the prepositions.

1	I haven't used MySpace	a	at risk if they use internet chatrooms.
2	Edward knows a lot	b	with someone I don't know.
3	I never share my personal details	c	for two years.
4	Identity thieves are a danger	d	to anyone who uses networking sites.
5	Young people are	e	about computers.

D **Read this information about online abbreviations. Then look at the discussion from an online chatroom and complete it with abbreviations from the list.**

When people are talking to each other in a chatroom, they often use abbreviations because they can type them more quickly and easily. For example, they write **u** instead of 'you', **r** instead of 'are' and **2** instead of 'to'. Words are often reduced to their phonetic components, so 'someone' could become **sum1**. Phrases can also be shortened to the first letter of each word. Here are some common abbreviated phrases that you might see used online:

AFK – away from (the) keyboard
ATM – at the moment
BTW – by the way
FYI – for your information
IMO – in my opinion
LOL – laughing out loud

OTT – over the top
PLS – please
TBH – to be honest
THX – thanks
TMI – too much information
TTYL – talk to you later

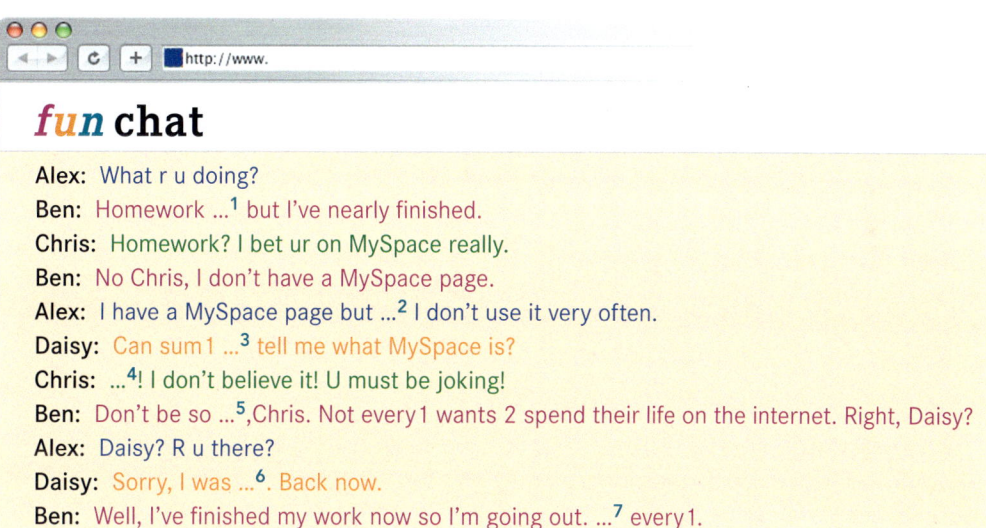

fun chat

Alex: What r u doing?
Ben: Homework …[1] but I've nearly finished.
Chris: Homework? I bet ur on MySpace really.
Ben: No Chris, I don't have a MySpace page.
Alex: I have a MySpace page but …[2] I don't use it very often.
Daisy: Can sum1 …[3] tell me what MySpace is?
Chris: …[4]! I don't believe it! U must be joking!
Ben: Don't be so …[5],Chris. Not every1 wants 2 spend their life on the internet. Right, Daisy?
Alex: Daisy? R u there?
Daisy: Sorry, I was …[6]. Back now.
Ben: Well, I've finished my work now so I'm going out. …[7] every1.

3 BUILDING SKILLS: MEDIATION

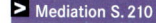
> Mediation S. 210

Write a two-paragraph article about social networking sites in German for your school newspaper.

1   For paragraph 1, collect information from text B on page 59 about:
    > what they are;
    > examples of sites;
    > how new members get started.

2   For paragraph 2, collect information about the possible dangers of these sites.

4 SPEAKING

Work with a partner. Talk about your own experiences with social networking sites.

1   Ask each other questions about the sites you have heard of and what you think of them.
2   If you are a member of a networking site, explain why you use it and whether you have had any bad experiences with the site.

5 SPEAKING

Say which of the points in the text the cartoon illustrates.

*"What shall I do?
She wants to meet for coffee."*

6 CULTURE CHECK: NETIQUETTE

Many young people in English-speaking countries like Britain and America use internet forums to have discussions online. These forums allow English speakers from around the world to talk about a wide range of topics, from politics and religion, to music and computer games.

English speakers are careful to sound polite in a face-to-face conversation and this is just as important in an online discussion. Most forums have their own rules but here are some general points on how to behave in an internet forum.

> Keep to the point – only write about the topic that is being discussed.
> Don't write everything in CAPITAL LETTERS. This is considered 'shouting' and is difficult to read. If you want to emphasize a word, you can use **bold** or <u>underline</u> it.
> Use capital letters for names, places and so on – otherwise you will seem lazy.
> Check your spelling and grammar and avoid using too many abbreviations, as other people may not understand them.
> Be polite to other users and do not be rude about them or their ideas.
> Use normal punctuation – don't write '!!!!' or '????' to emphasize a point, this is just unnecessary.

Read this discussion and say which users are not showing good 'netiquette' and why.

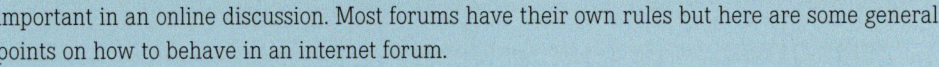

forum

we should do more to protect children who use the internet!!!! my brother jack is only 8 and i don't think he should go online. what do you think???? David

SHUT UP. That's STUPID. Kids can have so much FUN online. If you don't like the internet, why are you here? Ed

I think David is rite, we hav 2 b careful that kids don't spend 2 much time online. There r lots of things they can do instead of sittin in front of a computer all day! Georgia

PLS can we talk about something else? Did any1 c the football match on TV last night? Ben

Ben, if you want to talk about that, you can find a football forum. I think it's important to talk about this – if children use the internet, we need to make sure that they are safe. Laura

C Social options

Internet gaming addiction – swords, monsters and deadly danger

1 *I get dozens of calls from parents. They say, 'At first I thought it was a hobby and a phase but they won't stop. They think it's fine to play the game all day.'*

2 *It's unfortunate that certain games are chosen for criticism. I have never met a person who thinks this stuff is real and, if they do, they have got a mental health problem.*

3 *We feel that day-to-day life should be more important than entertainment.*

4 *This game twists people's minds. I think there should definitely be a warning on the box in stores – so when people buy it, they know what they're doing.*

Text adapted from: www.theage.com.au/news

1 MATCHING

Match the quotations (1–4) to the speakers (a–d).

a   Matt Hopkins,* internet gamer
b   Rachel Winters,* campaigner against internet games
c   Penny James,* psychologist, Centre for Internet Addiction Recovery
d   Employee of Blizzard Entertainment, maker of World of Warcraft

* Names have been changed

2 ROLE-PLAY

Work in a group of at least four. You are taking part in a TV panel discussion on this topic: 'Escape from reality: are internet games a danger?'

A   You are a 19-year-old internet gamer. You think that internet games are harmless.
B   You are 39 and the parent of a teenager who is addicted to internet games. You think they should be banned.
C   You are a primary school teacher. You are worried about the effect of internet games on young people, but you aren't sure whether they are really addictive.
D   You are a youth worker. You think internet games are OK for most people, but can be addictive for some. You think that schools and parents should educate children about the dangers.

3 WRITING

Write your own post for an internet forum about online games. You can start by using some expressions from the box below.

In my experience, From what I've heard, I feel that	internet games	are	highly addictive. harmless.	
	the media psychologists	have	exaggerated underestimated	the problem.

D Grammar checkpoint

1 MODAL VERBS

> Grammar summary S. 216

A Your school is planning a fundraising event. Write full sentences to make suggestions for the event.

> EXAMPLES *All of us should put up posters around town.*
> *Somebody ought to invite the TV news to film us.*

I We Somebody One of us Some of us All of us	can could should ought to must	put up posters around town. invite the TV News to film us. get an interview on local radio. ask local shops to sell tickets for us. put a special page on the school website. ask all the local bands to come and play. hire a bouncy castle for the children. have a barbecue and sell soft drinks. organize a car park for visitors.

B Think about how you can stay in touch with the world. Talk about good ways and ways that do not seem so good.

> EXAMPLES *I could go on the internet to do research for school projects.*
> *I shouldn't call friends on my mobile so much.*

Use these ideas.

> call friends on my mobile ❙ email my friends ❙ go on the internet to do
> research for school projects ❙ read celebrity magazines ❙ send friends text messages ❙
> watch TV during the week

2 *MUST, MUST NOT* AND *NEED NOT*

> Grammar summary S. 216

Complete the exchanges with *must*, *must not* and *need not*.

1 A My sister's getting her exam results today, so I .... get home and call her.
   B You .... wait till then. You can use my mobile to call her.

2 A We .... tell anybody about what has happened.
   B I agree. Sarah .... never hear about it, or she'll be really angry!

3 A Quick, turn on the TV! I .... miss the news.
   B But you've already heard the news on the radio, so surely you .... watch it as well!

4 A .... I really pay over the internet? It doesn't feel safe.
   B You .... worry: it's a secure website. And in fact, you .... pay this way, or they won't send you the goods!

5 A Come on! Hurry! We .... miss the big film, and that means we ....
      be at the cinema by 3.30.
   B But we .... watch it then because they're showing the film again at 6.00. So stop panicking!

On the move

FOCUS

1 Talk about the cartoons.

Today, we are free to travel where we want and when we want. Or are we? What do these cartoons say about various forms of transport?

"The salesman said that this was the ideal car for life in the fast lane."

"The flight is only 99p ... but it will be another £120 if you want to sit inside the plane!"

2 Think about it.

To what extent do these British and American cartoons also show the reality of travel in Germany?

3 Talk about your own travel experiences. Use words from the box.

1 Have you ever had any bad experiences while travelling at home or abroad? What happened? How did you feel?
2 What about good experiences? What happened? How did you feel?

> amazed **ı** angry **ı** annoyed **ı** anxious **ı** delighted **ı** depressed **ı** disappointed **ı**
> embarrassed **ı** excited **ı** exhausted **ı** frightened **ı** frustrated **ı** nervous **ı**
> pleased **ı** relaxed **ı** shocked **ı** surprised **ı** terrified **ı** upset **ı** worried

BEFORE YOU READ

1 22 Look at the photo. How do you think the people in this traffic jam probably feel?

TONY ASH green campaigner

Twenty years ago, there were 22 million cars on Britain's roads. Now there are over 30 million. And soon there will be 40 million if we don't take urgent action. Think of the pollution, and the environmental and health damage from the exhaust fumes. The world's choking to death on its tailbacks and gridlocks. And when you look up and down a traffic jam, 90% of those cars contain one driver and no passengers. It's mad, and it has to stop!

RUTH ROSS working mother

I'm a working mum, and I have to drive. If public transport could get me everywhere I need to go, I'd use it. But can it get me to the nursery after work to pick up my little girl? And to the supermarket or the dry-cleaner's? No. There isn't enough of it, and it's also far too expensive. Plus we pay a fortune to drive our cars! Surely, if the government spent all our road and fuel taxes on more and cheaper public transport, things would be better.

LAURA SMITH government transport minister

More roads aren't the answer. If we build one to reduce congestion on another, what happens? In five years, they're both congested. So, if we try to build our way out of road chaos, we will just build our way into more road chaos. As for public transport, this is improving, but it's a long and expensive job. And much of the money has to come from drivers, so the cost of driving can only increase. What we need is a better balance. People who must drive should be able to drive efficiently. Others must change to public transport. If that happens, life will be much better for everyone and CO_2 emissions will be much lower.

WAYNE SIMPSON office worker

OK, so I spend too much time in tailbacks, but I wouldn't give up my car even if you paid me. It says who I am. It means freedom and flexibility. I can go where I want when I want. It also means privacy. I've got my own space, and I can listen to the music I like. Cars give people the freedom to live and work where they want.

(412 words)

1 LOOKING AT THE TEXTS

A Make notes from the texts.

Give five reasons why the drivers do not want to change to public transport.

B Say what you think.

You and your partner live in the suburbs, and you both drive to work in the city centre.
1 Discuss the options below to save money. Talk about the pros and cons, e.g. costs, savings, flexibility, time and impact on the environment.
2 Decide what to do. Give reasons for your choice.

> Drive to work with friends/colleagues (= car sharing).
> Sell one or both cars and use public transport.
> Sell both cars; use bikes to get to work. Use public transport or hire a car for longer trips.

2 WORKING WITH WORDS

Find idiomatic expressions in Tony Ash's comments to complete the following sentences.

1 With everyone trying to leave the city, there was soon total … on every road: nothing could move for hours!
2 Just look at the … from that truck: emissions like that are illegal! (*word pair*)
3 If we don't take action to cut emissions, the world will … (*idiom*)
4 After the accident, there was a ten-mile … on the motorway.

3 LISTENING

1 23 **A Think about it.**

Distance and travel are the themes of many songs. Can you think of any? Brainstorm some ideas with a partner.

B Listen to the song *Route 66*. Route 66 is the famous road that runs through seven American states. Listen for general understanding and answer these questions.

1 Do you think that the singer likes travelling on Route 66? Why/Why not?
2 In which direction across the USA does the song travel?

C Listen for detail. Look at the map below, listen again and answer these questions.

1 Where does Route 66 start and finish? Identify cities A and E on the map.
2 What are the names of towns/cities B, C and D?
3 How long does the song say the road is?
4 Which city does the singer describe as pretty?

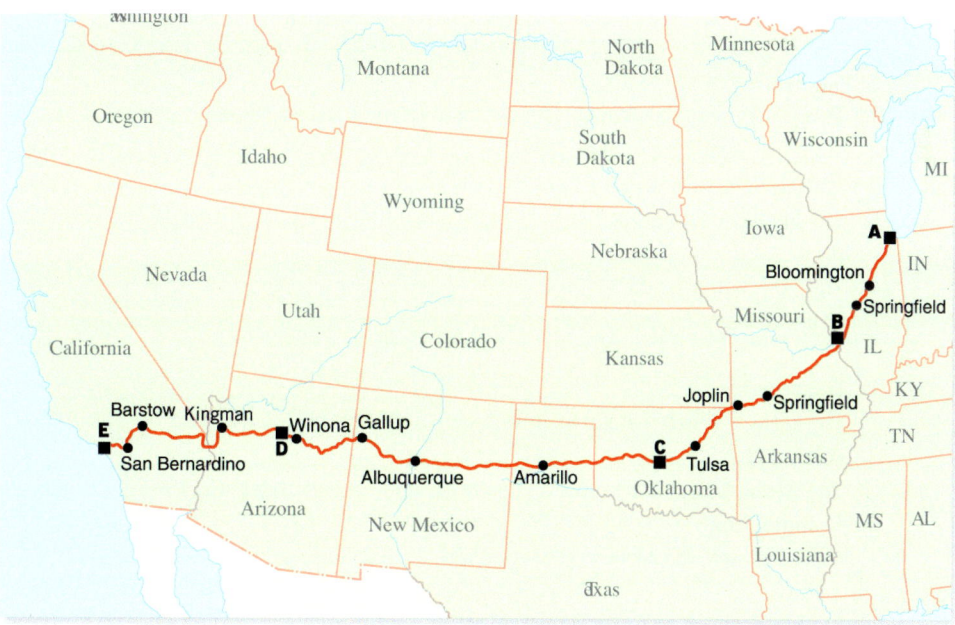

D Say what you think.

What differences are there between the image of travel in the song *Route 66* and the real situation that most commuters experience every day? Think about cartoon 1 on page 65.

4 BUILDING SKILLS: INTERPRETING CARTOONS

> **TIP**

Some cartoons are just visual jokes, but most deliver a serious message. When you prepare a presentation (see page 206), look out for cartoons that could help present a key point. This could make your presentation much more fun and memorable!

A With a partner, briefly talk about what is happening in the cartoon.

> Interpretation von Bildern und Karikaturen S. 207

B Now use the 'D-A-C method' (**D**escribing, **A**nalyzing and **C**ommenting) to discuss the cartoon in more detail.

1 First look at sentence beginnings a–e and decide if they are used for describing, analyzing or commenting on the cartoon.
   a This is something we know from personal experience. For example, we see that …
   b There is a smaller mountain …
   c The cartoonist is trying to show that SUVs …
   d The message behind the cartoon is that the number of SUV sales is falling because gas prices are …
   e The SUV is driving off …

2 Now complete the ideas in a–e and add them to the outline below.

   1 **D**escribing
      The cartoon shows a steep mountain with a vertical cliff down one side …
   2 **A**nalyzing
      The steep mountain is in fact a line graph labelled gas prices, and the SUV represents …
   3 **C**ommenting
      In my opinion, the cartoonist is quite right …, but I also think …

C Now use this method to write about another cartoon.

1 Choose one of the cartoons on page 65 and write your own analysis using the ideas above and phrases from the appendix, page 208.
2 Work with your partner again to discuss and improve your writing.

BEFORE YOU READ

If you were the German minister for transport, how would you try to reduce a) traffic congestion and b) vehicle emissions?

Satellite road pricing is on the way

Transport Minister Laura Smith has given new details of our future road tax system: road pricing.

If you drive in a road-pricing zone, you are charged according to where, when and how far you drive. On a quiet road in the country at night you will pay just 2p per mile. However, on a busy main road in the rush hour you can expect to pay £1.34 per mile. 'Unless we do this,' Smith says, 'there will be national gridlock by 2020.'

The technology is quite similar to the 'satnav' (satellite navigation) systems in many modern cars. In each case, satellites and a 'black box' in the vehicle communicate to record location, time and distance travelled. Your bill will arrive monthly.

For some people, this means a 'Big Brother' society, and they hate the idea. 'But,' Smith argues, 'as long as you've nothing to hide from the police, what's the problem?' Road hauliers say that the cost will destroy their businesses, but Smith believes that costs will balance – provided that hauliers avoid rush hour on the busiest roads. City commuters say their lives will be impossible. However, Smith says that people will turn to public transport and car sharing. 'Road use will become more efficient, and we estimate that traffic congestion will fall by 50%.'

(214 words)

THE ROAD TO ZERO EMISSIONS

Fuel prices have increased hugely, and CO_2 emissions have to decrease hugely. At last, car owners and environmentalists want the same thing – a car that does not 'cost the earth' to run. Engineers using several different technologies are racing to provide that car.

Some city dwellers are choosing electric vehicles like the tiny, zero-emission 'G-Wiz'. Joanna Page, actress, Londoner and G-Wiz owner, says: 'We've saved a small fortune in petrol.' Costing 40p (50 cents) to charge at night, it has a range of 80 kilometres. 'That's enough to drive round town all day.' The problem? The electricity comes from a traditional power station.

Hybrid petrol-electric vehicles like Toyota's best-selling Prius cleverly turn energy from the car's movement into electricity. The electric motor then supports the petrol engine, for example on hills. The technology is complicated and expensive,

but these cars give something like petrol-engine performance with much greater fuel efficiency.

Long in development, zero-emission fuel-cell technology finally entered commercial car production in 2008. The Honda FCX Clarity is the result. It combines hydrogen and oxygen to produce power – and the only waste is water. Amazing. But remember: we still have to manufacture the hydrogen. If, though, we can do this with renewable energy sources one day, we will finally have an environmentally friendly car with low running costs.

(217 words)

1 LOOKING AT THE TEXTS

A Do these tasks.

1 Read the first article and work out how much it will cost to drive ten miles on a main road into London at 8.00 a.m. on a Monday.
2 Calculate the future charge for driving ten miles on a country road at 8 p.m. on a Sunday evening.
3 Describe what today's car navigation technology and the road pricing technology of the future have in common.
4 Find the cost of a 40-kilometre journey in a G-Wiz.
5 Explain why, eventually, fuel cell technology will probably win against hybrid technology.
6 Describe what environmental problem both electric cars and cars powered by fuel cells have at the moment. Then state a possible solution to this problem.

B Say what you think.

Dad – why can't we have a proper car?

2 WORKING WITH WORDS

A There are several word pairs in the texts. Find partner words for 1–8.

	Text 1		Text 2
1	Paragraph 1: ... tax	5	Paragraph 1: ... prices
2	Paragraph 1: road ...	6	Paragraph 1: ... emissions
3	Paragraph 2: ... road	7	Paragraph 4: ... production
4	Paragraph 4: traffic ...	8	Paragraph 4: ... sources

B The same words can have other partners. Find more using the words in the box.

country ׀ diesel ׀ electricity ׀ haulier ׀ income ׀ jam ׀ lights ׀ oil ׀ power ׀ side

> **TIP**

Use this technique to help collect and learn vocabulary efficiently.
Use your dictionary to add partner words.

3 SPEAKING

A Follow these steps to prepare a role-play.

1 Read the following information about congestion charging.

London started congestion charging several years ago, and many other cities want to do the same. All vehicles (except public transport, taxis and 'green' cars like the G-Wiz) have to pay a daily charge if they enter the city centre. The aim is to reduce congestion as much as possible.

Positive results:
a) 30% congestion reduction in the central zone;
b) bus travel up by 38%;
c) 65% of charges go towards better public transport.

Negative results:
a) much more traffic now on roads around the zone: new areas of congestion;
b) reduced sales for 65% of small businesses in and close to the zone: many have considered moving away;
c) a lot of anger among people negatively affected.

Source: Times Online, Oct 29, 2006: Focus: How to get gridlock Britain moving again

2 As a class, choose a city near you which could benefit from congestion charging.
3 Imagine you are at a meeting on congestion charging. Work in groups of four and choose a role each.

Roles	
Businessperson	▶ File 9, page 194
City councillor	▶ File 5, page 192
Road commuter	▶ File 2, page 192
Government transport official	▶ File 12, page 194

B Do the role-play.

1 Put forward your point of view and try to persuade the others. Use these phrases:
If we do/don't ..., ... will/won't ...
Provided ...
As long as ...
Unless ...
2 Agree what to do.
3 Compare your decision with the other groups. Take a class vote to choose the best one.

CULTURE CHECK: APPROPRIATE GREETINGS

At the congestion charging meeting some people know each other and some do not.
Choose which greetings are appropriate in the following situations.

Situation 1

City councillor Jean Hayes and businessperson Bob Hill are not close friends, but they have met quite often before at meetings.
Which greeting might Jean Hayes use? How might Bob Hill reply?

HAYES
a Hi, Bob. How's it going?
b Hello, Bob. How are you?
c Hello, Bob. How do you do?

HILL
a How are you?
b Not bad.
c Very well, thank you.
   And you?

Situation 2

Jean Hayes is formally introducing Bob Hill to government minister Nick Redding.
How should he reply? How might she continue?

HAYES   Mr Redding, this is Mr Hill.

REDDING   How do you do?*

HILL
a Fine, thank you. How do you do?
b I'm fine, thanks. How are things going?
c How do you do?

REDDING
a Not bad, thanks. And you?
b It's nice to meet you.
c How fantastic to meet you!

* The greeting "How do you do?" is now becoming a little old-fashioned, but it is still used in some very formal situations.

DISCUSSION

> Diskussionen führen S. 210

In small groups, discuss the possible effects of an oil crisis.

Imagine a major oil and gas crisis during the winter. Both oil and gas are almost completely unavailable and extremely expensive. How would a crisis like this affect you personally? How might it affect the whole community? Use phrases like these:

If we had a crisis like that,	it might	mean ...ing ...
If something like that happened,	it could	make me / us ...

How walkable is your community?

Everyone benefits from walking. These benefits include improved fitness, cleaner air, reduced risk of certain health problems and a greater sense of community. But walking needs to be safe and easy, especially for children. Next time you are taking a walk, use this checklist to decide if your neighborhood is a friendly place for walking.

Walkability checklist

1. Did you have room to walk?

a Yes.

b No, because
- … paths started and stopped.
- … paths were broken or cracked.
- … paths were blocked with poles, signs, bushes, vehicles, etc.
- … there were no paths or pavements.
- … there was too much traffic.

2. Was it easy to cross streets?

a Yes.

b No, because
- … streets were too wide.
- … traffic signals made us wait too long.
- … traffic signals didn't give us enough time to cross.
- … there weren't enough pedestrian crossings.
- … trees, bushes or parked cars blocked our view of traffic.

3. Did motorists and cyclists behave well?

a Yes.

b No, because
- … motorists backed out of driveways without looking.
- … motorists did not stop for people crossing the street.
- … motorists drove too fast.
- … cyclists rode too fast on shared paths.
- … cyclists didn't keep to cycle paths.
- … cyclists were rude or aggressive.

4. Was your walk pleasant?

a Yes.

b No, because
- … there weren't enough green spaces, trees, etc.
- … there were scary dogs.
- … there were scary people.
- … there was offensive graffiti.
- … there was lots of litter.
- … there was too much air pollution from traffic.

(242 words)

Introduction and questionnaire adapted from www.walkinginfo.org

1 PAIRWORK

Do the following tasks:

a Use the checklist to evaluate the 'walkability' of the area where you live. Compare your results with a partner.

b What could be done about any problems that you have identified? Brainstorm solutions with your partner, then present your best solution(s) to the class.

2 WRITING

Write two more questions for the questionnaire to cover the needs of people with disabilities (e.g. in a wheelchair) and people with small children in prams/pushchairs.

D Grammar checkpoint

1 IF-SENTENCES TYPE 1

> Grammar summary S. 220

A Tomas, a student in London, has to travel to Paris. Use the table to help him decide how to get there. Use *if*-sentences type 1 and add information from the table where required.

Travel between London and Paris		
	Cost	Time
By plane	£122 return	1 hr 20 min (+ about 3 hours travel/waiting time)
By train & Eurostar	£159 return	2 hr 30 min
By car & ferry	£135 return	about 9 hr

TOMAS	What's the best way to get to Paris?
YOU	If you *go*[1] (*go*) by plane, it *will be*[2] (*be*) cheaper than by train or ferry.
TOMAS	Will it be faster to fly too?
YOU	Well, yes and no. If you ...[3] (*count*) just the flight time, it ...[4] (*take*) less time.
TOMAS	So why do you say 'yes and no'?
YOU	Because it ...[5] (*take*) longer if you ...[6] (*also allow*) time for travel to and from the airport.
TOMAS	Really? So if I ...[7] (*travel*) by plane, how much ...[8] (*it/cost*) and how long ...[9] (*it/take*)?
YOU	It ...[10] (*cost*) ...[11], and it ...[12] (*take*) about ...[13] altogether.
TOMAS	What about the train? How long ...[14] (*it/take*) if I ...[15] (*go*) by train?
YOU	Just ...[16] from the UK straight to Paris. But then there's also the cheaper ferry option. If you ...[17] (*take*) your car, it ...[18] (*cost*) ...[19]. Of course, the journey time is longer – about ...[20].
TOMAS	Well, I like ships and the sea, so perhaps I'll take the ferry. Thanks for your help.

B Work with a partner. Practise the dialogue together.

2 IF-SENTENCES TYPE 2

> Grammar summary S. 220

A Make *If*-sentences type 2 with the verbs in the right forms and the correct punctuation.

1 Wayne Simpson: the government (*build*) more roads | we (*not have*) road congestion | And | we (*not have*) congestion | everybody (*be able to*) get around faster
   If the government built more roads, we would not have congestion. And if we did not have congestion, everybody would be able to get around faster.

2 Tony Ash: car drivers (*carry*) more passengers | traffic jams (*disappear*) | And | traffic jams (*disappear*) | everybody (*be*) much healthier

3 Ruth Ross: transport services (*become*) cheaper | more people (*use*) them | And | more people (*use*) them | they (*expand*) and (*get*) better

4 Laura Smith: the government (*do*) nothing about transport | the situation (*go*) from bad to worse | And | that (*happen*) | the government (*lose*) the next election

B Imagine you are in London and in the following situations. Look at the table in exercise 1A again, and make statements using *If*-sentences type 2.

1 You need your car for a holiday in France.
   a How would you go?
      If I needed my car for ..., I would go by ...
   b Cost?
      If I went by ..., it ...

2 You have to get to Paris urgently.
   a How would you travel?
   b Time?

3 You need to connect with a flight from Paris to Tokyo.
   a How would you go?
   b Cost and time?

5

Green enough?

FOCUS

1 Compare the past and the present.

Thinking about the environment ...
> how are things worse now than, say, 50 years ago?
> could some things actually be better now than 50 years ago?

2 Work with a partner. Discuss some Hollywood views of the future.

a Look at pictures 1–4 and match them to titles a–d.

a Waterworld
b 28 Days Later
c The Day after Tomorrow
d Armageddon

b All of these films imagine future disasters. Are the disasters a) natural, b) man-made or c) a mixture of both?

c Briefly discuss what each film is about. The following words may be helpful.

asteroid ┃ catastrophe ┃ destruction ┃ disaster ┃ epidemic ┃ flood ┃
hurricane ┃ ice age ┃ tsunami

A *Armageddon is set in the (near/distant) future, and it's about (an asteroid which is going to hit Earth).*
B *That's right. And they have to (find a way of stopping it).*

BEFORE YOU READ

A Look at the pictures and say what is happening in each.

B Read the title of the text. Try to link the pictures to the title.

Going green: the final report

By Julie Price

A

B

C

D

We started our 'green year' exactly twelve months ago – on January 1st last year. Now, we have finished, and it is time to look back on the experience.

Like a lot of people, Paul and I had already made ourselves a little greener. For example, we had started recycling more carefully, and we had fitted low-energy light bulbs around the house.

But last year was a very different matter, and this is how it all began. As a journalist, I had written an article in December called *How to save the planet*. My boss had then asked me to turn my fine words into action for a year – and write monthly progress reports. Oh, dear! My boss is a woman you do not refuse.

Fortunately, Paul agreed, and so our new way of life began. First, we simply turned down the heating. That was not too difficult: we just suggested that visiting friends should wear sweaters! And we immediately started saving both energy and money.

We also considered changing to alternative energy sources. Should we put a wind turbine on the roof perhaps? No. Wind strength in a city crowded with buildings is too weak and unreliable. Well, then, what about solar power? Surely even under grey north European skies we could meet many of our energy needs. Well, yes, but the cost was far too high. In the end, we spent our limited budget on more roof insulation. This simple, sensible step has already paid for itself.

After we had done this, we faced our first hard decision. We loved our car, but we decided it had to go. Once we had finally sold it, things slowly got easier. After all, we live in a city, so we could walk, cycle and use public transport. Sometimes it took longer, but we learned to allow extra time. As for the money we got from selling the car, we decided to use it to finish double-glazing the house. (We had done most of the house previously but had run out of cash.)

The other difficult thing was the summer holiday. We had always loved going somewhere warm and exotic, especially India, but last year no. Instead, we took the train to Wales and had a walking holiday. We got wet but very fit, and we also discovered beautiful places we had never heard of in our own country. And, by avoiding those flights, we saved two tonnes of CO_2 emissions – the amount that two average cars produce in a whole year!

What about the future? Well, we're used to our new lifestyle now, and we aim to continue. The only thing is this: somehow we *must* find a way to travel the world again.

(454 words)

1 LOOKING AT THE TEXT

A Read the text quickly to match pictures A–D to different paragraphs.

B Copy and complete the tables using information from the text.

Timeline
December, the year before last
January 1st last year
Today, a year later

Events
1 JP wrote 'How to save the planet'.
2 …

Actions taken last year
1 Turned down …
2 …
3 …
4 …

Benefits mentioned in the text
1 Saved energy & …
2 …

Actions not taken
1 Put a …
2 …

Reasons mentioned
1 …

Plans/Hopes for the future
1 …
2 …

C Use your notes to give a spoken summary. You can use these ideas.

In December the year before last, Julie Price wrote …, and her boss then … And so, on January …, … Today, a year …, …

Julie and her husband took a number of actions last year. First of all, they …, and this immediately saved energy and … Then they … They also … Finally, they …

There were other actions that they considered but did not take. For one thing, they thought about putting a …, but they … because … For another, they wondered about …, but …

As for the future, they plan to … However, they really want to …

D Write an email in German.

> Mediation S. 210

A German friend asks for your advice on quick ways to save energy and money on heating her home. Write an email to her in German, suggesting two things she should do and two she should not. Use the information in the text to explain your advice.

E Say what you think.

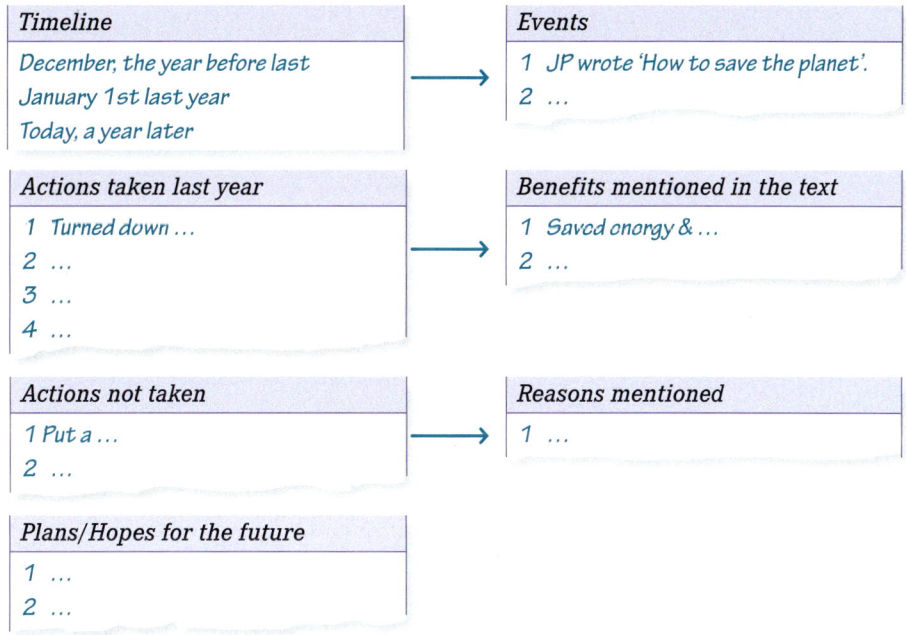

In my family, we couldn't do any of those things – except maybe put in more insulation.

At home, we've already done some of those things, but we would never get rid of our car. That would be going too far!

2 WORKING WITH WORDS

A **Find words or expressions in the text that have similar meanings to these expressions.**

1 every month (*lines 15–20*)
2 at once (*lines 20–25*)
3 finally (*lines 26–41*)
4 got used to (*lines 43–56*)

5 before that (*lines 43–56*)
6 particularly (*lines 57–69*)
7 quantity (*lines 57–69*)
8 way of life (*lines 70–74*)

B **Rewrite the sentences with the words and phrases from the box below and your own words.**

1 We started our 'green year' on January 1st last year.
2 My boss had asked me to write monthly progress reports.
3 We suggested that visiting friends should wear sweaters.
4 We also considered changing energy sources.
5 We learned to allow extra time.

> advised ▪ every month ▪ got used to ▪
> in addition ▪ was the start of

> **> TIP**
>
> When you use information from a text to write a comment or summary, you need to change the original words and phrases as much as possible. But be careful: changing a word might mean you need to change other parts of the sentence too, like the word order.

C **Read the dictionary section below on phrasal verbs with the verb *turn*. Then do the following tasks.**

1 Complete the following sentences from the text with the correct phrasal verbs.
  a My boss had then asked me to … my fine words … action for a year.
  b First, we simply … … the heating.

2 Complete the following with phrasal verbs from the dictionary section.
  a Every month last year, a lot of readers used to … … page 8 to read Julie Price's latest monthly report on her green year.
  b Her husband Paul was very interested in her project, and the many difficult changes to their way of life did not … him …
  c They quickly learned to … … all lights and appliances that they were not using.
  d They also used to … … the hot water system for fewer hours a day.
  e They were quite worried about going on holiday to Wales, but everything … … very well, and they loved their time there.
  f One cloudy day, they walked about two kilometres along a valley, and then … … the road and climbed a steep mountain path.
  g They nearly … … when it started raining heavily, but they kept going and came to a beautiful lake – just as the sun started shining again!

> **turn back** to go back in the same direction as you came: *The weather became so bad that they had to turn back.*
>
> **turn sb/sth down** to refuse an offer or request, or the person that makes it: *Why did you turn that job down? · He asked her to marry him, but she turned him down.*
>
> **turn off sth** to leave one road and and go on another: *We turn off the motorway at junction 10.*
>
> **turn (sb) off** to lose or make sb lose interest; to make sb feel bored or disgusted: *Men with beards turn me off.*
>
> **turn sth off** to move the switch, etc. on a piece of machinery, etc. to stop it working: *He turned the TV off.*
>
> **turn sth on** to move the switch, etc. on a piece of machinery, etc. to start it working: *Turn the lights on!*
>
> **turn out (to be sth)** to be sth in the end: *The weather turned out fine. · The house that they had promised us turned out to be a tiny flat.*
>
> **turn to sth** to find a page in a book: *Turn to page 45.*

B The bigger picture

BEFORE YOU READ

A Look at the two halves of the picture and describe each in turn.

B Say whether they seem to show versions of the past, present or future.

2 **3**

News from the future 1

Yesterday, entering the 2060s, we heard the news we desperately did not want to hear. Around the world, the airwaves were full of it: we have passed the figure of 560 parts per million of CO_2 in the
5 Earth's atmosphere, twice the level it was before the Industrial Revolution. More importantly, 99% of scientists agree that it is also the point of no return for climate change. We have just passed the last red danger light at high speed.

10 What will happen now? The answer is: a lot. Here in Europe, summers will get hotter and hotter and winters ever wetter. Sudden violent storms will become more and more common. And we are the lucky ones. In other parts of the world, life has
15 already become impossible because of climate change. Hurricanes are forcing people away from Central America and the USA's south-eastern coasts. In Asia, cyclones are doing the same from China to India. Africa's deserts are expanding fast. Thousands
20 are dying. Millions more are refugees. These regions are falling into chaos.

Moreover, the Greenland and Antarctic ice sheets are melting and sea levels are rising a centimetre a year. Many low-lying islands have disappeared, and
25 soon great coastal cities from Shanghai to Alexandria to New York will drown.

Scientists were warning the world about this 60 years ago. If people had acted quickly back then, they would have prevented today's disasters. But
30 they did nothing. Why?

(238 words)

2 **4**

News from the future 2

Yesterday, entering the 2060s, we heard the news we were hoping for. Champagne has become a rare luxury these days, but people happily paid €1,000 for a bottle to celebrate. For the world has again held
5 atmospheric CO_2 at 450 ppm. Moreover, the level will fall slightly this year – even though the world economy will continue growing by 4%.

CO_2 stabilization alternatives

Carbon emissions (billion tonnes a year) / Year

Historic
Begin action now
Delay action until 2056

There are many reasons for this success, and here are just a few. First, we have reduced our use of oil,
10 gas and coal by nearly 80% over the last 50 years, and it is these fossil fuels that produce most of the CO_2 emissions. We have replaced them with various alternative forms of energy, including 'renewables' such as solar, wind, tidal and hydroelectric power.
15 There is also fuel cell technology. Today this runs the world's three billion vehicles, and it produces no CO_2 at all – nor any other sort of pollution. Then there is nuclear fusion, the safe, cheap nuclear technology that EU members first
20 began developing 80 years ago.

These and other changes have happened thanks to the strength and vision of our grandparents' generation. Their governments understood the need to fight global warming. If they had not started – and continued – the fight to control CO_2 emissions then, severe climate change would have begun by now. Our world would have fallen into chaos if those wise leaders
25 had not been there. Today we owe them a big thank you as we emerge from human history's greatest crisis.

(248 words)

1 LOOKING AT THE TEXTS

A Read the texts quickly to match them to the two halves of the picture on page 79.

B Read the first text carefully. Choose the best answer or answers.

1 The writer tells us that before the Industrial Revolution …
  a there was half as much CO_2 in the atmosphere as in 2060.
  b there was twice as much atmospheric CO_2 then as in 2060.
  c there were about 280 ppm of CO_2 in the Earth's atmosphere.

2 According to the author, writing in 2060 about climate change, …
  a the effects are bad in Europe but much worse in other places.
  b it has become impossible to live in many regions such as Europe.
  c storms have forced people to leave their homes in Europe.

3 The writer believes that it would have been possible to stop climate change in the early 21st century, but …
  a people then did not do anything about it.
  b people back then did something but it was too little and too late.
  c people in those days did not know why they needed to do anything.

C Read the second text carefully and then write a letter in German to *Wissenschaft Heute*. Explain what we must do to make the world safe for our grandchildren in 2060 and beyond.

 **> Mediation S. 210**

2 WORKING WITH WORDS

A Use fractions and percentages from the box to complete the statements.

> a fifth (1/5) ∎ half (1/2) ∎ three-fifths (3/5) ∎ 20% ∎ 60% ∎ 100%

1 According to the first report, CO_2 levels before the Industrial Revolution used to be … of the 2060 figure of 560 ppm. In other words, they have risen by … %.

2 Turning to the second report, we can say that if the pre-industrial CO_2 level was 280 ppm, then that was about … of the 2060 figure of 450 ppm that this report notes. That is to say, the level of CO_2 shows an increase of roughly … %.

3 The second report goes on to say that today's use of fossil fuels is roughly … of the 2010 total, i.e. the use of fossil fuels now is only about … % of what it was.

B Practise saying fractions and percentages. Read out the statements in exercise A.

3 LISTENING

2 5 **A** Listen for general understanding. Listen once and say whether the statements are true or false.

1 The speakers are on either a radio or a TV show.
2 The guest writes for a magazine called *Science Now*.
3 Dr Parry is talking about CO_2 emissions around the world.
4 He believes that the whole world must immediately start reducing emissions.
5 If the world does what Dr Parry says, he believes that we will save ourselves from the worst possibilities of climate change.

B Listen for detail. Copy the chart, listen again and complete it.

C Make statements about the chart. Use fractions and percentages.

In the period to 2020, emissions have to …

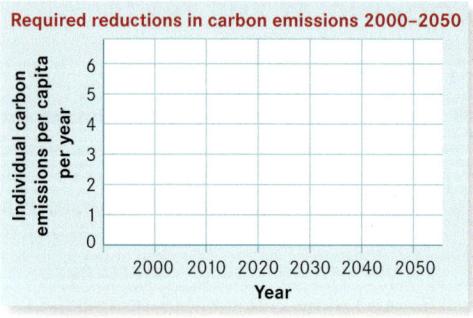

Required reductions in carbon emissions 2000–2050

(chart with y-axis "Individual carbon emissions per capita per year" from 0 to 6, x-axis "Year" from 2000 to 2050)

4 BUILDING SKILLS: SUMMARIZING

A Read the summary of *News from the future 1* and compare it with the original.

1 Note examples of rephrasing.
2 Find examples of new connectors to link ideas together.
3 Compare the lengths of the original and the summary.

(Yesterday, entering the 2060s, we heard the news we desperately did not want to hear.) (Around the world, the airwaves were full of it:) we have passed the figure of 560 parts per million of CO_2 in the Earth's atmosphere, twice the level it was before the Industrial Revolution. (More importantly, 99% of scientists agree that) it is also the point of no return for climate change. (We have just passed the last red danger light at high speed.)

(What will happen now? The answer is: a lot.) Here in Europe, summers will get hotter and hotter and winters ever wetter. Sudden violent storms will become more and more common. And we are the lucky ones. In other parts of the world, life has already become impossible because of climate change. (Hurricanes are forcing people away from Central America and …) Thousands are dying. Millions more are refugees. (These regions are falling into chaos.)

Moreover, the (Greenland and Antarctic) ice sheets are melting and sea levels are rising (a centimetre a year). Many low-lying islands have disappeared, and soon great coastal cities (from Shanghai to …) will drown.

Scientists were warning the world about this 60 years ago. If people had acted quickly back then, they would have prevented today's disasters. (But they did nothing. Why?)

(238 words)

Unnecessary anecdote

Unnecessary supporting figure & source of opinion
Simile
Rhetorical question

Unnecessary examples
Repetition
Unnecessary names
Unnecessary supporting figure & examples

Rhetorical finish

Summary

Now, in 2060, CO_2 in our planet's atmosphere has risen above 560 parts per million. This is 100% higher than it was before the Industrial Revolution, and it means climate change is out of control.

In Europe, we will see hotter summers, wetter winters and more violent, stormy weather. Things are even worse in other regions. There, life has already become very difficult because of climate change. Millions of people have become refugees, and many are dying.

The Earth's ice is melting, and sea levels are rising. Low-lying islands have flooded and soon so will important coastal cities.

If the world had responded to scientists' warnings 60 years ago, these catastrophes would have been avoided.

(115 words)

B Now write a summary of *News from the future 2*. It should be between a third and half of the original length.

> Zusammenfassung S. 204

4 3

VEG OUT*
Community GARDEN

In the middle of the busy suburb of St Kilda in Melbourne is an amazing oasis – the Veg Out Community Garden. It's an organic, chemical-free vegetable garden run by members of the local
5 community. It's a relaxed, friendly place with curving paths and crazy sculptures.

People are often drawn to the garden because they don't have the space at home to grow plants. It's also a great place to meet new people and learn from more
10 experienced gardeners.

The St Kilda community is multicultural and this is reflected in the range of fruit and vegetables which are grown here. Lenny Pastro's plot is like a little slice of his native Italy. He makes a nice pasta sauce with his
15 home grown herbs, and grows a good crop of egg plants.

Pensioner Margot lives in a flat with only a small balcony that doesn't get much sun, so Veg Out is a great opportunity for her to grow some vegetables.

For her friend Betty, the garden means she gets some 20
exercise, a social life with the other gardeners and the pleasure of growing her own food.

It's clear that gardening appeals to people of all ages. For young single mum Jaala and her daughter, Maya, it's a great way to connect with the community. 25
'Living in a flat can be lonely,' Jaala says, 'so I come down here and meet other kids and mums. And it's very relaxing.'

'Maya didn't eat tomatoes until we grew some, she didn't eat cucumber until we grew it, and she just loves 30
playing here and learning about growing things.'

A place like this community garden emphasizes how gardening can bring people together. As fewer families have their own gardens, places like this are becoming more and more important. Lively, multicultural 35
communities are growing up along with the vegetables.

(300 words)

* Wortspiel: to veg out (ugs.) = relaxen
  veg(etables) = Gemüse

Adapted from: www.abc.net.au/gardening

1 COMPREHENSION

How is the community garden beneficial ...

a for beginner gardeners? b for people who live in flats?
c for elderly people? d for young children?

2 MIND MAP

Copy the mind map and complete it with your own ideas.

- obesity
- junk food
- unhealthy diet
- CHILDREN'S DIET
- healthy diet
- behavioural problems
- vitamins and minerals

3 PROJECT

Write down some ideas for the following project.

You are a nursery nurse and you want to help plan a project to encourage young children to eat healthily. It could be a visit to a community garden, an organic farm, an allotment, etc. What resources will be needed? What arrangements need to be made?

D | Grammar checkpoint

1 PAST PERFECT

> Grammar summary S. 214

Make one sentence from each pair of sentences using the expression in brackets. Put one clause in the past perfect. Add a comma if necessary.

1 Julie and Paul changed to low-energy light bulbs. She wrote 'How to save the planet'. (*before*)
   Julie and Paul had changed to low-energy light bulbs before she wrote 'How to save the planet'.

2 Julie produced this piece for the *Daily News*. She and Paul also started recycling. (*before*)
3 Life began to change much, much more dramatically. She wrote about saving the planet. (*after*)
4 Julie's newspaper never said much about green issues. She wrote her article. (*until*)
5 Julie's boss Karen read the article. She began thinking hard about Julie's ideas. (*when*)
6 Karen decided that the *Daily News* should go green. She saw all the letters from readers. (*once*)
7 Karen made this decision. She picked up the phone and called Julie to her office. (*as soon as*)
8 Julie left Karen's office 30 minutes later. She agreed to live a 'green year' and write about it. (*by the time*)
9 Paul accepted the idea. He and Julie discussed it carefully that evening. (*once*)
10 They decided to begin their new lifestyle. They immediately took the first step and turned down the heating. (*after*)

2 IF-SENTENCES TYPE 3

> Grammar summary S. 220

Put the verbs in the right forms to make *if*-sentences type 3. (The *if* part may be in first or second position.) Add a comma if necessary.

1 Julie (*not write*) her article on 'How to save the planet' / her boss (*not ask*) her to go green for a year
   If Julie had not written her article on 'How to save the planet', her boss would not have asked her to go green for a year.

2 Paul (*not agree*) to go green for a year / Julie (*say*) no to her boss.
   If Paul hadn't agreed ...

3 Julie and Paul (*not be able to*) pay for efficient roof insulation / they (*spend*) their money on wind or solar power instead
   Julie and Paul would not have been able to ...

4 they (*keep*) their car / they (*not learn*) to get around the city in other ways
5 they (*not make*) some money from selling the car / they (*not be able to*) finish double glazing their house
6 they (*fly*) to India for their summer holiday / they (*add*) two tonnes of CO_2 emissions to the atmosphere
7 they (*not go*) to Wales instead / they (*not discover*) lots of beautiful places that were new to them

6

Modern ways to work

FOCUS

Holiday Club International operates ski and seaside resorts across Europe. Members buy points when they join, and these points allow them to use the resorts where and when they want.
Like other organizations, HCI needs a variety of staff and skills. Here are some of them.

1 accountant
2 bookings clerk
3 customer relations officer
4 IT technician
5 receptionist
6 publicity assistant
7 resort activities officer
8 salesperson
9 ski instructor
10 waiter

1 Match the people in the photos (A–F) to six of the jobs (1–10).

2 Say which of employees 1–10 you think said the following. Explain why.

My job is temporary because it's seasonal and it's not well paid. In high season, I have to work long, irregular hours. So it can be stressful. But I meet lots of people, and the job is fun. I love working outdoors, helping people to learn a new skill. I always have to be friendly and helpful, but that's me anyway. And I decide how to do things. I just love being independent.

My work is office-based and, with its regular routines, I suppose it's rather repetitive and not very challenging. But it's a responsible job and I have to be accurate. It's secure, permanent, full-time, and I like the regular hours. There's a reasonable salary with good fringe benefits. I work with numbers and don't have any customer contact, but I have to be a good team player in our small group.

3 Imagine you have a choice of jobs 1–10 at Holiday Club International. Say which you would or would not choose and why, using the highlighted vocabulary above.

I'd try the job of ... I think	it would be good	
I wouldn't try ... I don't think	I would enjoy it / be good at it	because ...
	I would like it / be good at it	

BEFORE YOU READ

A student from another country asks you this question: 'After Class 10 in Germany, what routes can you take to get a good, permanent job by your early 20s?' How would you answer?

2 7

Routes to the modern workplace: complex but flexible

ANNA	Haven't we met somewhere before? It's Ed, isn't it?
ED	That's right. You were at Oxford CFE, weren't you?
ANNA	Yes, I finished there a year ago, last July.
ED	Me too. I was there for two years.

5   ANNA   So was I. It's strange we didn't get to know each other.

      ED   Well, it's a big place, and we were on different courses. I did the one-year IT Diploma. And you did Business Studies, didn't you?

10   ANNA   Not in the first year. When I came over from Germany, I joined the International Study Programme.

      ED   That sounds very grand!

      ANNA   Well, it included lots of English – and some IT and basic Business Studies. It was a bridge to my

15   second year.

      ED   So what brought you over from Germany?

      ANNA   Well, after I left school, I did a one-year secretarial course in Dortmund. But then I found out I could get a business qualification over here for free, thanks to the EU. And I wanted to get some international work experience too.

20   ED   Is that what you're doing now?

      ANNA   Yes, I scanned the internet for suitable job adverts, sent out loads of CVs and letters of application towards the end of my course, and I got some interviews – and a job offer from Mediscan. I've been there for a year now, and they're a good employer. The hours are a bit longer than at home, but the salary's reasonable and there are good benefits. I'm training in Export Sales now, and it's quite

25   challenging. I'll probably stay for several years.

      ED   Great! Actually, your first year at CFE reminds me a bit of mine. I was on an 'access' programme.

      ANNA   What's that exactly?

      ED   It's for people who want to get back into education – and need some help getting there.

      ANNA   So what were you doing before that then?

30   ED   It was stupid really. I left school and just drifted into a temporary job at a local factory that made car seats for Honda in Swindon. They put me in stock control as I'd done some ICT at school. It was a boring, dead-end job, but the pay was OK.

      ANNA   What happened then?

      ED   Well, after three years, the company decided to move production to Bulgaria and make us all

35   redundant. Two months later, the factory was gone and so were 140 jobs! We were out of work!

      ANNA   Was that when you decided to go to CFE?

      ED   Yes, it was hard, but my redundancy pay helped, and I got a part-time job too. I upgraded my skills, and it worked. BSG, the solar heating company, were hiring as I was finishing. I applied for an IT job, and I got it. I'm finally in full-time, permanent work at last, the salary is good and I'm going to stay.

40   ANNA   Let's hope BSG doesn't decide to move to Bulgaria too!

(462 words)

1 LOOKING AT THE TEXT

A Compare and contrast Ed's and Anna's routes to their jobs today.

1 Contrast what they did after they left school.
2 Outline the college training that they each did in Oxford.
3 Compare their experiences since they finished their courses.

B Say what you think.

1 Who do you think was clearer and more organized at the beginning – Ed or Anna?
2 Do you think this mattered much?
3 Which person are you more like – Ed or Anna – and why?

2 BUILDING SKILLS: TAKING NOTES FROM READING

> **TIP**

When you take notes, organize them with sub-headings or dates (see below). Leave out unnecessary words such as pronouns and articles. Use abbreviations and symbols such as: *e.g., km, =, etc.*

A Copy and complete the notes about Ed and Anna from the past to now and to their future plans. (To work out dates in the past, work backwards from this year.)

1
> *Ed*
> *Summer 20..: Left school, got job at ...*
> *Summer 20..: Lost ...*
> *...   ...*
> *...   ...*
> *Future plans: ...*

2
> *Anna*
> *Summer 20..: Left school., started a ...*
> *Summer 20..: ...*
> *...   ...*
> *...   ...*
> *Future plans: ...*

B Use your notes to give an oral summary.

1 Work with a partner. Take turns to tell the stories of Ed and Anna.
2 Listen carefully to each other. Make sure that you have both noted the important information fully and accurately.

3 WORKING WITH WORDS

A Copy and complete the lists with 'employment' vocabulary from pages 85–86. Then add other words that you know.

Employment

Getting a job	Things an employer wants	Pay and conditions
job advertisement (advert/ad)	experience	wages
...	...	...
...	...	...

Describing work	Types of employment	Being out of a job
stressful	permanent	redundancy pay
...	...	...
...	...	...

B Rewrite the sentences using the words in brackets (all from pages 85–86) instead of the underlined words.

1 I had a lot of pressure in my old job. (*stressful*)
   My old job was very stressful.
2 Susie is paid very well. (*salary*)
3 Tina works full-time now. (*job*)
4 Tony has responsibility for all export sales. (*responsible*)
5 Helping people is part of my job. (*helpful*)
6 Jo doesn't meet many customers in her work. (*customer contact*)
7 They closed the factory and put everybody out of work. (*redundant*)

4 BUILDING SKILLS: TAKING NOTES FROM LISTENING

> Das Hörverständnis üben S. 199

2 8 **A** Listen for general understanding. Listen to Part 1 and answer these questions.

1 Who is speaking?
2 Use your notes from exercise 2A to say when this phone conversation happened.
3 What do you think the speakers are going to talk about in Part 2?

> **TIP**
>
> This is harder than taking notes from reading because you can easily fall behind as you write. But don't panic! Speakers often make false starts and repeat themselves.

2 9 **B** Listen for detail. Listen to Part 2 and do the following:

1 Listen once. Try to remember as many details as you can, but do not write notes.
2 Briefly, report details that you remember to the class. Do you all remember the same?
3 Prepare headings, referring to exercise 3A for help. Start like this:
   Job: Assistant IT ..., Marketing Support ...
   Type of employment: full-time, ...
4 Listen again and take notes.
5 Work with a partner. Take turns to talk about the job from your notes. Make sure that you have both noted the important information fully and accurately. Add to or change your notes as necessary.

B The bigger picture

BEFORE YOU READ

A What benefits beyond pay may temporary jobs in Germany offer?

B What further benefits do you expect when you get a permanent job?

2 10

A contract too good to be true?

The aptitude tests and the interview were over: after several false starts, Steve finally had the 'right' job. The starting salary was not great, but his career prospects were good. Who could tell? After many years of commitment, Steve might even become a director.

In return, the company was also making big commitments. When Steve showed his family his new contract of employment, his long-retired grandad could hardly believe his eyes. The overall terms and conditions of service were generous and the fringe benefits excellent. 'We didn't have all this when I was your age,' he said.

He recognized cheap cafeteria prices, but subsidized travel, the rise from two weeks' paid holidays to five and the long-term sick pay were new to him. So were the free private healthcare, travel insurance and gym membership.

Then there was the flexitime system to help employees create a good work-life balance. There was also generous paid maternity and paternity leave, and subsidized creche facilities encouraged mothers to return to part-time or full-time work when they were ready.

Such employee benefits have developed over many years. Some have been due to union pressure, and some to government and EU laws. Others have come from business itself. A modern employer invests a lot of money in training its employees. In return, it wants to keep them – and to keep them working hard. It knows that a happy worker is a harder worker. Its workforce is its most valuable resource.

'But how can they afford all these benefits?' Grandad finally asked.

In today's competitive world of work, this is a very good question, and many European business leaders and politicians are asking it.

The big problem is this: business in rich, expensive Europe has to compete globally, most of all with low-cost East Asia. There, working hours are long, pay is low and benefits are few. In order to compete, European business has been taking tough action. First, it has sent manufacturing and now also many white-collar clerical and IT jobs to East Asia and other low-cost regions. It has also been taking away some of its generous benefits. For example, Europe's short, 35-hour week is dying. British business never accepted it. German firms have forced employees to accept longer hours. Now the French are starting to work longer hours too.

* * * * *

After an increasingly hard working life, Steve may one day have to answer his grandad's question like this: 'They really *couldn't* afford all those benefits – at least not for very long.'

(416 words)

1 LOOKING AT THE TEXT

A Read quickly to find information.

1 List the fringe benefits that the photos on page 89 illustrate.
2 List the benefits Steve's grandad had when he was young and those he did not.

B Copy and complete the notes on the text.

1 Aspects of Steve's new job – good and bad:

a *starting salary: not great*
b *career: ...*
c ...
d ...

2 Examples of benefits:

a ...
b ...
c ...

3 Better benefits have come from:

a ...
b ...
c ...

4 Global pressure on European business means:

a ...
b ...

5 Conclusion:

...

C Work with a partner and write a summary.

Use your notes to write a summary of the text in five short paragraphs. Choose one of the following to start each paragraph.

> Better benefits for people like Steve have come from several sides. ▮
> However, there is great pressure on European employers like Steve's. ▮
> Steve's job offered many benefits, including the following. ▮
> After a hard working life, it is probable that Steve will reach an unhappy conclusion. ▮
> Most aspects of Steve's new job were very positive.

Start like this: *Most aspects of Steve's new job were very positive. Although ...*

2 WORKING WITH WORDS

A Use words from the text to complete Steve's answers to his family's questions.

1 *Does the company offer any help with children?*   *Yes, it gives ..., ... and ...*

2 *What about other paid time off work?*   *Well, we get ..., and we also get ...*

3 *And how about subsidized benefits? Is there anything like that?*   *Sure. They give us ..., and they offer ..., too.*

4 *And what about free benefits? Are there any completely free extras?*   *The answer's yes again. The company provides ..., ... and ...*

B Say what you think.

If you applied for Steve's job, which fringe benefits would interest you most/least? Why?

3 LISTENING

2 11 **A** Listen for general understanding. Listen to conversations 1–4 from Anna's first day at Mediscan. Match them to pictures A–D.

B Listen for detail. Listen to Anna's conversations again. Say which of these expressions you hear.

1 a Excuse me, but could you direct me to Marketing, please?
   b Excuse me, but can you tell me the way to Marketing, please?

2 a I'm sorry, but I need to see some form of ID, please.
   b I'm afraid I have to ask you for some kind of ID, please.

3 a I wonder if you could fill in some forms for me, please.
   b Perhaps you could fill in these forms for me, please.

4 a After that, would you like me to take you to your new office?
   b After that, shall I show you the way to your new office?

5 a If it's all right to ask, are you from Germany by any chance?
   b If you don't mind me asking, are you German perhaps?

6 a Shall I move it over to the window for you?
   b Would you like me to move it over to the window for you?

7 a Would it be all right if I came with you?
   b Would you mind if I came with you?

8 a Could you possibly wait for a moment while I save this document?
   b Do you think you could wait just a moment while I save this document?

4 CULTURE CHECK: POLITE EXPRESSIONS

Germans can often sound too direct, and even rude, to English speakers – especially the British. On the other hand, English speakers' politeness and indirectness can sound absurd to Germans. However, polite expressions are very important to English speakers, so use them!

please ▪ thank you ▪ certainly ▪ of course ▪ I'm afraid (that) … ▪ I'm sorry, but … ▪

Polite expressions for asking, requesting and offering are also very important. Try not to answer requests or questions with only 'Yes' or 'No'. Fuller replies are more friendly and polite.

May/Can I ask … ▪ If you don't mind me asking … ▪ Perhaps you could tell me … ▪
Could you/I (possibly) … ▪ Would you mind if … ▪ I wonder if you/I could … ▪
Do you think you/I could … ▪ Would you like (me) to … ▪ Shall I … for you?

A Work with a partner. Practise offering and requesting in these situations.

1 The room is very hot.
2 An elderly man is standing on the bus.
3 Your boss has given your colleague a lot of work.
4 You are carrying a heavy parcel.
5 You have forgotten to bring some money for lunch.

B Work with a partner and act out the situations in exercise 3. You can vary the language from what you heard on the CD, but try to use expressions from exercises 3B and 4.

5 DISCUSSION

▶ Diskussionen führen S. 210

Work in a group. Use the questions to guide your discussion.

1 What sort of work have you done up to now, and when did you do it?
2 What did you enjoy, and what did you not like so much?
3 Are you going to look for a job in the summer?
4 What sort of job would you like to have ten years from now?
5 What steps will you need to take to get there?

C Social options

Crisis in the caring professions?

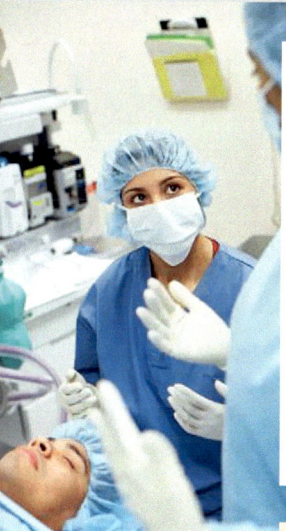

1

UK urgently needs doctors and nurses

The UK has not been producing enough healthcare workers to meet its needs. Despite increased training and recruitment numbers, shortages of 10,000 nurses and 25,000 doctors are anticipated for 2020.

Report for UK Migration Commission

2

Nursing shortage is critical

American hospitals are in a serious crisis. There are now over 120,000 open positions for nurses nationwide. At the same time, the nurses we do have are getting older; the average age is now 45.

Over the next 20 years, this country is going to be short of 400,000 nurses, unless something is done to change things.

CBS Broadcasting, USA

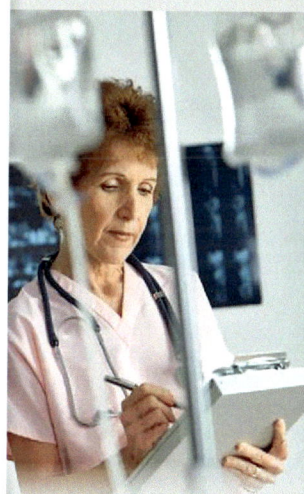

3

Childcare shortage stops parents from working

Almost 200,000 extra childcare places are needed and their non-existence is stopping parents from working, a comprehensive childcare report has found.

Sydney Morning Herald, Australia

4

Social worker crisis puts children at risk

Some of the most vulnerable children in Britain are at risk because of a nationwide shortage of suitable social workers, the co-president of the Association of Directors of Children's Services has warned.

The Observer, UK

1 MEDIATION

You are preparing to take part in a radio debate called 'Crisis in the caring professions'. Select relevant information from the newspaper extracts and write some notes in German. Do not translate word for word.

2 GROUP DISCUSSION

Discuss in small groups.

What is the situation in Germany? What shortages are you aware of? Do you think that any of the reasons in the box have led to people leaving the caring professions? Can you think of any other reasons for shortages of care workers?

job stress ı long hours ı
low pay ı negative image ı
opportunities abroad ı
too much responsibility

D Grammar checkpoint

1 PRESENT PERFECT PROGRESSIVE

> Grammar summary S. 214

Write replies to the questions. Use the words in brackets and the present perfect progressive.

1 A Clara started her training course about two months ago, didn't she? (*do*)

   B *Yes, she has been doing her training course for about two months now.*

2 A Alex joined Altman GmbH about a year ago, didn't he? (*work for*)

   B *Yes, …*

3 A Maria and Nick began studying German around ten weeks ago, didn't they? (*learn*)

   B …

4 A Eva and her sister moved into the apartment roughly a month ago, didn't they? (*share*)

     …

5 A Tomas started looking for a new job nearly a month ago, didn't he? (*search*)

   B …

6 A Jenny asked for a college application form over a week ago, didn't she? (*wait for*)

   B …

2 PRESENT PERFECT PROGRESSIVE AND PRESENT PERFECT

Complete the dialogue. Sometimes more than one tense is possible. > Grammar summary S. 214

TONY Hi, Emma! How are you?

EMMA Oh, hi, Tony! Fine, thanks. And how *have you been keeping*?[1] (*you/keep*)

TONY Really well. I …[2] (*not see*) you for ages.

EMMA No, we …[3] (*not meet*) since Lucy's party last summer. What …[4] (*you/do*) since then?

TONY I …[5] (*travel*) in South America. What about you?

EMMA Oh, I …[6] (*not do*) anything as exciting as that. I …[7] (*take*) a business studies course at college.

TONY …[8] (*it/go*) well?

EMMA Yes, and I …[9] (*just finish*) the first year. And guess what! I …[10] (*pass*) with top grades! I found out this morning.

TONY That's really great! Let's go and celebrate!

3 GENERAL REVISION OF TENSES

> Grammar summary S. 212–216

It is 10th December, and Stefanie is in Ireland to study English. Use appropriate tenses to describe Stefanie's year.

Start like this: *In late May, after she had …*

late May	finish her final school exams, decide to study English in Ireland for a year
June – Sept	take a holiday job and save as much as possible
	do this job, book a place at the Language Centre in Dublin
10th Sept	fly to Ireland to start her course
then – now	go to classes five days a week
every morning	study at the Centre for three hours
this morning	different – meet some friends to do some Christmas shopping
Christmas	plan to visit her family in Dortmund and stay for 10 days
Easter	if have enough money, travel round Ireland
June	take her English exam and then travel home via London
autumn	want to go to college

Going global

FOCUS

Perhaps you have a laptop like this at home. If so, how did it get there? How was it made? This laptop and the products that run on it are the work of many people in many places.

1 **Read the introduction above, and then make sentences like the one below.**

The hardware was designed in Japan, and it was ...

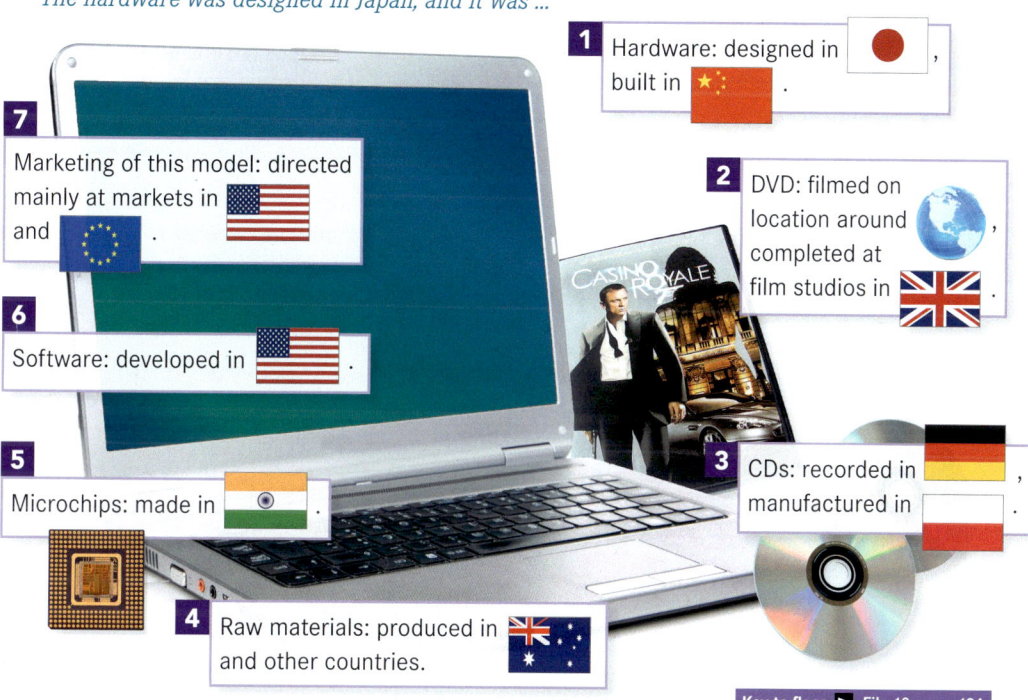

1 Hardware: designed in [flag], built in [flag].

2 DVD: filmed on location around [globe], completed at film studios in [flag].

3 CDs: recorded in [flag], manufactured in [flag].

4 Raw materials: produced in [flag] and other countries.

5 Microchips: made in [flag].

6 Software: developed in [flag].

7 Marketing of this model: directed mainly at markets in [flag] and [flag].

Key to flags > File 10, page 194

2 **Discuss things that you have at home.**

Accessories: e.g. bags, hats, shoes
Clothes: e.g. jeans, trainers,
Electronic goods: e.g. laptop, mobile phone, sound system, TV
Sports equipment: e.g. fitness machine, sports shoes
Transport: e.g. car, motorbike, scooter

1 Use this checklist and note your 'Top 5' favourite things.

2 Also note the brand name of each item, and where you think the following took place: development, design, production.

3 Work with a partner. Take turns to talk about things on your list like this:
(First) on my list is my ... It's a (brand name), and I think it was (produced) in ...

3 **When you get home, check the labels on your favourite things. Were they made where you thought?**

BEFORE YOU READ

2 12 You see lots of goods from around the world in the shops. What other effects of globalization can you also see?

news news news
MONEY MATTERS

Globalization – good or bad?

WITH LISA HALL

They say globalization is good. But how good is it for ordinary people? Let's start by hearing from some ordinary people.

1 ARAND KRISHNAN
senior software programmer, InfoXL, India
Here in Bangalore, India's IT capital, we support the team in Houston, Texas. At the end of their working day, they send us
5 problems, ready for our working day here. We process the material and send back solutions, ready for their next day.

Lots of western companies do this. It works well because we have good English and IT skills, and because data transmission is very cheap. But it's not
10 all foreign companies here now. India is developing fast, and many local IT companies are being set up. In fact, I've been asked to help set one up now. It's a big risk, but a big opportunity too.
(108 words)

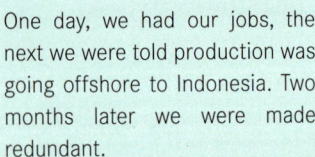

2 NICK BELL ex-furniture factory worker, Galax, Virginia, USA
One day, we had our jobs, the next we were told production was going offshore to Indonesia. Two months later we were made
5 redundant.

Our factory was the main employer in town, and since it closed every other business has been hit hard. So there are no other jobs for us, and people are leaving to find work somewhere else.
10 They say globalization puts cheap goods in the shops from places like China, but it's also taken my job away. If I could just get it back, I'd give up cheap goods tomorrow. What good are they if you don't have a paycheck? They're still too expensive!
(112 words)

3 MALIKA AL-MAGRABI
textile worker, Tangier, Morocco
When I started here at 15, I was glad to find full-time work. But now it's terrible. Before, we were given 14 days to fill orders, but
5 now we usually only get five. We're often required to work 16 hours a day, and we're sometimes forced to work through the night. People get ill, but that isn't allowed. I nearly lost my job when I was off sick for a day.

They're supposed to pay overtime for all the extra
10 hours, but they never do. But what can we do? When my friend Fatima asked for her money, she was sacked immediately. We're just slaves.
(105 words)

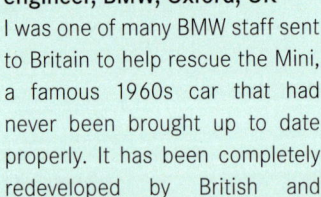

4 BORIS STEIN production engineer, BMW, Oxford, UK
I was one of many BMW staff sent to Britain to help rescue the Mini, a famous 1960s car that had never been brought up to date properly. It has been completely
5 redeveloped by British and German engineers, and now the reborn Mini is as popular as ever. We're working flat out, and nearly 250,000 are being produced every year.

The Mini certainly isn't cheap, so price is not the
10 main competitive advantage. Instead, it wins hearts and minds because it's fantastic to drive, it's beautifully made with cutting-edge technology, and it's one of the world's great brands. It shows that we can still win the globalization game right here in
15 Europe.
(121 words)

1 LOOKING AT THE TEXTS

A Complete the summaries with words from the first two texts.

Arand Krishnan is a senior software ...[1] with InfoXL in ...[2], India. His team provides overnight ...[3] for colleagues in America. InfoXL and other foreign ...[4] came to India because people speak English and have good ...[5] skills, and because the cost of sending ...[6] is very low. Now, many local IT businesses are appearing, and Arand may take the ...[7] and help ...[8] one up.

Nick Bell used to make ...[9] in Galax, Virginia in America, but then ...[10] moved to Indonesia and he became ...[11]. The factory was the biggest local ...[12], and its loss hit every other ...[13] in the town. People are now moving away to find work. Nick does not want the cheap ...[14] that globablization brings. He just wants the ...[15] back that ...[16] took away. Without it, he cannot buy these goods anyway.

B Use the third text to do a mediation task.

> Mediation S. 210

You are a Moroccan union official and a guide for a visiting group of German union officials. Write a short explanation of the situation at Malika's factory – past and present.

C Compare and contrast Boris Stein's experience with that of Nick Bell.

Find one similarity and several differences between them. Use this language:
Both of them have ... However, ... while ...
Concerning their recent experiences at work, ... but ...
Looking at the future, ... whereas ...

D Say what you think.

Our cutting edge technology means German jobs are safe.

Don't you believe it! Plenty of German jobs have gone abroad.

2 WORKING WITH WORDS

A Find opposites of these words in the text.

Text 1	Text 2	Text 4
1 problems (*lines 1–7*)	4 earlier (*lines 1–5*)	6 out of date (*lines 1–9*)
2 expensive (*lines 8–14*)	5 employee (*lines 6–9*)	7 loses (*lines 10–16*)
3 close down (*lines 8–14*)		

B Use pairs of opposites from exercise A in the correct form to complete the following.

1 In countries such as Morocco, most ... do not allow their ... to join unions.
2 This IT equipment is ten years old, so it's completely .... If we want to stay in business, we'll have to buy equipment that's ...
3 All sorts of electronic equipment used to be much more ... than it is now. It is amazing to see how ... today's very powerful computers are.
4 Sadly, European manufacturers have ... a lot of business to Chinese producers. However, they can still ... new customers in world markets when they offer excellent quality.
5 Because of global competition, older, less efficient European industries have had to ....
At the same time though, new high-tech industries have continued to ... successfully.
6 Many developing countries still have big ... such as disease and poor infrastructure. But most are slowly finding ... to them – often with help from the west.

3 **CULTURE CHECK: BODY LANGUAGE AND PERSONAL SPACE**

Globalization is bringing together more and more people from different parts of the world. However, different cultures have different ideas about such basic things as body language and personal space. Something acceptable in one culture may be unacceptable in another.

You have probably already noticed some of the differences, for example through meeting people from other cultures, and you have certainly seen different cultural behaviours in films and on TV.

So try this quiz and see how culturally sensitive you are. Decide who you think is making each point.

EA = an East Asian, LA = a Latin American, NA = a North American, NE = a northern European, SE = a southern European

> *We don't like making too much eye contact when we talk. We feel that's quite rude and 'pushy'. If somebody does that while speaking, we feel that person is trying to dominate or control the listener.*

A EA | LA

> *I don't feel comfortable with somebody who doesn't look me in the eye when we talk. Rightly or wrongly, I feel there's something dishonest about that person – something that I can't quite trust.*

D EA | NA

> *It's just natural to touch the other person's arm or shoulder when we're talking. It shows the warmth that we feel towards each other.*

B EA | LA

> *It's not polite in our culture to stand too close when we talk. We need to give each other as much personal space as possible. That's at least 80 centimetres.*

E SE | EA

> *When I meet somebody new, I like to shake hands firmly to show that I want to have a warm, friendly relationship with that person.*

C NA | EA

Answers > File 4, page 192

4 **DISCUSSION**

> Diskussionen führen S. 210

Discuss these questions in small groups.

1 Whatever the activists say, do you think any government can or should try to stop or slow down globalization?
2 How might globalization affect you in the future? Are you more likely to be a 'winner' or a 'loser' in the globalization process?

BEFORE YOU READ

A What do you think Martin Luther King meant when he said, 'Before you've finished breakfast this morning, you'll have relied on half the world'?

B Have you seen products in the shops with a FAIRTRADE label on them? What do you think it means?

Let's be fair about trade by Sally Pearson

2 13

The not-so-fair trading

We are told that free trade is a good thing. But is it? For many people it is not, and they are some of the poorest in the world.

5 'Always low prices' promises Walmart, America's – and the world's – largest retailer. Consumers like this, of course, and so sales rise. But the big retailers do not cut their own profits to reduce prices. They pass those 'low prices' along the supply chain to the producers, who are
10 forced to compete with each other globally to be the cheapest. The producers are 'free' only to pass on the cost pressures to their workers.

It happens all over the world, in factories and on farms, and the results are the opposite of freedom.

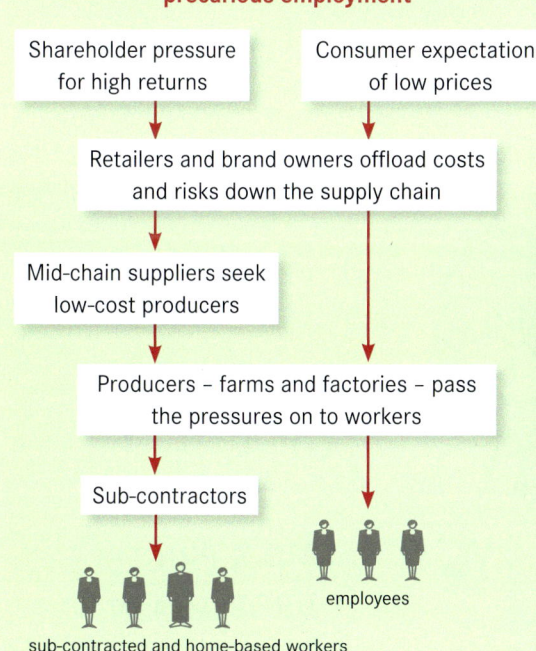

Supply chain pressures create precarious employment

Shareholder pressure for high returns

Consumer expectations of low prices

Retailers and brand owners offload costs and risks down the supply chain

Mid-chain suppliers seek low-cost producers

Producers – farms and factories – pass the pressures on to workers

Sub-contractors

employees

sub-contracted and home-based workers

'We used to be well paid for meeting our targets,' 15 Chandrika, a Sri Lankan textile worker reports. 'But now the targets they give us just cannot be met, so the bonus is never paid.'

'As a casual worker, I don't get a bonus, paid holidays or redundancy pay,' says Ragel, a fruit picker from South 20 Africa.

Ana, a Bolivian factory worker, despairs: 'We have buried our dreams. Our only concern for the future is to make sure that the same thing doesn't happen to our children.' 25

The FAIRTRADE way

FAIRTRADE, with sales now expanding rapidly in Europe and North America, offers hope instead of despair. Coordinator Jack Carson explains:

'We visit potential suppliers to look at their products 30 and their business strengths and weaknesses. If we are happy about these things, we develop an action plan. They may need design or technical support, for example, to get their products right for western markets. We also agree to buy directly and pay a fair, guaranteed price – 35 and some of this immediately. This helps workers with things like paying for their children's education.

We later offer training in marketing and other skills so that producers can gradually become 40 independent.

As for the products, these range from food produce like coffee and bananas to crafts and fashion clothing. They are sold through our own shops and increasing numbers of other stores, including big 45 supermarket chains. Sales are growing by nearly 50% per year. Consumers recognize the FAIRTRADE label and know that it promises quality products at competitive prices – and help for the producers. Instead of rising profits for middlemen, FAIRTRADE brings rising living 50 standards to some of the world's poorest people.'

(401 words)

1 LOOKING AT THE TEXT

A **Read the text carefully. Choose the best answer or answers.**

1 Walmart sells more than …
   a any other supermarket in the USA.
   b any other retailer in North America.
   c any other retail business in the world.
2 The three workers who speak about their problems …
   a come from three different continents.
   b all work in factories.
   c all do badly under the free-trade system.
3 FAIRTRADE helps its suppliers by …
   a helping them to improve their products.
   b helping them to help themselves as exporters.
   c building schools for their children's education.
4 More and more people are buying from FAIRTRADE because …
   a its products are cheaper than normal supermarket products.
   b they want to pay a fair price for quality products.
   c they know this helps to improve life in poor parts of the world.

B **Read the text again and do these activities.**

1 Explain the 'word play' in the title of the text.
2 Find one similarity between each of the workers who speak in the text and Malika's situation – see page 96.
3 Identify the three sentences that relate to the diagram on page 99.
4 In your own words, explain the process that the diagram in the text illustrates.
5 Find the sentence that the photos represent.
6 Copy and complete the diagram on the right.
7 Cover the diagram and describe the process it illustrates.

> Consumers buy more FAIRTRADE quality products at fair …
>
> FAIRTRADE coordinators find more … in poor …
>
> Producers export directly to … for sale through …
>
> FAIRTRADE helps them to …
>
> They agree & pay fair …

C **Say what you think.**

So, we just need to start growing coffee and then we join FAIRTRADE. What do you think?

FAIRTRADE SALES UP AND UP

MILK PRICES DROP AGAIN

2 WORKING WITH WORDS

A Match words from the box to 1–12 to form word pairs. Then look for the expressions in the text to check your answers.

1 free (*paragraph 1*)
2 supply (*paragraph 2*)
3 cost (*paragraph 2*)
4 paid (*paragraph 5*)
5 redundancy (*paragraph 5*)
6 fruit (*paragraph 5*)

7 factory (*paragraph 6*)
8 action (*paragraph 8*)
9 food (*paragraph 10*)
10 fashion (*paragraph 10*)
11 supermarket (*paragraph 10*)
12 living (*paragraph 10*)

> chain **ı** chains **ı**
> clothing **ı** holidays **ı**
> pay **ı** picker **ı**
> plan **ı** pressures **ı**
> produce **ı** standards **ı**
> trade **ı** worker

B Complete the following sentences with word pairs from exercise A. Use plural forms where necessary.

1 Every good employer should offer its employees good pay and conditions, including … … and, if jobs have to be cut, fair … …

2 The big … … like Walmart sell fresh … … as well as thousands of products in cans, packets and bottles.

3 The problems of poor working conditions apply to … … making trainers in Indonesia as well as to … … who gather oranges and lemons in countries around the Mediterranean.

4 Thanks to today's … … between different countries, there are huge … … that bring products to us from right around the world.

3 LISTENING

2 14 A Listen for general understanding. Then answer these questions.

Sally Pearson visited Guatemala with Jack Carson to write more about FAIRTRADE.
1 Who is Felipe Castro?
2 What is Manos Campesinas?
3 Has FAIRTRADE been a positive or a negative experience for Felipe and his colleagues as a group?
4 Has it been positive or negative for Felipe and his family?

B Listen for detail. Listen again and note points 1–12 missing from Sally's notes.

> *Felipe Castro:*   age 48; wife & 3 children
> *Farm:*   1) _____ a hectare; 2) _____ coffee trees
> *Co-operative – Manos Campesinas (= 'Workers' Hands'):*
>   3) _____ members; 4) started in _____
> *What it does:*   5) sells to _____
>   6) gives _____
>   7) offers _____
> *Higher earnings allow farmers to build a new coffee mill:*
> *What it will do:*   8) add _____
>   9) create _____
> *Higher earnings are also changing people's daily lives:*
> *Farmers can now:*   10) install _____
>   11) keep _____
> *Felipe hopes to:*   12) send _____

4 BUILDING SKILLS: WRITING A COMMENT

> Eine Stellungnahme schreiben S. 203

A Prepare to write a comment:
Global competition is the only way.

1 Make a note of your own opinion. Consider first the views and experiences of everybody in this unit.
2 Copy and complete this mind map using words from the box.

> **TIP**

When you write a comment, it is very important to collect and present the arguments for and against the topic. You can do this with notes and tables, but a mind map may be the most useful tool of all.

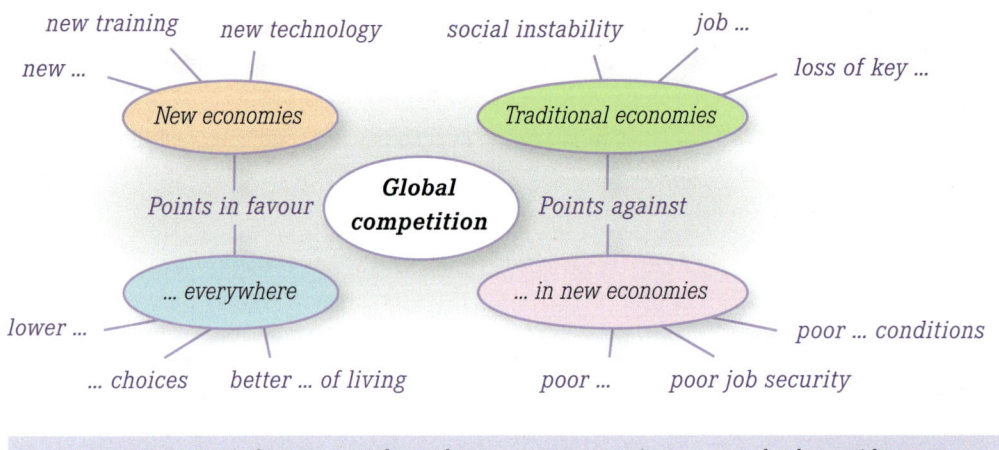

| consumers ▪ industries ▪ jobs ▪ losses ▪ pay ▪ prices ▪ standard ▪ wider ▪ |
| workers ▪ working |

B Write your comment.

1 Write a draft. Use this outline and keep to the point. Use the language shown to help you get started.

Introduction	Statement of the issue and your own opinion
	We live in a world that is rapidly globalizing, and this is creating both benefits and great problems. It is therefore important to consider whether globalization is the only possible way forward. In my opinion, ...
Development	Arguments for or against your own opinion, with evidence/examples
	On the one hand, we should note the many good things that ... First of all, ... Secondly, ... For example,
	On the other hand, we must remember the huge difficulties that ... First, ... For instance, ...
Conclusion	Restatement of opinion and brief summary of reasons
	When I weigh up the good and the bad effects of globalization, I feel that on balance, it is ... My main reasons for this conclusion are that ...

(For further useful connectors to help you in your writing, see **Language for writing** on the back cover flap.)

2 Check your draft for ideas. Make sure that it a) keeps to the point and b) is clear and logical.
3 Check your draft for correctness. Check a) language, including word order, b) vocabulary, c) spelling and d) punctuation.
4 When your draft is as good as possible, make a neat copy.

C Social options

Tips for responsible travel

Before you travel

- Plan your route to minimize your carbon footprint. You should travel by train and then local public transport where possible.
- It's a good idea to read about local cultures and learn as much as you can of the local language. Remember: travelling with respect earns you respect. 5
- Ask your tour operator whether there are local conservation or social projects that you could visit and how you could help support them.

While on holiday

- Buy local produce in preference to imported goods. However, you should never buy products that may 10 be made from endangered plants or animals.
- Hire a local guide – you'll discover more about local culture and lives, and the guide will earn an income.
- Respect local cultures, traditions and holy places 15 – if in doubt, ask advice or don't visit.

- Use public transport, hire a bike or walk when convenient – it's a great way to meet local people and reduce pollution.
- Use water sparingly – it's very precious in many 20 countries and tourists tend to use far more than local people.
- Remember that local people may have different ways of thinking. This just makes them different, not wrong! 25

When you get back

- Write to your tour operator or hotel with any comments or feedback about your holiday. Include suggestions on reducing the environmental impact and increasing the benefits for local communities. 30

- If you've promised to send pictures or gifts to local people, remember to do so – many are promised and not all arrive!
- Enjoy the memories, reflect on your experience and start planning your next trip! (260 words) 35

Abridged and adapted from: www.responsibletravel.com

1 MIND MAP

Use information from the text to draw a mind map about 'responsible tourism'.

2 ROLE-PLAY

Work in groups of four.

In today's globalized economy, poorer countries often need foreign money to fund development. Tourism often seems like a quick and easy solution.

A You work for a tourism company. You want to set up an eco-tourism resort in Chad, Africa. You are sure that it will bring money into the local area and it won't harm the environment. You have travelled to the village to talk with local people.

B You are an African teenager. You think that the resort will mean jobs and a better future for local people.

C You are an aid worker from Germany. You are worried that local people will stop growing their own food and work for the resort instead. If the resort isn't a success, they will go hungry.

D You are an environmentalist from Chad. You are concerned that even an 'eco-tourism resort' will damage the environment.

D | Grammar checkpoint

1 THE PASSIVE: MIXED TENSES

> Grammar summary S. 219

Jack Carson often interviews and writes reports about possible new FAIRTRADE suppliers. Write part of his report on 'Fruits of Africa' for him.

> Put the underlined sections into the passive.
> Use *by* + agent only where necessary.
> Think carefully about word order.

Start like this: *'Fruits of Africa' was started by Mr James Kasozi and some …*

JACK	Mr Kasozi, thanks for seeing me.
JAMES	You're very welcome, but please call me James.
JACK	Fine, well, when did you begin this project?
JAMES	Some other fruit farmers and I started 'Fruits of Africa' five years ago.
JACK	What made you do that?
JAMES	Well, before that, we always lost our fresh fruit if we did not sell it quickly at the local market.
JACK	And now?
JAMES	Now we don't waste these valuable mangos, bananas and pineapples – we dry them instead in very cheap, simple dryers.
JACK	Who supplies the dryers?
JAMES	Our own organization is now making and selling these dryers as cheaply as possible.
JACK	Do they run on electricity?
JAMES	No, they don't use electricity. The natural heat of the sun does the drying.
JACK	Are they popular?
JAMES	Yes, farmers in the local area have already bought hundreds of the dryers. And we are now also receiving orders from all over the country.
JACK	So what about the future?
JAMES	If FAIRTRADE accepts our dried-fruit products, it will help a lot of poor farmers in this very poor part of Africa towards a much better life.

2 THE PASSIVE WITH MODAL VERBS

> Grammar summary S. 219

Jack and a colleague are summing up their ideas on another project. Use the underlined points and the passive to complete Jack's email to his boss.

JACK	So let's sum up our ideas on the 'Baskets of Bengal' project.
LISA	Right. First, they must improve their production quality control.
JACK	And to help them do that, we should send our Technical Support Officer, Stephen Carter.
LISA	Good idea. We could ask him to visit them early next month.
JACK	Next, they have to supply a sample order so that we can test the market here.
LISA	Right, and the next thing: we may need further basket designs at a later date.
JACK	If so, we might supply a specialist product designer to work with them.
LISA	And finally, about payment: we can make an immediate 30% payment with our first order, and we'll pay the rest 60 days after receipt of order.

Email

Dear Margaret

Lisa and I have reached the following conclusions re. 'Baskets of Bengal':

1 Their production quality control must be improved.

8

Finding a job in the EU

FOCUS

1 Work with a partner or in a small group.
Answer the questions and then check your score.

A quiz about the EU

1 How many countries signed the original Treaty of Rome on 25 March 1957?
   A 4   **B** 6   **C** 9

2 Where is the headquarters of the European Commission?
   A Brussels   **B** Luxemburg   **C** Strasbourg

3 When was the euro introduced?
   A 2000   **B** 2001   **C** 2002

4 The voters of which two countries rejected the EU constitution in 2005?
   A Britain and Sweden   **B** France and the Netherlands   **C** France and Italy

5 Which country is not a member of the EU?
   A Belgium   **B** Norway   **C** Sweden

6 How many members does the EU have?
   A 25   **B** 27   **C** over 27

7 What is the Schengen Agreement about?
   A Cross-border policing   **B** Open frontiers   **C** The introduction of the euro

8 Who wrote the music to the 'European anthem'?
   A Edward Elgar   **B** Guiseppe Verdi   **C** Ludwig van Beethoven

Answers ▶ File 3, page 192

2 What is your own attitude to the EU? Choose the statement you agree with most and then do a class survey.

> *I don't have an 'attitude'. The EU means nothing to me.*

> *The EU has brought peace and prosperity to Europe, but I think that's enough. I don't want a United States of Europe with Brussels as its capital.*

> *I'd like the EU to become like the USA. At the moment, national governments have more say than the people of Europe and that's a real problem.*

A Personal perspectives

BEFORE YOU READ

What do you think applying for a six-month internship at a tourist information office involves?

An internship in the UK

Lisa Bach, 20, from Münster is studying tourism in Bremen. As part of her studies, she has to do six months' practical training as an intern in an English-speaking country. Lisa decides to look for an internship in the UK. She contacts a German online agency, SEC, that specializes in arranging internships abroad, and finds this offer:

Tourism internship

Location	Norwich, Norfolk, UK
Sector	tourism
Duties	dealing with enquiries, incl. accommodation; general office duties; occasional 'meeting & greeting' duties
Length	6 months, 1 April to 30 September 20..
Qualifications	18 or over; fluent English, one other major European language; MS Office; car driving licence; friendly, outgoing personality; ability to work well in a team
Remuneration	no salary; accommodation arranged; contribution towards travel/living expenses (by negotiation)
Application	email application, CV as attachment; host's name/email address and job reference number provided by SEC; phone interview will be arranged by email

Lisa fills in the SEC form, pays a fee and receives further details, including the name/email address and the job reference number.

Email

Betreff:	Application for tourism internship
Von:	Lisa Bach <lisa.bach@okipost.de>
Datum:	10 November 20.. 21:32
An:	Norwich City Council <human-resources@norwich.gov.uk>

Dear Sir or Madam

I refer to your offer of a tourism internship on SEC's website, reference ncc-tic-2064.

As you will see from my CV, I am studying Tourism Management at the University of Applied Sciences in Bremen, Germany. Students on this course are required to have a minimum of six months' practical work experience in an English-speaking country.

I am hoping to find an internship next year and would like to apply for the post you are offering. The dates 1 April to 30 September are fine, as are the duties you list in the job description. I worked for two months at the tourist office in Münster this summer, where I gained experience of similar work.

As requested, I attach my CV. If you have any further queries, please contact me by phone or email.

If you are interested in my application, I look forward to arranging a phone interview.

Yours faithfully

Lisa Bach

1 LOOKING AT THE TEXTS

A Do the following tasks.

1 What is Lisa's reason for applying for an internship?
2 Find information in the ad and email to show why Lisa chose this internship.
3 Say whether you think Lisa got a phone interview and explain your answer.

B Say what you think.

1 Could you imagine doing an internship abroad like Lisa? Say why / why not.
2 How would you feel about doing an unpaid internship?

2 WORKING WITH WORDS

A Find words or expressions in the ad (1–3) or email (4–6) to fit these definitions.

1 period of training – often unpaid
2 friendliness, enthusiasm for meeting new people
3 discussion to reach an agreement
4 department responsible for employees
5 opposite of 'theoretical'
6 summary of applicant's personal details, qualifications and work experience

B Write four sentences using some of the words and phrases from exercise A.

LISA BACH

Personal details

Name:	Lisa Bach
Address:	Kreuzstraße 15, 48142 Münster, Germany
Date and place of birth:	28 May 1989, Münster
Nationality:	German
Daytime phone number:	+49-2571-547821
Email address:	lisa.bach@okipost.de

Education

10/2007–present	Fachhochschule Bremen (University of Applied Sciences); 7-semester course, Touristik (Tourism Management)
08/2004–06/2007	Adolf-Kolping-Berufskolleg, Münster (vocational school); 3-year course, Hotelfachfrau (Hotel Administration); grade average: 1.9 on 6-point scale from 1 (very good) to 6 (very unsatisfactory)
08/1999–07/2004	Realschule im Kreuzviertel, Münster (secondary school); school-leaving certificate (equivalent of GCSE); grade average 2.1

Work experience

2003	Altenzentrum St. Josef; assistant carer in home for the elderly
2002	Presto Supermarkt, Münster; sales assistant

Paid employment

Summer 2009	vacation job, Verkehrsverein Münster; assistant in tourist information office
Summer 2008	vacation job, Hotel am Stadtgarten, Münster; assistant receptionist

Interests and skills

Languages	English, advanced (some knowledge of business English)
IT skills	MS Office (Word, Excel, PowerPoint); HSTeam 2006 (hotel software); eComBot Travel (e-Tourism software)
Other	driving licence, EU class C
References	references can be supplied on request

3 LOOKING AT THE CV

Which part of a CV contains this information? Be careful: some information is not given in a CV at all.

1 ability to speak a foreign language
2 applicant's grade at end of Year 10
3 details of driving licence
4 details of unpaid jobs
5 how long an applicant went to primary school

6 information about paid holiday jobs
7 job applicant's email address
8 job applicant's name and address
9 names and addresses of referees
10 information regarding marital status and number of children

4 WORKING WITH WORDS

A Find the English equivalents of the following German words and expressions in the CV. They are not necessarily in the same order.

1 *Abschlusszeugnis*
2 *auf Wunsch*
3 *Berufserfahrung*
4 *bezahlte Beschäftigung*
5 *Empfangsassistentin*

6 *Ferienjob*
7 *fortgeschritten*
8 *Führerschein*
9 *Notendurchschnitt*
10 *Computerkenntnisse*

B Use some of the words and expressions from exercise A to explain the following in English.

Sie möchten jemandem sagen, dass …
1 Sie etwas Berufserfahrung in der Touristikbranche haben.
2 Ihr Ferienjob als Empfangsassistentin Ihnen gut gefallen hat.
3 Sie nach einer bezahlten Beschäftigung suchen, bei der Sie Ihre Computerkenntnisse einsetzen können.
4 auf Wunsch Empfehlungsschreiben eingereicht werden können.
5 Sie fortgeschrittene Englischkenntnisse besitzen.
6 Sie seit zwei Jahren einen Führerschein haben.

5 MEDIATING

> Mediation S. 210

Explain Lisa Bach's CV in German.

You work in the human resources department of a big German tour operator. The company wants to hire an assistant to arrange hotel accommodation for its European tours. Use Lisa's CV to explain to your boss in German why you think she would be a good candidate for the job.

6 WRITING

Write an English letter of application and CV based on your personal profile.

Imagine you are applying for a three-month internship in any country or field of your choice. Write the letter of application and your CV in English. Include information about your school career, work experience, skills, etc.

7 LISTENING

3 2 **A Listen for general understanding. Read the email and then listen to the extract from the telephone interview. How did the interview go: *well*, *badly* or *all right*?**

Email

Subject:	Application for tourism internship
Date:	21 November 20.. 10:12
From:	Norwich City Council <human-resources@norwich.gov.uk>
To:	Lisa Bach <lisa.bach@okipost.de>

Dear Lisa Bach

Further to your application for an internship, I would like to arrange a date and time for a telephone interview. This should take place during our office hours, which are 9:00 a.m. to 6:00 p.m. (local time), Monday to Friday.

Could you please let me have a date and time this week when I can reach you on a landline phone?

Thank you and I look forward to hearing from you.

With regards

Ruth Morgan

B Listen for detail. Read the statements below. Then listen again and say if they are true or false. Correct the false statements.

1 Ruth suggested that they both use first names.
2 Lisa didn't react to Ruth's request for an interview date very promptly.
3 Ruth's first question was about Lisa's course in Bremen.
4 Lisa worked at the tourist information office in Münster last summer.
5 Lisa's main job at the tourst information office was dealing with callers' enquiries.
6 Almost all of these callers were only interested in accommodation.
7 Usually, Lisa just gave dog-owners the addresses of suitable accommodation.
8 Lisa's duties in Norwich will be very different from what she did in Münster.

C Summarize the phone interview in German.

8 ROLE-PLAY

Work with a partner. Read the suggestions below and add any ideas or information of your own to complete the interview. Then act out the interview together.

Ruth asks:
... about Lisa's knowledge of French.
... what Lisa hopes to get out of her internship.
... what Lisa thinks she can offer the tourist information centre in Norwich.
... how Lisa got on with co-workers/managers in Münster.
... how Lisa handled difficult customers/callers.

Lisa asks:
... about her accommodation in Norwich.
... what she will be expected to do on a typical day.
... if she will be allowed to deal with callers herself.

B The bigger picture

BEFORE YOU READ

3 3 In this extract from *Now it's your turn*, a radio phone-in show, Helen Wood is asking callers about Britain and the EU. What opinions do you expect to hear?

HELEN   Is the EU good or bad for Britain? Or is it a mixture of both? That is the topic of our programme this evening. And my first caller is John Harris from Bristol. John, now
5   it's your turn.

JOHN   Hello. Uhm ... Yes, well, first I want to say that I'm certainly not anti-European, but I'm totally against the EU.

HELEN   Oh yes. Why's that, John?

10 **JOHN**   Well, I think the EU's a waste of time and money – just corruption, bureaucracy and interference in our affairs. What right has Brussels to tell us what to do? And it's so undemocratic. Just a bunch of unelected
15 foreign bureaucrats. And who pays for it all? We do! I say we should leave tomorrow!

HELEN   Phew! Well, we've certainly got off with a bang. Now our next caller is ... Oh, yes. Jane Garner from Hull, right?

20 **JANE**   That's right, Helen. Good evening.

HELEN   Hi. And what's your opinion, Jane?

JANE   Well, my brother works for the EU in Brussels, and I think your last caller was very unfair – what he said was misleading, frankly.

25 **HELEN**   Oh? And what makes you say that?

JANE   Well, for example, the so-called 'Brussels bureaucracy'. Believe it or not, the EU is run by fewer people[1] than it takes to run a medium-sized city like Leeds[2].

30 **HELEN**   Really? So why do so many people say that the EU is too bureaucratic, then?

JANE   Well, it's all a question of perception. The trouble is that a lot of people blame Brussels for things that national governments
35 do. The fact is that the European Commission has no legislative power at all. It can only inform, advise and recommend. The rest is up to the Council of Ministers.

HELEN   In other words, national
40 governments, right?

JANE   Right – and unfortunately national

politicians just defend their own national interests, that's the problem. The UK is particularly bad there, I'm sorry to say.

HELEN   Well, thank you for that, Jane. And   45
now my next caller is Dr Peter Brown from Manchester University. What's your take on this, Peter?

PETER   Well, we've been doing research into corruption in Europe, and our findings   50
show that the EU is much less corrupt than nearly all national governments. In actual fact, it's relatively clean.

HELEN   Yes, but the media is full of stories about corruption, isn't it, Peter? They can't all   55
be wrong, can they?

PETER   Well, it's like the last caller said, I'm afraid. All too often, the EU gets the blame for the wrongdoing of national governments. It's like in sport. Where there's money, there's   60
corruption. But the EU doesn't pay out any money directly, to farmers, for example. The member states are responsible for that, and there you really do find some corruption.

HELEN   OK. Thanks, Peter. And now a caller   65
from Europe is on the line. Beate König from Aachen in Germany. What would you like to say, Beate?

BEATE   Good evening everybody. Well, I think the EU is much more than just trade and   70
so on. It's open frontiers, a common currency, the freedom to live and work where we want.

And it's peace, stability and a European identity, too. I value those things a lot, that's all.

75 **HELEN**   Fine. So you have no problem with Brussels interfering in German affairs?

BEATE   Well, no, I don't. I think that in our globalized world, 'national sovereignty' doesn't mean much anyhow.

HELEN   Oh yes? Why's that? 80

BEATE   Well, what about global threats like climate change, scarcity of raw materials, terrorism, mass migration, cross-border crime and so on? No single country can fight those alone. We have no choice. We must integrate 85 to survive.

(608 words)

1 The EU has just over 23,000 employees (2007)   2 Leeds City Council employs about 33,000 people (2008)

1 LOOKING AT THE TEXT

A Do the assignments.

1 List arguments the callers give for and against the EU.
2 Explain why many people have a negative view of the EU.

B Read the speech bubbles and say who is speaking.

1 *There are dishonest politicians in every country.*

2 *It's unfair that our taxes support these foreign politicians.*

3 *National governments alone can't solve international problems.*

4 *Individual countries decide how money from the EU is spent.*

5 *The EU doesn't control us, they make suggestions and recommendations.*

6 *People should stop and think about all the opportunities the EU offers.*

7 *The running of the EU is actually quite efficient if you look at the figures.*

8 *The British government should run our country – not the EU.*

John

Jane

Peter

Beate

C Say what you think.

1 Say which opinion is closest to your own, John Harris's or Beate König's, and why.
2 Which of the statements (a, b or c) do you agree with most? Give reasons for your choice.

I would like to see …
a a further widening of the EU to include all European countries.
b no further widening but greater integration of the present members.
c the EU remain as it is at the moment – no further widening, no further integration.

2 WORKING WITH WORDS

A Complete the table with the missing forms from the phone-in.

	verb	noun	adjective
1	mix	...	mixed
2	corrupt	...	...
3	...	...	interfering
4	perceive	...	perceptive
5	...	advice, adviser	advisory
6	...	recommendation	recommended
7		responsibility	...
8	threaten	...	threatening

B Complete the sentences with some of the words that you found in exercise A.

1 You'll find that all opinion is based on a ...[1] of fact and ...[2]
2 Ask Jane Baker. She's ... for European affairs.
3 Unfortunately, where there's money, there's ...
4 I'm sorry. I can't help you. I strongly ... that you find a good lawyer.
5 Government ...[1] in our private lives is getting worse because of the ...[2] of terrorist attacks.

C Explain these sentences or phrases from the phone-in.

1 '... we've certainly got off with a bang.' (*line 17*)
2 '... what he said was misleading, frankly.' (*line 24*)
3 'The rest is up to the Council of Ministers.' (*line 37*)
4 'What's your take on this ...?' (*line 47*)
5 'In actual fact, it's relatively clean.' (*line 52*)

3 WRITING

> Eine Stellungnahme schreiben S. 203

Use these ideas to write a comment evaluating arguments for and against a fully united Europe.

For:
> balance power of USA/Russia/China
> threats now global, not national (climate change, terrorism, etc.)
> federal system more democratic
> more efficient/effective single market

Against:
> member states too diverse to unite
> differences in size/economies too great
> no official language
> too much power to bigger countries
> people prefer nation states

Use these expressions to emphasize or moderate what you say:

Emphasizing expressions
> it is clear that ...
> there can be no/little doubt that ...
> no matter how ...
> to begin/start with ...
> on top of that ...

Moderating expressions
> as far as I can see ...
> on the one hand ..., on the other (hand) ...
> perhaps/maybe ...
> it seems to me ...
> most would perhaps admit ...

4 5

Mc Nurses come to Germany

For years, workers from eastern Europe have filled a gap in Germany's overstretched healthcare system by providing care at home for the country's old and sick.

5 Approximately 4.5 million households in Germany include people in need of care at home. Nursing care can be expensive, and so home care assistants do the rest. That includes shopping, cooking, giving medication and 10 generally providing time and company.

An estimated 100,000 Bulgarians, Czechs, Hungarians and Poles work in the healthcare sector in Germany. Many of them are working illegally.

15 Seeing a business opportunity, a nursing company from Bremen called 'McPflege' now plans to use cheap, legal healthcare workers from eastern Europe to offer 24-hour personal care for just two euros an hour.

20 Depending on the kind of care needed, patients would spend between €1,500 and €1,700 a month. In comparison, a typical German healthcare provider costs up to €5,000 euros a month.

Union leader Ralf Krüger said, "The company 25 name makes people think of fast food and suggests 'fast care'. Krüger told reporters that McPflege could not provide the high quality of care that is needed.

On the other hand, 30 experts point out that German nursing care providers have no solutions of their own to the problem of 35 home care shortages. Nursing care expert Claus Fussek said the whole debate was hypocritical. 'When a 40 75-year-old woman

takes care of her 80-year-old husband day and night, nobody asks whether she can manage it or is qualified for it.'

The McPflege-type care is a useful addition, 45 Fussek said, adding that it provided desperate relatives with quick help at affordable prices.   (265 words)

Adapted and abridged from *Deutsche Welle*

1 COMPREHENSION

Make two lists: (a) arguments for 'McNurses' in the text
(b) arguments against them

2 ROLE-PLAY

You are taking part in a TV debate about 'McNurses'.

A   You are Ralf Krüger. You are against the McPflege care model.
B   You are Claus Fussek. You believe that 'McNurses' are a good idea.

3 WRITING

Write down some ideas for how more young people could be encouraged to become nurses and care assistants.

D Grammar checkpoint

1 GERUND OR INFINITIVE?

> Grammar summary S. 221

Choose the correct form, a) or b).

1 We really enjoy a) travelling | b) to travel[1] within the Eurozone because we dislike a) having to | b) to have to[2] change money all the time. In fact, I think the UK should consider a) giving up | b) to give up[3] the pound and a) adopting | b) to adopt[4] the euro.

2 We chose a) joining | b) to join[1] the EU, didn't we? In my opinion, we should stop a) opting out | b) to opt out[2] of everything and start a) playing | b) to play[3] a full role in the union. If we don't, we risk a) becoming | b) to become[4] isolated on the edge of Europe. We really must avoid a) letting | b) to let[5] that happen.

3 My sister wants a) studying | b) to study[1] German so my dad suggested a) applying | b) to apply[2] to a university in a German-speaking country. Anyhow, she decided a) going | b) to go[3] to Dresden and she plans a) moving | b) to move[4] there in August.

4 Both Austria and France have promised a) holding | b) to hold[1] a referendum about Turkey joining the EU. If they do, I can't imagine Turkey a) winning | b) to win[2] the vote. Personally, I would like a) avoiding | b) to avoid[3] a referendum at any cost. I would prefer Turkey a) stopping | b) to stop[4] negotiations to join the union before that happened. Just think about it! It could mean a) closing | b) to close[5] the door to Europe in Turkey's face!

5 I will never forget a) visiting | b) to visit[1] the EU headquarters in Brussels for the first time. I had read so much about the 'gigantic EU bureaucracy' that I expected a) seeing | b) to see[2] huge office blocks and so on. I remember a) being | b) to be[3] very surprised at what I found. In fact, the EU building did not seem a) being | b) to be[4] any bigger than that of many big international firms. But when I tried a) telling | b) to tell[5] people back home, many of them simply refused a) believing | b) to believe[6] me. Some even told me to stop a) talking | b) to talk[7] such nonsense.

2 GERUND OR INFINITIVE?

> Grammar summary S. 221

Use the infinitive or -ing form to complete this dialogue.

A radio producer, Nick West, is talking to a reporter, Sue Green, about a request from a listener.

NICK Hi, Sue. Look, do you remember ...[1] (*interview*) that guy about opening an office in Germany?

SUE Yes, of course. Greg Cox. Nice man but he just couldn't stop ...[2] (*talk*). He's trying ...[3] (*find*) an agent in the Ruhrgebiet, I think.

NICK Well, this email is from a guy called Lothar Moers in Bochum. He'd like ...[4] (*get*) in touch with Greg Cox but he says he forgot ...[5] (*note*) down his address. I meant ...[6] (*deal*) with it yesterday, but I just didn't manage ...[7] (*do*) it, I'm afraid. And I can't stop ...[8] (*reply*) to it now. Do you think you could answer it for me?

SUE Sure. I'll stop ...[9] (*work*) on this report and do it immediately.

NICK Thanks, a lot, Sue. I suppose it just means ...[10] (*tell*) Greg Cox Mr Moer's email address and then he can take it from there. I don't want ...[11] (*do*) it the other way round.

SUE Of course not. We always avoid ...[12] (*give*) other people somebody's address. Anyhow, luckily, I decided ...[13] (*keep*) Greg's contact details just in case anybody got in touch. I'll try his mobile number first and if I have no luck, I'll try ...[14] (*get*) him on his office number.

9

Social challenges

FOCUS

1 Do awareness activity 1: *Who are you?*

1 Work with a partner - someone you do not know well. Copy the chart below. Add extra writing space in columns 2-4.
2 Silently, fill in column 2 about yourself. Then guess your partner's answers and fill in column 3.
3 Next take turns to ask the questions and fill in column 4.
4 Discuss differences between your column 3 and 4 answers.

Who are you?	Myself	Partner (my guesses)	Partner (his/her answers)
1 What is your father's cultural heritage? (e.g. national /regional /ethnic /religious background)			
2 What is your mother's cultural heritage?			
3 Where were you born?			
4 What's your favourite school subject?			
5 What's your favourite sport?			
6 Who's your favourite musician /band?			
7 What's your favourite food?			
8 What's your biggest fear?			
9 What do you consider your best quality?			
10 How do you see yourself in ten years' time?			

2 Do awareness activity 2: *How does society help make me who I am?*

1 Use the diagram below to help you organize your thoughts. Think how different parts of society can benefit, control and influence you.

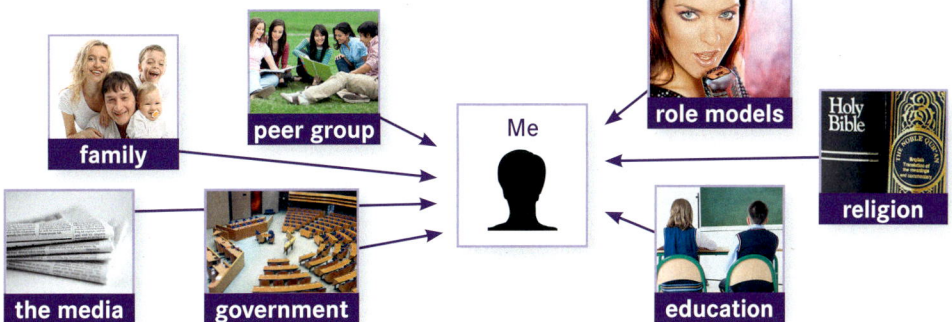

2 Work with a partner. Present your ideas to each other and discuss any differences.

BEFORE YOU READ

3 4 The first picture is from an old advert. What view of family life does it show?
Is this your view?

What's in a family?

Do you remember the 'perfect' family? You know, the one with the happy husband going off to his steady job in his clean, white shirt. And the happy wife looking after the perfect home while bringing up the perfect children.

5 Perhaps that family only ever existed in 1960s washing powder ads. Certainly, life today is much less tidy. The pressures on families are often huge. Few fathers have a steady job for life, and quite often there is no father. And the mother often works. Who then polishes the home and the children?

10 In fact, quite often there is no father *or* mother: in America about 4.5 million young people live with grandparents, and many more live with other relatives.

So can the family still do its traditional job for children? Can it still provide the steady structure, rules and role models that socialize the young, bringing them up to be responsible members of adult society? Every day the media seem to prove that street gangs have taken over – have become the only 'family'

15 many teenagers have.

But there is better news too. When families break down, alternative arrangements with relatives can work well, as the stories of Brittany Hicks and Arianna Bianco show. Both have fathers they have never known. Brittany's mother could not look after her because of emotional problems. Arianna's mother had a drug addiction, making childcare impossible.

20 You might expect Brittany and Arianna to feel abandoned and angry. But both girls say they don't feel that way. 'I just deal with it,' says Arianna. 'I don't get mad at my mom. Being addicted to drugs was obviously a thing she couldn't stop.'

Brittany says she used to feel rejected by her mother, but, 'As I grew up, I came to realize that she loved me a lot. She told me, "I never abandoned you. I always knew where the best place was for you." And

25 now I believe her.'

Brittany and Arianna both agree that they have to live by a tougher set of rules than kids in traditional families. 'My aunt is definitely stricter,' says Arianna. 'All my friends agree.' Brittany says her grand-parents check her activities more closely than she thinks they need to. 'I guess it's because they don't want me to run into the same problems my

30 mom did.'

Talking about life outside the traditional family structure, Brittany speaks for both girls when she says, 'People think it's really different, but it's not. You're living with

35 people who love you and want you to have a good life – just like any family.'

(426 words)

Brittany, who lives with her grandparents

Arianna, whose aunt and uncle care for her

1 LOOKING AT THE TEXT

A Read the text and do the following tasks.

1 Contrast the 'fantasy family' of the 1960s with the way that many real-world families are today.
2 Note things that Brittany and Arianna have in common in the way that they have been brought up.
3 Compare the way that Brittany and Arianna are being brought up with a more normal family upbringing.

B Say what you think.

"The only way I could get him to take any notice of me was to put myself on DVD."

"Couldn't you at least wait until half-time so we could discuss our communication problem?"

2 WORKING WITH WORDS

A Use the correct form of these phrasal verbs from the text to complete the story below.

> break down ∎ bring up ∎
> deal with ∎ go off ∎ grow up ∎
> look after ∎ run into ∎ take over

When Tony was three and his younger sister Lucy just two, their parents' marriage ... ...¹ big problems, and it ... ...² so badly that one day their father just disappeared. Years later, the family learned that he had ... ...³ to start a new life in Australia.

For the next three years, their mother seemed to be able to ... ...⁴ the situation. A child-minder ... ...⁵ the children every day while she went to work. In the end, though, the problems of ... ...⁶ two small children as a single mother were too much for her, and she had a nervous breakdown. Social Services then ... ...⁷ from her, and the children were taken into care for several months. Then, after recovering, their mother was able to take them back again. She also met a new partner who soon became a real father to the children. So, in the end, Tony and Lucy ... ...⁸ quite normally and happily.

B Find words or expressions in the text to express the underlined parts of the sentences below more efficiently.

The old ways and the new

1 It has gradually become clear to people that the old ways of family and working life have changed forever. (*paragraph 7*)
   People *have come to realize* that the old ways of family and working life have changed forever.
2 For example, people often change jobs these days, and nobody expects to find a job that will continue until one retires at the age of 65. (*paragraph 2*)

Becoming a member of society

3 It is essential for every community to <u>bring up</u> its young people <u>to become good members of that community</u>. (*paragraph 4*)

4 Young people need to learn to <u>do things according to</u> the rules and customs of their community. (*paragraph 8*)

Helping a boy called Sam

5 It is clear that Sam's mother, Carrie, has severe psychiatric problems and that <u>looking after her child</u> has become impossible for her. (*paragraph 5*)

6 Carrie's illness is a big problem and Sam's father has lost contact with the family, and so we have been trying to make <u>other plans for dealing with the situation</u>. (*paragraph 5*)

7 Although his situation is very bad, <u>I can tell you something more positive</u>. It seems that his aunt and uncle are happy to give him a home. (*paragraph 5*)

3 LISTENING

A **Listen for general understanding. Listen to someone else talking about his experiences and answer these questions.**

1 What is the family situation?

2 Does the speaker feel that he is dealing with it
   a very well?   b as well as can be expected?   c very badly?

3 What is often the problem at the end of the working day?

B **Listen for detail. Listen again and choose the correct answers.**

1 Note which activities a–d the father believes his daughter and he are doing enough together.
   a watching football   c playing board games
   b playing with Barbie dolls   d talking

2 Say which of the following the father hopes that people outside the family can help to provide.
   a understanding of make-up   c knowledge of the facts of life
   b knowledge of hairstyling   d a female role model

3 Which problems a–d does the father say he has in finding a new partner?
   a ability to trust someone new   c having a daughter
   b lack of time to find someone   d inability to find a good role model

C **Say what you think.**

Imagine yourself as the girl above thinking back at the age of 18. What would you say to 'your' father about his efforts? Write your thoughts in the form of a letter to him. Use these ideas:

When I look back at those years after Mum left us, I (sometimes/often) feel …
I (often/always) remember that (I/we/you) used to …
I'm sure it was very (hard/depressing/tiring) for you to …
I wish (you/we/I) (had/hadn't) …
Finally, I'd just like to say …

BEFORE YOU READ

Work with a partner. Try to decide which of these groups you trust most and least. Make a list from 1 (most trusted) to 7 (least trusted).

business managers ▪ politicians ▪ doctors and nurses ▪ journalists ▪ priests and ministers ▪ teachers ▪ solicitors and lawyers

Changing society

In a recent survey, Britons showed that the people they trust least are politicians (and journalists). Membership of political parties has dropped to record low levels, and numbers voting in elections have fallen. In a recent national election, only 55% of voters took part and just 42% of these voted for the winning party. The new government was chosen by roughly a quarter of the adult population!

Election numbers are falling across most of the western world. And, worryingly, the people who are least likely to vote are the young. Does this mean that young people have turned away from politics? For many the answer is yes but for others, no. The thing that these young people have turned away from is traditional party politics. Political parties work by bringing together many shades of opinion, and then uniting these into policies covering all areas of government. But these young people have a narrower focus – the environment, for example, or animal rights.

They live in the world of single-issue politics, and they see their particular issue as one requiring urgent action. They want to force the government to understand it and to act. This often means direct action to get public opinion on their side. They organize campaigns that may include demonstrations, marches and other ways of attracting attention. They may use non-violent acts of civil disobedience that lead to arrest by the police. Sometimes, they might even use violence – although this very often actually reduces rather than increases sympathy for their cause.

'There is nothing so powerful as an idea whose time has come,' Victor Hugo said, and this is true of some single-issue campaigns. Think of the suffragette movement that won women's right to vote in the early 20th century. Think of the Civil Rights movement in the 1950s and 1960s, finally bringing Black Americans their full freedom. Think of the students' movement of the late 1960s, which gave the voice of the young new power. These were campaigns that changed history.

Not every battle shakes the world though: smaller successes are possible too. Take the case of Julia Butterfly Hill, for example. Aged 23, she climbed a 180-foot, 1,000-year-old redwood tree in Stafford, California with the aim of preventing further logging in the area. She stayed there month after month, her friends supplying her with food by rope. After remaining in the tree for two years, she won. The loggers signed an agreement promising to save the tree and the surrounding forest forever.

Can traditional politicians attract people like Julia to join them? Sadly for mainstream politics they usually cannot.

(432 words)

1 LOOKING AT THE TEXT

A **Read the text quickly and say what these numbers refer to.**

55% ∎ the early 20th century ∎ the 1950s and 1960s ∎ 23 ∎ 180-foot

B **Say whether these statements are true or false. Correct the ones that are false.**

1 British people prefer to believe politicians rather than people in business.
2 Not so long ago, about 50% of the British population voted for the new government.
3 Young people are often more interested in single-issue politics than in traditional party politics.
4 The Civil Rights movement won the right to vote for American women.
5 Julia Butterfly Hill achieved nothing when she went to live up a tree.

C **Say what you think.**

1 Look again at the list of groups in Before you read.
   > Are politicians the only ones who can influence and change society?
   > Are they even the main influencers and changers?
   > Are there other groups in society that you would like to add to the list?

2

Sure I believe in change and I'll even go on a demo or two, but I'll never break the law or do anything violent. That's got to be wrong.

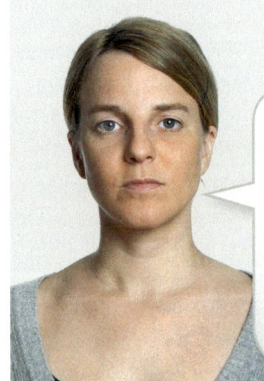

Look, sometimes you have to take the law into your own hands to make the world take notice and actually do something!

2 WORKING WITH WORDS

A **Form adjectival compounds from the highlighted words.**

> **TIP**
> • When plural nouns are used adjectivally, e.g. *a 180-foot tree*, they usually become singular, e.g. *feet > foot*.
> • Adjectives disappear if the meaning is obvious, e.g. *tall* when talking about the height of a tree.

1 Julia climbed a tree that was 180 feet tall.
   Julia climbed a 180-foot tree.

2 She climbed a tree that was 1,000 years old.
3 She was a student who was 23 years old.
4 She began a protest that lasted for two years.
5 She was a good example of an activist who is concerned with a single issue.
6 In 1918, the suffragettes finally won the women's vote after a battle that had lasted 29 years.
7 The suffragettes and the Civil Rights movement were both important forces for change in the twentieth century.

B Find words or expressions in the text to express the underlined parts of the sentences below more efficiently.

1 Membership of political parties has recently fallen to <u>the smallest numbers that there have ever been</u>. (*paragraph 1*)
Membership of political parties has recently fallen to record low levels.

2 Our festival is a great community event, and everybody in the village <u>has a role to play</u> in the various activities. (*paragraph 1*)

3 Our party is a very broad political group, and in it you can find <u>lots of slightly different ideas</u>. (*paragraph 2*)

4 Barbara is not interested in traditional political parties. She believes that <u>fighting for just one political cause</u> is the only way to change anything. (*paragraph 3*)

5 We believe that our new party is one <u>that the world is now ready to listen to and follow</u>. (*paragraph 4*)

6 The Civil Rights movement in America in the 1950s and 1960s was one that <u>deeply affected everybody everywhere</u>. (*paragraph 4*)

C Make statements from the notes. Use language from the table to turn the percentages into appropriate expressions of proportion.

Some statistics from the recent city elections:

1 Population registered to vote: 79%
Just under four-fifths of the population were registered to vote.
Or:
Approximately four out of five of the population were registered to vote.

2 Electorate who actually voted: 62%
3 Those over 50 who took part in the election: 76%
4 Voters aged 18–30 who voted: 25%
5 Those in the age range 30–40 who took part: 34%
6 Votes for the winning candidate, Sally Driscoll: 42%
7 Electors voting for the runner-up, David May: 39%
8 Votes going to the other five candidates: 19%

fewer than	(one) out of (five)
just under	(three) out of (eight)
a little under	(seven) out of (ten)
nearly	
almost	half
	a third
exactly	a quarter
about	a tenth
around	
roughly	(two) thirds
approximately	(three) quarters
	(four) fifths
just over	(five) sixths
a little over	(six) sevenths
more than	(seven) eighths
well over	(nine) tenths

3 LISTENING

A Listen for general understanding. Two people are giving their opinions on an issue which is extremely important for them. Listen and answer these questions.

1 What are they talking about?
2 What are they both against?
3 What are they both for?
4 Which presentation of their case is better?

B **Listen for detail. Listen again to decide why one speaker is better than the other. Consider these points and give examples.**

> clear delivery in simple English that the listeners can understand;
> organization of the presentation: introduction, presentation of ideas, summary;
> inclusion of relative ideas and information that is clearly connected (using *first of all, secondly, however, therefore,* etc.).

4 BUILDING SKILLS: GIVING A PRESENTATION

> Die Arbeitsergebnisse präsentieren S. 206

A **Work with a partner. Look at the cartoon and do these activities.**

1 Describe the cartoon.
2 Identify all the single-issue campaigns the man supports.
3 List more single-issue campaigns that you know about.
4 Discuss them and agree on one you would like to present.

B **Prepare a 90-second presentation.**

1 For the short introduction: collect essential information on the background to the campaign – why it was needed and how/when it was started.
2 For the main development: collect essential information on things that the campaign has done, with its successes and failures.
3 For the conclusion: agree on how you will re-state your opinion with a summary of supporting reasons.
4 Write notes for your presentation. Then practise and time it. Make necessary changes. Now you are ready to give your presentation, following the guidelines on page 206–07.

> **TIP**

- You may know all that you need to know for your presentation. However, you may want to collect information from books, magazines, campaign leaflets and from related websites.
- Sort and choose only the most important information to use. Remember: you have only a short time and every word must matter!

5 WRITING

> Eine Stellungnahme schreiben S. 203

Write a comment.

Choose an issue from the cartoon or any other that you do <u>not</u> support. Write a comment evaluating general arguments for and against it. Conclude with a short summary of your personal view. Try to use some of the expressions that Julie used in her spoken presentation in exercise 3, for example:

First let's consider …   *However, I believe that …*   *Moreover, …*
They also make the point that   *First of all, …*   *So, to summarize, …*
…   *Therefore, …*

C Social options

1 COMPREHENSION

Say where the following ideas can be found in the song. Give line numbers.

a Adults can't force teenagers to do what adults want.
b Growing up is difficult.
c Teenagers and adults are always arguing.
d Teenagers don't want to become like their parents.
e Will today's young people still be rebels when they are older?
f Young people see the world differently to older generations.

Teenage Politics by MXPX

4 6

No I'm not mad, but I think they forget
what it's like and how hard it is to be a teenager.
This is a new day and age, we read a different book
where Elvis ain't the rage and polyester ain't the look.
5   And will we change at all when we get old?
Or will we be the same? Never do what we're told?
Well that depends on you, are you doing the right thing?
It's not about control, it's about you and me and understanding.

Teenage politics, it's too confusing!
10 Politics shmolitics, it's too confusing!

Is it time again to disagree
about anything and everything and what's on TV?
It's a vicious circle, never ending,
a linear equation worldly extending.

15 Teenage politics *etc.*

No I'll never be like you, I'll never ever be like you.
Oh no! I'm just like you!

2 ROLE-PLAY

Work in groups of four.

A multinational corporation has got permission from the government to build a theme park in a local woodland area. This means cutting down the trees and draining a lake. Debate what you are going to do about it.

Student A You are a radical activist. You want to chain yourself to a tree in protest against the plans.
Student B You believe in lawful protest. You want to organize a peaceful demonstration outside the headquarters of the company involved.
Student C You don't believe in demonstrations and protests, but you want to email your local council.
Student D You don't think that ordinary people can change these things. Hopefully stories in the media will make the politicians and business people change their minds.

3 WRITING

Do one of the following tasks.

Either: a Examine the songwriter's attitude in 'Teenage politics'. What is the songwriter's view of today's teenagers? Write a paragraph.
Or: b Write a third verse expressing your own view about how today's teenagers relate to their parents' generation.

1 PARTICIPLE CLAUSES 1

> Grammar summary S. 224

Join the pairs of sentences. Use the word in brackets with the correct sentence and change the following verb into an *ing* participle.

1 Joey first got high on medical drugs at the age of 13. He grew up in a small town in Vermont. (*while*)
   Joey first got high on medical drugs at the age of 13 while growing up in a small town in Vermont.

2 He had used these drugs for two years. He finally allowed peer-group pressure to push him into trying heroin. (*after*)

3 He took this dangerous step. He had always been determined to avoid heroin because of all the frightening stories about it. (*before*)

4 He took the powerful new drug. He quickly found himself 'on the clouds'. (*on*)

5 He began selling heroin to pay for his $400-a-day habit. He moved from 'snorting' to using a needle. (*after*)

6 He studied at the University of Vermont. He knew he was reaching 'the bottom' and decided to visit the university's drug treatment centre. (*while*)

7 Soon after that, he realized that he really must break his addiction. He saw his best friend die of a drug overdose. (*on*)

8 He finally got clear of heroin ten months ago. He looks back on the whole experience now and says, 'I wouldn't wish it on my worst enemy.' (*after*)

2 PARTICIPLE CLAUSES 2

> Grammar summary S. 224

Change the relative clauses (starting with *who*, *which*, *that*) to *ing* or *ed* participle clauses. See the example below.

Sheena Alston, social worker

Sheena Alston is an experienced social worker who works for Redbridge Social Services and who is employed in the Children's Services Department.

For many years her job was to find suitable homes for children who had been taken into care from broken homes and from families which had a history of violence. She had special responsibility for children who came from ethnic backgrounds, and it was her job to find 'foster' families which offered these children similar ethnic backgrounds.

More recently, she has taken over a newly created section that is called 'Friends and Family' and that is tasked with the job of placing children with relatives or with family friends. The children who are brought into the system often have serious psychological problems, and their successful placement is a job which requires hard work and great care both by Sheena and by the new families. However, a good result also brings great happiness to the child, to the family – and of course to Sheena herself.

*Sheena Alston is an experienced social worker **working** for Redbridge Social Services and **employed** in the Children's Services Department.*

10

Multiculturalism

FOCUS

1 Look at the picture of a typical London market scene. Use the words in the box to talk about the ethnic minorities you can see.

> Afro-Caribbean **ı** black **ı** British Asian **ı** Indian **ı** Pakistani **ı** white
> +
> bindi (red spot) **ı** hijab (headscarf) **ı** sari **ı** turban

2 Which different cultures live in your region or neighbourhood? Which do you belong to?

3 Do you have social contact with people of other cultures? Where? When?

BEFORE YOU READ

A Read the title and say what the story could be about.

B How would you expect a 'fanatic' to behave?

My Son the Fanatic

Hanif Kureishi's short story is set in East London. Parvez, a 40-year-old Pakistani taxi driver, has been living in England for almost 20 years. He is worried about his son, Ali, who is behaving strangely. Now, Parvez has taken a night off to take Ali out for a meal. In this extract he is telling Bettina, his friend and confidant, about that evening ...

This time Parvez was trembling. Bettina put her arms around him.

"What's happened?"

"I've just had the worst experience of my life."

As Bettina rubbed his head Parvez told her that the previous evening he and Ali had
5 gone to a restaurant. As they studied the menu, the waiter, whom Parvez knew, brought
him his usual whisky and water. Parvez had been so nervous he had even prepared a
question. He was going to ask Ali if he was worried about his imminent exams. But first,
wanting to relax, he loosened his tie, crunched a popadom and took a long drink.

Before Parvez could speak, Ali made a face.
10 "Don't you know it's wrong to drink alcohol?" he said.

"He spoke to me very harshly," Parvez told Bettina. "I was about to castigate the boy
for being insolent, but managed to control myself."

He had explained patiently to Ali that for years he had worked more than ten hours
a day, that he had few enjoyments or hobbies and never went on holiday. Surely it
15 wasn't a crime to have a drink when he wanted one?

"But it is forbidden," the boy said.

Parvez shrugged, "I know."

"And so is gambling, isn't it?"

"Yes. But surely we are only human?"
20 Each time Parvez took a drink, the boy winced, or made a fastidious face as an
accompaniment. This made Parvez drink more quickly. The waiter, wanting to please
his friend, brought another glass of whisky. Parvez knew he was getting drunk, but he
couldn't stop himself. Ali had a horrible look on his face, full of disgust and censure. It
was as if he hated his father.
25 Halfway through the meal Parvez suddenly lost his temper and threw a plate on the
floor. He had felt like ripping the cloth from the table, but the waiters and other
customers were staring at him. Yet he wouldn't stand for his own son telling him the
difference between right and wrong. He knew he wasn't a bad man. He had a
conscience. There were a few things of which he was ashamed, but on the whole he
30 had lived a decent life. "When have I had time to be wicked?" he asked Ali.

In a low monotonous voice the boy explained that Parvez had not, in fact, lived a
good life. He had broken countless rules of the Koran.

"For instance?" Parvez demanded.

7 imminent
   bevorstehend
8 crunch *kauen, im
   Mund zerbrechen*
   popadom *Papadam
   (knuspriger dünner
   Fladen)*
11 castigate *züchtigen*
12 insolent *unverschämt*
17 shrug *mit den
   Schultern zucken*
20 wince *zusammen-
   zucken*
   fastidious *nörgelnd*
26 rip *reißen*
30 decent *anständig*
   wicked *böse, gottlos*

Ali hadn't needed time to think. As if he had been waiting for this moment, he asked
35   his father if he didn't relish pork pies.

"Well ..."

Parvez

Parvez couldn't deny that he loved crispy bacon smothered with mushrooms and mustard and sandwiched between slices of fried bread. In fact, he ate this for breakfast every morning.

35   Ali then reminded Parvez that he had ordered his own wife to cook pork sausages, saying to her, "You're not in the village now, this is England. We have to fit in!"

Parvez was so annoyed and perplexed by this attack that he called for more drink.

40   "The problem is this," the boy said. He leaned across the table. For the first time that night his eyes were alive. "You are too implicated in Western civilisation."

Parvez burped; he thought he was going to choke.

"Implicated!" he said. "But we live here!"

45   "The Western materialists hate us," Ali said. "Papa, how can you love something which hates you?"

"What is the answer then?" Parvez said miserably. "According to you."

Ali addressed his father fluently, as if Parvez were a rowdy crowd that had to be quelled and convinced. The Law of Islam would rule the world; the skin of the infidel

50   would burn off again and again; the Jews and Christians would be routed. The West was a sink of hypocrites, adulterers, homosexuals, drug takers and prostitutes.

As Ali talked, Parvez looked out of the window as if to check that they were still in London.

"My people have taken enough. If the
55   persecution doesn't stop there will be *jihad*. I, and millions of others, will gladly give our lives for the cause."

"But why, why?" Parvez said.

"For us the reward will be in paradise."

60   "Paradise!"

Finally, as Parvez's eyes filled with tears, the boy urged him to mend his ways.

"How is that possible?" Parvez asked.

"Pray," Ali said. "Pray beside me."

65   Parvez called for the bill and ushered his boy out of the restaurant as soon as he was able. He couldn't take any more. Ali sounded as if he'd swallowed someone else's voice.

Parvez' son Ali

On the way home the boy sat in the back of the taxi, as if he were a customer. "What
70   has made you like this?" Parvez asked him, afraid that somehow he was to blame for all this. "Is there a particular event which has influenced you?"

"Living in this country."

"But I love England," Parvez said, watching his boy in the mirror. "They let you do almost anything here."

75   "That is the problem," he replied.

(830 words)

35 relish *genießen*
37 smother *bedecken*
42 be implicated in
   Teil von etw sein
43 burp *aufstoßen*
   choke *ersticken*
49 quell *bezwingen,*
   beherrschen
   infidel *Ungläubige / r*
50 be routed *besiegen*
51 sink *hier: Sumpf*
   hypocrite
   Heuchler / in
   adulterer *Ehebrecher*
55 persecution *Hetzjagd*
62 urge *drängen*
   mend one's ways
   sich bessern
65 usher out
   hinausführen

1 LOOKING AT THE TEXT

A **Read the text and do the following activities.**

1 Describe the setting of the incident and say from whose point of view it is told.
2 Copy and complete the table below. Outline Parvez's and Ali's conflicting opinions.

Parvez	*Ali*
drinks alcohol (whisky)	*rejects alcohol because it's against the Koran*

B **Say what you think.**

1 Explain the conflict between Parvez and Ali.
2 Describe Ali's idea of Muslim cultural identity in Britain and compare it to his father's.
3 Why do you think Ali has become a fanatic?

2 WORKING WITH WORDS

A **Collect verbs and verb phrases that Hanif Kureishi uses to describe Ali's reaction to his father's behaviour.**

Think about body language (facial expressions or gestures) that shows Ali's attitude, e.g. *(to) make a face*, as well as expressions such as *(to) speak harshly to sb, (to) be forbidden,* etc.

B **How does Parvez defend himself against Ali's criticisms?**

Find expressions Parvez uses to persuade his son that he is a hard-working and decent man who has integrated into English society, e.g. *(to) have few enjoyments/hobbies,* etc.

3 WRITING

Write a paragraph summarizing how you think the story could go on.

Work with a partner or in small groups. First, collect ideas on what happens when Parvez and Ali get home. Here are some ideas:

The argument continues and intensifies at home ...
Ali's mother tries to mediate ...
Finally, Ali leaves the house ...
His parents ...

Or

Ali goes up to his room ...
Parvez continues to drink ...
He feels misunderstood and unfairly treated ...
He works himself up into a rage and goes up to Ali's room ...

You could start like this:

For some time, they continued their journey in silence. "Can't we at least talk to each other?" Parvez asked miserably. "No," said Ali. "I have nothing more to say to you." When they got home, ...

BEFORE YOU READ

A How would you describe the racial make-up of America?

B What do you think the 'new face of America' (see the title of the text) could be like?

3 10

Leo Jimenez

Vin Diesel

Jessica Alba

The New Face of America

Leo Jimenez, 25, is a New York model. His high cheekbones and jet-colored black hair and eyes suggest Asian or American-Indian ancestry. In fact, Jimenez ⁵ is Colombian by birth, a product of the mixed racial heritage of that Latin-American country. He says his melting-pot looks have ¹⁰ definitely opened doors for him.

People like Jimenez are both defining and benefiting from a big shift in American attitudes ¹⁵ to race, a shift that has led Louis Vuitton, YSL Beauty and H&M to employ racially-mixed models. The popularity of movie stars like Vin Diesel and Jessica Alba ²⁰ with young audiences is due in part to their diverse ethnic backgrounds – and the same applies to sports stars like Derek Jeter and Tiger Woods.

²⁵   "Today what's ethnically neutral, diverse or simply unclear has tremendous appeal," says Ron Berger, the chief executive of a New York advertising and trend-research company.

The new attitudes are evident not only in fashion, the ³⁰ media and entertainment. Nearly 7 million Americans said they were members of more than one race in the 2000 census. In addition, more than 14 million Hispanics – about 42 percent of Hispanic respondents – ticked "some other race".

³⁵   The increasingly multiracial American population, demographers say, is due to intermarriage – which has become much more common and socially acceptable since the ending of segregation in the 1960s – and to waves of mixed-race immigrants, particularly from ⁴⁰ Latin America.

The multiracial bonus

For decades, art directors, magazine editors and casting agents wanted tall, blond, blue-eyed models and actors. But now the demand for the "Nordic look" is on its way out. Vin Diesel, 36, the star of action movies like ⁴⁵ *The Fast and the Furious* (2001) once hid his racial heritage by saying that his mother is Irish and his father's race unknown. But now he admits that his racial mix has been a big career asset that has enabled him to play all types of roles and many ethnicities. ⁵⁰

Even megastars like Jennifer Lopez and Christina Aguilera borrow from diverse cultures and ethnic backgrounds. Lopez, who is Puerto Rican, features as a mixed-race Latina-Asian princess in the latest Louis Vuitton ad, while Aguilera, half Ecuadorean, poses as ⁵⁵ an Indian film star on a recent cover of *Allure* magazine.

According to Linda Wells, the magazine's editor- ⁶⁰ in-chief, this reflects a current fascination with the racial hybrid. "Uniformity just isn't appealing ⁶⁵ anymore," she says.

A recent study by the Lewis Mumford Center at the State University of New York ⁷⁰ at Albany noted that while nearly half of Hispanics chose the "some other race" category in the 2000 census, a big majority of Hispanics had chosen the ⁷⁵ "white" category 20 years earlier. "There used to be a sense that to be white was to have arrived," says John R. Logan, the Mumford Center's director. "Today there's a trend towards rejecting whiteness as a badge of success." (479 words) ⁸⁰

1 LOOKING AT THE TEXT

A Read the article quickly to find and explain the following numbers. They are in the same order.

1	nearly 7 million	**4**	about 42 percent	**7**	36
2	2000	**5**	the 1960s	**8**	nearly half of
3	more than 14 million	**6**	for decades		

B Find information in the article to support the following quotations.

1 Ron Berger: "Today what's ethnically neutral, diverse or simply unclear has tremendous appeal."
2 Linda Wells: "Uniformity just isn't appealing anymore."
3 John R. Logan: "Today there's a trend towards rejecting whiteness as a badge of success."

C Say what you think.

1 Do you agree with Ron Berger and Linda Wells? Say why (not).
2 Can you name any German racially-mixed celebrities? Think particularly of sport and pop music.

2 WORKING WITH WORDS

A The words in the table are all from the text. Give the missing verb or noun forms.

B Use some of the words from the table to write six sentences.

Leave gaps where the words should go. Then swap your sentences with a partner. Can you complete each other's sentences?

	Verb	Noun
1	(to) suggest	…
2	…	product
3	(to) employ	…
4	…	entertainment
5	…	respondent
6	…	marriage
7	…	segregation
8	…	action
9	…	fascination
10	(to) choose	…
11	(to) arrive	…
12	…	director

3 MEDIATION

> Mediation S. 210

Read the dialogue. Then pick out the main points and explain them in German.

KATE I think a lot of Europeans have a completely out-dated idea of what America's really like.

MIKE Oh? What makes you say that?

KATE Well, just to start with, a lot of people think that black Americans make up the biggest minority. But that's no longer true. I read that people of Spanish origin – you know, "Hispanics" – now outnumber African-Americans.

MIKE Really? I didn't know that.

KATE Today, about 15% of the total population say that they are Hispanic. The comparable figure for Blacks is just over 13%.

MIKE OK. And the hispanic population is growing much faster, isn't it?

KATE Right. The black – and by the way also the white – share of the population is actually shrinking. But what I really wanted to say is that people of mixed race are becoming just as important as the traditional minorities.

MIKE Oh, yes. Now you mention it, I remember reading something about that. That was one finding of the last US census, wasn't it?

KATE Yes, it was. For the first time, people were allowed to name more than one race in the 2000 census. And a lot of people did so.

MIKE What, before 2000 you could only give Black or White?

KATE Of course not, Mike. But you could only give one race. You know, African-American, Caucasian, Hispanic, Asian, Native American and so on. Take sports stars like Derek Jeter and Tiger Woods, for example. They're both a fairly complicated racial mix, but until 2000 they were just Black.

Derek Jeter   Tiger Woods

4 LISTENING

A Listen for general understanding. Read the questions, then listen and answer them.

1 What is the main topic of the radio discussion?
2 Who is taking part in the discussion?
3 Which speaker takes a hard, "anti-immigrant" line?
4 You are a big farmer in southern California. Which speaker seems to have most understanding of your situation?

B Listen for detail. First, make sure you understand the multiple-choice questions below. Then listen again and choose the correct answer, a), b) or c).

1 Frank claims that there are about **a)** 7 – **b)** 9 – **c)** 12 million illegal Mexican immigrants in the USA.
2 Julia thinks that a figure of about **a)** 5 – **b)** 7 – **c)** 9 million illegal immigrants is more accurate.
3 Julia says that the government has tolerated poor illegal immigrants for a long time for **a)** humanitarian – **b)** economic – **c)** religious reasons.
4 The majority of illegal immigrants work in **a)** farming, construction and manufacturing – **b)** their own business – **c)** domestic service and restaurants.
5 Julia feels that illegal immigrants should be allowed to stay in the USA provided that they **a)** have a home and a job – **b)** are willing to become US citizens – **c)** have nowhere to go in Mexico.
6 Frank argues that illegal immigrants should be deported because they **a)** have broken the US immigration laws – **b)** are taking jobs from Americans – **c)** are the Mexican government's responsibility.
7 Julia disagrees with Frank partly because immigrants **a)** work long hours for very low wages – **b)** do jobs that Americans aren't qualified to do – **c)** have become essential to the US economy.
8 Frank says that **a)** Americans wouldn't do immigrants' jobs even for a better wage – **b)** immigrants are taking jobs from Americans – **c)** immigrants are responsible for a rise in crime.

5 SPEAKING

Describe and interpret the cartoons.

> Interpretation von Bildern und Karikaturen S. 207

1 Work with a partner. Describe one cartoon each. Your partner should not look at the cartoon while you are doing so. Then look at the cartoons together and pick out any missing or incorrect details.

> on the right/left ▮ in the middle ▮
> in the foreground/background ▮
> (to) close ▮ (to) dig a hole ▮ (to) cart sth
> away ▮ (to) represent/stand for ▮ to build ▮
> border ▮ fence post ▮ barbed wire ▮
> wire-netting (fence) ▮ spade

> **TIP**
>
> Use the **present progessive** for what is happening now:
> *Two Mexicans **are talking**.*
> Use the **present perfect** for what has just or recently happened:
> *The Americans **have built** a fence.*

2 Now interpret the cartoons. Present your results to the rest of the class.
> ➤ *... stands for/represents ...*
> ➤ *The cartoonist's message is ...*
> ➤ *... shows the contradictory positions of ... and ...*
> ➤ *On the one hand, the US government ..., on the other, employers ...*

6 WRITING

Read the press report and write the story from Lee's point of view.

Start like this: *I don't know how the accident happened. One minute we were on the road, the next we were crashing down the side of this canyon. Maybe Mom went to sleep for a moment, I don't know ...*

The life of 12-year-old Lee Wilson was saved by an illegal Mexican immigrant who found him wandering in the southern Arizona desert after his mother, 45-year-old Joan Wilson, had driven their car off the road and down the side of a canyon.

Lee crawled out of the wreck to get help. He was found frightened and confused about four hours later by Jesus Manuel Cordova, 26. After trying unsuccessfully to free the mother, Cordova cared for Lee while they waited for somebody to come by. Joan died a short time later.

As temperatures dropped, Cordova gave the boy his jacket, lit a fire and stayed with him until some hunters passed by and radioed for help. The boy was flown to a hospital in Tucson but was found to be unhurt.

C Social options

Celebrating diversity or 'political correctness'?

4 7

1 A row erupted when St Anne's Infant School in Bristol decided to hold a Diwali day last month, marking the Hindu festival of light as part of its religious education curriculum … The school does not have any Hindu pupils. *(Daily Mail)*

2 Knowland Grove Community First School in Norwich caused outrage among parents last week by cancelling its traditional nativity play in favour of a festival of lights, showcasing the Jewish holiday Hanukkah and the Hindu festival of Diwali as well as Christmas. *(Daily Mail)*

3 A survey of 100 schools has found only one in five opting to stage the traditional Christmas story. One in three will stage a religion-free Christmas play or have no event at all.

'This is a reflection of society,' says Keith Porteous Wood of the National Secular Society. 'We should celebrate it. It shows a greater sensitivity to our more multicultural society.'

Not everyone agrees. 'Muslims do not take offence at nativity plays,' says Manzoor Moghal, chairman of the Leicester-based Muslim Forum.

'Britain is a Christian country and the majority of people are Christians. We enjoy your festivities and we like to learn about them.' *(BBC News)*

1 COMPREHENSION

Outline how the celebration of festivals has changed in UK schools.

Contrast the views of the following people about the changes:
> Parents at Knowland Grove   > Keith Porteous Wood
> Manzoor Moghal

2 INTERNET RESEARCH

Use the internet to find out about these festivals:

Bodhi Day ▪ Eid al-Fitr ▪ Guy Fawkes' Night ▪ Holi ▪
Human Rights Day ▪ International Day of Peace ▪
Kwanzaa ▪ Rosh Hashanah ▪ Saint Patrick's Day ▪
Thanksgiving ▪ Vasaikhi

> When are they?   > Where are they celebrated?
> Are they linked with a particular religion or culture?

3 WRITING

Write a paragraph.

Which of the above festivals might be celebrated in schools in your area to teach students about other faiths and cultures? Write down some ideas for events that schools could arrange for celebrating these festivals.

4 CARTOON

Comment on the message of this cartoon.

D Grammar checkpoint

1 REPORTED SPEECH – STATEMENTS

> Grammar summary S. 217

Read the statements and report the information.

1 There will soon be over ten million illegal immigrants in California alone.
   Governor Schwarzenegger complained that ...
2 Fewer immigrants crossed the Rio Grande last year.
   However, he added that ... the year before.
3 The US government has decided to build a fence along the border.
   The Mayor of San Diego said that ...
4 Surveillance cameras have been installed at every crossing point.
   An immigration official told reporters that ...
5 Maria Sanchez: "To be effective, the fence must be at least eight feet high."
   Ms Sanchez pointed out that ...
6 Maria Sanchez: "They are also going to introduce much stricter border controls."
   She went on to say that they ...

2 REPORTED SPEECH – QUESTIONS

> Grammar summary S. 219

**A border guard has stopped a Mexican driver at a crossing point near San Diego.
Report his questions.**

1 "Can you understand English?"
   The guard asked the truck driver ...
2 "Do you have a valid entry visa?"
   He inquired ...
3 "May I see your vehicle papers, please?"
   The guard asked politely ...
4 "What is the purpose of your visit to the USA?"
   Then he wanted to know ...
5 "Where are you staying in California?"
   After that, he asked ...
6 "How long do you plan to stay in California?"
   He was interested to know ...

3 REPORTED SPEECH – INTRODUCTORY VERBS

> Grammar summary S. 217

Report the comments using as many different introductory verbs as you can.
These comments were made at a citizens' meeting in San Diego to discuss the problem of illegal
immigration in southern California.

JEB DALE: In my opinion, the only answer is to build a high fence along the whole border. I'm a border guard and it's impossible to seal off a virtually open frontier.

SALLY-ANN MORRIS: Yes, but is that feasible? The fence would have to be at least eight feet high and the border's 1,400 miles long, for goodness' sake.

TOM BARNS: And it's not just the fence, either. There's the infrastructure, too – surveillance cameras and so on. And I know what I'm talking about, folks. I read something once about the iron curtain in Europe. You wouldn't believe it!

CARL HARMS: Well, I sure am glad that somebody has at last mentioned work, because that's what this is all about. I'm a fruit farmer and I'd go bust without the Mexicans, legal or illegal. The fact is, we need these people as much as they need us.

ANNA GARCIA: I agree with that. No way! I think we need to do two things. First, a general amnesty for all illegal immigrants who already live and work here and, second, a fair quota system for poor Mexicans like for anybody else.

MADDY BARNS: It's good you mentioned the iron curtain. Is that what we really want? I mean do we want to build an iron curtain right across America?

11

Crime

FOCUS

1 Link the captions a–c to the cartoons 1–3.

> **a** "... and our patience is exhausted. If you don't pay the ransom this year, we will ..."
> **b** "You must admit, a strict diet, no alcohol and early to bed certainly keep you fit."
> **c** "Open up, Benny. We know you're there. Fraud Squad."

2 Use the words and expressions below and the captions to describe the cartoons.

> (to) be like a film set | (to) become an adult | breakout | (to) break out of / escape from prison | (to) deceive/trick sb into thinking sth | in captivity | kidnapper | (to) look over one's shoulder | victim (of a crime)

3 Which of these crimes do the cartoons focus on?

> > graffiti-spraying
> > kidnapping
> > burglary
> > escaping from prison
> > drink driving
> > shoplifting
> > fraud
> > armed robbery

4 Which of the eight crimes above do you think is the most/least serious? Why?

> (to) be irresponsible | (to) be (relatively) trivial | minor/serious/trivial crime | (to) cause death/serious injury | (to) often involve children | (to) only involve property

BEFORE YOU READ

A Look at the headline and photos. What do you think the press report could be about?

B The US Constitution forbids 'cruel and unusual punishment' but the Supreme Court ruled that the death penalty is constitutional. What, then, do you think is meant by 'cruel and unusual punishment'?

Karla Faye Tucker has an important place in American legal history. Her execution for murder broke the convention that women were not given the death penalty. Read on to find out more.

Execution by lethal injection
In this variety of the death penalty, the person is strapped down and given a series of injections which are supposed to be painless. However, this procedure has gone wrong many times and resulted in a lot of pain.

A step too far?

1 ...

On the morning of Karla Faye Tucker's execution by lethal injection on 3 February 1998, the Governor's Office in Austin, Texas, received over 3,000 phone calls, faxes and emails, 80% of them asking the then governor, George W. Bush, to spare her life.

But nothing helped. Even if he had wanted to, Governor Bush felt he couldn't spare a convicted murderer's life 'just because she's a woman'. So the execution went ahead as planned, although even Texans – who routinely execute their killers without a thought – were troubled by it.

2 ...

By far the most important result of Ms Tucker's execution was to put an end to the legal convention that women may not be subjected to the death penalty. The last 'act of state' that discriminated between men and women simply because of their sex died with her. Since then, all attempts to save women from execution have similarly failed.

For feminists, Karla Faye's death was an awkward victory in the ongoing battle for equality with men. Whatever logic may say, many feel that equal wages and opportunity are one thing, capital and corporal punishment quite another. As civil rights activist Anna-Marie Barfield said, "Come on. We don't want to be that equal."

3 ...

The campaign for Karla Faye's life saw some surprising alliances. Civil rights campaigners, fundamentalist religious groups and male conservatives joined forces, although for widely differing reasons.

A large majority of civil righters are opposed to the death penalty on principle, seeing it as a 'cruel and unusual punishment' and hence unconstitutional. They also find the apparent racial bias repugnant. They would like to see the lives of all 369 offenders currently* on death row in Texas, of whom 40.9% are black and 27.9% Hispanic, spared.

Most fundamentalists are not opposed to capital punishment on principle – indeed, many are among its biggest fans – but nonetheless they thought that Ms Tucker's life should be spared. This was because during her 14 years on death row she had shown true remorse, had married a priest and had become a devout Christian. (The then Pope, John Paul II, agreed and sent a note to Governor Bush, himself a devout Christian, asking for clemency.)

Meanwhile, confused male conservatives just felt that women are, well, women and ought not to be executed. The more thoughtful among them pointed out that "as women don't kill by nature, those few that do must be insane".

4 ...

Although many liberals also felt, at least in private, that executing women "somehow stinks", they were deeply worried by the passions aroused by the Tucker campaign. Would a reformed and repentant male have received such international attention? Would a black man who had killed an eldery white couple but then become a devout Muslim in prison have received such high-profile support? Almost certainly not. It was her sex and her prettiness and her uncanny natural ability to tear hearts on TV that made Karla Faye Tucker the campaigners' pin-up. (489 words)

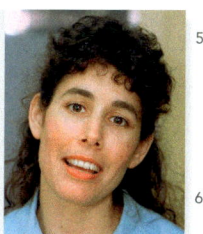
Karla Faye Tucker

*15 February 2008

1 LOOKING AT THE TEXT

A Put four of these sub-headings into the text at the points shown.

Strange bedfellows | Public opinion | Women's lib? |
What about victims' rights? | The liberal dilemma | Pleas for clemency

B Link the speech bubbles 1–8 to the people in the box. Say how you know.

an assistant in the Governor's Office, Austin, Texas | an aunt of Karla Faye's victim |
a civil rights activist | a Christian fundamentalist | a feminist |
Karla Faye's husband | a liberal | a male conservative

1 Yes, gender equality can be really tough, but I believe inequality is even worse.

2 Being strapped to a bed and given a lethal injection is a cruel punishment. I believe humans deserve much better.

3 I'm not against capital punishment, but this is different. God has spoken to her. She's seen the Light.

4 I just feel that women – all women – should have our special protection and respect.

5 Look, Karla Faye Tucker's Christian, pretty and white, but what about the other 52 women on death row, not to mention the men?

6 This note has just arrived for the Governor. Guess who it's from?

7 What about victims' rights, I'd like to know? This woman killed our Jerry with an axe because she wanted to steal his motorcycle, for Pete's sake!

8 We didn't touch each other. We were only allowed to talk through a glass wall using microphones.

2 WORKING WITH WORDS

A **Show that you understand these expressions by using them in sentences of your own.**

1 (to) spare sb's life (*line 8*)
2 act of state (*line 17*)
3 corporal punishment (*line 24*)

4 high-profile support (*line 66*)
5 (to) tear hearts (*line 68*)
6 campaigners' pin-up (*line 69*)

B **Choose the most suitable connector, a) or b).**

The US Supreme Court abolished the death penalty **a)** also | **b)** as[1] unconstitutional in 1972.
a) However | **b)** Moreover[2], it was reintroduced in 1976 **a)** because of | **b)** because[3] a rise in
violent crime **a)** what | **b)** which[4] many people saw **a)** as | **b)** like[5] being one result of abolition.

a) Furthermore | **b)** However[6], here we should be careful. The Supreme Court itself did not
reintroduce capital punishment, **a)** and | **b)** but[7] only said that it was not unconstitutional –
a) if | **b)** whether[8] to use it was for the states to decide.

Today, 36 states have reintroduced the death penalty, **a)** as a rule | **b)** in fact[9] by lethal
injection **a)** because | **b)** while[10] this method is said to be more humane. **a)** But | **b)** Thus[11]
this number can be a little misleading **a)** also | **b)** as[12] six of these states have not used the
death penalty at all since reintroducing it, **a)** and | **b)** whereas[13] four more have only used
it once. **a)** Moreover | **b)** Though[14] two-thirds of all executions since 1977 have been carried
out in just five states, by far the most, 408, in Texas.

a) Although | **b)** Nonetheless[15], these states are not evenly spread throughout the country.
a) For example, | **b)** Whereas[16] the northern and eastern states tend to be against capital
punishment, those in the south and west make use of it.

3 WRITING

> Eine Stellungnahme schreiben S. 203

**Comment on the suggestion that capital punishment should be used for particularly
serious crimes such as murder and terrorism.**

Think about the pros …
> can never kill again
> cheaper than lifelong imprisonment
> retribution
> 'deterrent effect'
> enables victim's loved ones to 'draw a
  line'

and cons …
> some innocent people will certainly be executed
> 'two wrongs do not make a right'
> suffering of guilty person's innocent family
> no rehabilitation possible
> most murders committed in the heat of the moment
> problem of mental instability at time of crime

According to FBI data, the murder rate in Non-Death Penalty States (green) has remained consistently
lower than the rate in Death Penalty States (red).

BEFORE YOU READ

A What do you associate New York City with? Try to name at least three things.

B Have you ever come across the New York Police Department (NYPD)? Where?

Although the New York Police Department (NYPD) features in many films and TV dramas, in fact until quite recently it was not much better than the criminals it was supposed to bring to justice. Read the article to find out more.

A stitch in time saves nine

In the early 1990s, New York City was sliding into lawlessness and chaos. South Bronx was just one of several 'no-go areas'; even the police only went there in heavily-armed groups. In 1991, the worst year for crime, the New York Police Department (NYPD) registered 2,245 murders, 2,818 rapes and 100,280 robberies. Few New Yorkers dared to use the subway or go into Central Park after dark. The city was fast becoming ungovernable.

Ten years later, New York had gone from being among America's most dangerous big cities to being one of its safest. In 2001, there were 633 murders, a drop of over 70%, 1,530 rapes and 27,229 robberies. And the subway? It had become one of the cleanest, safest and most efficient transport systems in the country.

What made this turnaround possible? First, there was a sea change in public opinion. Ordinary, decent, tolerant New Yorkers wanted their big apple back – and were willing to support a tough new mayor, Rudolph Giuliani, and a tough new police chief, William J. Bratton, to do it.

Bratton's first step was to clean up the NYPD itself. The force was rotten with drug abuse, bribery, racism and nepotism. That is one reason why Giuliani hired Bratton from Boston. He was a stranger to New York; he owed no favours. And Bratton was merciless. Corrupt officers were weeded out with 'zero tolerance'. That is where the term really comes from. They were not only sacked with the loss of all pension rights, but they were also prosecuted and given tough sentences. The 'bad apples' were replaced by 2,000 better-educated officers taken from all of New York's communities.

After cleaning up the police, Bratton then introduced a policy called 'Crimes and Quality of Life' (CQL). "In the past, we just cut down trees," said Bratton. "But that's not enough. You must kill the seeds, so that the trees never grow. That's what CQL is all about."

To stop the seeds from growing into trees, the new and reformed NYPD focused on seven main areas: drug dealing, domestic violence, bad and threatening behaviour in public places, car theft, guns on the street, school violence and graffiti spraying. "I told my officers never ever to look the other way," said Bratton. "It's like in school. The biggest deterrent isn't getting punished, but getting caught."

And it worked. As the seeds of crime were weeded out, the incidence of more serious crimes fell as well. "There's no such thing as a trivial crime," Bratton told his officers. "Never forget that most armed robbers started out as shoplifters."   (431 words)

1 LOOKING AT THE TEXT

A Explain the title by referring to information in the article.

B Answer the questions.

1 Why is it possible to say that New York was 'becoming ungovernable' in the early 1990s?
2 What evidence is there to show that the situation in New York had improved radically by 2000?
3 How did Bratton go about reforming the NYPD?
4 Why was Bratton's policy of 'Crimes and Quality of Life' so successful?

2 WORKING WITH WORDS

A Link the words or expressions on the left with their meanings on the right.

1	no-go area (*line 3*)	a	completely different way of looking at a situation
2	turnaround (*line 19*)	b	catch criminals
3	sea change (*line 20*)	c	corrupt people
4	big apple (*line 21*)	d	diametrically opposed direction
5	zero tolerance (*line 30*)	e	nickname of New York City
6	bad apples (*line 34*)	f	part of city too dangerous to enter
7	cut down trees (*line 41*)	g	stop people becoming criminals
8	kill the seeds (*line 42*)	h	absolute refusal to show understanding in any circumstances

B Choose four more words or expressions from the text and write definitions – make sure they are in a different order. Swap with a partner. Can he/she match them?

3 SPEAKING

A Look at the photos and read the offenders' details. Which crimes do you think are most serious? Which are less serious or more understandable?

An eye for an eye?

1  **Chloe Martin, 35:** caught stealing petrol from neighbour's car; single parent with two young children; first offence; says she can't afford to buy all the petrol she needs to drive to work

2  **Jake Wilson, 32:** broke into warehouse to steal electronic equipment; injured security guard with flick knife; history of burglary/violence; resisted arrest

3  **Wim De Graf, 45:** caused bad road accident (two people injured, one seriously) by dangerous driving; in UK on business and returning to Holland at end of week; first known offence; claims he was late for very important appointment

4  **Holly Chang, 19:** stole £400 from employer to finance gambling habit; second offence in six months; refuses to accept help from Gamblers Anonymous

5  **Luke Hall, 15:** sprayed graffiti on luxury villa; did it because "my dad says they should build more cheap homes"; says he won't do it again but he still agrees with his dad

B **Study the possible punishments in the box and find one to fit each crime. Report your verdict to the class and give reasons for it.**

> Let the person off with a warning not to do it again ▮
> Put him/her on probation with a suspended sentence (say how long) ▮
> Make the offender do community service (say number of hours per week and for how long) ▮
> Impose a fine of up to £3,000 ▮
> Sentence person to prison for at last three years ▮
> Make him/her repair or pay for any damage

4 GIVING A TALK

> Die Arbeitsergebnisse präsentieren S. 206

In small groups of three or four prepare a talk on crime trends in the USA.

Use the outline below (making any changes you wish) and the information in File 7, page 193. You may add any further information you have. Present your results to the rest of the class.

Outline: Crime trends in the USA

1 You could start your talk like this:
What impression do many Europeans have of crime in the US? Probably that the USA is a particularly violent and criminal place. But is this picture ...?

2 Go on:
We wonder whether this is supported by the latest statistics for the period ...
(= bridge to development sections)

3 Development I:
Refer to and explain nationwide general trends; point out biggest/smallest decrease(s)/increase(s) by region; speculate about possible causes, e.g. better policing, poverty, ...
Crime trends vary widely from region to region. For example, ...

4 Development II:
Refer to more detailed trends, including homicides; point out difference between crimes committed, crimes reported, crimes prosecuted, i.e. police involvement in fighting crime.
It is extremely important to recognize the difference between ...

5 Conclusion:
Conclude by referring back to your opening remarks and giving your group's opinion.
It is clear that Europeans' perception of crime in the USA is ...

3 14 **A** Listen for general understanding. Listen to a story about an old lady who was stopped for speeding. Then put the drawings into the correct order.

A

B

C

D

E

F

B Listen for detail. Listen again, then choose the correct statement, a), b) or c).

1 The deputy stopped the old lady because she …
   a) was speeding.
   b) went through some red lights.
   c) was driving a stolen car.

2 The old lady said she had lost her licence because she had driven …
   a) without vehicle registration papers.
   b) dangerously and caused an accident.
   c) while drunk.

3 The deputy sheriff …
   a) called the sheriff.
   b) called for back-up.
   c) arrested the old lady for murder.

4 The punch line is …
   a) 'I bet the liar told you I was speeding, too.'
   b) 'And I killed and hacked up the owner, too.'
   c) 'I'm sure everything's quite in order.'

C Social options

1 MIND MAP

Use the information from the text to draw a mind map on the subject of cyberbullying.

2 ROLE-PLAY

Work in groups of three. You are taking part in a debate about ways to prevent 'happy slapping'.

Gangs of youths sometimes attack an innocent person without warning and film the attack on a mobile phone. They may make DVDs of the attack or upload the clip onto the internet. The British press call this shocking practice 'happy slapping,' even though it is anything but funny and some victims have even died.

Student A	You are a victim of happy slapping. You think that happy slapping gangs and the owners of websites that show their videos should be punished. You also want these websites to be shut down.
Student B	You are a police officer. You want to be able to check teenagers' mobile phones for illegal videos and photos.
Student C	You were once involved in happy slapping yourself. You regret your actions and think that educating the offenders would help to prevent the problem.

3 WEBSITE

Write the text for an anti-cyberbullying website.

You decide to set up a website for victims of cyberbullying. You want other young people to contribute their own stories and advice. Include the following:

> A welcoming message which will encourage teenagers to share their stories
> An explanation of the aims of the site
> A warning about the seriousness of cyberbullying

THE AGE

Cyberbullying

Elissa Baxter

If 16-year-old Jessica Jones had received a black eye in the playground, her school would have been forced 5 to deal with the attacker. But when the schoolgirl received a text message from a schoolmate threatening to hurt her, her school told her that she just had to learn to live with it.   10

'I felt completely shocked,' Jessica says. 'It was also very scary because I thought I was going to be physically hurt.'

Cyberbullying takes many forms. Some bullies prefer threatening text messages. Others use 15 email. Instant messaging, internet chat rooms and social networking sites such as MySpace are prime breeding grounds for exclusion, abuse and threats. Some bullies even set up websites to ridicule their victims.   20

Jessica took the matter to the police who responded immediately and the bullying stopped. Jessica then started a campaign in the local media to raise awareness of cyberbullying.

'It's really amazing how many people are affected 25 by it,' says Jessica. 'Victims often don't tell anyone, they think it's embarrassing or are too upset to talk about it.'

Jessica's advice for victims of cyberbullying: 'Talk to someone you trust about the problem. Tell 30 the school, tell your parents or tell the police. Make sure it's someone who's going to do something about it.'

'Second, don't engage with it. Keep the messages to prove what's happened but don't 35 respond. That will only make the problem worse.

'Third, don't accept that it's your fault. Cyberbullying is a crime and you don't have to accept it.'   (249 words)

Adapted and abridged from www.theage.com.au

D Grammar checkpoint

1 ADVERB ORDER

> Grammar summary S. 223

Copy the table with eight writing lines into your exercise book and complete it with adverbs from the box. Sometimes more than one position is possible.

> ~~always~~ I ~~beautifully~~ I as a rule I at 6 o'clock I in the lesson I each spring I
> every day I fast I fortunately I in New York I in prison I last summer I loudly I
> naturally I nowadays I of course I often I once a month I on the whole I seldom I
> silently I since 2008

Front	Mid	End-Position		
		manner	place	frequency/time
	always	beautifully		

2 FORMING SENTENCES

> Grammar summary S. 223

Put the words or expressions in the correct order to make sensible sentences.

1 two hours' exercise | research | need | that | at least | a day | healthy prisoners | suggests
2 occupy | sometimes | a cell | two prisoners | unfortunately | designed for one
3 often | complain | critics | that | 'academies of crime' | are | prisons | in fact just
4 in street crime | has caused | mobile phones | it is said | that | a big increase | the theft of
5 clearly | a 'must have' status symbol | mobile phones | amongst | this is because | the young | have become
6 occur | or social group | most murders | within the family
7 no longer there | I returned | my car | to the car park | when | was
8 after dark | it's scandalous | many women | that | nervous | of walking | are | through our parks
9 in reality | crime | is falling | is increasing | it | many people | think | unfortunately, | when
10 FBI statistics | in states | less murders | perhaps surprisingly | show that | the death penalty | there are | without

3 TRANSLATING

Translate the sentences into English. Be careful about word order.

1 Vor dreißig Jahren war es noch möglich, ungefährdet auf der Straße zu spielen.
2 Viele New Yorker hatten Angst, nachts ihre Wohnungen zu verlassen.
3 Einige Wissenschaftler behaupten, dass Armut der Hauptgrund für Kriminalität ist.
4 Die Erfahrung zeigt, dass harte Bestrafung selten wirksam ist.
5 Leider ist eine große Mehrheit dafür, die Todesstrafe wieder einzuführen.
6 In der Tat wurde die Null-Toleranz hauptsächlich gegen korrupte Polizisten angewendet.
7 Selbstverständlich wollte der Polizist wissen, wo wir uns zur Tatzeit aufgehalten haben.
8 Man sagt, dass der Dieb sich während der Flucht schwer verletzt hat.
9 Im Interesse der Gleichbehandlung werden heutzutage Frauen in den USA genauso hart bestraft wie Männer.
10 Laut einer Meinungsumfrage aus dem Jahre 2007 sind 74 % der Wahlberechtigten (*electorate*) in Texas für die Todesstrafe.

12

Future life, future living

FOCUS

1 Link the photos 1–8 to the captions a–h.

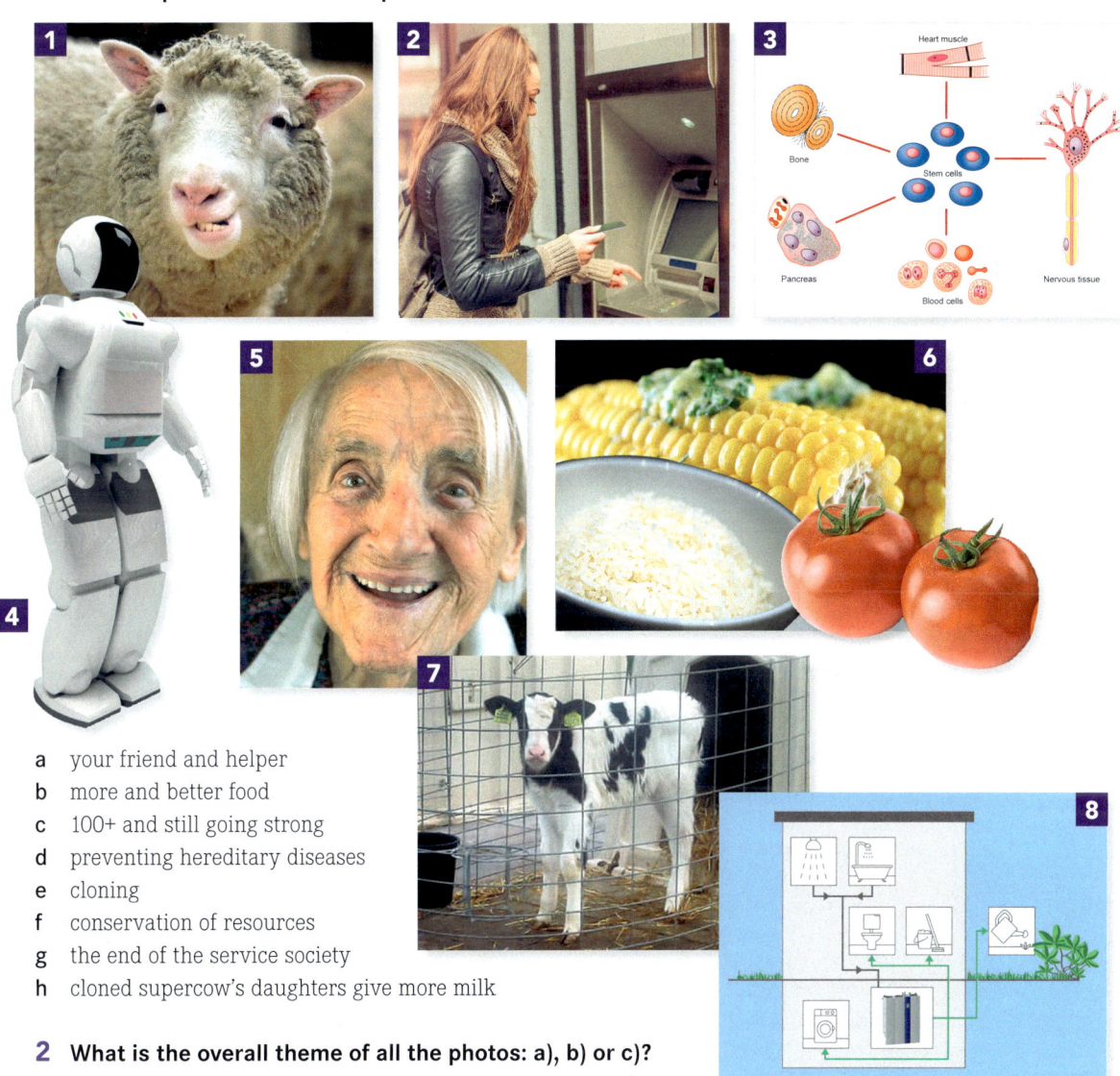

a your friend and helper
b more and better food
c 100+ and still going strong
d preventing hereditary diseases
e cloning
f conservation of resources
g the end of the service society
h cloned supercow's daughters give more milk

2 What is the overall theme of all the photos: a), b) or c)?
a) Future fears – b) Future developments – c) Future hopes

3 Which two developments do you find most interesting or useful? Say why.
Then do a class survey.

4 How do you think life in Germany will have changed by, say, 2050?

BEFORE YOU READ

A What boycotts have you heard of, for example the USA's boycott of Iran?

B Do you think boycotts work or do they hurt the wrong people?

C Have you ever taken part in a boycott? If not, can you imagine doing so? Why (not)?

According to this report from the Daily Mail*, the media and the big supermarkets are doing more to protect British consumers from the unknown risks of genetically-modified (GM) food than their government is.*

British supermarkets call for a boycott of 'cloned' meat and milk

Britain's biggest supermarkets last night announced a boycott of meat and milk from cloned farm animals and their offspring. The move follows Daily Mail revelations that a calf, the daugher of a US cloned cow, has been born on a British farm.

Separately, the government's Food Standards Agency (FSA) plans to hold emergency talks with EU officials tomorrow over the policing of food from cloned animals and their offspring.

Current food and health laws require the investigation and approval of any meat or milk from cloned farm animals. However, a loophole in the law means that there are no such controls on food which is produced by their offspring. As a result, meat and milk from animals who have a clone for a mother could be in the shops within a few years.

Last night, super-markets, including Tesco, Sainsbury's, Asda, Morrisons and Marks & Spencer, reacted to this threat by announcing their own boycott. Tesco said: "We would not stock any products derived from cloned animals or their offspring." Marks & Spencer said: "We have long had a ban on all genetically modified ingredients in our food. That ban will now apply to any food from cloned animals and their offspring."

A Holstein calf called Dundee Paradise, the daughter of a US cloned cow, was born on a farm in Shropshire last month. This made clear that clone farming and the genetic modification of animals has now moved from science fiction to the reality of the supermarket.

In an astonishing failure, the government knew nothing at all about Dundee Paradise and the future birth of other calves from the same cloned cow.

Supporters of cloning claim that calves like Dundee Paradise will form the nucleus of the country's future dairy herds. And cloned and GM animals could, they say, provide cheap food for future generations. The idea is that 'supercows' will be capable of producing vast quantities of milk, as much as 70 pints (about 40 litres) a day.

However, the history of cloning and genetic modification is full of examples of animal suffering. The first cloned mammal, Dolly the sheep, died prematurely at the age of six in 2003 from a lung infection. She had also been diagnosed with the early onset of severe arthritis, and there are many more examples of miscarriages, ill health and abnormal organs.

Dundee Paradise and her sisters will start producing milk in around two years' time. As the law now stands, there is nothing to stop this going into stores without any form of labelling.   (424 words)

from the *Daily Mail*, London, 10.01.07, abridged

1 LOOKING AT THE TEXT

A Do the assignments.

1   Explain why the *Daily Mail* can claim that British supermarkets and the media are doing more to protect consumers than the government is.
2   Point out the difference between Tesco's and Marks & Spencer's policy on GM food.
3   Say why the *Daily Mail* speaks of 'an astonishing failure' on the part of the British government.
4   Describe what role Dolly the sheep plays in the text.

B Use information from the text and any ideas of your own to list the pros and cons of cloning farm animals.

pros	cons
provide cheap food	*unpopular among consumers*

2 WORKING WITH WORDS

A Replace the highlighted words or phrases with a synonym from the text. They are not necessarily in the same order.

1   Supermarkets announced a refusal to sell[1] meat and milk from cloned animals or their young[2].
2   A serious omission in the regulations has allowed such meat to get into supermarkets.
3   This showed beyond a doubt[1] that the genetic alteration[2] of animals has now shifted[3] from science fiction to supermarket reality.
4   Dolly suffered an early death at the age of only six.
5   Exceptionally productive cows[1] will be able to deliver huge amounts[2] of milk.
6   As the law now stands, there is nothing to prevent[1] this milk finding its way[2] into stores without any type[3] of labelling.
7   The UK intends[1] to hold emergency discussions[2] with EU officials over the supervision[3] of food from cloned animals.
8   This calf and ones like her will make up the heart of Britain's future dairy herds.

B Work with a partner and complete the table.

The words in the table are all from the press report. If necessary, use a dictionary to find the missing forms. Please note: for some words, more than one noun is possible.

	Verb	Noun(s)	Adjective
1	announce	...; ...	
2	...	revelation	...
3		law; ...	...
4	require	...	
5	...	investigation	...
6	...	approval	...
7	produce	...; ...	...
8	...	threat	...
9	apply	...; ...	...
10	...	modification	...
11	...	...	astonishing
12	...	infection	...

C Replace the German words with words that you have found in exercise B.
Be careful with tenses, etc.

1 The ... (*Ankündigung*) shocked supporters of GM farming.
2 Cloned cows are said to be more ... (*leistungsfähig*) than their natural sisters.
3 It is a ... ... (*gesetzliche Auflage*) to get approval for food from cloned animals.
4 The *Daily Mail* ... (*untersuchen*) food from cloned animals in Britain and ... (*aufdecken*) a loophole in the law.
5 The EU ... (*drohen*) to introduce stricter labelling.
6 The findings ... (*erstaunen*) the journalists.
7 Farmers ... (*verändern*) plants by natural selection for thousands of years.
8 Is it true that cloned animals suffer from more ... (*ansteckende*) diseases than natural ones do?

3 WRITING

Write an email to the editor of the *Daily Mail* saying whether you would eat the meat of a cloned animal or its offspring.

Give reasons why or why not. You can use the outline on the right, adding any ideas of your own.

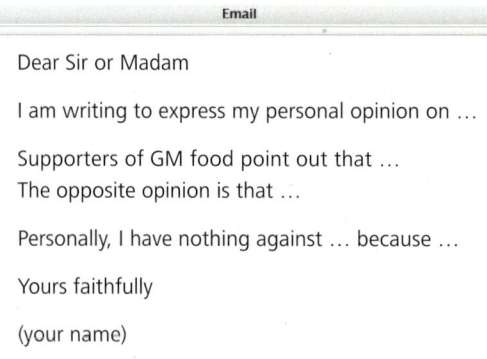

Email

Dear Sir or Madam

I am writing to express my personal opinion on ...

Supporters of GM food point out that ...
The opposite opinion is that ...

Personally, I have nothing against ... because ...

Yours faithfully

(your name)

B The bigger picture

BEFORE YOU READ

A Have you ever made use of FAQs yourself? If so, what did you want to find out?

B Work with a partner. Read this list of FAQs about gene technology. Then, skim the text and match as many questions as possible to the answers. Finally, read the text and match the remaining FAQs.

a Can we trust the food we eat?
b How do genetic engineers answer these arguments?
c How does gene technology differ from selective breeding?
d What are the ecological arguments against GM crops?
e What are the medical applications of GM?
f What is GM food?
g Why do some people think GM food may be harmful?

3 16

1 ...

GM food is produced from plants or animals whose genes have been changed by scientists. All living organisms have genes written in their DNA.
5 They are the chemical instructions for creating and maintaining life. By changing the genes, scientists can alter the characteristics of an organism. Maybe, for example, we want a plant to produce bigger yields or an animal to produce
10 more meat. Gene technology can do this.

2 ...

A tendency to suffer from many illnesses is 'genetically programmed' by the genes in a person's DNA. By changing the right genes, it
15 becomes possible to get rid of this tendency. At present, such techniques are very promising in the treatment of dementia and diabetes in old age. A further, more distant, medical application of gene technology could be the production of
20 transplant organs.

3 ...

Farmers have used selective breeding to improve crops and animals for thousands of years. They have also created new plants and animals by
25 cross-breeding closely-related species. This is how they produced wheat and mules, for example. However, this was a very time-consuming business. Gene technology delivers much faster and more predictable results because it enables
30 scientists to select a single gene for a single characteristic.

4 ...

Critics argue that we do not know enough about how genes interact with each other and with the environment. This means that we can't say with 35 certainty what the long-term result of any modification will be. They worry that manipulations could accidentally lead to substances being produced that are poisonous, or could trigger allergies. Critics also argue that 40 antibiotic-resistant genes in plants and farm animals could be passed to the micro-organisms that make us ill. If this happens, we might not have effective antibiotic drugs to fight back.

5 ...

They point out that there is no evidence that GM food has any bad effects. They argue that a lot of non-GM food is processed to remove unwanted or toxic substances – and that the regulations that govern GM foods are far stricter than those for non-GM products. Genetic modification might cause new allergies but so, too, can traditional selective breeding. In fact, gene technology may make it possible to rid our food of such problems altogether. Furthermore, GM enables us to improve not only the flavour, texture and shelf life of food, but also its nutritional value.

▶

6 ...

All food is subject to regulation to ensure that it is safe for human consumption. Everybody involved in the production, processing and marketing of food, from farmers through to shopkeepers, must obey these strict rules. Food poisoning is usually caused by poor practice somewhere between the farm gate and the supermarket shelf. But consumers also have a responsibility. One of the main reasons why food poisoning has increased so dramatically in recent years is that we, the consumers, have not stored and prepared food properly in our own kitchens.

7 ...

The green lobby fears that certain genes from GM crops could be passed on to other species, with harmful results. For two reasons, they are particularly worried about genes that make GM plants resistant to herbicides. Firstly, these genes could produce 'superweeds' that are resistant to all but the most powerful herbicides and, secondly, they could destroy insects and birds as their food becomes contaminated. But is this really new? The fact is that 'factory farming' is already playing havoc with nature. On the contrary, bioengineers argue, GM technology offers a real chance of improving the situation in the countryside – GM crops require less of the fertilizers and pesticides that are later washed into the rivers. And because GM crops produce higher yields, they need less land. This could save the few surviving uncultivated habitats.

(607 words)

1 LOOKING AT THE TEXT

A Pick out arguments for and against the use of genetic technology.

What do you think of the arguments? Sort them into three categories: *most convincing – quite convincing – least convincing*. Then compare your results with others and see what the class thinks.

On an annual basis, about 6 million pre-school kids die because they don't have access to enough food. GM technology should be used to increase the production of main food staples, improve the efficiency of production and provide access to food for small-scale farmers.

B Use the arguments and information you have picked out in exercise A to write a comment on the opinion on the right.

2 WORKING WITH WORDS

A Explain the following in your own words.

1 get rid of sth (*paragraph 2*)
2 more distant (*paragraph 2*)
3 time-consuming business (*paragraph 3*)
4 long-term result (*paragraph 4*)
5 trigger sth (*paragraph 4*)
6 toxic substance (*paragraph 5*)
7 shelf life (*paragraph 5*)
8 be subject to sth (*paragraph 6*)
9 poor practice (*paragraph 6*)
10 play havoc with sth (*paragraph 7*)

B Complete the sentences with the missing prepositions.

1 GM tomatoes, ...[1] example, are produced ...[2] plants that have been genetically modified ...[3] scientists.

2 DNA is often referred ...[1] as 'the blueprint ...[2] life', implying that it contains all the information needed to create life.

3 It is possible to get rid ...[1] a tendency to suffer ...[2] a particular illness by modifying the right genes ...[3] a person's DNA.

4 Critics are worried ...[1] the fact that not enough is known ...[2] how genes interact ...[3] each other ...[4] the long term.

5 The spread ...[1] seeds from GM crops could lead ...[2] the unintentional production ...[3] toxic substances ...[4] the natural environment.

6 Supporters ...[1] GM techniques point ...[2] that selective breeding can also result ...[3] the creation ...[4] new allergies.

7 The genetic modification ...[1] DNA is very promising ...[2] the treatment ...[3] conditions like dementia that occur ...[4] old age.

8 The control ...[1] so-called 'superweeds' depends ...[2] the use ...[3] very powerful herbicides because they are resistant ...[4] conventional methods ...[5] weed control.

3 TRANSLATION

> Übersetzung S. 211

Translate the text into German.

After climate change and the energy crisis, the world is now facing another catastrophe: the death of its bees. Almost 90% of bees have already died in some regions of the USA. In Germany, too, bee numbers
5 have virtually halved in the last 15 years.

Maybe this would be sad rather than bad if bees just made honey. But honey is a by-product of a much more important job. Bees are essential for the pollination – and hence the growth – of over
10 90 different kinds of fruit and vegetable worldwide. The fact is that without bees, traditional farming is no longer possible.

But what are the causes of this catastrophe? The answer to this question is that nobody really knows.
15 However, possible causes are new insecticides, that may kill bees as well as less friendly insects, air pollution, the destruction of natural habitats and, more recently, even radiation from mobile telephone masts. GM crops have also been named as a possible
20 cause.

According to Manfred Hederer, a German expert, bee deaths could be caused by a highly toxic substance that still has to be identified.

(184 words)

4 LISTENING

17 You are going to listen to an extract from the radio show *Be my guest*. Presenter Judy Patterson is talking to Ruth Morse and Luke Wilson about the use of gene technology (GT).

A Listen for general understanding. Listen once and say what two main uses of GT are being discussed.

B Listen for detail. Read the ten statements below. Then listen to the extract again and say whether they are true or false. Correct the false statements.

1   Judy asks Ruth whether she thinks GT is a useful development.
2   Ruth is very sceptical about the medical value of GT.
3   Ruth says that GT will definitely enable scientists to produce transplant organs.
4   Luke sees human cloning as a big danger.
5   Ruth describes the excitement about human cloning as 'media hype'.
6   Ruth says that growing GM crops is the only answer to food shortages.
7   Luke agrees with Ruth that GM crops could help feed the world's growing population.
8   Judy thinks one benefit of GM crops is that they produce more food than natural ones.
9   Luke claims that GM crops are responsible for the destruction of the world's bees.
10 Ruth agees with Luke that the death of bees is a big disadvantage of GM farming.

5 SPEAKING

Hold a debate on the motion 'Gene technology is of great benefit to humankind'.

> **INFO**

- A **debate** is a **formal discussion** on a **clearly-defined motion** before an audience.

- In this kind of debate, there are normally four active **speakers**: the **proposer**, who argues for the motion, and the **opposer**, who argues against the motion, each with **seconds**, who support them with additional arguments or information.

- The debate is led by a neutral **chairperson**, who a) introduces the motion, b) calls on the participants to speak, c) makes sure that the speakers keep to the given time and d) calls on the audience to vote for or against the motion at the end of the debate. The chairperson may allow the audience to ask questions at the end.

- Debates make use of **formal spoken language**. In practice this means:
  > avoid very colloquial language
  > use full sentences
  > never 'get personal'
  > use emphasizing and moderating language, as necessary.

1   Choose the speakers and a chairperson.
2   The speakers prepare their 'speeches' for or against the motion by collecting arguments and ideas from the texts in this unit. (Don't forget the translation text!) Add any other information you may have.
3   Hold the debate. The proposer and opposer should speak for about three minutes each, their seconds for about two minutes.
4   Take a class vote for or against the motion at the end.

Elderly get to grips with gadgets

Designers might think the elderly need 'smart homes' full of computer technology to make their lives easier, but it's the simple things like can openers that really count.

For many elderly people, technology in daily life centres around tasks like opening cans, pouring hot water into a mug without scalding yourself, bathing and washing safely. The stereotype is that older people can't cope with technology. But in many cases the reality is that they have made the perfectly sensible decision that they don't need to use more high-tech gadgets like mobile phones.   5

Tools that help people who are elderly or have disabilities to live normal lives are called 'assistive technology'. Not all assistive items are exciting, but they still need someone to recognize a problem and find an innovative way to solve it.   10

David Sinclair, of British charity Help the Aged, says that product designers often don't talk to the people who will use their designs until it's too late. 'Younger people are designing things for older people and not consulting us until the marketing stage,' he says. 'Older people don't have input into these products.'

15   Sinclair points to *Magiplug* as a good example of assistive technology for elderly people. The *Magiplug* is a bath plug that goes red when it's too hot (prevents scalding) and has a pressure-sensitive plate that automatically lets excess water out (prevents flooding).   (228 words)

The *Magiplug*

Adapted and abridged from *The Guardian*

1   MEDIATION

You work in a home for the elderly. You have been asked to address a conference of young German designers on the subject of how modern design can help the elderly.

Select relevant information from the text and write a list of suggestions. Do not translate word for word.

2   ROLE-PLAY

You are taking part in a radio debate on 'What does old age mean in the 21st century?'

Student A   You are 83 and have all kinds of health problems. The healthy, energetic 80-year-old is an advertising myth. That person doesn't exist in real life.

Student B   'Age is in the mind.' Your grandmother is 78, but she still runs her own business.

Student C   'You are only as old as you feel.' Unfortunately many people have to struggle with health problems, like your father who is 59 but can't walk upstairs.

Student D   You are 50 and thinking about retirement. You are worried that 'you get old when you retire'.

3   WRITING

Think of a new item of assistive technology and design an advertisement for it. Explain what it is and why it will make life easier/safer/better for elderly people.

D Grammar checkpoint

Here is a grammar quiz on what you have learned in this course. In each case, choose the correct alternative – a) or b).

1 MIXED TENSES

1 The firm a) makes | b) has been making bikes for over a hundred years.
2 Work on genes a) became | b) has become possible when they discovered DNA.
3 They a) publish | b) are publishing a new magazine next year.
4 a) Did you make | b) Have you made back-up copies of these files yesterday?
5 Luke a) talked | b) was talking to Maria when I arrived.
6 They met after they a) have both left | b) had both left university.
7 Sarah a) is often travelling | b) often travels to the US on business.
8 We a) aren't going to have | b) won't have a holiday this year.
9 I a) didn't see | b) haven't seen that movie yet.
10 According to the timetable, our train a) leaves | b) will leave at 10:32.
11 The minister expects the EU a) is going to allow | b) will allow GM crops soon.
12 We read the documents while we a) waited | b) were waiting for the meeting to begin.

2 MIXED STRUCTURES

1 Frank has avoided a) going | b) to go to a doctor for years.
2 Do you remember a) seeing | b) to see your girlfriend for the first time?
3 Humans can only survive a short time without a) drinking | b) they drink.
4 Jack a) told | b) told me that he'd be late for the meeting.
5 If you hadn't called the police, the thieves a) had got away | b) would have got away.
6 I'm sorry, but stamps a) can only bought | b) can only be bought at post offices.
7 We a) don't have to | b) mustn't finish the project this week – next week is fine.
8 The car's OK, but it would be better if it a) didn't use | b) wouldn't use so much fuel.
9 Somebody at the bus stop told a) me the way | b) the way to me.
10 I'm sure we a) have already seen | b) have seen already this film.
11 Frank stopped a) buying | b) to buy some petrol on his way home.
12 The mechanic a) explained | b) explained me how to switch on the lights.

3 FORMS OF WORDS

1 You can earn a) a lot of | b) much money designing websites.
2 The Greens don't seem to like a) each other | b) themselves very much.
3 Can you lend me a) any | b) some money, please? – Sure. How much?
4 This project has been a) good organized | b) well organized.
5 The customs officer spoke to us a) friendly | b) in a friendly way.
6 We enjoyed a) ourselves | b) us a lot at the party.
7 Do you think a) there is water | b) water is on Mars?
8 Do you have to wear a) a | b) an uniform at school?
9 Please try a) not to be | b) to not be late.
10 The news a) are | b) is not very good, I'm afraid.
11 You will find some more a) information | b) informations on the next page.
12 Joshua's dad doesn't want a) him to get married | b) that he gets married so young.

Social Topics

④ ⑩ Youth Cafés

In your town, how many places can you go where you can just relax and

5 have a good time, without adults telling you what to do and without the pressure of alcohol? Not many? Have

10 you ever been to a Youth Café?

Youth Cafés are showing up in towns across the country. They're places where you can hang out, however you like to hang out.

How they start

15 Youth Cafés start in the brains of young people who are tired of the old options in their community. They want their own space, a place that's stress-free and alcohol-free. Somewhere they can be themselves, be with their mates and do what they want.

20 When young people decide to set up a Youth Café, they quickly find others like them, willing to help. They also find help from people in their community – adult volunteers, local government, police and so on – who also see the benefits of a place you can

25 call your own.

It's yours

Youth Cafés are places for young people. But better still, they're run by young people. They manage the café, making sure everyone has a say and picking up

30 skills they can take into careers later.

Each Youth Café has a committee that decides activities, policies, what to sell at the snack bar, when to open, how to raise funds and more. The committee usually gets its ideas from the other

35 young people that use the café.

Help if you need it

Youth Cafés usually have qualified youth workers on hand, who are either on the café's staff or stopping by regularly. So if you're having problems with anything, you can get it off your chest and get some 40 help.

Success story: Barcode

A Youth Café in Weston-super-Mare is providing young people with a safe, non-alcoholic place to hang out in the evening and at weekends. 45

Like many seaside towns, Weston-super-Mare in Somerset is a great place to be in summer. But during the winter, the lack of places to go can be a problem for young people. 50

The local Youth Council was asked for ideas on how to improve facilities for young people in the area. Gillian Crouch, 14, was chair of 55 the council at the time. 'We sent out questionnaires for young people asking what they wanted and they all wanted a Youth Café,' she recalls. 60

The café, Barcode, is open from Wednesday to Sunday, normally from 2.30pm to 9.30pm, although the hours change in the holidays.

Barcode also runs themed evenings. Friday night is party night, which is an under-18s club night without 65 alcohol, and there is a monthly showcase for local young bands. About 60 young people come in on a Friday night and up to 150 visit on a Saturday. The bar is proving most popular with 11–15-year-olds – some of whom go every night. (470 words) 70

Adapted and abridged from www.princes-trust.org.uk

1 LOOKING AT THE TEXT

Choose the correct answer(s).

1 At a Youth Café you can …
  a buy cheap beer.
  b enjoy yourself with other young people.
  c chat with friends.

2 Youth Cafés are set up …
  a by young people.
  b by qualified café managers.
  c with the help of adults in the community.

3 If teenagers at the café have personal problems …
  a they should tell the café committee.
  b they can discuss them with youth workers.
  c they should talk to the café manager.

4 Teenagers in Weston-super-Mare …
  a didn't have enough places to go.
  b asked for a Youth Café.
  c wanted Barcode to sell alcoholic drinks.

5 The Youth Council in Weston-super-Mare …
  a asked Gillian Crouch to run a Youth Café.
  b asked young people for their views.
  c didn't want a Youth Café.

6 Barcode …
  a is open every evening.
  b sometimes has live music.
  c is busiest on Saturday evenings.

2 WORKING WITH WORDS

Explain these words and expressions from the text in your own words.

1 community (*line 16*)
2 volunteer (*line 23*)
3 to have a say (*line 29*)
4 snack bar (*line 32*)
5 to raise funds (*line 33*)
6 youth worker (*line 36*)
7 seaside (*line 46*)
8 Youth Council (*line 51*)

3 MIND MAP

Copy and complete this mind map using information from the text.

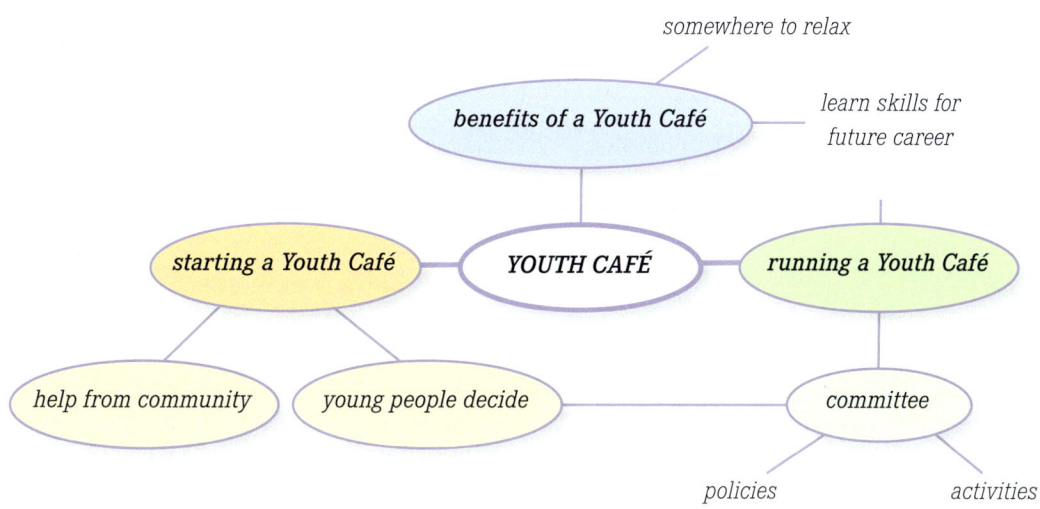

4 DISCUSSION

Use points from your mind map to answer these questions with your partner.

1 What benefits can Youth Cafés bring to young people?
2 What potential problems could affect Youth Cafés?
3 How would you deal with these problems?

I'm	in favour of against	Youth Cafés	because ...
The great thing about The problem with	Youth Cafés	is ...	
Youth Cafés	are	all very well, OK, I suppose,	but ...

5 PRESENTATION

Work in a group. Brainstorm ideas for a youth project in your area. Present the best idea to your class. Include the following information:

> **What** is the project? > **How** will it work?
> **Why** is it needed?   > **What resources** (money, staff, location, etc) will be needed?

Some useful vocabulary

Youth work

advice	Rat(schlag)
advise sb	raten, empfehlen
community centre	Gemeindehaus, -zentrum
deal with an issue	sich mit einem Problem auseinandersetzen
reach out to sb	sich an jdn wenden
earn sb's ...	jds ... gewinnen
confidence	Zuversicht, Vertrauen
trust	Vertrauen

Youth projects

advertise	werben für, ankündigen
anti-drugs campaign	Antidrogenkampagne
art exhibition	Kunstausstellung
band showcase	Bandvorstellung
course	Kurs, Lehrgang
drama group	Theatergruppe
get involved in	sich mit etw befassen, sich für etw engagieren
get sth off your chest	etw loswerden
have a say	mitreden dürfen
magazine	Zeitschrift, Magazin

prove popular	sich als populär erweisen
raise funds	Gelder aufbringen
rap competition	Rapwettbewerb
run	(durch)führen
set up	aufstellen, aufbauen
themed evening	Themenabend
youth club	Jugendzentrum

Social problems

abuse	Missbrauch
alcoholism	Alkoholismus
alienation	Entfremdung, Isoliertheit
boredom	Langeweile
crime	Verbrechen
drug abuse	Drogenmissbrauch
drug dealing	Drogendealen, Drogenhandel
drunkenness	Trunkenheit
poverty	Armut
social exclusion	soziale Ausgrenzung
truancy	Schuleschwänzen
unemployment	Arbeitslosigkeit
vandalism	mutwillige Sachbeschädigung, Vandalismus
violence	Gewalt

Childcare: young consumers

Advertising and pester power

4 11

Over 95% of kids have pestered their parents for a product promoted on TV, according to a recent survey*. But only 12% of parents think advertising to children should be banned and 30% think ads are a valuable way of teaching children about marketing.

5   Most parents are no strangers to 'pester power' – when children keep on asking for something until they get it. Toys and games are the leading 'pester products' with 83% of parents being nagged to buy them, particularly in the run-up to Christmas. Snacks (68%) are a close second, and around 30% of kids pester parents for entertainment in the form of movies, days out and restaurant treats.

Parents are surprisingly tolerant of advertising to kids. The majority of parents see it as a useful tool
10 for teaching children the difference between desirable and necessary. 'I think it is down to parents to ensure their kids realize that just because something is available doesn't mean they can have it,' commented one parent.

Another mum remarked 'I think marketing to children is OK, as long as parents help children understand that they can't have everything they want. Life is full of disappointments as well as the
15 good stuff. Teach them there is a balance and it stops them being spoiled.'

Child psychologist and parenting expert Dr Pat Spungin adds: 'Advertising is such a huge part of our lives that it's inevitable that children will have to learn how to handle it sooner or later. Today's parents are the first generation that grew up with TV advertising, and this media-literate generation think that passing on media-awareness to their children is important.'

*Research Method: Online survey hosted on www.raisingkids.co.uk. 525 parents responded

20 ## MARKETING TECHNIQUES

As well as ads, marketing experts use the following techniques to reach children and teenagers:

▶ **Product placement** is when particular products are shown in films and TV shows, e.g. a popular character eats a particular brand of
25 chocolate bar, drinks a particular brand of fizzy drink or uses a particular brand of mobile phone. The use of the product is supposed to appear 'natural' – not like advertising. However, it encourages consumers to associate the product and the brand with a positive image.

▶ **Tie-ins** are links between entertainment (e.g. films, TV shows or computer games) and products (e.g. toys, fast food or drinks). Kids see
30 the film, then they can buy the toy and eat the snack too! Coca Cola reportedly paid Warner Bros. Studios $150 million for the marketing rights to the film *Harry Potter and the Sorcerer's Stone*.

Adapted and abridged from: www.raisingkids.co.uk

(425 words)

1 LOOKING AT THE TEXT

You are taking part in a radio talkshow about the impact of advertising on children. Select relevant information from the text and answer the following questions in German. Do not translate word for word.

1 Wie beeinflusst TV-Werbung das Verhalten von Kindern ihren Eltern gegenüber?
2 Für welche drei Produkte/Unternehmungen interessieren sich Kinder vorwiegend?
3 Was finden viele Eltern an Kinderwerbung eher positiv?
4 Was ist laut Dr Spungin unvermeidbar und welche Konsequenzen sollte man daraus ziehen?
5 Was versteht man unter Produktplatzierung *(product placement)* und wie unterscheidet sie sich von Werbung?
6 Was versteht man unter Kombinationswerbung *(tie-ins)*?

2 WORKING WITH WORDS

Jill Osmond from Birmingham disagrees with the article on page 159. In this email, she explains why.

Complete her email with words from the box. There are three words that you don't need.

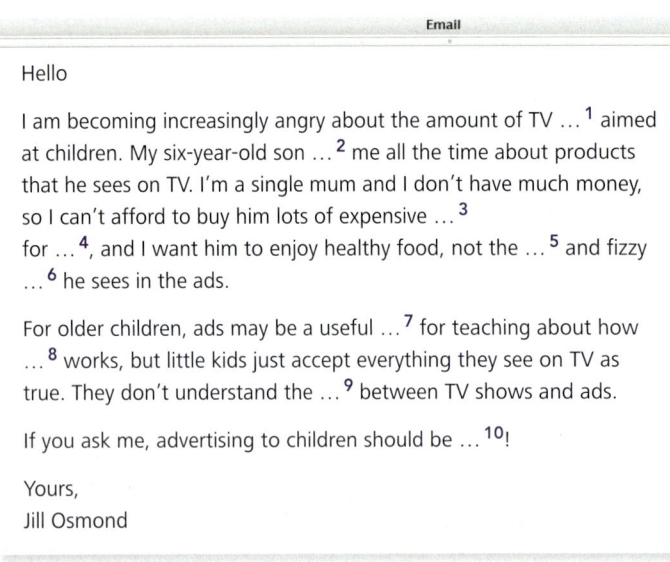

Email

Hello

I am becoming increasingly angry about the amount of TV … [1] aimed at children. My six-year-old son … [2] me all the time about products that he sees on TV. I'm a single mum and I don't have much money, so I can't afford to buy him lots of expensive … [3] for … [4], and I want him to enjoy healthy food, not the … [5] and fizzy … [6] he sees in the ads.

For older children, ads may be a useful … [7] for teaching about how … [8] works, but little kids just accept everything they see on TV as true. They don't understand the … [9] between TV shows and ads.

If you ask me, advertising to children should be … [10]!

Yours,
Jill Osmond

adverts ¦ banned ¦ brand ¦ Christmas ¦ difference ¦ drinks ¦ marketing ¦ necessary ¦ parents ¦ pesters ¦ snacks ¦ tool ¦ toys	

3 ROLE PLAY

Work with a partner.

A You are the parent of a young child. You think that advertising to children should not be allowed. Tell your partner how you feel and why.
B You are also the parent of a young child. You think that advertising to children is OK. Try to persuade your partner.

I	think feel	advertising on children's TV advertising to children	is	bad, OK,	because …

Don't you	think agree	(that)	it's important it's bad	to teach kids about … ? for kids to expect … ?

4 LOOKING AT STATISTICS

Comment on the statistics shown in the pie chart.

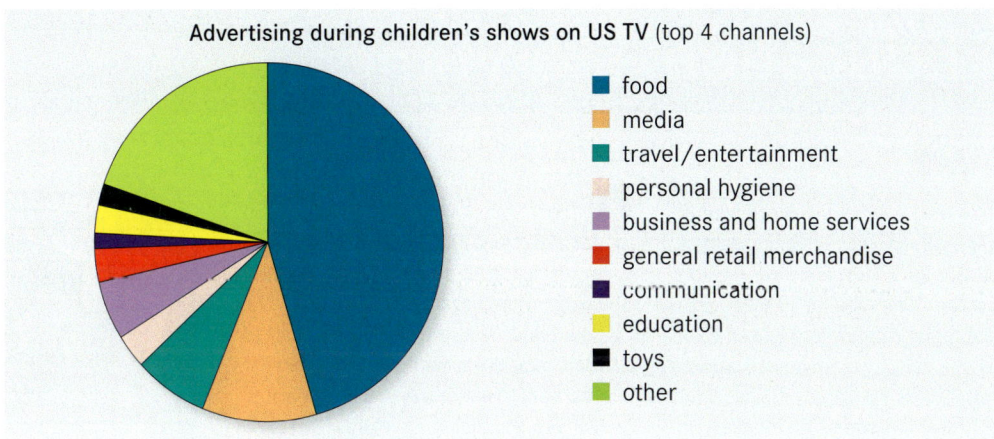

Advertising during children's shows on US TV (top 4 channels)

- food
- media
- travel/entertainment
- personal hygiene
- business and home services
- general retail merchandise
- communication
- education
- toys
- other

Source: *Food for thought: Television Food Advertising to Children in the United States*, Kaiser Family Foundation

Well over Slightly less than	... per cent	of advertising	is for ...

This	trend fact	is	worrying alarming surprising	in the context of when we consider	childhood obesity. household debt etc.

5 WRITING

How should Jill Osmond deal with her son's 'pester power'? Respond to the email in exercise 2 with your own suggestions.

Some useful vocabulary

Upbringing	
allow sb to do sth	jdm erlauben etw zu tun
bring up a child	ein Kind aufziehen/ erziehen
educate sb about sth	jdn über etw aufklären
give in to sb	nachgeben
nag	(herum)nörgeln
pester sb for sth	jdn um etwas anbetteln, jdm mit etw keine Ruhe lassen
set rules	Regeln aufstellen
teach sb the value of sth	jdm beibringen, welchen Wert etw hat

Advertising	
advertise sth	werben für
advertisement	Werbung
brand	Marke

competitive	konkurrierend
encourage sb to buy sth	jdn ermutigen/bestärken etw zu kaufen
increase sales	den Umsatz steigern
influence sb	jdn beeinflussen
persuade sb	jdn überzeugen/ überreden
promote sth	für etw werben
target sb	auf jdn abzielen

Negative consequences of consumerism	
be dissatisfied	unzufrieden sein
become overweight	übergewichtig werden
become greedy/ materialistic	(hab)gierig/materialistisch werden
childhood obesity	Fettleibigkeit im Kindes- alter
get into debt	sich verschulden

3

Education: storytime

1 They made their way to the place where the light was, and soon saw it shine brighter and grow larger, until they came to a well-lit robber's house. The donkey, being the
5 biggest, went to the window and looked in.

'What do you see, my grey horse?' asked the cockerel.

'What do I see?' answered the donkey, 'a table covered with good things to eat and
10 drink, and robbers sitting at it enjoying themselves.'

'That would be the sort of thing for us,' said the cockerel.

'Yes, yes! Ah, how I wish we were there!'
15 said the donkey.

Then the animals discussed how they could drive away the robbers. At last they thought of a plan. The donkey would put his forefeet on the window ledge, the dog would
20 jump on the donkey's back, the cat would climb on the dog, and lastly the cockerel would to fly up and stand on the head of the cat.

Adapted extract from *Grimm's Fairy Tales* by Frances Jenkins Olcott

2 The woman had brought two daughters into the house with her, who were beautiful, but wicked in their hearts. Now began a bad time for the
5 poor child. 'Will the stupid goose sit in the sitting room with us?' said they. 'If you want to eat bread, you must earn it. Out you go, kitchen servant!'

They took her pretty clothes away
10 from her, put an old grey dress on her and gave her wooden shoes. 'Just look at the proud princess, how well dressed she is!' they laughed, and led her into the kitchen.

15 There she had to do hard work from morning till night, get up before daybreak, carry water, light fires, cook and wash. Besides this, the sisters did their best to upset her — they laughed at
20 her and emptied her peas and lentils into the ashes of the fire, so that she was forced to sit and pick them out again.

Adapted extract from *Grimm's Fairy Tales* by Frances Jenkins Olcott

3 The third little pig met a man with a heavy load of bricks, and said:

'Please, man, give me those bricks to build a house with.'

So the man gave him the bricks, and he built his house with them. So the wolf came, as he did to the other little pigs, and said:

5 'Little pig, little pig, let me come in.'

'No, no, by the hair on my chinny chin chin.'

'Then I'll huff, and I'll puff, and I'll blow your house down.'

Well, he huffed, and he puffed, and he huffed and he puffed, and he puffed and huffed. But he could not blow the house down.

Adapted extract from *The Rainbow Book of Fairy Tales for Five-Year-Olds* by Lisa Ripperton

1 LOOKING AT THE TEXT

Match the illustrations and titles to the extracts from fairy tales. There are two titles and illustrations you don't need.

a Cinderella
b Little Red Riding Hood
c The Bremen Town Musicians
d Hansel and Gretel
e The Three Little Pigs

2 WORKING WITH WORDS

The words below are all from the texts. Find their opposites.

1 light (*text 1, line 2*)   3 beautiful (*text 2, line 3*)   5 proud (*text 2, line 11*)
2 lastly (*text 1, line 21*)   4 wicked (*text 2, line 3*)   6 heavy (*text 3, line 1*)

3 DISCUSSION

Which of these statements about fairy tales is closest to your own view? Compare ideas with your partner.

Brendan, 30, father of Liam, 3

> Fairy tales? I don't read them to my son. Not the old, traditional Brothers Grimm ones, anyway. They're too scary for young children. There are cruel punishments, wicked stepmothers and far too much death and violence!

Sarah, nursery nurse, 20

> Cinderella for example, well, she's patient and kind and she gets the Prince in the end, doesn't she? Or the Bremen town musicians – they're a bunch of misfits, but because they work together, they're successful. So I think there are some useful core values that you can teach with fairy tales.

Phil, primary school teacher, 29

> They're great for early literacy development – kids soon pick up the repetitive elements and memorize them. The stories and characters are vivid and exciting, so they offer lots of opportunities for acting out episodes, drawing pictures, making masks and so on.

Melissa, student, 17

> Don't you think that fairy tales are, well ... old-fashioned and irrelevant? I mean, what relevance do princesses and castles have for today's kids? There's so much gender-stereotyping in fairy tales, too.

4 ANALYZING AN AUSTRALIAN ABORIGINAL STORY

This story is told by the Ngarrindjeri, one of the Aboriginal peoples of Australia. Read the story, then comment on the following aspects:

1 Reasons why Ngarrindjeri adults might tell the story to their children
2 Universal themes in the story
3 How it might be used in a European kindergarten or primary school

4 13

The Thukeri*

Long ago, in the time of the dreaming stories, there lived a group of Aboriginal people. They were hungry so three men decided to go fishing. They told the other people to light the fire and that they would be back in the evening.

So they got their canoe and went fishing where there were really juicy fish.

They caught so many fish that their boat nearly sank. So they decided to go back to their camp.

When they were at the edge of the shore an old man came along. The fishermen said, 'Quick – hide the fish.'

The old man said, 'I haven't eaten fish for a year.' Then the fishermen said, 'Sorry, we don't have enough fish to feed our people.' ▶

* *thukeri* – Ngarrindjeri word for a kind of fish that has a lot of bones

So the old man walked away and turned back and said in a tired voice, 'You will never enjoy those fish again.'

So the men went back to their camp to feed their children and the rest of their people.

The first one to taste a fish was a little girl. She started to choke. Then the mum tried some and choked as well.

Then the leader of the group of Aboriginal people said, 'Did you see anyone when you went fishing?' The fishermen said, 'Yes, we saw an old grandpa.'

'That wasn't just an old grandpa, that was Ngurunderi*, you silly men! Because you didn't share, Ngurunderi has made all the fish bony, so now we can never eat them again.'

Ngurunderi – creator spirit of the Ngarrindjeri people

Slightly adapted from: *Thukeri: a Ngarrindjeri Dreaming story*, Education Department of South Australia

5 WRITING

Choose a fairy tale or other short story that you know well. Alternatively, use the internet to find a non-European story, e.g. African, Aboriginal Australian or Native American. Outline the plot and comment on whether it is suitable for reading to/with the following age groups:

> 1–3 year-olds   > 4–8 year-olds   > 8 year-olds and older

Useful vocabulary

Ethics		decode	entschlüsseln
be justified	gerechtfertigt sein, Recht haben	character	Persönlichkeit
brave	mutig, tapfer	engage a child's attention	die Aufmerksamkeit eines Kindes erregen
bravery	Mut, Tapferkeit	excite a child's imagination	die Fantasie / Vorstellungs-kraft eines Kindes anregen
carry a moral message	eine moralische Botschaft tragen		
deal with ethical questions	sich mit moralischen Fragen befassen	match spoken words with print	den Zusammenhang zwischen Laut und Schrift erkennen
(dis)honest	(un)ehrlich		
(dis)honesty	(Un)Ehrlichkeit	nursery rhyme	Kinderlied, -reim, -vers
get one's just rewards	das bekommen, was man verdient hat	plot	Handlung
		read a story aloud	eine Geschichte (laut) vorlesen
promote positive values	positive Werte voran-treiben, anpreisen		
		reading age	Lesealter
right and wrong	Recht und Unrecht	have the ~ of an eight-year-old	beim Lesen auf dem Stand eines Achtjährigen sein
(un)ethical behaviour	(un)moralisches Verhalten		
		read to a child	einem Kind vorlesen
		recite a poem by heart	ein Gedicht auswendig aufsagen
Literacy development			
act out a story	eine Geschichte vorführen, spielen	retell a story	eine Geschichte nach-erzählen
become a fluent reader	fließend Lesen lernen	sound recognition	Lauterkennung
		text comprehension	Textverständnis
broaden a child's understanding / experience of the world	das Weltverständnis / den Erfahrungsschatz eines Kindes erweitern	word recognition	Worterkennung

4

Caring: blind people

How people who are visually impaired cross streets

4 14

Crossing a street is something that people with full vision take for granted. For people who are visually impaired (blind or partially sighted), it can be
5 difficult and dangerous and requires the learning of special techniques.

The first information that visually impaired pedestrians need is: 'Have I arrived at a street?' They use a combination of clues to recognize the
10 street edge. These may include tactile clues such as feeling the kerb with their cane or foot, and auditory clues such as the sound of the traffic on the street next to or in front of them.

The next information needed for decision-making at
15 unfamiliar intersections is: 'Which street is this?' This information is rarely available to visually impaired people. They need to develop a mental map and keep track of where they are within that map, usually by counting street crossings. If they are unsure, they
20 need to ask other pedestrians.

The next information needed is: 'How is the intersection laid out?' For example, how wide the street is, if there is an island in the middle of the
25 street, and where exactly the pedestrian crossing is.

It may not be possible for pedestrians who are visually impaired to work out this information by listening to the traffic sounds. If the person makes the wrong choice, he or she may walk out of the
30 pedestrian crossing area and into waiting or moving traffic. Again, help may be needed from sighted pedestrians.

Next, they need to identify the type of traffic control system at this intersection: Does the intersection have
35 traffic lights? Is there a button to press, and if

so, where is it? Can cars turn right during the Walk interval?

Techniques for gathering this information include listening to traffic sounds for some time before
40 crossing and searching the pavement for poles with pushbuttons. This task has become difficult or impossible at many intersections. Missing information for any of these questions may result in crossing the road at the wrong
45 time.

Changes in the travel environment

In the past twenty years, changes in intersection layout, signals, driver behaviour and car technology have made life more
50 difficult for visually impaired pedestrians. At the same time, the walkability of our towns has generally decreased.

Wider streets are more difficult to cross in a straight line. Traffic islands make it more difficult to find your
55 way. Raised crossings may mean that there is no clear difference between the pavement and the street. Aggressive drivers are moving faster and are less likely to stop for pedestrians who do not follow the rules. The technology of cars, including electric
60 cars, has become quieter, making them harder to hear. (444 words)

Abridged and slightly adapted from www.walkinginfo.org

1 LOOKING AT THE TEXT

Choose the correct sentence ending(s).

1   When blind people cross the street ...
   a   they have to use special techniques.
   b   they have to ask sighted people to help them.
   c   they are at greater risk than sighted people.

2   To find out exactly where they are in town, blind people ...
   a   use an electronic map.
   b   often need to ask a sighted person.
   c   use special street signs.

3   For blind people, using a pedestrian crossing ...
   a   is easy and safe.
   b   requires a lot of information about the type and layout of the crossing.
   c   is safer if a sighted person helps them.

4   In the past 20 years ...
   a   crossing the street has become more difficult for blind people.
   b   motorists have become more tolerant towards blind people.
   c   pedestrian crossings have become a lot easier for blind people to use.

2 WORKING WITH WORDS

Match the words (a–m) to the definitions (1–10). There are two words you don't need.

a	auditory	1	the ability to see
b	clue	2	prevented from doing something properly
c	kerb	3	a particular way of doing something
d	impaired	4	a small piece of information that helps you to realize something
e	intersection	5	to do with the sense of touch
f	pavement	6	to do with hearing
g	pedestrian	7	a place where two or more roads meet
h	tactile	8	a person who travels on foot
i	technique	9	all the vehicles on the road
j	technology	10	the place next to the road where people walk
k	traffic		
l	vision		

3 FLOW CHART

Use the information from the text to complete this flow chart.

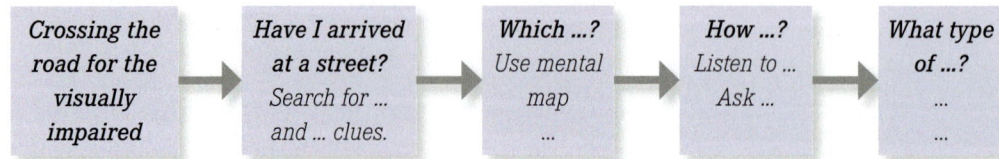

| Crossing the road for the visually impaired | → | Have I arrived at a street? Search for ... and ... clues. | → | Which ...? Use mental map ... | → | How ...? Listen to ... Ask ... | → | What type of ...? ... ... |

MEDIATION

You a preparing to give a talk in a German youth club about how to help pedestrians who are blind or visually impaired. You have found the following short text on a British website.

 Select the relevant information from the text and write some notes in German. Do not translate word for word.

KERBS AND ROADS Assisting someone across the road

When you are approaching a kerb, say so and say whether it's a 'kerb up' or 'kerb down'. Pause at the kerb before stepping up or down and the person you are guiding will feel the change in your body movement through your guiding arm.

Take care when approaching a rounded kerb to make sure the person you are guiding reaches it at the same time that you do.

It is important not to assume that just because someone is standing by a roadside they want to cross and your offer of help may be declined.

Always cross roads using the shortest distance, i.e. go straight across rather than crossing at an angle.

Do use a pedestrian crossing if there is one, but if not, allow plenty of time for the person you are guiding to cross at a normal pace and don't take risks.

If you are parting company after crossing a road, do tell the person you are guiding where they are and which way they are facing.

Source: *Royal National Institute for the Blind*, www.rnib.org.uk

5 PROJECT

Design a poster to alert sighted pedestrians or motorists to the needs of visually impaired pedestrians or people with other disabilities.

Useful vocabulary

Disabilities		Traffic and street furniture	
able-bodied	*körperlich gesund, nicht behindert*	car driver	*(Auto)Fahrer/in*
blind	*blind*	curb (AE); kerb (BE)	*Bordstein, Seitenstreifen*
blindness	*Blindheit*	cyclist	*Radfahrer/in*
deaf	*taub*	dangerous	*gefährlich*
deaf-mute	*gehörlos*	entrance	*Einfahrt*
impaired	*beeinträchtigt, behindert*	exit	*Ausfahrt*
hearing	*hörgeschädigt*	footbridge	*Fußgängerbrücke*
speech	*sprachbehindert*	HGV (heavy goods vehicle)/lorry/ truck	*Lkw (Lastkraftwagen)*
vision	*sehbehindert*		
in a wheelchair	*in einem Rollstuhl*	intersection	*Kreuzung, Verzweigung*
mute	*stumm, Stumme/r*	lamppost	*Laternenpfahl*
partially sighted	*sehbehindert*	motorist	*Autofahrer/in*
visually impaired	*sehbehindert*	obstacle	*Hindernis*
with a disability	*mit einer Behinderung*	parked vehicle	*geparktes Fahrzeug*
with learning difficulties	*mit Lernschwierigkeiten*	pavement (BE)	*Bürgersteig*
		pedestrian	*Fußgänger/in*
with limited mobility	*mit eingeschränkter Beweglichkeit/Mobilität*	pedestrian crossing	*Fußgängerüberweg*
		roundabout (BE); traffic circle (AE)	*Kreisverkehr*
⚠ It is better to refer to *people with disabilities* than *disabled people* – the disability does not define the person!		sidewalk (AE)	*Bürgersteig*
		subway	*(Fußgänger)Unterführung, (BE), U-Bahn (AE)*

5

Health: being overweight

How can I help my overweight daughter?

My 17-year-old daughter Abi* is putting on weight rapidly and I don't know whether I should intervene. The rest of our family is slim and healthy. She is pretty, has many friends, and has a good idea of where she is going in life. She knows about healthy eating but cannot seem to apply this knowledge to herself. When she was a toddler, she refused to eat vegetables, and now she overeats, and her diet consists mainly of carbohydrates.

I have tried to help her in various ways –

by not keeping biscuits in the house, paying for her gym membership and reminding her to eat fruit.

I worry a lot about her. We are very close, though our relationship is sometimes difficult. I can't bear to watch her risking her health and happiness.

I feel I have done everything in my power to help but I realise she has to make up her own mind to help herself.

Debbie*, London

*Names have been changed

What the expert thinks

It sounds as if you have done a great deal to help your daughter lose weight and to eat healthily.

However, perhaps you should accept that you and your daughter have different ideas about a healthy weight and diet. It sounds as if it's easy for you and the other members of your family to stay slim. Your daughter, however, may not have the same body frame or metabolic rate as the rest of you.

The second problem is the way you perceive your daughter. You claim that she is risking her health and her happiness. How can her weight alone have such an effect if she is pretty and popular? Could it be that you are confusing good health and happiness with being slim? The truth is, happiness and body weight are not directly linked.

The best way to deal with your assumptions and concerns would be to arrange for your daughter to have a thorough health check. Let the doctor decide what a healthy weight and a healthy diet should be for her.

Adapted and abridged from *Guardian News and Media*

(340 words)

1 LOOKING AT THE TEXT

Decide whether the statements are true (T), false (F) or not mentioned in the text (N).

1 Debbie is worried because her daughter is too thin.
2 Debbie's daughter Abi is popular with other teenagers.
3 Abi wants to become a nursery nurse when she leaves college.
4 Debbie encourages Abi to eat healthily and get exercise.
5 The expert thinks that Debbie has not done very much to help her daughter.
6 The expert thinks that a doctor should decide what is a healthy weight for Abi.
7 The expert says that it's difficult to be happy if you aren't slim.
8 Abi goes to the gym twice per week.

2 WORKING WITH WORDS

Complete the two readers' answers with the words and phrases in the box. There are three items you don't need.

> accept ∎ gym ∎ health ∎ healthy eating ∎ mind ∎ overeat ∎ overweight ∎
> popular ∎ put on weight ∎ sport ∎ reminded ∎ slim ∎ worried

She'll take action when she's ready

I was in the same situation as your daughter when I was 16. I had always been an ...**1** child and continued to ...**2** at secondary school.

It wasn't until I left school that my appearance became more important to me, so I learned about ...**3** and started to go to the ...**4** regularly. I've lost nearly 10 kilos now.

You need to realize that there's nothing you can do until your daughter makes up her own ...**5** to help herself.

IR, Cardiff

Love her for who she is

I grew up with healthy food and exercise, yet I was always bigger than other children. As I reached my teens, my self-esteem got worse and I turned to food for comfort. My mother ...**6** about my ...**7** and constantly ...**8** me to eat healthily. This didn't help – it just made me believe that I wasn't good enough. I still have problems with my weight.

Does your daughter ...**9** for emotional reasons? You say you have been trying to 'help' her, but that means that she has been getting the message that her body is a problem for you. Be proud of who she is now and let her know that you love and ...**10** her – that is absolutely the best support that a parent can give.

HF, Glasgow

(Letters adapted and abridged from *Guardian News and Media*)

3 WRITING

Compare and contrast the ideas expressed by IR and HF in their letters.

∎ Both IR and HF feel that ...
∎ Whereas IR thinks that ..., HF ...
∎ Where IR and HF differ is ...

4 STATISTICS ON OBESITY

Study the three charts, then answer the questions. The language in the box may help you.

1 What do they tell us about obesity in German teenagers compared to English teenagers?
2 What do they tell us about obesity in German adults compared
   a   to English adults?
   b   to German teenagers?
3 What factors can you think of that might explain these differences?

> On average, English/German teenagers … ▮
> Compared to their peers in Germany/England, … ▮
> When we come to adults, on the other hand, we find that … ▮
> There appears to be a major difference between … ▮
> A possible explanation for this might be found in … ▮

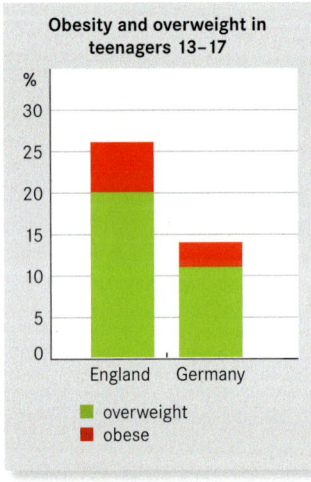

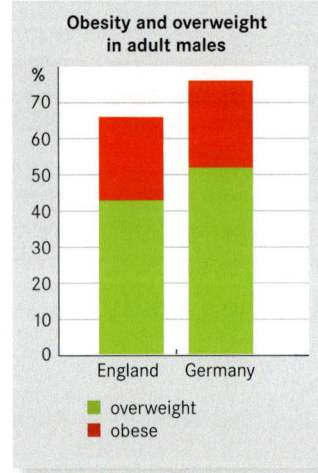

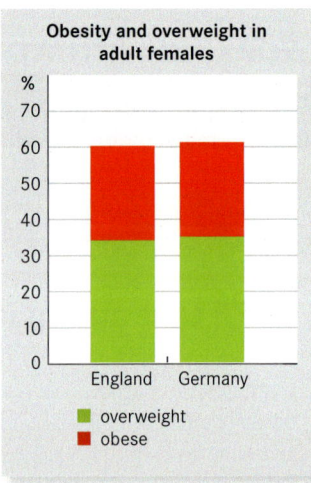

Source: *International Association for the Study of Obesity*

Useful vocabulary

Diet and lifestyle	
be at one's ideal weight	*Idealgewicht haben*
be overweight	*übergewichtig sein*
be underweight	*untergewichtig sein*
body image	*Auffassung über den Körper*
carbohydrates	*Kohle(n)hydrate*
diet	*Ernährung(sweise)*
a poor ~	*schlechte, mangelhafte Ernährung*
a balanced ~	*ausgewogene Ernährung*
emaciated	*abgemagert*
fat (adj.)	*dick*
fat (n.)	*Fett*
go on a (crash) diet	*eine (Radikal)Diät machen*
get exercise regularly	*regelmäßig Sport treiben, sich regelmäßig bewegen*
lifestyle	*Lebensweise, Lebensstil*
active ~	*aktive Lebensweise*
sedentary lifestyle	*sitzende Lebensweise, sehr viel sitzen*

metabolic rate	*Stoffwechsel*
minerals	*Mineralien*
nutrition	*Ernährung*
obese	*fettleibig*
obesity	*Fettleibigkeit*
overeat	*sich überessen, überfressen*
overweight	*übergewichtig*
protein	*Eiweiß / Protein*
self-esteem	*Selbstwertgefühl, Selbstachtung*
high ~	*hohes Selbstwertgefühl*
low ~	*niedriges Selbstwertgefühl*
slim	*schlank*
suffer from	*unter … leiden*
anorexia	*Magersucht*
bulimia	*Bulimie*
an eating disorder	*Essstörung*
thin	*dünn, mager*

6

Childcare: training and careers

BackChat YouthForum

Kaz07   posts: 2   2 hours ago

I'm REALLY interested in a career in childcare, but I don't really know where to start. Has anyone got any advice for me? I think I might like to become a children's nurse or a nursery nurse.

I'm 17 by the way and I finish school in June.

5 **samvincent   posts: 109**   1 hour 50 minutes ago

Kaz – children's nurse and nursery nurse are two completely different jobs!

A children's nurse looks after children and young people up to 18 who need medical care because they are sick or injured or have a disability. You may work in a hospital or in the community. You work together with doctors and you provide practical nursing care – checking temperatures, giving
10 drugs, things like that.

A nursery nurse usually looks after children who aren't sick. They can be very small babies or older children to about six or seven years of age. The job involves taking care of the children's daily needs – bathing and changing the little ones, keeping the older ones happy and safe – and educating them and helping them to develop their social skills. You usually work in a nursery.

15 **Kaz07   posts: 3**   30 minutes ago

Thanks for that info. Being a children's nurse sounds really cool! What training do you have to do?

matto   posts: 32   25 minutes ago

You'll need to do a diploma or a degree in nursing to become a children's nurse. That's what I'm
20 doing now – I'm in the second year of my diploma course. It's a 3-year full-time course. The first year was all about general nursing. For the rest of the course I am concentrating on paediatrics (children's health care) and childhood development. Like all nursing courses it's very hard work, but I love it :-)

skatergirl26   posts: 79   13 minutes ago

I decided to do nursery nursing because I didn't want to spend 3 years training to be a nurse :-(

25 As a nursery nurse, you can start in a nursery straight away as a trainee and attend college part-time to work towards an NVQ in childcare, learning and development.

Gummiadler   posts: 8   8 minutes ago

Sorry, what's an NVQ? I live in Germany. I don't think we have them here.

skatergirl26   posts: 80   2 minutes ago
30 An NVQ is a 'National Vocational Qualification'. It's a competence-based qualification. In other words, you don't sit an exam, you provide evidence to an assessor that you can do the various parts of the job. The assessor observes you at work and asks you questions. When you have passed all the units, you get your qualification.

(400 words)

1 LOOKING AT THE TEXT

Copy the mind map and complete it with information from the text.

babies to 6/7 years

nursery nurse

children + teenagers to 18 years

children's nurse

part-time training

Jobs in childcare

full-time training

2 WORKING WITH WORDS

Copy and complete the table.

Noun	Verb	Adjective
care (line 7)		...
competence (line 30)		...
development (line 22)	...	...
...	...	different (line 5)
...	to train (line 24)	

3 LOOKING AT CASE STUDIES

The following case study was published by a British childcare organisation to give school leavers an idea of what working in a nursery is like.

Working in a day nursery

Jamie – senior nursery nurse

Jamie, 22, has worked at a day nursery for the last four years, gaining qualifications and working his way up the career ladder.

1 I studied Health and Social Care at college. After leaving college I became a trainee nursery nurse.
2 I am qualified at NVQ Level 3 in Early Years Childcare. I worked towards the NVQ on a day release basis, attending college one day a week, whilst getting practical experience working at the nursery.
3 I am now 'third in charge' (most senior person after the deputy manager) at the nursery and I hope to work my way up to be deputy manager. One day I'd like to be a nursery manager or, perhaps, to run my own nursery.
4 It's hard work, so you need to be serious about working in a nursery. This is a career with opportunities and the chance to progress. You can make a real difference to children's lives. I would advise other men to be determined and go for it!
5 The children are the best thing about the job – it's just great seeing them grow up.

Slightly adapted from: *National Day Nurseries Association*, www.ndna.org.uk

Insert the questions at the most appropriate points. One of the questions was not asked.

a What qualifications did you gain as a trainee nursery nurse?
b How many staff work at your day nursery?
c What are the highlights?
d How would you advise other men thinking about working in a day nursery?
e How did you get started in childcare?
f What are your plans for the future?

4 WRITING

Where do you see yourself working when you are Jamie's age? Write a career case study for yourself at the age of 22, using Jamie's as a model. You could also record the case study as an audio or video interview with a partner.

OR

Write a forum post telling Kaz about a childcare job that you know about in Germany. Make sure you include the following information: typical tasks, place of work, age range of children, length of training, type of assessment (e.g. competence-based or exam-based).

Useful vocabulary

Childcare professions	
childminder	*Tagesmutter*
children's nurse / paediatric nurse	*Kinderkrankenschwester*
nanny	*Kindermädchen*
live in ~	*ein Kindermädchen, das mit im Haus lebt*
nursery nurse	*Kinderpfleger/in, Erzieher/in*
nursery teacher	*Erzieher/in (mit Studienabschluss)*
paediatrician	*Kinderarzt/ärztin*
playworker	*Angestellte/r in einem Spielprojekt*
pre-school education	*Vorschulerziehung*
primary school teacher	*Grundschullehrer/in*
social worker	*Sozialarbeiter/in*
teaching assistant for children with special educational needs	*Lehrassistent/in für Kinder mit besonderen pädagogischen Bedürfnissen*
youth and community worker	*Jugend- und Sozialarbeiter/in*

Qualifications and training	
certificate	*Zeugnis*
commit oneself to sth	*etw mit voller Überzeugung tun*
course	*Kurs, Lehrgang*
full-time ~	*Vollzeitkurs*
part-time ~	*Teilzeitkurs*
diploma	*Abschlusszeugnis, Diplom*
education	*Ausbildung*
primary ~	*Primarstufen/Grundschulausbildung*
secondary ~	*Sekundarstufenausbildung*
further ~	*höhere (meistens berufliche) Schulbildung*
higher ~	*Hochschulbildung*
experienced	*erfahren, sachkundig*
graduate	*(Hoch)Schulabsolvent*
qualification	*Zeugnis, Abschluss, Qualifikation*
qualified	*ausgebildet, qualifiziert*
responsible	*verantwortlich, verantwortungsvoll*
responsibility	*Verantwortung*
specialized	*spezialisiert, fachkundig*
trained	*geschult, ausgebildet*

Where childcare workers work	
after-school club	*Kinderhort*
community healthcare centre	*Gemeinde- und Gesundheitspflegezentrum*
crèche	*Krippe*
general hospital	*allgemeines Krankenhaus, Kreiskrankenhaus*
holiday play-scheme	*Spielprojekt während der Ferien*
infant school	*erste 3 Jahre der Grundschule*
nursery school	*Kindergarten*
paediatric hospital	*Kinderkrankenhaus, Kinderklinik*
playgroup	*Spielgruppe*
primary school	*Grundschule*
secondary school	*weiterführende Schule*
special school	*Sonderschule*

7

Education: volunteering abroad

Raleigh is a youth and education charity that provides adventurous and challenging expeditions for people of all backgrounds, nationalities and ages. Over the past 24 years, 30,000 people have been

5 involved in more than 250 expeditions in 43 countries, developing their skills and making a real difference to local communities and environments around the world.

A Raleigh 5 or 10-week expedition is unique in giving

10 venturers the opportunity to work on three different phases:

1 Community project
In our host countries there is a severe lack of community infrastructure such as schools, medical centres and

15 housing. You may be involved in building a school or developing a fresh water supply. You will live and work alongside local people.

2 Environmental project
The work is often renovating or building ranger

20 stations and trails in national parks. These projects are important for the conservation of eco-systems and biodiversity.

3 Adventure
We aim to give our participants a challenging 19-day

25 trekking or canoeing experience which takes them through a variety of different scenery.

Destinations include Borneo, Costa Rica and Nicaragua, and India. We run between 10 and 12 expeditions a year.

CASE STUDY: Barry
My name is Barry, I am 26 and from Partick in Glasgow.

Before I joined Raleigh I had got in with a bad crowd. During this time I became addicted to
5 heroin and valium. I got caught up in crime, shoplifting, car theft and assault and robbery and got sentenced to 30 months in a young offenders' institute.

When I got out I lived in supported
10 accommodation but due to experiences in jail I became depressed and suffered from anxiety. I did not like what I had become, I didn't believe in myself and didn't think I would amount to anything.
15

I heard about Raleigh from a friend and thought it would be a great experience to help me increase my self-confidence and to give me more experience for a career in the care sector. I was able to work on my communication skills
20 and gain the motivation to face challenges head on.

I feel that doing Raleigh has taught me more than college did. Other young people should try the overseas programme because it can
25 change the way you feel about yourself and other people. It can help you work with all sorts of people from different backgrounds.

Adapted extracts from www.raleighinternational.org

(390 words)

1 MEDIATION

Your friend is thinking about taking a gap year to do voluntary work abroad between finishing school and starting work.

Write down some points from the text (in German) which could be useful for him/her. Do not translate word for word.

2 LOOKING AT THE TEXT

Read the case study and choose the correct answer(s).

1 Barry received a prison sentence …
   a because he committed a lot of crimes.
   b when his friends stole a car.
   c after he left Raleigh.

2 After leaving the young offenders' institute, Barry …
   a had no self-confidence.
   b lived with his parents.
   c felt anxious and depressed.

3 When Barry first heard about Raleigh, he …
   a didn't think he would be successful.
   b thought it might help him to start a new career.
   c thought that it wasn't right for him.

4 Now that he has completed his Raleigh programme, Barry …
   a believes that he has learned a lot.
   b wants to go to college overseas.
   c would recommend the programme to other people.

3 WORKING WITH WORDS

Match the words in the box to the definitions below. There are three words too many – write your own definitions for them.

> adventurous ▪ anxiety ▪ assault ▪ challenging ▪ charity ▪ conservation ▪
> destination ▪ local ▪ robbery ▪ scenery ▪ shoplifting ▪ trail ▪ variety

1 willing to try new things
2 difficult to achieve
3 from the nearby area
4 a rough path
5 protecting the natural environment
6 the landscape you can see around you
7 taking goods from a shop without paying
8 taking property from a person or place illegally
9 a violent attack on someone
10 a feeling of worry or nervousness

4 ROLE PLAY

Work with a partner.

A You are Barry. You have heard about Raleigh from a friend and have decided to ask a careers advisor about volunteering abroad. You think it could give you useful experience.

B You are Barry's careers advisor. You want to know about the following things:
> what Barry hopes to learn from volunteering abroad
> what kind of volunteering interests Barry
> whether Barry has the right skills for volunteering abroad (e.g. work with others, communicate with others, work hard, want to help people in poorer countries)

5 FUNDRAISING IDEAS

Raleigh venturers have to pay a fee to cover the cost of their participation in the programme. Many of them can only afford this by getting sponsorship from friends, family and the public.

Work in a group. Brainstorm fundraising ideas, then present your best idea to the class. The class votes on the best idea overall.

Useful vocabulary

Social/psychological problems

addict	Süchtige/r, Abhängige/r
addicted to	süchtig nach
addiction	Sucht
dependent on	abhängig von
drugs	Drogen
anti-depressants	Antidepressiva
depressed	deprimiert, nieder-geschlagen
pessimistic	pessimistisch
suffer from ~	an ... leiden
~ depression	Depressionen
~ anxiety	Angstzuständen
~ a lack of self-confidence	mangelndem Selbst-bewusstsein
~ low self-esteem	geringer Selbstachtung

Crime

shoplifting	Ladendiebstahl
theft	Diebstahl
robbery	Raubüberfall
assault	Körperverletzung
young offenders' institute	Jugendvollzugsanstalt
sentencing	Verurteilung

Life skills

believe in oneself	an sich selbst glauben
communication skills	Kommunikationsfähigkeiten

determination	Entschlossenheit
encourage	ermutigen, bestärken, unterstützen
face challenges head on	Herausforderungen realistisch/praktisch annehmen
motivate	motivieren
outgoing	aufgeschlossen
overcome difficulties	Schwierigkeiten bewältigen
positive attitude	positive Einstellung
rise to a challenge	sich einer Herausforderung stellen
self-confidence	Selbstbewusstsein
self-belief	Selbstvertrauen

Fundraising

car boot / jumble sale	Flohmarkt, Trödelmarkt
donate	spenden
donation	Spende
door-to-door collection	Haustürsammlung
raffle	Lotterie, Tombola
sponsor	Förderer/in, Sponsor/in
sponsored event	gesponserte Veranstaltung
sponsorship	Sponsoring, Unter-stützung

Education: Waldorf teaching

4 17

Outdoor activities in a Waldorf kindergarten

by Karen Smith

As Waldorf early childhood educators, our goal is to teach by example. Through our work, the children learn important lessons to prepare them for the academic subjects they will begin in grade one. This teaching method is quite different from the trend in m a i n s t r e a m education, where abstract concepts provide the basis for learning, and there are no opportunities for shared work activity with adults.

There is much work to be done in a Waldorf kindergarten. The teacher places him/herself in the centre of all the activity, showing purpose and enthusiasm for his/her work. Preparing the food, dusting, polishing, repairing toys, folding the laundry, washing the dishes, sewing and mending are all jobs the children can learn to accomplish.

In today's mechanized world, most of the tasks that formerly were completed by humans are now done by machines. Children have little opportunity to see adults use their hands to wash dishes or bake bread. Objects that in days long ago would have been repaired are now thrown away and replaced.

Observing the work of the adult engaged in meaningful activity serves to boost the children's energy, helping them to develop an 'I can do it' attitude.

In my first year as a Waldorf kindergarten teacher, I felt that the time I spent outside with my class was aimless. I spent a great deal of time preparing for activities inside the classroom, but outside interests were always an afterthought. I asked my fellow trainee teachers for ideas. The idea of making a wooden spoon to use for cooking in our classroom appealed to me most.

Undertaking a long-term project teaches by example the value of perseverance and a job well done. At the beginning of the school year, I began carving a branch from an apple tree.

Throughout the months as I worked on the branch, I never directly answered the children when I was asked what it would become. As it is much more interesting for a child to think about the outcome of a project, 'What do you think it might be?' was my reply.

Some thought it might be a paddle for a boat, a sword, a hammer, a fork, or a walking stick. My response to their thoughts was: 'Perhaps, but I am not sure yet what this tree wants to become.' Only in the spring did a few children think it might become a spoon. At the end of the project, as it was becoming a real spoon before their eyes, the children were eager to have me finish it to use to serve our porridge.

I was delighted in their excitement when we were finally able to use the spoon in the last week of class, completing the lesson that work has a purpose.

(470 words)

Abridged and adapted from *'The role of purposeful work in a Waldorf Kindergarten'* by Karen Smith

1 LOOKING AT THE TEXT

Complete the sentences in your own words.

1 Whereas Waldorf kindergarten teachers …
2 The role of the teacher in a Waldorf kindergarten …
3 Karen was dissatisfied with the way …
4 Although the children wanted to know what Karen …
5 When the spoon was finished, it …

Remember!
Übersetzung von Kindergarten
= kindergarten (AE);
* nursery school (BE)*

2 WORKING WITH WORDS

Find antonyms (words of opposite meaning) for these words from the text.
Use a dictionary to help you if necessary.

1 work (*line 3*)
2 abstract (*line 14*)
3 formerly (*line 28*)
4 repair (*line 32*)

5 meaningful (*line 35*)
6 aimless (*line 42*)
7 response (*line 60*)
8 excitement (*line 67*)

3 DISCUSSION

Work in a group.

Here are some ideas for outdoor activities at a Waldorf kindergarten. Put them into three categories, according to your group's opinion:

A definitely suitable for young children
B only suitable under close supervision by the teacher
C not suitable for young children

Autumn
> Harvest vegetables, herbs and flowers to make dyes for fabric.
> Sweep fallen leaves.

Winter
> Build and maintain a bird feeder.
> Shovel snow from the paths.

Spring
> Plant seeds of flowers and vegetables.
> Make flower necklaces.

Any time of year
> Pick up rubbish.
> Sweep walkways.
> Care for kindergarten animals.
> Nail a plank across two logs to make a bench.
> Saw wood or branches.
> Sand (*schmirgeln*) wooden toys.
> Mend toys, fences, furniture, etc.
> Build a climbing ladder.

Summer
> Wash outdoor tools, toys, furniture.
> Weed the garden.
> Water the plants.

4 WRITING

Your British friend is a trainee kindergarten teacher. He has asked you about the German childcare system.

Write an email to your friend.

1 Define these terms and any others that you think would be useful.

> Kinderkrippe ▪ Kita ▪ Schulhort ▪ Spielgruppe ▪ Waldorfkindergarten ▪ Waldkindergarten

> Our children are here from the age of ... to ...

> In our nursery, we look after ...

> This kind of nursery is for children who ...

2 Describe the daily routine (including activities) in a kindergarten that you know.

> The day starts at ...

> In the morning, ...

> The children's favourite activities are ...

> At break time, the children like to ...

> In the afternoon ...

Useful vocabulary

Types of pre-school education	
crèche	Krippe
kindergarten	Kindergarten
nursery school	Kindergarten
playgroup	Spielgruppe

Activities in pre-school education	
acting	Schauspielerei
art and craft	Kunsthandwerk
board game	Brettspiel
break time	Pause
building bricks	Backsteine bauen
colour in a picture	ein Bild ausmalen
counting	Rechnen
cuddly toy	Kuscheltier
cutting and sticking	Schneiden und Kleben
doll	Puppe
doll's house	Puppenhaus
dress up	sich verkleiden
excursion	Ausflug
fire drill	Probealarm
modelling clay	Knete, Knetmasse
nursery rhyme	Kinderlied, -reim, -vers
painting	Malerei
play cooperatively	gemeinschaftlich, kooperativ spielen
playground	Spielplatz

playground equipment	Spielplatzausstattung
puppet	Puppe, Marionette
sandpit	Sandkasten
singalong	gemeinsames Lieder-singen
slide (n.)	Rutsche
snack time	Brotzeit, Zwischenmahlzeit
storytime	Geschichtenzeit
structured play	strukturiertes Spielen
supervise	beaufsichtigen
supervision	Aufsicht
swimming lesson	Schwimmstunde
toy	Spielzeug-
~ boat	boot
~ car	auto
~ plane	flugzeug
~ train	zug
traffic safety	Verkehrssicherheit

Developing skills in pre-school education	
learn ... skills	... Fertigkeiten lernen
creative	kreative
motor	motorische
literacy	Lese- und Schreib-
numeracy	rechnerische
social	soziale

9

Social work: creativity

4 18

Tales of the unexpected

Contributions to a creative writing project for unemployed people reveal the rich stories 'ordinary' people have to tell, and the diversity of their experiences.

5 It is 2.30 on a grey Thursday afternoon and a dozen people are gathered around a long, low table in a plain-looking room. Before them lie files, A4 printouts and handwritten notes. A middle-aged man is reading out a short story about his memory of a
10 childhood trip to Butlins holiday camp.

A unique collection of autobiographical stories by people who have experienced poverty, mental illness, addiction and other forms of hardship, *Salt and Vinegar* is the result of a series of workshops at
15 the Brighton Unemployed Centre Families Project. The charity is run by and for the unemployed, unwaged and low-waged.

Like most of his fellow contributors to *Salt and Vinegar*, James* has experienced difficult, lonely times. 20

'I've been coming to creative writing classes since 1993,' James says. 'The centre was a friendly and cheap place to go for someone who didn't have a lot of money, and provided some structure to the day.'

For others, it has been even more of a lifeline. 25 'I was in despair, lower than low,' explains Chris, 54, recalling the day, nine months ago, when he first visited the centre in search of help with his CV. 'I wanted to come alive again. Within three hours, I'd had a hot meal. I came here full of sorrow, 30 and left with a smile on my face.'

Chris is dyslexic and learned to read and write in his 20s. Four years ago, his marriage broke down. He struggled with depression, insomnia and alcoholism. 35

His stories, all short ('I don't like to be complicated'), have an honesty and clarity that more experienced writers might envy. In one piece, 'Home', he writes of his former home: 'The front door as it opened it gave me a feeling of being wanted. And at times that door 40 frame seemed to smile at me after a hard day's work.'

Jenny couldn't be more of a contrast to Chris. She's 29, confident and streetwise. She has written four pieces describing her experiences of abortion and 45 heroin addiction. 'The abortion was in London when I was 18,' she says. 'I was with someone at the time. I really loved the guy, but he wasn't very nice.'

As one contributor says, 'Salt and Vinegar proves 50 you don't have to be famous to tell your story. Ordinary people have stories to tell, too.'   (413 words)

Adapted and abridged from: www.guardian.co.uk/society   *People's names in this article have been changed

1 LOOKING AT THE TEXT

Match these speech bubbles to the people from the text.

Jenny
James
Chris
the project leader
a reader of *Salt and Vinegar*

> **1** *The writers may be "ordinary" people, but I found their stories extraordinary.*

> **2** *The workshop has really helped me to fight depression.*

> **3** *While working on this project, I think I've probably learned as much as the participants have.*

> **4** *Drugs used to be a big part of my life.*

> **5** *I have been learning creative writing for many years now.*

2 WORKING WITH WORDS

Copy and complete the table.

	Noun	Verb	Adjective
1	...	...	creative (line 1)
2	memory (line 9)	...	...
3	help (line 28)	...	...
4	...	...	alive (line 29)
5	clarity (line 37)	...	...
6	...	describe (line 46)	...

3 DISCUSSION

Discuss in a group.

1 How can writing be a form of therapy for people who have had difficult experiences?

2 Why is it better for such people to take part in a writing workshop, rather than writing alone?

4 WRITING

Write a short story based on Chris's or Jenny's experiences. You can use the key words below and/or your own ideas.

Chris

argue with wife ▪ divorce ▪ drink too much ▪ lose job ▪
become homeless ▪ visit Brighton Unemployed Centre ▪
get involved in creative writing project ▪
write articles for local paper ▪
start to have hope for the future

meet Josh at a nightclub ▪
quarrel with parents about Josh ▪
leave home ▪ find out that pregnant ▪
Josh – refuse to take responsibility ▪
have an abortion ▪ leave Josh ▪
suffer from depression ▪
starts taking drugs ▪
parents – persuade to come back home ▪
forgive each other

Jenny

5 MEDIATION

 You are very impressed by the work of the Brighton Unemployed Centre Families Project. In the future, you and some other students would like to set up a similar project where you live.

You are a preparing a letter to your local authority, in which you want to outline the basic features of the British project. Select relevant information from the text below and draft your letter in German. Do not translate word for word.

Brighton Unemployed Centre Families Project

◆ The Centre was set up in 1981. Brighton Unemployed Centre Families Project became a registered charity in 1994 and is run by the unemployed for the unemployed. We provide practical support, education and recreation for those in poor housing, claimants, unwaged people and those on low incomes.

◆ We provide a wide range of courses and classes, a crèche, refreshments and lunches, welfare and benefit advice, temporary housing support, volunteer opportunities and much more.

◆ Our courses are run for unemployed and unwaged people. This includes all benefit claimants (including pensioners and those in low-paid work who receive benefits) and anyone who doesn't have a wage coming in (e.g. travellers, people whose partners work but don't themselves, 16 – 18 year olds not in work, etc.). Other people may come on our courses if there is a space not required by an unwaged person.

◆ Although regular attendance is encouraged, for most courses we run there is no need to book in advance, simply turn up on the day (with the exception of computer courses, which must be booked in advance). Unless stated in the individual course information, each session costs £2, £2.50 or £3 for some longer sessions.

Source: www.bucfp.org

Useful vocabulary

Psychological problems

addiction	*Sucht, Abhängigkeit*
addict	*Abhängige/r, Süchtig/er*
alcoholism	*Alkoholismus*
alcoholic	*Alkoholiker/in*
binge drinking	*Besäufnis/Sauferei*
despair	*Verzweiflung*
desperate	*verzweifelt*
hopelessness	*Hoffnungslosigkeit*
mental illness	*psychische Erkrankung*
social isolation	*soziale Isolation*
suicide attempt	*Selbstmordversuch*

Unemployment and low-paid work

unemployed	*arbeitslos*
unwaged	*ohne Einkommen*
low-waged	*mit niedrigem Einkommen*
low-paid	*schlecht bezahlt*
claimant	*Antragsteller/in*

Therapy

argue	*sich streiten*
counselling session	*Beratungsgespräch*
detox clinic	*Suchtklinik*
get sth off one's chest	*etw loswerden*

life coach	*Lebensberater/in*
mentor	*Mentor/in, Berater/in*
occupational therapy	*Beschäftigungstherapie*
self-help group	*Selbsthilfegruppe*
share one's experiences	*seine Erfahrungen jdm anvertrauen*
support group	*Selbsthilfegruppe*
therapist	*Therapeut/in*

Outcomes of therapy

become drug-free/ alcohol-free	*clean werden*
change one's behaviour	*sein Verhalten ändern*
find closure	*etw verarbeiten können*
get clean (sl.)	*clean werden*
get one's life back together	*sein Leben wieder in den Griff bekommen*
have a relapse	*einen Rückfall erleiden, rückfällig werden*
have hope for the future	*Zukunftsaussichten haben*

10

Education: multicultural schools

20

Schools can only benefit from bilingual pupils

Amanda Livingstone,* headteacher of Fordbridge primary school* in Newham

Like many schools across the capital, Fordbridge, in Newham, East London, is a large multicultural primary school. More than 70% of our children speak English as a second language and we have 42 languages represented from 35 different countries – a reflection of the diversity of Newham's population.

Some may feel concerned about this mix of languages and cultures, but as headteacher of this lively learning community, I see this linguistic and cultural diversity as one of our greatest strengths.

It inspires me that the majority of my pupils are bilingual or multilingual. The knowledge and skills that the children have in their first language can be a great help when they learn English.

In fact, the children's bilingualism is a real positive factor in their education, and their thirst for knowledge and learning is something their monolingual classmates benefit greatly from. We need to firmly squash this urban myth that limited language ability is the same as limited ability to think.

In London, it is pleasing to see that many of our highest achieving schools have large numbers of children who speak English as a second language. Walking into these schools, there is a happy buzz of learning, and the teaching is innovative and exciting. A culturally-inclusive curriculum promotes equality of access to learning.

Our families new to the UK fully understand that a good education will increase their children's life choices. Our parents are very supportive and keen to promote education within their households. This is a well-trodden path, followed by economic and political migrants into this country over several generations.

We have a lot to learn from the excellent practice that we see in our multicultural schools. Funding is necessary to support children in the earliest stages of learning English.

It is right that the government emphazises the importance of modern foreign language teaching in our schools. In this respect, our multicultural schools with many bilingual pupils have a head start in their learning. These pupils are highly skilled and have much to offer our communities.

(338 words)

*Names in this blog have been changed. Adapted and abridged from guardian.co.uk

1 MEDIATION

You are preparing to take part in a panel discussion about multiculturalism in primary education. You want to take Amanda Livingstone's school as an example of a successful multicultural primary school.

Answer the following questions in German, using relevant information from the text.
Do not translate word for word.

1 Who is Amanda Livingstone and to what extent is his school multicultural?
2 In what ways are the bilingual and multilingual pupils different, and why is this also beneficial for their monolingual fellow pupils?
3 What do many successful London schools have in common?
4 How are equal opportunities promoted in these schools?
5 Historically, what have immigrant families always clearly understood?
6 What is the British government trying to promote, and why do Amanda Livingstone's pupils have an advantage here?

2 WORKING WITH WORDS

Define these words and expressions from the text in your own words in English.

1 diversity (*line 8*)
2 bilingual (*line 16*)
3 urban myth (*line 25*)
4 culturally-inclusive curriculum (*line 34*)
5 promote (*line 35*)
6 migrant (*line 44*)
7 emphasize (*line 52*)
8 head start (*line 55*)

3 GROUP WORK

Work in a group.

In contrast to Amanda Livingstone, some parents are worried about multicultural schools and feel that their children might not get the best education by attending them. Is this purely prejudice, or are there good arguments for not sending your children to a multicultural school?

Write a list of possible advantages and disadvantages of multicultural schools.
For each disadvantage, write down some ideas for how the problem could be solved.

4 LOOKING AT STATISTICS

The chart shows exam results for 2,279 11-year-old pupils in Lambeth, a part of London. Comment on the statistics. To what extent do they support Amanda Livingstone's argument?

*Level 4 = the expected level for pupils at age 11

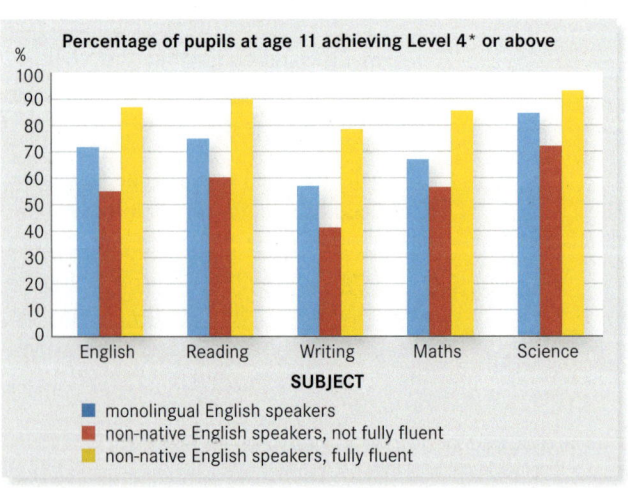

Percentage of pupils at age 11 achieving Level 4* or above

■ monolingual English speakers
■ non-native English speakers, not fully fluent
■ non-native English speakers, fully fluent

5 ROLE-PLAY

Work with a partner.

Student A You are working in London. You have a young son and you want him to go to a school where he will learn good English. You have heard that the local primary school is very multicultural and that many of the pupils don't speak English as their first language. You are worried about this.

Student B You are a teacher at the local primary school. Listen to the parent's concerns and explain the advantages of a multicultural school to him/her.

6 WRITING

Imagine you are working as a nursery nurse in an inner-city nursery in Germany where many of the children's first language is not German. How will you help them to prepare for the pre-school German test? (Even if your region hasn't introduced this test, imagine what you would do to help the children to prepare.)

Write a post about your ideas on an international internet forum for nursery nurses. The language of the forum is English.

Useful vocabulary

Multicultural society

asylum seeker	*Asylbewerber/in*
bilingual	*bilingual, zweisprachig*
break down barriers	*Hindernisse aus dem Weg räumen*
cultural heritage	*Kulturerbe*
cultural melting pot	*kultureller Schmelztiegel*
discriminate against	*diskriminieren, benachteiligen*
diversity	*Vielfalt*
ethnic minority	*ethnische Minderheit*
ignorance	*Unwissenheit, Ignoranz*
ignorant	*unwissend, ungebildet*
integrate	*integrieren, eingliedern*
mainstream society	*Mainstream-Gesellschaft*
multi-ethnic	*Mehrvölker-…, multi-ethnisch*
multilingual	*mehrsprachig, multilingual*
prejudice	*Vorurteil*
question stereotypes	*Stereotypen/Klischees in Frage stellen*
race relations	*Beziehungen zwischen ethnischen Gruppen*
racial harmony	*Harmonie zwischen verschiedenen ethnischen Gruppen*
racial tension	*Spannung zwischen verschiedenen ethnischen Gruppen*

racism	*Rassismus*
refugee	*Flüchtling*
stigmatise	*brandmarken*
tolerance	*Toleranz*
urban myth	*moderne Legende*

Teaching and learning

be disadvantaged	*benachteiligt sein*
communication skills	*kommunikative Fertigkeiten*
culturally inclusive	*kulturell eingeschlossen*
encouragement	*Ermutigung, Unterstützung, Förderung*
evaluate	*bewerten, beurteilen*
intellectual development	*geistige Entwicklung*
language acquisition	*Spracherwerb*
literacy	*Lese- und Schreibfertigkeit*
numeracy	*Rechnen*
proficiency	*Leistung, Können*
reading skills	*Lesefertigkeit*
reasoning ability	*Fähigkeit, logisch zu denken*
stretch a student	*eine(n) Schüler(in) fordern*
teaching strategy	*Lehrstrategie*

11

Youth work: foster care

You call this home?

by Laura Gomez*, 16

My mom and I don't get along. When I lived with her, we were always arguing. When things got really bad, she'd kick me out at night with nowhere to go but the park. Finally, a year and a half ago, I moved out of my house and went into foster care.

It's hard for the foster care system to find foster homes for teenagers because most foster parents want young kids, so a social worker asked me if I wanted to live with a family member or go to a group home. At my family members' houses there would still be problems, so I chose to go to a group home.

My group home is a big house where six girls, who are in foster care, live with staff members who change shifts every eight to 10 hours. The staff are responsible for watching us, making sure the house is clean and cooking dinner. Each girl has a roommate. We have chores and eat together at the dinner table, but that's about all my group home has in common with living like a family.

There are some good things. I get a therapist to talk to and I know the group home can't kick me out, like my mom would. I also like getting to know the girls who move in.

But in a group home there are too many rules and no freedom to do what normal teenagers do, like hang out with friends. And most of the staff members are not respectful.

You have to ask permission for everything, like to get food from the fridge, cook, watch TV, use the phone, go in the backyard or take a shower (the staff say there is a schedule). How can you feel at home when you have to ask to eat or can't go outside unless you have a staff member with you? It feels like a place where people go to work instead of a normal home.

During the school year we can't go out after school, unless we have an educational activity and then we have to be home by 7p.m. We can go out on the weekends but we have to be back by 10p.m.

Also, the clothing allowance is $50 a month, which isn't that bad if I save it. But my weekly allowance is only $7 to $10. Being a teenager I have a lot of expenses, like hygiene products, my cell phone, movies and buying things from the mall. Seven dollars doesn't get me anywhere.

I interviewed another housemate, Jade*, who suggested ways to make the group home better. She said, "Minimize some of the rules and restrictions, take us out more to places we enjoy, give us a responsible amount of money per week and make us feel at home instead of in jail. Give us more freedom and let us enjoy our lives as kids."

Not all group homes are bad. But a lot of group homes are not run with as much care as they should be. Group homes should be a place where foster youth can grow up, feel like they belong and get help with their issues of being away from their families. But all they are is a place to sleep. A group home doesn't feel like a home.

(555 words)

Lightly adapted and abridged from *LA Youth*   (*Names in this article have been changed)

1 WORKING WITH WORDS

A newspaper journalist is interviewing Laura about her experience of the group home.
Complete the dialogue with terms from the box. There are three terms that you don't need. (The words are all used in the text.)

freedom ▪ group home ▪ in jail ▪ place to sleep ▪ respectful ▪ responsible ▪ restrictions ▪ schedule ▪ staff ▪ staff member ▪ teenagers

REPORTER So do you regret your decision to move into a ...**1**?

LAURA Well, I wouldn't say that exactly. The problem is that it feels like just a ...**2** and it should be more like a real home.

REPORTER How do you mean?

LAURA Well, the ...**3** aren't as ...**4** as they should be.

REPORTER I see. And is there anything else?

LAURA Yes. There are too many rules and ...**5**. Sometimes it feels like being ...**6**. We just want to be normal ...**7** and have the same amount of ...**8** as other kids of our age.

2 LOOKING AT STATISTICS

Interpret the statistics shown in the two charts. Use the phrases below.

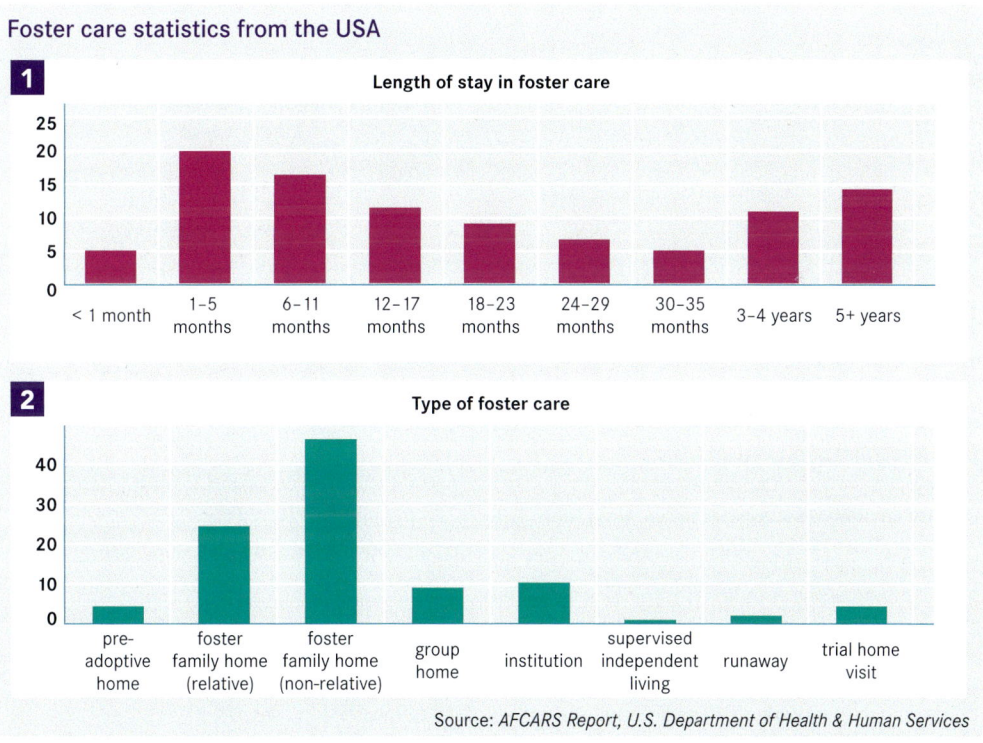

Foster care statistics from the USA

1 Length of stay in foster care

2 Type of foster care

Source: *AFCARS Report, U.S. Department of Health & Human Services*

In ... per cent of cases, children The most/least common type of ...	stay in foster care foster care is	for a short/long period.
This This	is might be	worrying because	when we consider that ...

3 ROLE PLAY

Work with a partner.

Student A You are a young person in a group home. You would like more freedom and some improvements to the home. Speak to a member of staff. Be polite and make positive suggestions.

Student B You are a staff member in the home. You have to maintain discipline in the home and ensure that the housemates are safe. Respond to your partner's complaints in a friendly way, but make sure he/she understands your point of view. Try to reach a compromise.

4 DISCUSSION

Work in a group. Choose either Task A or Task B.

Student A How do you think that care for people like Laura could be improved? Make a list of recommendations.

Student B Write a list of social rules that you think are suitable for a group home.

Useful vocabulary

In a group home

antisocial behaviour	*unsoziales Verhalten*
atmosphere	*Atmosphäre*
be a friend to s.o.	*jdm ein/e Freund/in sein*
caring	*fürsorglich, liebevoll*
considerate	*rücksichtsvoll*
curfew	*Ausgangssperre, Sperr-stunde*
environment	*Umfeld, Umgebung*
get along well/badly	*sich gut/schlecht vertragen, auskommen*
help someone with problems/issues	*jdm helfen, der Probleme hat*
housemate	*Mitbewohner/in*
inconsiderate	*rücksichtslos*
neighbour	*Nachbar/in*
offer a shoulder to cry on	*sich anbieten als jd, bei dem man sich ausweinen kann*
petty	*kleinlich*
rebel against sth	*gegen etw rebellieren*
responsible	*verantwortlich, verant-wortungsvoll*
roommate	*Zimmernachbar/in (AE), Zimmergenosse/in (BE)*
set boundaries/guidelines	*Grenzen, Richtlinien setzen*
share the good times and the bad	*gute und schlechte Zeiten miteinander verbringen*

sociable	*gesellig, umgänglich, gesellschaftsfähig*
supportive	*unterstützend*
take responsibility for one's actions	*für sich selbst die Verant-wortung übernehmen*
tense	*angespannt*
thoughtful	*bedacht, nachdenklich, rücksichtsvoll*
unsociable	*nicht umgänglich, ungesellig*

Household chores

do one's fair share	*den gerechten Anteil übernehmen*
do the cooking	*kochen*
do the shopping	*einkaufen*
do the dishes / washing up	*Geschirr spülen*
do the washing/laundry	*Wäsche waschen*
draw up a rota	*einen Dienstplan aufstellen*
lay the table	*den Tisch decken*
mow the lawn	*Rasen mähen*
prepare meals	*Essen machen*
sort the rubbish (BE)/garbage (AE) for recycling	*den Müll zum Recycling trennen*
tidy up	*aufräumen*

Social projects: success!

The Youth Hall of Fame
Young people who are making a difference

Rachel May*, 17, from Vienna, Virginia, is the founder of ROAR (Reach Out and Read), an organization of student volunteers who collect and distribute used books to homeless shelters and facilities where there are children who cannot afford books of their own.

Rachel, who has overcome dyslexia, knows how important it is for children to read. 'Reading is the basis of knowledge,' she said, 'so I wanted to help make sure that needy children would have books to read.'

She began by contacting homeless shelters to see if they needed books, and when several responded, Rachel held her first drive four years ago. Its success prompted her to begin recruiting student volunteers to help her promote future book drives, collect and sort donated books, and get them into the hands of under- privileged kids.

Now she has collected more than 20,000 books and set up libraries at shelters, daycare centers, and elementary schools in Virginia, Washington, D.C., and Maryland. She also sent 400 books to a small town in South Dakota after a tornado destroyed its library.

Jeremy Leon*, 17, from Phoenix, Arizona, survived a rough childhood in an inner-city neighborhood and went on to develop a program that is now helping to keep other at-risk teens in his old school away from crime and drugs.

When he was young, Jeremy's mother struggled with drug and alcohol addiction and an inability to care for her children. Jeremy was recruited by neighborhood gangs, but was ultimately 'saved' by a school counselor who later adopted him.

In his new family, Jeremy began to think of the kids in his old neighborhood who did not have the opportunities he now enjoys. 'I decided to do something to help them and to honor my parents,' he said. He approached a police officer working at his former school and became a volunteer mentor. He soon put together a plan to organize neighborhood clean-ups and to teach kids swimming, soccer, healthy eating and CPR**. Other students have since signed on to help Jeremy, and his program, *School Buddies*, now also offers after-school tutoring and recreation activities during school breaks. Jeremy plans to start a foundation soon, named after his adoptive parents, to provide college scholarships to children from his old neighborhood.

Adapted extracts from www.thekidshalloffame.com
(380 words)
*People's names in the article have been changed   ** Cardio Pulmonary Resuscitation

1 LOOKING AT THE TEXT

Choose the correct answer(s).

1 Rachel understands the value of reading because …
   a her parents couldn't afford any books.
   b she didn't have any books when she was homeless.
   c she had to struggle with a learning difficulty as a child.

2 ROAR began when …
   a homeless people asked Rachel for books.
   b Rachel found out that homeless shelters were eager to have books.
   c students donated some books to Rachel.

3 Jeremy spent his childhood …
   a in a tough part of town.
   b partly with a mother who was addicted to drink and drugs.
   c in a home for young criminals.

4 When he was older, Jeremy …
   a decided to help underprivileged kids like himself.
   b went back to his old school as a full-time teacher.
   c went to college on a scholarship paid for by a police officer.

5 The *School Buddies* programme …
   a needs more financial support.
   b provides things for children to do during school breaks.
   c provides scholarships for students to go to college.

2 WORKING WITH WORDS

Complete the sentences with the opposites of the <u>underlined</u> words. There may be more than one correct answer.

1 After initial <u>success</u>, the programme turned out to be a …
2 Hopefully my … mistakes will be the basis for <u>future</u> success.
3 When they have <u>collected</u> enough books, they'll … them to homeless people.
4 His <u>childhood</u> was difficult, and unfortunately things didn't get much easier for him in …

3 CARTOON

Analyze this cartoon and contrast its view of young people with the real teenagers featured on page 189.

The language in the box may help you.

At first glance, the cartoon seems to suggest that … ▮
However, the caption below the cartoon makes it clear that … ▮
Whilst the young people featured in … may not be typical, … ▮
In my opinion, it is unfortunate that … / important to …

4 PRESENTATION

Work in groups.

Can you think of somebody who should be in the Youth Hall of Fame? He/she should be under 20 and should have achieved something extraordinary. The achievement can be in any area.
It could be someone you know (or yourself!), a person in the media or a person from history.
In your presentation, explain who the person is, his/her background, what the achievement is and what you think is extraordinary about it.

Useful vocabulary

Family background		find a way to do sth	eine Möglichkeit finden, etw zu tun
adopt	adoptieren	improve the lives of others	das Leben anderer verbessern
advantaged/ privileged background	privilegierte Familien-verhältnisse	invent sth	etw erfinden, sich etw ausdenken
broken home	zerrüttetes Zuhause	make a contribution to ~	einen Beitrag ... leisten
difficult childhood	schwierige Kindheit	~ art	zur Kunst
disadvantaged/ underprivileged background	benachteiligte Familien-verhältnisse/ Vergangenheit	~ the community	zur Gemeinschaft
		~ music	zur Musik
encourage	ermutigen, unterstützen, fördern	~ science	zur Wissenschaft
foster	in Pflege nehmen	~ society	zur Gesellschaft
poor neighbour-hood	arme Wohngegend	overcome	... überwinden
		~ difficulties	Schwierigkeiten
		~ disadvantages	Benachteiligungen
Personal qualities		~ setbacks	Rückschläge
determined	entschlossen	put together ~	... aufstellen, erstellen
generous	großzügig	~ a plan	einen Plan
gifted	begabt, talentiert	~ a programme	ein Programm
highly motivated	hochmotiviert	receive ~	... bekommen, erhalten
independent	unabhängig	~ an award	eine Auszeichnung
inventive	einfallsreich	~ a medal	eine Medaille, einen Orden
show initiative	Initiative zeigen		
selfless	selbstlos, uneigennützig	~ a prize	einen Preis
		set up ~	... aufbauen, organisieren
Achievements		~ a charity	eine Wohltätigkeits-organisation
donate sth	etw spenden		
		~ foundation	Stiftung

Files

FILE 1 Unit 3, exercise 3C, p. 58

Debbie

Personally, you would prefer the romantic comedy, and you particularly dislike science fiction, but you will watch it if that's what Dave wants. And anyway, you will accept the majority decision. You agree with Dave that a late movie would be a bad idea.

You would like to eat something before the film as you haven't had anything since breakfast.

role card

FILE 2 Unit 4, exercise 3, p. 71

Road commuter

You want much better public transport *before* congestion charging starts. You know that as things are, public transport can only carry up to 13% of commuters like you. You cannot afford to pay the daily congestion charge – (you know the figure for London is about £15 per day) – and you do not want to fight to find a place on public transport buses or trains every day.

role card

FILE 3 Unit 8, Focus, p. 105

1B | 2A | 3B | 4B | 5B | 6B (2008) | 7B | 8C

FILE 4 Unit 7, Culture Check, p. 98

a) EA | b) LA | c) NA | d) NA | e) EA

FILE 5 Unit 4, exercise 3, p. 71

City councillor

As the chairperson of the meeting, you must make sure everyone speaks and help the meeting come to an agreement. You think that congestion charging is necessary, but you worry that it will cause terrible problems. You need the government money to help develop public transport, but you can only provide the city's 50% of the money from congestion charges. The city has no other spare money.

role card

FILE 6 Unit 3, exercise 3C, p. 58

Dave

You are more interested in driving than anything else today, and you don't really mind which film you go to – although you would quite like to see *Journey to the Stars*. However, you don't want to go to a late showing because you know your dad will be worried about the car. (You want to make sure he will lend you it many, many more times!)

role card

1 Nationwide general trends

U.S. crime statistics

According to the FBI's Preliminary Semiannual Uniform Crime Report, the nation experienced a 1.8 percent drop in violent crime and a 2.6 percent drop in property crime during the first six months of 2007 compared to the same period in 2006.

■ **Crime by region**
Percent change by geographic region

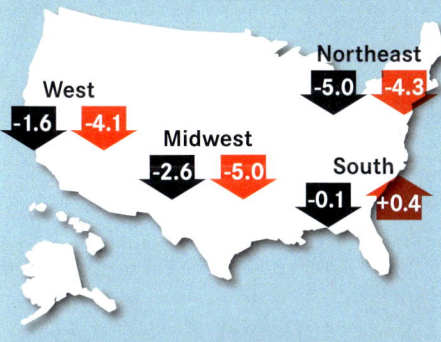

⬇ Violent crime   ⬇ Property crime

■ **Violent Crime**
Each of the violent crime offense categories decreased nationwide from January 2007 when compared to the corresponding months in 2006.

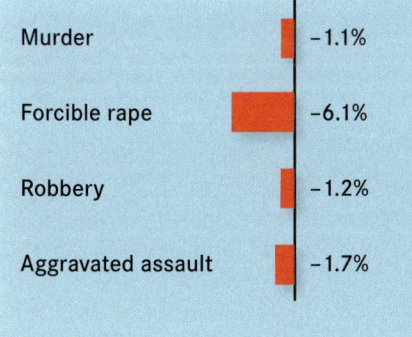

Murder — 1.1%

Forcible rape — 6.1%

Robbery — 1.2%

Aggravated assault — 1.7%

Source: U.S. Department of Justice, Bureau of Justice Statistics, http://www.ojp.usdoj.gov/bjs/

2 Violent crime

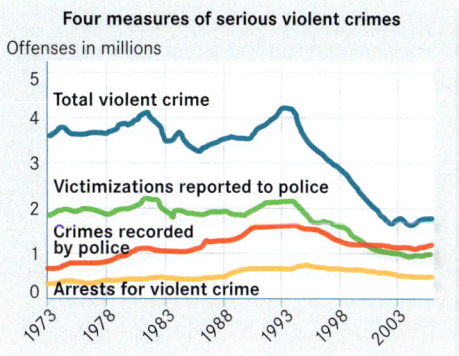

Serious violent crimes are 1) rape, 2) robbery, 3) armed assault and 4) homicide

Source: National Crime Victimization Survey

3 Homicide

4 Crime reported to the police

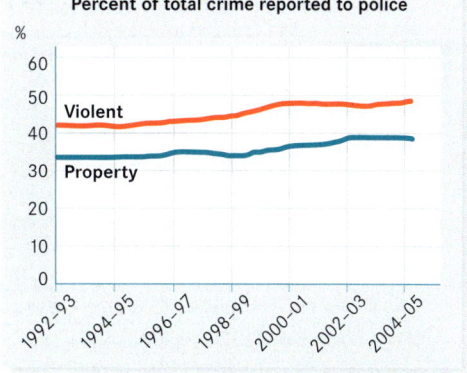

Source: http://www.fbi.gov/headlines/uscrimestatistics

FILE 8   Unit 3, exercise 3C, p. 58

Steve

You helped yourself to several things from the fridge before Claire arrived, so you're not hungry at all at the moment. Of all three films, you would much prefer to see *Pirates of the Caribbean*. (You have seen all the other 'Pirates' films at least twice each.) However, you know that Claire doesn't like *Pirates of the Caribbean*, and you don't want to have an argument with her. On the other hand, if you can quietly persuade Steve, then Debbie will probably agree with him – and then Claire will have to agree too.

role card

FILE 9   Unit 4, exercise 3, p. 71

Businessperson

You fear a large loss of trade, especially as car parking is already expensive in the city centre and the costs of running the business are high. You want the city councillor to understand clearly that if you have to close down, the city will lose your business rates (= local taxes). There may be thousands more like you.

role card

FILE 10   Unit 7, Focus, p. 95

 Australia   China   the EU

 Germany   India   Japan

 Poland   the UK   the USA

FILE 11   Unit 3, exercise 3C, p. 58

Claire

You would much prefer *One Night in New York*, and you think *Pirates of the Caribbean* is very silly – definitely something for 13-year-old boys. You are hungry and would quite like to eat before the film.

role card

FILE 12   Unit 4, exercise 3, p. 71

Government transport official

You accept that congestion charging will cause problems for some people but believe that it must be part of the answer to the congestion problem. You can provide government money to help develop public transport if the city council provides the other 50%.

role card

Appendix

Skills

REZEPTION

Lesen schwieriger Texte

Texte werden zu unterschiedlichen Zwecken gelesen. Manchmal braucht man nur zu wissen, worum es geht, dann reicht in der Regel ein aufmerksames Überfliegen des Textes. Oft müssen gezielt Informationen herausgesucht werden, dann kommt es darauf an, die richtigen Schlüsselwörter zu finden. Will man sich gründlich mit einem Text auseinandersetzen, um z. B. Fragen zu beantworten oder einen Aufsatz dazu zu schreiben, ist gründliches, möglicherweise zweimaliges Lesen erforderlich.

Grobverständnis: Sich einen schnellen Überblick über einen Text verschaffen

Manchmal werden Sie im Buch aufgefordert, einen Text schnell zu lesen, um das Thema grob zu erfassen.

1. Schritt: Suchen Sie nach Anhaltspunkten, die Ihnen Aufschluss über den Textinhalt geben: Titel und Zwischenüberschriften, fett gedruckte Wörter, Bilder und Bildunterschriften.

2. Schritt: Sind Sie noch unsicher, lesen Sie die ersten und letzten Sätze jedes Absatzes. Bleiben Sie nicht an Einzelwörtern, schwierigen Zitaten usw. hängen.

Suche nach Einzelinformationen im Text

Bei vielen Textverständnisfragen oder Aufgaben vom Typ *True or false* geht es darum, schnell bestimmte Informationen im Text zu finden und nicht jedesmal den ganzen Text neu zu lesen.

1. Schritt: Suchen Sie den Text nach Schlüsselbegriffen für die gesuchten Informationen ab. Geht es etwa um die Meinung des Autors zu einem bestimmten Thema, halten Sie nach Wörtern wie *think, believe, opinion* usw. Ausschau. Geht es um Informationen zu einem Thema, rufen Sie sich ein paar Schlüsselbegriffe in Erinnerung, nach denen Sie Ausschau halten. Manchmal hilft es, sich den gesuchten Begriff als gedrucktes Wort vor dem geistigen Auge vorzustellen.

2. Schritt: Gehen Sie falls nötig mit dem Finger die Zeilen entlang, während Sie suchen. Wenn Sie sich wie oben beschrieben vorbereitet haben, springen Ihnen die gesuchten Begriffe sofort ins Auge.

Detailverständnis: Gründliches Lesen

Lesen Sie nicht einfach drauflos. Ein paar einfache Schritte helfen Ihnen, den Text besser zu verstehen, ohne sich in Details zu verlieren.

1. Schritt: Der erste Schritt sollte darin bestehen, sich ein grobes Verständnis vom Textinhalt zu verschaffen (siehe oben). So werden Sie unklare Stellen besser in den Gesamtzusammenhang einordnen können. Es ist hilfreich, sich die wichtigsten Stichwörter kurz zu notieren. Zu dem Text *A step too far* auf S. 136 etwa könnten Sie nach kurzem Überfliegen aufschreiben: *The text is about the death penalty in the United States, in particular about the first woman who was executed.*

2. Schritt: Machen Sie sich die Struktur des Textes bewusst. Wo ist die Einleitung? Welcher Teil enthält die Hauptinformationen, und wie sind sie aufgebaut (Zwischenüberschriften, Absätze usw.)? Achten Sie auf Strukturwörter wie *only, but while, that's why, while, however* usw., mit denen der Verfasser seine Argumentation gliedert.

3. Schritt: Lesen Sie den Text nun aufmerksam. Notieren Sie sich Schlüsselstellen, z.B: *Karla Faye Tucker – first woman to be executed in the US; executed in Texas on 3 February 1998; case attracted a lot of interest – some felt because she was white, attractive and showed remorse (married a priest and became a Christian); many pleas for clemency to Governor Bush from different groups and even from the Pope.* Schlagen Sie Wörter beim ersten Lesen nur nach, wenn die Bedeutung des ganzen Satzes an ihnen hängt. Oft lässt sich die wesentliche Bedeutung durch den Kontext erschließen.

4. Schritt: Notieren Sie sich den Textinhalt in strukturierter Form, etwa einer Mind Map oder einer Liste (Themen, pro/kontra). Fügen Sie auch Formulierungen hinzu, die Ihnen später helfen, sich in eigenen Worten über den Textinhalt zu äußern. Schlagen Sie jetzt das notwendige Vokabular nach. **>** Note Making S. 201, Mind Mapping S. 202

Umgang mit unbekannten Vokabeln

Fragen Sie sich bei neuen Vokabeln immer, ob sie für das Verständnis des Zusammenhangs unbedingt notwendig sind. Nachschlagen kostet Zeit und hilft oft nicht beim Verständnis des wirklich Wichtigen.

Erschließen der Bedeutung aus dem Kontext

> Ein Wort, das unbekannt scheint, kann z.B. mit einem anderen, Ihnen bekannten Wort verwandt sein (Ableitungen wie *aggressor* von *aggressive*). Oder das Wort hat einen bekannten Wortstamm und einen angehängten Wortteil, mit dessen Hilfe Sie die Bedeutung erkennen können (*formal – **in**formal, clockwise – **anti**clockwise, change – change**able**, stupid – stupid**ity***). Manche Wörter haben Ähnlichkeiten mit einem deutschen Wort (vgl.etwa *initial* und „Initialen", *potential* und „potenziell").

> Sind Sie sich immer noch nicht sicher, kann der Satzzusammenhang Aufschluss geben. Machen Sie sich zunächst die Wortart bewusst: Suchen Sie nach einem Substantiv? Wofür steht das gesuchte Substantiv wahrscheinlich – für ein Gebäude? Eine Person? Handelt es sich um ein Adjektiv, das die Situation näher beschreibt oder jemanden charakterisiert?
> Schauen Sie sich den folgenden Absatz an und versuchen Sie die Bedeutung der fett gedruckten Wörter aus dem Zusammenhang zu erschließen:
> *Business is bad at the moment and we don't expect it to **rally** for at least a year. All the signals are very **inauspicious**, I'm afraid.*
> Auch wenn man *rally* und *inauspicious* nicht kennt, kann man aus dem Kontext erschliessen, dass *rally* ein Verb ist, das eine positive Entwicklung beschreibt und *inauspicious* ein Adjektiv mit negativer Bedeutung ist

Umgang mit dem einsprachigen Wörterbuch

Machen Sie sich mit Ihrem Wörterbuch vertraut, so dass Sie die Symbole, Abkürzungen und die Lautschrift verstehen und die Hilfen, die vorne und hinten im Wörterbuch oder auf Zusatzseiten angeboten werden, nutzen können. Auf der folgenden Seite sehen Sie ein Beispiel eines typischen Wörtbucheintrags.

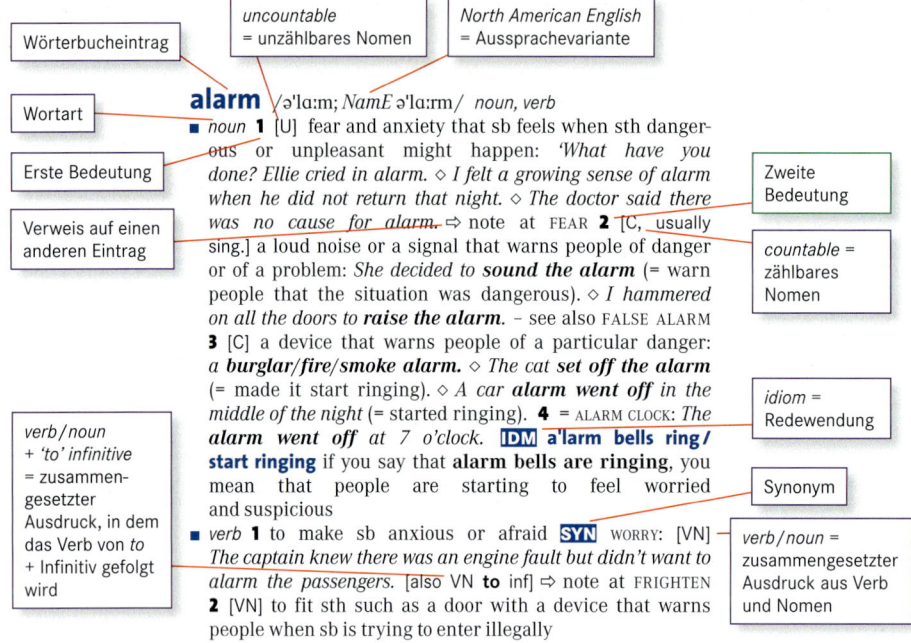

The following diagram labels point to parts of a dictionary entry for "alarm":

- Wörterbucheintrag
- uncountable = unzählbares Nomen
- North American English = Aussprachevariante
- Wortart
- Erste Bedeutung
- Verweis auf einen anderen Eintrag
- verb / noun + 'to' infinitive = zusammengesetzter Ausdruck, in dem das Verb von *to* + Infinitiv gefolgt wird
- Zweite Bedeutung
- countable = zählbares Nomen
- idiom = Redewendung
- Synonym
- verb / noun = zusammengesetzter Ausdruck aus Verb und Nomen

alarm /ə'lɑːm; *NamE* ə'lɑːrm/ *noun, verb*
- *noun* **1** [U] fear and anxiety that sb feels when sth dangerous or unpleasant might happen: *'What have you done? Ellie cried in alarm. ◇ I felt a growing sense of alarm when he did not return that night. ◇ The doctor said there was no cause for alarm.* ⇨ note at FEAR **2** [C, usually sing.] a loud noise or a signal that warns people of danger or of a problem: *She decided to* **sound the alarm** (= warn people that the situation was dangerous). ◇ *I hammered on all the doors to* **raise the alarm.** – see also FALSE ALARM **3** [C] a device that warns people of a particular danger: *a* **burglar/fire/smoke alarm.** ◇ *The cat* **set off the alarm** (= made it start ringing). ◇ *A car* **alarm went off** *in the middle of the night* (= started ringing). **4** = ALARM CLOCK: *The* **alarm went off** *at 7 o'clock.* **IDM a'larm bells ring/ start ringing** if you say that **alarm bells are ringing**, you mean that people are starting to feel worried and suspicious
- *verb* **1** to make sb anxious or afraid **SYN** WORRY: [VN] *The captain knew there was an engine fault but didn't want to alarm the passengers.* [also VN to inf] ⇨ note at FRIGHTEN **2** [VN] to fit sth such as a door with a device that warns people when sb is trying to enter illegally

> Notieren Sie sich alle Wörter, deren Bedeutung Sie suchen, und schlagen Sie dann alle hintereinander nach.

> Lesen Sie nicht den gesamten Eintrag, sondern beschränken Sie sich auf die Verwendung Ihres Stichworts in der gesuchten Wortart (z. B. Sie suchen *alarm* als Verb, also ignorieren Sie den ersten Teil des oben stehenden Eintrags). Den entsprechenden Abschnitt mit allen zusammengesetzten Ausdrücken und den Beispielsätzen, die Ihnen helfen zu unterscheiden, in welchen Zusammenhängen welche Bedeutung zutrifft, müssen Sie dann allerdings gründlich lesen.

> Schauen Sie sich auch die Einträge in der unmittelbaren Umgebung Ihres Stichworts an, um eine Vorstellung von dem Wortfeld zu bekommen.

> Notieren Sie sich die passende Bedeutung, damit Sie sie nicht wieder vergessen.

Lernen neuer Vokabeln

Es gibt verschiedene Möglichkeiten, Vokabeln zu lernen – suchen Sie sich die, die Ihnen am besten liegt. Eines gilt jedoch für alle Methoden: Wörter prägen sich am besten ein, wenn man nicht nur das Stichwort aufschreibt, sondern auch noch dazugehörige Ausdrücke, Synonyme, Gegenteile, verwandte Wörter und Verwendungsbeispiele, evtl. auch Aussprachehinweise. Besonders wichtig sind zusammengesetzte Ausdrücke. Dazu gehören auch *phrasal verbs* (*set about, put off* usw.). Der Eintrag für das Stichwort *pay* könnte z. B. so aussehen:

pay (noun)	–	*Bezahlung, Gehalt, Lohn*
payslip	–	*Gehaltsabrechnung*
pay day	–	*Zahltag*
pay-off	–	*Abfindung*
pay (verb)	–	*zahlen*
pay for sth	–	*etw bezahlen*
pay off	–	*auszahlen*
pay as you go (phone)	–	*Prepaid(-Handy)*

Natürlich brauchen Sie nicht gleich komplette Wörterbucheinträge aufzuschreiben. Überlegen Sie sich jedoch, welche Ableitungen Ihnen zu dem neuen Wort schon bekannt sein könnten oder in welchem zusammengesetzten Ausdruck es Ihnen begegnet ist. Lassen Sie Platz für spätere Hinzufügungen, so dass die Einträge nach und nach „wachsen".

Karteikarten: Sie benötigen Karteikarten und einen Karteikasten mit mehreren Abteilungen. Schreiben Sie das englische Wort mit den dazugehörigen Ergänzungen auf eine Seite einer Karteikarte und die deutschen Bedeutungen auf die Rückseite. Sobald Sie ein Wort wissen, wandert es von der ersten in die zweite Abteilung des Karteikastens. Die Wörter in der zweiten Abteilung schauen Sie sich in größeren Abständen nochmal an, um diejenigen, die Sie wissen, dann in die dritte Abteilung fürs Langzeitgedächtnis abzulegen. Was Sie nicht wissen, kommt zurück in die erste Abteilung, die Sie sich möglichst oft anschauen sollten.

Vokabelheft: Wenn Sie im Unterricht neue Vokabeln mitschreiben wollen, bietet sich ein Vokabelheft an. Benutzen Sie ein zweispaltiges Heft, damit Sie eine Spalte leicht bedecken können. Gestalten Sie das Lernen weniger schematisch, indem Sie die Seiten, die Sie lernen wollen, zufällig auswählen und ab und zu mal Deutsch–Englisch statt Englisch–Deutsch lernen.

Wortfamilien: Fertigen Sie Listen mit Wortfamilien an, um sich zusammen mit einem neuen Wort auch noch seine Ableitungen einzuprägen (*approve – approval – approving – disapprove – disapproval*).

Wortfelder: Die beste Methode, Wortfelder, also zusammenhängende Wortgruppen zu einem Thema zu lernen, sind Mind Maps, also grafisch angelegte Wortnetze. Diese Methode ist gut geeignet, um den Themenwortschatz für eine Klassenarbeit zu lernen. Um den Schlüsselbegriff herum werden einzelne Oberbegriffe für die wichtigsten Aspekte des Themas angeordnet. Um jeden Oberbegriff werden nun die dazugehörigen Vokabeln herumgeschrieben.   > Mind Mapping S. 202

Vokabeltrainer: Wer gerne am Computer lernt, findet problemlos einen geeigneten Vokabeltrainer im Handel. Solche Software enthält meistens vielerlei Übungen, die das Vokabellernen unterhaltsam und spielerisch gestalten. Achten Sie darauf, dass es sich um eine Software handelt, die auf Ihre Schulart abgestimmt ist. Es gibt auch zahlreiche kostenlose Online-Vokabeltrainer im Internet.

Das Hörverständnis üben

Um gesprochenes Englisch zu verstehen, z. B. in Unterhaltungen, Telefongesprächen, Vorstellungsgesprächen, im Fernsehen u. a., sollten Sie sich gut auf die jeweilige Situation vorbereiten. Oft beeinträchtigen der Akzent, Hintergrundgeräusche und andere Störungen das Verständnis so, dass man sich auf das Wichtigste konzentrieren muss. Eignen Sie sich die unten beschriebene Methode an, wenn Sie die Hörverständnisaufgaben in *Focus on Success* bearbeiten. Damit lassen sich Barrieren bei schwierigen Hörtexten leicht abbauen.

Vor dem Hören
> Lesen Sie die gesamte Aufgabenstellung sorgfältig durch. Nutzen Sie alle Hilfen, die Ihnen zur Verfügung stehen – Abbildungen, Überschriften usw.
> Schreiben Sie wenn möglich **Schlüsselbegriffe** auf und rufen Sie sich, wenn genug Zeit ist, kurz wichtige Wortfelder zum Thema in Erinnerung.

Während des Hörens
> Hören Sie sich den gesamten Hörtext zunächst in Ruhe an, um zu verstehen, worum es geht. Machen Sie in dieser Phase keine Notizen.
> Achten Sie bei einem zweiten Hören nur auf die für die Aufgabe wichtigen Informationen. Konzentrieren Sie sich nicht auf einzelne Wörter und Ausdrücke, die Sie nicht verstehen.

> Achten Sie auf Ausdrücke, die den logischen Gedankengang verdeutlichen, z. B. *however, in my view, in conclusion* usw. Sie helfen Ihnen, den roten Faden nicht zu verlieren.
> Notieren Sie Informationen nur **stichpunktartig**, nie in ganzen Sätzen. Dabei kann ein Raster sehr hilfreich sein. In diesem Beispiel handelt es sich um den Wandel der Geschlechterrollen in unserer Gesellschaft:

	changed role	*reasons*	*consequences*
men			
women			

> Verwenden Sie Zeichen, Abkürzungen und Wortverkürzungen, um beim Notieren Zeit zu sparen:

Zeichen		**Abkürzungen**		**Wortverkürzungen**	
=	*the same as*	e.g.	*for example*	govt	*government*
≠	*not the same as*	km	*kilometres*	impt	*important*
+	*and*	w., w/o	*with, without*	kids	*children*

Nach dem Hören
> Formulieren Sie Ihre Stichpunkte so schnell wie möglich aus – vielleicht können Sie später Ihre Aufzeichnungen nicht mehr lesen oder Ihre Wortverkürzungen nicht mehr verstehen.
> Versuchen Sie, alle Fragen zu beantworten. Wenn Sie einige Informationen nicht verstanden haben, stellen Sie eine begründete Vermutung an.

Suche nach Informationen im Internet

Das Internet bietet riesige Ressourcen für die Recherche, z. B. für Aufsätze oder Präsentationen, aber es ist wichtig zu wissen, wo und wie man am besten sucht.

1. Schritt: Notieren Sie, wonach Sie genau suchen, und halten Sie passende Suchbegriffe fest. Ohne eine solche Vorgabe, die so spezifisch wie möglich sein sollte, gerät man vom Suchen leicht ins Surfen.

2. Schritt: Überlegen Sie sich, wo Sie mit der Suche beginnen sollten. Es ist sinnvoll, sich mit der Zeit einen Grundstock an englischsprachigen Ressourcen zusammenzustellen, z. B. *online encyclopedias* (etwa www.encyclopedia.com), *online dictionaries* (z. B. www.leo.org), *facts and figures about different countries* (etwa https://www.cia.gov/cia/publications/factbook/), *news sites* (z. B. www.bbc.co.uk), *science and technology sites* (etwa www.howstuffworks.com).

3. Schritt: Suchen Sie sich die beste Suchmaschine und geben Sie möglichst spezifische Suchbegriffe ein. Machen Sie sich mit allen Suchfunktionen vertraut. Schränken Sie die Sprache der angezeigten Ergebnisseiten auf Englisch ein.

4. Schritt: Achten Sie darauf, nur verlässliche Quellen zu benutzen. Im Durchschnitt ist das Internet nicht sehr zuverlässig, da jeder Nutzer beliebige Informationen einstellen kann. Prüfen Sie immer, wer für die jeweiligen Inhalte verantwortlich ist, und verlassen Sie sich nicht auf die nächstbeste Information.

5. Schritt: Bevor Sie einzelne Artikel Satz für Satz lesen, überfliegen Sie sie. Sind nur einzelne Abschnitte für Ihr Thema relevant, suchen Sie sich diese heraus und ignorieren Sie die übrigen Teile. > Grobverständnis S. 196

6. Schritt: Anstatt ganze Textabschnitte in Ihr Dokument herüberzukopieren, machen Sie sich gezielt Notizen. Speichern Sie die Seite unter Ihren Favoriten, wenn Sie später noch einmal darauf zurückkommen oder Materialien bzw. Zitate von der Seite verwenden möchten. > Note Making S. 201

PRODUKTION

Note Making

Es ist sinnvoll, sich beim Lesen und Hören eines Textes Notizen zu machen. So können Sie später leichter auf die Informationen zurückgreifen.

Beim Lesen

Auf den ersten Blick scheint es ziemlich leicht, sich beim Lesen eines Textes Notizen zu machen. Trotzdem fällt es vielen schwer, wirklich kurze, sinnvolle Stichpunkte zu notieren. Oft führt die Sorge, etwas Wichtiges auszulassen, dazu, dass ganze Sätze des Originaltextes abgeschrieben werden. Damit verliert man nicht nur Zeit, sondern es wird später auch schwierig, seinen Text in eigenen Worten zu formulieren.

Hier einige Tipps, damit Sie diese Falle umgehen:

> Geben Sie Ihren Notizen eine Überschrift, die Ihr Thema klar umreißt, z. B. *Effects of genetic engineering on the environment*.

> Gehen Sie den Text durch und filtern Sie die wesentlichen Unterthemen heraus, die Sie als Überschriften verwenden können. Denken Sie daran, unter den Überschriften genug Platz für Ihre Stichpunkte zu lassen. > Detailverständnis S. 196

> Halten Sie Ausschau nach Signalen wie Hervorhebungen, Wiederholungen und bedeutungstragenden Adjektiven wie *huge, incredible, devastating* usw. Diese zeigen, was der Verfasser für wichtig hält.

> Notieren Sie nur Stichwörter, nicht ganze Sätze.

> Verdeutlichen Sie den logischen Aufbau der Informationen, z. B. indem Sie bestimmte Punkte in einer Liste untereinanderschreiben, Themen durch Leerzeilen voneinander abheben oder die wichtigsten Begriffe unterstreichen.

> Kontrollieren Sie, ob Sie alle notwendigen Informationen zusammengetragen haben. Vergessen Sie nicht, dass sie oft über den gesamten Text verstreut sind.

Beim Hören

In diesem Fall ist es schwieriger Notizen zu machen, da man oft sehr schnell schreiben muss. Man muss sich auf das Wesentliche konzentrieren und sollte Abkürzungen verwenden, damit man den Faden nicht verliert. > Das Hörverständnis üben S. 199

Mind Mapping

Eine Mind Map ist eine sinnvolle Methode, Begriffe und Angaben übersichtlich in einem Netz um einen Oberbegriff herum anzuordnen. Sie eignet sich z. B. zum Vokabellernen, zum Brainstorming, zum Ideensammeln und zur Vorbereitung eines Aufsatzes oder einer Präsentation.

> Umgang mit unbekannten Vokabeln S. 197

Materialien: Ein großes Blatt (z. B. DIN A3), farbige Stifte.

1. Schritt: Schreiben Sie den Oberbegriff (wenn es um Wortfelder geht) bzw. das Thema (wenn es um eine Ideensammlung geht) deutlich und groß in die Mitte.

2. Schritt: Schreiben Sie die wichtigsten Begriffe zum Thema um den Oberbegriff herum; sie sollten durch starke „Äste" mit dem Oberbegriff verbunden sein.

3. Schritt: Fügen Sie nach demselben Prinzip weitere Wörter und Ideen zu den einzelnen Unterthemen hinzu. Je spezieller, desto kleiner die Verzweigungen, d.h. der Weg vom Thema nach außen führt vom Allgemeinen zum Speziellen. Sie können jederzeit und überall neue Ideen hinzufügen.

4. Schritt: Heben Sie wichtige Begriffe durch farbige Markierungen und Symbole hervor.

Fragen zum Text beantworten

> Lesen schwieriger Texte S. 196

Bevor Sie mit dem Schreiben beginnen, vergewissern Sie sich, dass Sie den gesamten Text verstanden haben. (Nicht jedes Wort ist wichtig – überlegen Sie sich, ob Sie die Bedeutung des Satzes auch verstehen, ohne jedes Wort zu kennen.) Lesen Sie die Aufgabenstellung immer genau, um zu verstehen, worauf es bei der Beantwortung genau ankommt – ein häufiger Fehler ist das „Vorbeischreiben" an der Frage. Achten Sie auch darauf, keine Informationen zu „verpulvern", die Sie möglicherweise für die Beantwortung einer anderen Frage benötigen.

> Wenn Sie im Buch nichts anstreichen dürfen, machen Sie sich Notizen in Form von Stichpunkten und Listen, anstatt ganze Sätze aus dem Text herauszuschreiben. In der Klassenarbeit bzw. Prüfung sollten Sie die wichtigsten Passagen im Text markieren. Am besten markieren Sie alles, was für eine Textverständnisfrage wichtig ist, mit einer bestimmten Farbe, und nehmen dann eine andere Frage für die nächste Textverständnisfrage.
> Verwenden Sie in der Antwort die Zeitform der Fragestellung.

> Verwenden Sie so viele Synonyme und Umschreibungen der Begriffe und Formulierungen aus dem Text wie möglich, z. B. *recently – in recent years; violent crime – crime involving violence; think – believe; to a great extent – greatly; when she was a child – in her childhood* usw.

> Suchen Sie Signale im Text wie Hervorhebungen, Wiederholungen und bedeutungtragende Adjektive und Adverbien wie *absolutely, unbelievably, amazing*. Dies sind Signale dafür, was der Verfasser für wichtig hält.

> Versuchen Sie nicht, Ihre eigene Meinung einzubringen, wenn dies nicht in der Fragestellung gefordert ist.

Formulierungen für das Schreiben über den Text
> *According to the author, ...*
> *The article goes on to say that ...*
> *The text says that ...*
> *The author makes the point that ...*

Aus dem Text zitieren

Wenn Sie wirklich einmal eine wichtige Aussage aus dem Text zitieren möchten, um einen Punkt zu unterstreichen, so tun Sie dies nicht, indem Sie einfach die Formulierung des Textes übernehmen, sondern zeigen Sie, dass Sie bewusst zitieren und dies auch sprachlich deutlich machen können. Zitieren Sie in Ihrer Antwort höchstens einmal aus dem Text.

Zitate in die Antwort einbauen
> *To quote the author, ...*
> *According to the article, many stars are 'both defining and benefiting from a big shift in American attitudes to race'.*
> *Ron Berger highlights the positive aspects of this shift by saying 'what's ethnically neutral, diverse or simply unclear has tremendous appeal'.*

Eine Stellungnahme (*comment*) schreiben

Bei einer Stellungnahme geht es darum, Ihre Meinung zu einem bestimmten Thema darzulegen. Wichtig ist, dass Ihre Meinung begründet und mit Beispielen belegt ist.

1. Schritt: Machen Sie sich genau bewusst, worüber Sie schreiben sollen. Lesen Sie die Aufgabenstellung mehrmals durch.

2. Schritt: Machen Sie sich Notizen. Ordnen Sie Ihre Stichwörter übersichtlich an, z. B. in einer Mind Map, einer Liste oder einer Übersicht. > Note Making S. 201, Mind Mapping S. 202

3. Schritt: Schreiben Sie einen Einleitungssatz, der sich auf die Aufgabenstellung beziehen sollte.

4. Schritt: Behandeln Sie jedes Argument in einem Absatz. Handelt es sich um ein Pro-/Kontra-Thema, können Sie erst die Pro- und dann die Kontra-Argumente anführen. Verdeutlichen Sie Ihre Argumentation durch die Verwendung von Strukturwörtern; hierzu siehe die Liste auf der hinteren Umschlagklappe dieses Buches (*Language for writing*). > Einen Text sinnvoll gliedern S. 205

5. Schritt: Bringen Sie Ihre Argumentation in einem prägnanten Schlusssatz auf den Punkt.

Einen Text zusammenfassen

Die Fähigkeit, einen gelesenen Text zusammenzufassen, ist nicht nur wichtig, um den Text richtig zu verstehen, sondern sie hilft auch bei anderen Situationen, in denen Sie Informationen aus einem Text auf das Wesentliche reduzieren müssen. Zu solchen Situationen gehören z. B. die Beantwortung von Textverständnisfragen oder eine Mediation.

> Fragen zum Text beantworten S. 202, Mediation S. 210

1. Schritt: Lesen Sie den Text so oft wie möglich, bis Sie sicher sind, alles verstanden zu haben.

> Detailverständnis S. 196, Umgang mit unbekannten Vokabeln S. 197

2. Schritt: Fassen Sie in ein oder zwei einleitenden Sätzen zusammen, worum es in dem Text geht, z. B.: *The text is an extract from a radio phone-in show which is looking at people's attitudes to the EU.*

3. Schritt: Machen Sie sich bewusst, welche Informationen für den Leser wichtig sind, indem Sie *Wh*-Fragen beantworten: *Who? What? When? Where? Why?*, z. B.:
> *Who: Dr Peter Brown from Manchester University*
> *What: has been doing research into corruption in the EU*

4. Schritt: Machen Sie sich Notizen in Form von Stichwörtern. > Note Making S. 201

5. Schritt: Schreiben Sie Ihren Text. Beachten Sie dabei folgende Punkte:
> Lassen Sie Unwesentliches weg. Dazu gehören etwa Beispiele, Aufzählungen, Namen, Zitate usw.
> Verwenden Sie so weit wie möglich Ihre eigenen Worte.
> Vermeiden Sie es, zu dem Text Stellung zu nehmen. Dies gehört in der Regel nicht zur Aufgabenstellung.
> Denken Sie daran, Zitate in indirekte Rede umzuwandeln. > Reported speech S. 217

6. Schritt: Kontrollieren Sie Ihren Text auf Fehler und vergewissern Sie sich, dass Sie alle wichtigen Aspekte des Textes berücksichtigt haben.

Einen Aufsatz schreiben

Im Laufe der Oberstufe, in der Abschlussprüfung und auch später, z. B. im Studium, werden Sie immer wieder Aufsätze zu unterschiedlichsten Themen schreiben müssen. Es ist sinnvoll, sich von Anfang an einige Regeln zu eigen zu machen, um das Vorgehen möglichst zu automatisieren und sich gleich auf den Inhalt konzentrieren zu können. Dies ist besonders wichtig, wenn es – wie in der Abschlussprüfung – auf die Zeit ankommt.

1. Schritt: Verschaffen Sie sich Klarheit über Ihr Thema. Welche Aspekte gehören dazu, welche nicht?

2. Schritt: Machen Sie ein Brainstorming, indem Sie alle Ideen aufschreiben, die Ihnen zum Thema in den Kopf kommen. Wichtig: Die Ideen sollten Sie gleich in eine Struktur bringen, um nicht in einem Wust von ungeordnetem Gekritzel zu enden. Zur Strukturierung eignen sich z. B. Listen oder Mind Maps. ➤ Note Making S. 201, Mind Mapping S. 202

3. Schritt: Überlegen Sie sich einen Aufbau für Ihren Text. Dies kann z. B. in Form einer Mind Map geschehen. Eine andere Möglichkeit ist eine Übersicht (*outline*) wie die folgende:

> #### Should old towns be closed to private vehicles?
>
> **Einleitung:** Umreißen des Themas
> **Hauptteil:** Ausführung zum Thema, z. B.:
> **1.** *Disadvantages for business*
>   **1.1** *Job losses*
>   **1.1.1** *retail trade*
>   **1.1.2** *fewer tourists*
>   **1.1.2.1** *less money for tourist attractions*
>   **1.1.2.2** *job losses in cafés, etc.*
>   **1.2** *What about town centre residents, delivery vehicles, etc.?*
> **2.** *Advantages, positive effects on town and people*
> ...
> **Schluss:** Zusammenfassung, Fazit

4. Schritt: Schreiben Sie Ihren Text. Lassen Sie Platz für Korrekturen, Änderungen oder Ergänzungen. Wichtig: Verdeutlichen Sie Ihre Argumentation durch die Verwendung von Strukturwörtern; hierzu siehe die Liste auf der hinteren Umschlagklappe dieses Buches (*Language for writing*) und den Abschnitt unten „Einen Text sinnvoll gliedern".

5. Schritt: Überprüfen Sie Ihren Entwurf auf:
- **Rechtschreibfehler** (z. B. gleichlautende Wörter wie *there/their*, *meet/meat* usw.)
- **Grammatikfehler** (z. B. Gebrauch der Zeitformen; *-ly*-Endung für Adverbien)
- **Wortwahl** (z. B. Wiederholungen; *False friends* wie „aktuell" ≠ *actual*, „eventuell" ≠ *eventual*, „spenden" ≠ *spend*)
- **Satzbau** (z. B. unvollständige Antworten, die mit *Because* beginnen)
- **Gedankenführung** (z. B. Klarheit des Ausdrucks; Verwendung von Strukturwörtern wie *However, On the other hand, In addition, As a result* usw.)

Einen Text sinnvoll gliedern

Wann immer es darum geht, einen zusammenhängenden Text zu schreiben, sei es eine Antwort auf eine Frage zum Text, einen Aufsatz, eine Zusammenfassung o. Ä., ist es ganz wichtig, die Gedanken in einen logischen Zusammenhang zu bringen, damit der Leser den Faden nicht verliert. Dies alles gilt ebenso für mündliche Präsentationen, nur werden Sie dabei Ihre Materialien nicht Wort für Wort ablesen, sondern frei sprechen. Daher ist es wichtig, Formulierungen für die Gliederung auch mündlich parat zu haben.

Die wichtigsten Strukturwörter finden Sie auf der hinteren Umschlagklappe dieses Buches (*Language for writing*). Im Folgenden sehen Sie einige Beispiele, wie man diese Formulierungen in einen Text einbauen kann.

Argumente gliedern

> *In his text 'The world's changing energy supplies' Knapp discusses many aspects of energy and the environment. <u>Firstly</u>, he states that ... <u>Secondly</u> / <u>Then</u> he goes on to say that ... <u>Another point</u> he makes is that ... <u>Finally</u>, ...*

Eine Begründung anführen

> *<u>Due to</u> / <u>Because of</u> / <u>As a result of</u> all the discussions about renewable sources of energy ...*
> *Renewable energy has been talked about a lot. <u>Therefore</u>, the public ...*
> *Renewable energy has been talked about a lot, <u>so</u> the public ...*

Aspekte ergänzen

> *Brian Knapp states that many renewable sources of energy include high development costs. <u>In addition,</u> / <u>Moreover</u>, he points out that they these energy forms still only offer a small amount of the world's rising energy requirements.*
> *<u>In addition to</u> / <u>Besides</u> / <u>As well as</u> mentioning the high development costs of many renewable forms of energy, Knapp points out that these energy forms still only offer a small amount of the world's rising energy requirements.*

Einen Gegensatz ausdrücken

> *<u>Although</u> the demand for cheap energy is continuing to rise, our current main sources of energy – fossil fuels – are running out.*
> *<u>In spite of</u> the rising demand for cheap energy, our current main sources of energy are running out.*
> *<u>While</u> / <u>Whereas</u> the demand for cheap energy is continuing to rise, our current main sources of energy are running out.*
> *Our current main sources of energy are running out. <u>However,</u> / <u>But nevertheless,</u> the demand for cheap energy is continuing to rise.*
> *<u>On the one hand</u>, our current main sources of energy are running out; <u>on the other hand</u>, the demand for cheap energy is continuing to rise.*

Beispiele anführen

> *The writer is of the opinion that nuclear fusion is a safe energy source compared with other energy sources, <u>for example</u> / <u>for instance</u> / <u>such as</u> / <u>e.g.</u> ...*

Ein Fazit ziehen

> *<u>As a consequence,</u> / <u>All in all,</u> / <u>Consequently,</u> Brian Knapp thinks that ...*
> *<u>To sum up</u> / <u>To conclude</u>, I would like to say that ...*

Diese Strukturwörter (*connectors*) sollten Sie sich so zu eigen machen, dass Sie sie möglichst in jedem Text verwenden. Dadurch gewöhnen Sie sich eine genaue und logische Ausdrucksweise an. Achten Sie auch beim Lesen von Texten auf Strukturwörter; so können Sie der Gedankenführung leichter folgen.

Die Arbeitsergebnisse präsentieren

Die Fähigkeit, wirkungsvoll vor einem Publikum zu referieren, ist wichtig im Berufsleben und zunehmend auch in der Schule. Dabei kommt es nicht nur auf den Inhalt an, sondern auch darauf, wie anschaulich Sie den Inhalt „verpacken", d.h. dass Sie Ihren Vortrag leicht nachvollziehbar gliedern, abwechslungsreich gestalten und lebendig illustrieren.

Vor der Präsentation

1. Schritt: Bereiten Sie Ihr Thema gründlich vor und machen Sie sich dabei schon Notizen auf Englisch.

2. Schritt: Prüfen Sie Ihre Stichpunkte sprachlich und vergewissern Sie sich, dass Sie alles richtig aussprechen (anhand der Lautschrift in einem Wörterbuch oder der Aussprachebeispiele in gängigen Online-Wörterbüchern oder auf Wörterbuch-CD-ROMs).

3. Schritt: Überlegen Sie sich, wie Sie Ihren Vortrag interessanter und lebendiger machen können (Anschauungsmaterial, Audiobeispiele, Anekdoten usw.).

4. Schritt: Organisieren Sie alle Hilfsmittel, die Sie benötigen (OHP, Flipchart usw.).

5. Schritt: Üben Sie die Präsentation, am besten vor Zuhörern.

Während der Präsentation

1. Schritt: Steigen Sie nicht gleich mitten ins Thema ein, sondern geben Sie einen Überblick über Ihre Präsentation.

2. Schritt: Machen Sie es den Zuhörern leicht, indem Sie sich klar ausdrücken, kurze Sätze benutzen und langsam sprechen.

3. Schritt: Die Zuhörer bleiben am ehesten interessiert, wenn Sie Ihre Präsentation so abwechslungsreich wie möglich gestalten: Ziehen Sie zwischendurch Anschauungsmaterial (OHP, Beamer usw.) heran und teilen Sie Handouts aus. Wenn Sie Folien benutzen, halten Sie sie klar und übersichtlich, anstatt sie mit Grafiken zu überladen.

4. Schritt: Achten Sie auf Ihre Körpersprache: Wenden Sie sich dem Publikum zu, halten Sie Blickkontakt mit den Zuhörern, sprechen Sie langsam und deutlich und benutzen Sie Gesten, um den Inhalt zu verdeutlichen.

5. Schritt: Fassen Sie zum Schluss das Wichtigste zusammen. Bedanken Sie sich bei den Zuhörern für ihre Aufmerksamkeit und ermuntern Sie sie, Fragen zu stellen.

Interpretation von Bildern und Karikaturen

Am besten eignen Sie sich einen Grundstock an Formulierungen zur Beschreibung und Interpretation von Bildern und Karikaturen an. Achten Sie darauf, sich auf die wesentlichen Bildaussagen zu konzentrieren, anstatt sich in Details zu verlieren.
Halten Sie die folgenden Schritte ein, um Ihre Antwort sinnvoll zu gliedern:

1. Schritt: Beschreibung des Bildes. Betrachten Sie alle Einzelheiten der Bildvorlage, aber beschränken Sie sich bei der Beschreibung auf die Elemente, die für die Aussage wichtig sind.
Verwenden Sie bei der Beschreibung der Bildinhalte das *Present progressive* (außer bei Verben, die gewöhnlich nicht in dieser Zeitform vorkommen). Zu dem Cartoon auf S. 62 könnten Sie z. B. schreiben: *The cartoon shows two dogs in an office. The bigger dog is sitting at a computer. he is explaining to the smaller dog how safe the internet is because ...* Aber Vorsicht: Das *Present progressive* gilt nur für die Handlungen und Situationen, die im Bild dargestellt sind, nicht für die Verben, mit denen Sie den Cartoon beschreiben und interpretieren (*The cartoon **shows**/**describes** ... / It **seems** as if the dog on the left ...*).

> Present progressive S. 212

2. Schritt: **Interpretation des Bildes.** Wenn Ihnen das Bild nicht viel sagt, können Sie dies in Ihre Interpretation miteinbeziehen, indem Sie es als *ambiguous* oder *unclear* bezeichnen.

3. Schritt: **Stellungnahme zur Bildaussage.** Bringen Sie die Hauptaussage der Bildvorlage auf den Punkt und/oder beziehen Sie Stellung, indem Sie z. B. die Wirkung des Bildes auf den Betrachter beurteilen.

1. **Beschreibung des Bildes**
   > *In the foreground/background/centre there is …*
   > *The speech bubble (Sprechblase)/thought bubble (Denkblase)/caption (Bilduntertitel)/label (Aufschrift) says that …*
   > *The cartoon shows/appears to show …*
   > *The scene depicts/shows …*
   > *In the foreground/background, there is/are …*
   > *On the left/right you can see …*
   > *The … looks as if …*
   > *The person on the left appears to …/It seems as if the person …*
   > *He/She is wearing/holding …*

2. **Interpretation der Bildaussage**
   > *The picture/cartoon deals with the recent discussion of …*
   > *I think the cartoonist's/artist's/photographer's use of irony/exaggeration is intended to create …/is aimed at making …/conveys …*
   > *The person in the centre represents/symbolizes/shows …*
   > *This indicates/shows/reveals that …*
   > *The … represents/is in fact/stands for …*
   > *The cartoonist/artist/photographer criticizes/wants to say/express the idea that …*
   > *Because the foreground/background is …, the impression is given that …*
   > *From the way the people are depicted, it is obvious that …*
   > *The point of the cartoon seems to be that …*

3. **Stellungnahme, Beschreibung der Wirkung auf den Betrachter**
   > *I think the cartoon is quite right/makes a fair point.*
   > *I agree with the cartoonist/artist, but …*
   > *In my opinion, the cartoonist is partly right/exaggerates a little/a lot/is quite wrong.*
   > *For example,/For instance, …*
   > *Because of …, the picture touches me/leaves me cold.*
   > *I think the … is a symbol of …*
   > *The … helps to create a … atmosphere, which forces you to/has the effect of …*

Interpretation von Grafiken, Diagrammen und Tabellen

Wie im Falle von Cartoons ist es auch bei Grafiken, Diagrammen und Tabellen sinnvoll, einen Grundstock an Formulierungen zur Beschreibung und Interpretation parat zu haben. Halten Sie die folgenden Schritte ein, um Ihre Antwort sinnvoll zu gliedern:

1. Schritt: **Beschreibung der Vorlage.** Hier geht es nicht darum, alle Details aufzuzählen, sondern zu beschreiben, worum es in der Vorlage geht und welche Daten dargestellt werden.

2. Schritt: **Zusammenfassung der dargestellten Tendenzen, Entwicklungen bzw. Größen.** Welche Schlussfolgerungen ergeben sich aus den Daten? Kann man zusammenfassend ein Ergebnis oder Fazit formulieren?

Typen von Diagrammen

Tabelle (*table*)

	USA	UK
1995	*495*	*105*
2005	*718*	*85*

Kurvendiagramm (*graph, line graph*)

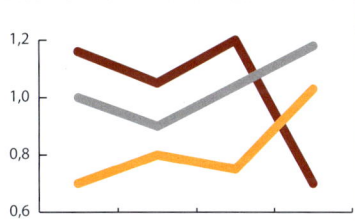

Balkendiagramm (*bar chart*)

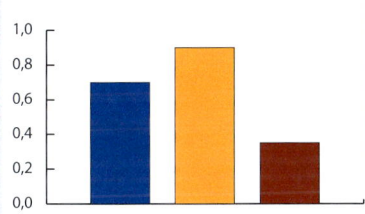

Kreis-/Tortendiagramm (*pie chart*)

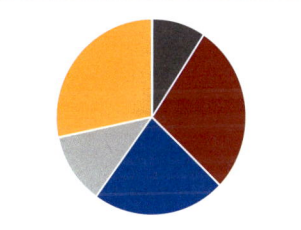

Sprechen über Zahlen und Mengenangaben (*values, amounts*)

> *more / less than …*
> *no less than …*

> *eighty-five per cent (said that …)*
> *On the other hand, almost …*

Sprechen über Proportionen (*proportions, shares, percentages*)

> *(over) half of*
> *more / less than one third / quarter of …*

> *the (vast) majority of*
> *a mere third of …*

Sprechen über Entwicklungen (*developments*) und Tendenzen (*tendencies*)

> *a huge / sharp increase / decrease*
> *a small / slight raise / dip*
> *levels out, remains constant*
> *drastically, gradually, sharply, steadily*

> *rises / increases / hits a maximum*
> *drops / decreases / falls / plunges*
> *over a period of …*
> *between 2000 and 2008*

INTERAKTION

Gruppengespräche und Diskussionen führen

Ob es um Gruppengespräche, Diskussionen oder Rollenspiele geht: Machen Sie das meiste daraus, indem Sie die folgenden Punkte beherzigen.

> Lernen Sie die Formulierungen auf der hinteren Umschlagklappe dieses Buches (*Language for discussion*). Klappen Sie diese während des Unterrichts aus. Die Formulierungen helfen Ihnen, sich klar und logisch auszudrücken.

> Bereiten Sie sich inhaltlich vor, indem Sie sich einzelne Aspekte des Themas nochmal in Stichworten ins Gedächtnis rufen und Schlüsselbegriffe auf Englisch notieren.

> Legen Sie sich, wenn genügend Zeit ist, ein paar Fragen/Antworten zum Thema zurecht.

> Bleiben Sie immer ruhig und denken Sie nach, bevor Sie sprechen.

> Bleiben Sie beim Thema und schweifen Sie nicht ab.

> Gehen Sie auf Ihre Gesprächspartner ein und halten Sie Blickkontakt.

> Beteiligen Sie sich und hören Sie nicht bloß still zu: Gruppenarbeit ist eine hervorragende Gelegenheit zum freien Sprechen.

Melden Sie sich auch immer mal wieder spontan zu Wort und lassen Sie Ausdrücke einfließen, die Interesse, Überraschung, Skepsis usw. äußern – so etwas macht das Gespräch gleich viel lebendiger:

Sich zu Wort melden	
> *Can I just say that ...*	> *Well, if you ask me ...*

Jemand anderen ins Gespräch einbringen
> *What do you think, Sven / Svenja?*

Verständnis, Erstaunen usw. ausdrücken	
Ach so. / Ah ja.	*I see. / Right. / Oh, right.*
Oh je!	*Oh dear!*
Echt?	*Really?*
Gut. / Okay.	*Fine.*
Alles klar.	*OK then.*
Das ist doch wohl nicht dein Ernst!	*You're kidding!*

MEDIATION

Mediation

Schriftliche Mediation bedeutet das sinngemäße Übertragen von Texten in eine andere Sprache für jemanden, der das Original nicht versteht. Wichtig bei einer Mediation ist immer die Konzentration auf das Wesentliche, im Unterschied zur Übersetzung. Einzelheiten sind bei einer Mediation ebenso zweitrangig wie stilistische Feinheiten.

1. Schritt: Lesen Sie genau, **für welche Situation** Sie den Text zusammenfassen müssen und **für wen**. Meist bestimmt die jeweilige Situation, worauf es ankommt.

2. Schritt: Lesen Sie den gesamten Text durch, ohne sich dabei auf Einzelwörter zu konzentrieren. Ignorieren Sie unbekannte Vokabeln wenn möglich, oft sind sie für das Verständnis des Hauptinhalts nicht wesentlich.

3. Schritt: Lesen Sie nochmals, worauf es in der Aufgabenstellung ankommt und in welcher Form die Lösung abgefasst sein soll. Wenn es einzelne Fragen gibt, markieren Sie die für die jeweiligen Fragen wichtigen Textpassagen in unterschiedlichen Farben.

4. Schritt: Fassen Sie die Hauptpunkte des Textes zusammen. Drücken Sie sich klar und verständlich aus; vereinfachen Sie die Sprache des Originals, indem Sie sich darauf konzentrieren, **was** gesagt wird, nicht **wie** es gesagt wird.

5. Schritt: Lesen Sie Ihren Text nochmals durch und vergewissern Sie sich, dass der Inhalt des Originals angemessen und verständlich ausgedrückt ist.

Übersetzung

Im Gegensatz zur Mediation ist bei der Übersetzung jedes Wort des Originaltextes wichtig. Oft muss im Deutschen jedoch eine andere Satzkonstruktion gewählt werden. Besonders knifflig sind z. B. die folgenden Konstruktionen; übersetzen Sie die Beispielsätze ins Deutsche:

> Partizipialkonstruktionen
> z. B. *The jobs done by women are often badly paid. / Some people say that feminism has been a great success pointing to the progress in the last 30 years.*
> Konstruktionen mit Gerundium
> z. B. *I avoided looking at her. / She achieved her aims by working very hard.*
> Passivkonstruktionen
> z. B. *He was offered a good job. / He is said to be rich.*

Außerdem muss häufig die Wortart geändert werden, z. B. *There is a need to …* (Es ist notwendig, zu …) oder *She used to work in France.* (Früher arbeitete sie in Frankreich.).

Eine weitere Schwierigkeit sind kleinere Partikel und Ausdrücke, die sich vom Deutschen oft unterscheiden, z. B. *after all, as, as to, as for, at all, at least, however, neither … nor, not … either, not … until, unless.*

1. Schritt: Lesen Sie den gesamten Text einmal zügig durch.

2. Schritt: Lesen Sie den Text nun Wort für Wort und schlagen Sie schwierige Wörter nach. Vergewissern Sie sich, dass Sie den Satzbau jedes Satzes richtig erfasst haben (siehe die Liste schwieriger Konstruktionen oben).

3. Schritt: Fertigen Sie eine Rohfassung an, die Sie am besten doppelzeilig schreiben, um Korrekturen einfügen zu können.

4. Schritt: Bevor Sie die Reinschrift anfertigen, prüfen Sie Ihren Text auf:
Rechtschreib- und Grammatikfehler (z. B. Partizipien, Gerundien, Zeitenfolge)
Ausdruck (z. B. Sätze, an denen man noch das englische Original erkennt)
Verständlichkeit (z. B. zu lange oder verschachtelte Sätze)
Vollständigkeit (ausgelassene Wörter oder Satzteile).

Grammar Summary

THE SIMPLE PRESENT

1 I **go** to the disco once a week.
2 We **live** in Bavaria.
3 Mr Brown **teaches** us English every day.
4 **I don't like** chocolate.
5 **Does** he **like** chocolate?

> Man gebraucht das **simple present** für regelmäßige, sich wiederholende Ereignisse oder Handlungen (1, 3) und für Dauerzustände (2, 4, 5).
> Mit Ausnahme der 3. Person Singular (*he, she, it*) hat das **simple present** dieselbe Form wie der Infinitiv (1, 2).
>   ⚠ Die **3. Person Singular** endet auf *-(e)s* (3).
> Ist **kein Hilfsverb** im Satz vorhanden, werden **Verneinung** und **Fragen** mit der entsprechenden Form von *to do* gebildet (4, 5).

Das **simple present** wird häufig mit den folgenden **Zeitangaben** benutzt:

> *always, never, often, rarely, seldom, sometimes*
> *generally, mostly, normally, regularly, usually*
> *every day/week/month/..., every morning/afternoon/...*
> *on Mondays/Tuesdays/..., on weekdays*
> *in (the) summer/winter/...*
> *at Christmas/Easter, at weekends*

THE PRESENT PROGRESSIVE

1 **I'm calling** to say that Ben's ill.
2 He**'s staying** in bed today.
3 The computer **isn't working**.
4 **Are** you **sleeping**?

> Man benutzt das **present progressive** (auch **present continuous** genannt) für Vorgänge oder Handlungen, die im Moment des Sprechens oder Schreibens passieren und noch nicht abgeschlossen sind (1, 3, 4).
> Es wird auch für vorübergehende Situationen gebraucht (2).
> Das **present progressive** wird mit dem Präsens von *to be* und der *-ing*-Form des Vollverbs gebildet.
> Da beim **present progressive** immer ein Hilfsverb vorhanden ist, wird die **Verneinung** mit *not/n't* gebildet (3).
> Fragen werden durch Umstellung gebildet (4).

Das **present progressive** wird oft mit den folgenden **Zeitangaben** benutzt:

> *at the moment, at present, now, this week/month*

⚠ Diese Verben bilden normalerweise **keine progressive-Form**:

be, believe, doubt, feel (meinen), *hate, hear, imagine, know, like/dislike, love, mean, notice, prefer, realize, recognize, remember, see* (begreifen), *seem, suppose, think* (meinen), *understand, want, wish*

THE SIMPLE PAST

1 We **wanted** to go to the USA last year.
2 She **went** on a school trip to London.
3 Jasmin **did not enjoy** her holiday in Rimini last summer.
4 Where **did** you **go** last year?

> Man benutzt das **simple past**, um über Vergangenes zu berichten.
> Das **simple past** wird auch gebraucht, wenn man sagen will, **wann** etwas geschehen ist (1, 3, 4).
> Bei **regelmäßigen** Verben wird das **simple past** durch das Anhängen von *-ed* an den Infinitiv gebildet (1).
> ⚠ Die unregelmäßigen Verben haben eine Sonderform (2), die man sich merken – auswendig lernen! – muss. > Irregular Verbs (S. 298)
> Ist **kein Hilfsverb** im Satz vorhanden, bildet man die **Verneinung** und **Fragen** mit *did/didn't* (3, 4).

Das **simple past** wird häufig mit den folgenden **Zeitangaben** benutzt:

> *yesterday, the day before yesterday, the week/month/... before last*
> *last night/week/month/summer/December/Easter/...*
> *two/three/... hours/days/years/... ago*
> *in 2005 / in the 20th century ...*
> *at that time, in those days*

THE PAST PROGRESSIVE

1 The teacher **was talking** to Heather **during the break**.
2 The tourists **were taking** photos when a lion (suddenly) **sprang** towards them.
3 I **wasn't doing** anything particular when he **arrived**.
4 **Were** you **having** breakfast when I **phoned**?

> Wenn man ausdrücken möchte, dass eine Handlung zu einem bestimmten Zeitpunkt oder während eines bestimmten Zeitraumes in der Vergangenheit **im Gange** war, benutzt man das **past progressive** (auch **past continuous** genannt)(1).
> Das **past progressive** wird auch benutzt, um zu verdeutlichen, dass eine Handlung im Gange war, als ein neues Ereignis (plötzlich) eintrat (2-4).
> Man bildet das **past progressive** mit *was/were* und der *-ing*-Form des Vollverbs (1).
> Die **Verneinung** wird mit *was not / wasn't* bzw. *were not / weren't* gebildet (3).
> **Fragen** bildet man durch Umstellung (4).
> ⚠ Einige Verben haben **keine progressive-Form** (siehe die Liste unter **present progressive**).

THE PRESENT PERFECT

1 I've **bought** a new car.
2 I **haven't seen** the new film yet.
3 How long **have** you **had** a laptop?
4 We**'ve had** snow **for** two weeks.
5 She**'s had** a cold **since** December.

> Wenn man ausdrücken will, dass etwas geschehen ist, ohne dass der genaue Zeitpunkt des Ereignisses wichtig ist, wird das **present perfect** benutzt (1, 2).
> Man gebraucht das **present perfect** auch, um zu sagen, seit wann oder wie lange ein Zustand oder eine Handlung schon andauert (3–5). Dafür wird sehr oft *for* bzw. *since* verwendet. (Im Deutschen steht dafür „seit" plus Gegenwart.)
> Das **present perfect** wird mit *have/has* und der 3. Form des Vollverbs gebildet (1, 4, 5).
> ⚠ Die unregelmäßigen Verben haben eine Sonderform (1, 2), die man auswendig lernen muss.

> Irregular verbs (S. 298)

> Die **Verneinung** wird durch das Einfügen von *not/n't* nach *have/has* gebildet (2).
> **Fragen** bildet man durch Umstellung (3).

Das **present perfect** wird oft mit den folgenden Zeitangaben benutzt:

> *already, still (not), (not) yet*
> *(not) ever, just, lately, never, recently*
> *so far this week/month/…, till/until now*

THE PRESENT PERFECT PROGRESSIVE

1 I**'ve been learning** English since I was 10.
2 They**'ve not been speaking** to each other lately.
3 **Has** he **been singing** in the choir for long?

> Das **present perfect progressive** (auch **present perfect continuous** genannt) benutzt man für Handlungen und Vorgänge, die in der Vergangenheit begonnen haben und zum Zeitpunkt des Sprechens bzw. Schreibens noch nicht beendet sind.
> Das **present perfect progressive** wird mit *have/has been* und der *-ing*-Form des Vollverbs gebildet (1).
> Die **Verneinung** bildet man durch das Einfügen von *not/n't* unmittelbar nach *have/has* (2).
> **Fragen** werden durch Umstellung gebildet (3).
> ⚠ Einige Verben haben normalerweise **keine progressive-Form** (siehe die Liste unter **present progressive**, S. 212).

THE PAST PERFECT

1 Laura couldn't pay. She **had forgotten** her purse.
2 Nina **had** already **left** the coffee bar by the time I arrived.
3 When I visited John in hospital, he **had been** there for ten days.

> Mit Hilfe des **past perfect** drückt man aus, dass zwei Handlungen oder Vorgänge in der Vergangenheit aufeinander folgten (1, 2). Die Handlung, die zeitlich voranging, steht im **past perfect**.
> Das **past perfect** wird auch verwendet, um auszudrücken, dass ein Zustand vor einem Zeitpunkt der Vergangenheit begann und zu diesem Zeitpunkt noch andauerte (3).

⚠ Wenn zwei oder mehrere kurze Handlungen in der Vergangenheit direkt aufeinander folgen, wird für alle Handlungen das **simple past** verwendet:
*The cat **ran** out when Joanne **opened** the door.*

THE PAST PERFECT PROGRESSIVE

1 Rod **had been travelling** for three months when he ran out of money.
2 When I found Mary, I could see that she **had been crying**.

> Das **past perfect progressive** (auch **past perfect continous** genannt) wird verwendet, wenn man ausdrücken will, dass eine Handlung oder ein Vorgang vor einem Zeitpunkt in der Vergangenheit begonnen hatte und bis (oder fast bis) zu diesem Zeitpunkt andauerte.

THE FUTURE

A will

1 In the future people **will use** public transport more often.
2 We can only hope that everyone **will accept** this shift in attitudes.
3 You've forgotten your purse? Don't worry. **I'll lend** you some money.
4 Ms Smith **will not be** at the meeting this afternoon.
5 I **won't come** either.
6 **Will** he **get** the job?

> Das **will future** benutzt man, um Vorhersagen zu machen (1) oder Vermutungen über die Zukunft zu äußern (2).
> Man benutzt es auch, wenn man sich spontan zu etwas entschließt, Angebote oder Versprechen macht (3).
> Das **will future** wird mit *will* + Infinitiv des Vollverbs gebildet. Es hat für alle Personen die gleiche Form (1–3).
> Die **Verneinung** bildet man durch das Einfügen von *not* unmittelbar nach *will* (4). Im gesprochenen Englisch sagt man häufig *won't* (5).
> **Fragen** werden durch Umstellung gebildet (6).

Das **will future** kommt häufig mit den folgenden einleitenden Verben und Ausdrücken vor:

> *believe, expect, forecast, hope, imagine, suppose, think*
> *It's clear/obvious that ..., There's no doubt that ...*

B going to

1 Look at these clouds. It**'s going to rain** soon.
2 This time I**'m going to get** good marks in the class test.
3 Tom **isn't going to work** at the club any more.
4 When **are** you **going to take** your driving test?

> Das **going to future** benutzt man für Ereignisse und Situationen, die nach Meinung des Sprechers bald eintreten werden (weil es bereits Anzeichen dafür gibt) (1).
> Es wird auch für Pläne und Absichten gebraucht (2).
> Das **going to future** wird mit *am/is/are* + *going to* + Infinitiv gebildet (1, 2).
> Die **Verneinung** bildet man durch das Einfügen von *not/n't* unmittelbar nach *am/is/are* (3).
> **Fragen** werden durch Umstellung gebildet (4).

⚠ Der **Gebrauch des Futurs** hängt in gewissem Maße von der Absicht oder Sichtweise des Sprechers ab. Dies gilt insbesondere für das **going to future** und für zukünftige Ereignisse. Daher ist es im Zweifelsfall ratsam, das neutralere **will future** zu benutzen.

C The present progressive / The simple present

1 We**'re leaving** the house at 10.30.
2 The bus **goes** at 11 o'clock.

> Man kann das **present progressive** auch **mit einer Zeitbestimmung der Zukunft** (*at 10.30, this afternoon, on Sunday*) für bereits feststehende Pläne und Verabredungen verwenden (1).
> Genau wie im Deutschen wird auch im Englischen das **simple present mit einer Zeitangabe** benutzt, um fest terminierte Vorgänge (Fahrpläne, Stundenpläne, Programme usw.) anzugeben (2).

MODAL AUXILIARY VERBS

1 He **can speak** several languages.
2 You **must accept** your new situation.
3 We **needn't go** to work today.
4 **May** I **interrupt** you?

> Um zu sagen, was geschehen kann, muss, darf, soll usw., benutzt man ein modales Hilfsverb in Verbindung mit einem Vollverb (1–4).

⚠ Im Englischen steht ein Hilfsverb – anders als im Deutschen – nie ohne Vollverb:
- Lena kann Spanisch. ⟶ *Lena can speak Spanish.* NICHT: ~~Lena can Spanish.~~

> Modale Hilfsverben – nicht jedoch die Ersatzverben (siehe unten) – haben bei allen Personen immer die gleiche Form, einschließlich der 3. Person Singular (keine *-s*-Endung) (1, 2).
> Die **Verneinung** wird durch das Einfügen von *not/n't* unmittelbar nach dem Hilfsverb gebildet (3).
> **Fragen** bildet man durch Umstellung (4).
> Abgesehen von *could* (wenn es für eine Fähigkeit gebraucht wird) kann man modale Hilfsverben nur im Präsens und – mit einer geeigneten Zeitangabe – mit zukünftiger Bedeutung benutzen, zum Beispiel:
>   – *You **can go** home now.* (Präsens)
>   *You **can go** home an hour early tomorrow.* (Futur)
>   – *I **must write** these letters now.* (Präsens)
>   *I **must write** a long report next week.* (Futur)

⚠ Um andere Zeitformen bei modalen Hilfsverben zu bilden, z. B. die Vergangenheit, muss ein geeignetes Ersatzverb gebraucht werden:

must	*The provider **had to block** access to the internet last December.*
can	*I **couldn't start** the car yesterday.* (Fähigkeit)
	*We **weren't allowed to go** home early last Friday.* (Erlaubnis)

Übersicht der modalen Hilfsverben nach Funktion

Funktion	Modale(s) Hilfsverb(en)	
Fähigkeit	*He **can** speak several languages.*	
	*The first satellites **could** only transmit sound.*	
Möglichkeit	*With your qualifications you **could** work abroad.*	
	*The boss **may** come in at any moment.*	
	*He **might** ask you what you are doing.*	
Bitte	***Can** I have a word with Ms Sims, please?*	(neutral)
	***Could** I speak to Ms Sims, please?*	(höflich)
	***May** I interrupt you?*	(betont höflich)
	***Might** I ask you a personal question?*	(äußerst höflich)
Erlaubnis	*You **can** go in now.*	(neutral)
	*The boss is free. You **may** go in now.*	(gefällig)
Verbot	*We **mustn't** be late for work tomorrow.*	
Pflicht	*You **must** wear a hard hat in the factory.*	
Wahl	*Most shop workers **needn't** work on Sundays.*	
Empfehlung	*You **should** get better qualifications.*	(neutral)
	*You **ought to** get better qualifications.*	(betont)
	*You **must** get better qualifications.*	(streng)

REPORTED SPEECH

A Aussagesätze

1 Some people **claim** that 'servant' robots **are putting** people out of work.
2 The speaker **reminded** his audience that there **were** some jobs robots **couldn't do**.

> Wenn man einem Dritten berichten möchte, was während eines Gespräches gesagt wurde, benutzt man die **indirekte Rede**.

> Bei Verwendung der indirekten Rede benutzt man ein einleitendes Verb wie *claim, say, remind, answer, think, mention* usw., um zu verdeutlichen, dass eine Äußerung wiedergegeben wird.
Steht das einleitende Verb in der Vergangenheit – also *said, answered, mentioned* usw. –, dann verschieben sich die Zeiten wie folgt:

direkte Rede		indirekte Rede
simple present	⟶	simple past
she works hard		*she worked hard*
present progressive	⟶	past progressive
she is working hard		*she was working hard*
simple past	⟶	past perfect
she worked hard		*she had worked hard*
past progressive	⟶	past perfect progressive
she was working hard		*she had been working hard*
present perfect	⟶	past perfect
she has worked hard		*she had worked hard*

present perfect progressive	→	past perfect progressive
she has been working hard		*she had been working hard*

past perfect	(keine Verschiebung)
she had worked hard	–

past perfect progressive	(keine Verschiebung)
she had been working hard	–

will	→	would
she will work hard		*she would work hard*

am/is/are going to	→	was/were going to
she is going to work hard		*she was going to work hard*

would/might etc.	(keine Verschiebung)
she would work hard	–

would have/might have etc.	(keine Verschiebung)
she had been working hard	–

⚠ Die modalen Hilfsverben werden folgendermaßen verschoben:

Modalverb	Bedeutung	indirekte Rede
can	Fähigkeit	*could, was/were able to*
can	Erlaubnis	*was/were allowed to*
may	Möglichkeit	*might*
may	Erlaubnis	*was/were allowed to*
must	Pflicht	*had to*
mustn't	Verbot	*was/were not allowed to*
needn't	freie Wahl	*did not/didn't have to*

> Außer wenn man über ein Gespräch berichtet, das am selben Tag stattgefunden hat, müssen fast alle **Zeit**- und einige **Ortsangaben** entsprechend der folgenden Tabelle geändert werden. (Angaben, die nicht aufgeführt sind, bleiben unverändert.)

direkte Rede		indirekte Rede
today	→	*on that day*
tomorrow	→	*the next day*
yesterday	→	*the day before*
the day after tomorrow	→	*two days later*
the day before yesterday	→	*two days before*
next day/Friday/week/Christmas/...	→	*the following day/Friday/week/Christmas/...*
last Friday/week/summer/...	→	*the Friday/week/summer/... before*
two years/months/weeks/... ago	→	*two years/months/weeks/... before*
now, at present	→	*then*
at the moment	→	*at that moment*
at this time	→	*at that time*
here	→	*there*
in this place	→	*at that place*
this	→	*that*
these	→	*those*

B Fragesätze

1 A member of the audience **asked what had led** to the widespread use of robots in factories.
2 She **wanted to know if/whether** her job **was endangered**.

> Bei indirekten **Fragen** unterscheidet man zwischen Fragen mit Fragewort (1) und Fragen ohne Fragewort (2).
> Bei Fragen **mit Fragewort** wird das Fragewort übernommen (1).
> Bei Fragen **ohne Fragewort** benutzt man *if* bzw. *whether* (= ob), um zu verdeutlichen, dass es sich um eine Frage handelt (2).
> Alle anderen Änderungen erfolgen wie bei den Aussagesätzen (siehe **Aussagesätze** S. 217).

C Bitten, Aufforderungen und Befehle

1 Lucy **asked the engineer to show her** the robot.
2 He **told her not to go** too close to it.

> **Bitten** werden meist durch *asked* (= bitten) (1), **Aufforderungen** und **Befehle** durch *told* (= sagen) (2) eingeleitet.
> Bei **positiven Sätzen** erscheint das Verb als *to* + Infinitiv (1).
> Bei **negativen Sätzen** setzen wir *not* unmittelbar vor *to* (2).

⚠ Die beiden Verben *to tell* und *to ask* stehen immer mit einem Objekt, das die angesprochene Person erwähnt (1, 2). Ist dies vom Kontext her nicht erkennbar, wird einfach ein passender Begriff eingesetzt:

– *Ben said, 'Don't enter the studio when the red light is on.'*
  *Ben **told everybody** not to enter the studio when the red light was on.*

THE PASSIVE

1 Measures **are being introduced** to reduce traffic pollution.
2 Pollution **is caused by** some thoughtless people.

> Ist der Verursacher einer Handlung unbekannt oder zweitrangig, benutzt man das Passiv. Im Vordergrund steht also das Ergebnis des Vorgangs (1).
> Möchte man den Verursacher doch angeben, benutzt man einen *by agent* (2).
> ⚠ Der Verursacher wird mit *by* – auf keinen mit Fall *from* – eingeleitet.
> Das Passiv wird mit einer Zeitform von *to be* und der 3. Form des Vollverbs gebildet:

Zeit	Zeitform von *to be*	3. Form
simple present	*am/is/are*	*caused*
present progressive	*am/is/are being*	*introduced*
simple past	*was/were*	*buried*
past progressive	*was/were being*	*built*
present perfect	*has/have been*	*installed*
will-Futur	*will be*	*blocked*
going to-Futur	*am/is/are going to be*	*sacked*

> Beim Gebrauch von modalen Hilfsverben wird nach folgendem Muster verfahren:

bei Aussagen	Hilfsverb + *to be* + 3. Form	*must be displayed*
bei Fragen	Hilfsverb + Subjekt + *to be* + 3. Form	*Can ... be persuaded?*

⚠ Das Verb *to be* bleibt im Infinitiv immer unverändert.

THE IMPERSONAL PASSIVE

1 **It is said that** petrol will soon cost more.
2 He **is thought** to have gone to hospital.

> Das **impersonal passive** wird vor allem dann benutzt, wenn man sich objektiv bzw. unbeteiligt ausdrücken möchte. Daher kommt diese Struktur oft in Polizeiberichten, seriösen Zeitungsartikeln usw. vor.

> Bei Verben des Berichtens, Denkens usw. benutzt man häufig das Satzmuster:
It is/was/... + 3. Form des einleitenden Verbs + *that*-Satz (1).
Hier sind weitere Beispiele dieses Musters:

Aktiv	*Some **say** that companies which cause pollution should be heavily fined.*
Passiv	***It is said that** companies which cause pollution should be heavily fined.*
Aktiv	*Experts **recommended** that more be spent on public transport.*
Passiv	***It was recommended** that more be spent on public transport.*

> Um das Subjekt des *that*-Satzes zu betonen, kann man folgendes Muster benutzen:
Subjekt + *is/was/...* + 3. Form + *to be* + andere Satzteile (2):

Aktiv	*Many **believe** that the minister is thinking of raising fuel taxes.*
Passiv	*The minister **is believed to be** thinking of raising fuel taxes.*

⚠ Der *by agent* wird in solchen Passivsätzen folgendermaßen verwendet:

Aktiv	*The speaker felt that the idea was too radical.*
Passiv	*The idea was felt to be too radical **by** the speaker.*

CONDITIONALS

1 If we **invest** in new technology, a lot of people **will lose** their jobs.
2 A lot of people **will lose** their jobs if we **invest** in new technology.
3 If more people **took part** in re-training schemes, they **wouldn't have to worry** about finding new employment.
4 We **won't have** political censorship if we **don't start** to censor the internet.
5 **Will** we soon **have** political censorship if we **start** to censor the internet?

> Ein **Konditionalsatz** besteht aus zwei Teilen: dem *if*-**Teil** und dem **Hauptteil**.
Der *if*-**Teil** drückt eine **Bedingung** aus, der Hauptteil eine **Folge**.
> Bei **Konditionalsätzen** kommen folgende **Zeitmuster** am häufigsten vor:

Typ I	*If + simple present*	+ *will*-Futur
Typ II	*If + simple past*	+ *would* + Infinitiv
Typ III	*If + past perfect*	+ *would have* + 3. Form des Verbs

Der *if*-Teil kann hinter dem Hauptteil stehen. In diesem Fall steht kein Komma dazwischen (2).
> Je nach Sinn kann der *if*-Teil, der Hauptteil oder beide Teile des Satzes **verneint** werden (3, 4).
> Bei **Fragen** kann nur der **Hauptteil** zu einer Frage geformt werden. Dann steht dieser Teil **an erster Stelle** (5).

> *if*-Sätze werden gemäß der **Wahrscheinlichkeit** der zu erwartenden Folge eingesetzt:
Typ I: Folge (fast) sicher.
*If we **invest in** new technology, a lot of people **will lose** their jobs.*
D.h. viele Leute werden (vermutlich) ihre Stellen verlieren, da wir (sehr wahrscheinlich) in die neue Technologie investieren werden.
Typ II: Folge theoretisch möglich, aber kaum wahrscheinlich.
*If we **invested in** new technology, a lot of people **would lose** their jobs.*
D.h. es ist kaum zu erwarten, dass viele Leute ihre Stellen verlieren werden, da wir (wahrscheinlich) nicht in die neue Technologie investieren werden.
Typ III: Folge unmöglich, da die Bedingung nicht erfüllt wurde und bereits in der Vergangenheit liegt.
*If we **had invested in** new technology, a lot of people **would have lost** their jobs.*
D.h. der Sprecher weiß schon, dass keiner den Job verloren hat, da wir in die neue Technologie nicht investiert haben.

GERUND/INFINITIVE

1 Max **enjoys playing** football.
2 Can you **afford to buy** that DVD collection?
3 Cem and Julie **continued to meet** even though they had spilt up.
4 Cem and Julie **continued meeting** even though they had split up.
5 Alison **normally likes going** to parties, but **today** she would **prefer to stay** at home.

> Nach einigen Verben folgt immer die *-ing*-Form **(gerund)** (1).
Am wichtigsten sind:

admit, avoid, consider, deny, enjoy, finish, give up, imagine, mention, (not) mind (etwas/nichts dagegen haben), *miss, practise, recommend, risk, stop, suggest*

> **Nach einigen Verben** folgt immer der Infinitiv **(infinitive)** (2).
Die **wichtigsten** Verben dieser Gruppe sind:

afford, choose, decide, expect, hope, manage, mean, plan, promise, refuse, want

⚠ Nach den Verben *begin*, *continue*, *intend* und *start* kann der **Infinitiv** oder die *-ing*-Form **beliebig benutzt werden** (3, 4).

> Einige Verben werden **je nach Bedeutung** entweder mit dem **Infinitiv** oder mit der *-ing*-Form benutzt. Die **wichtigsten** Verben dieser Gruppe sind:

like, dislike, love, hate, prefer

> Wenn von einer **allgemeingültigen Situation** die Rede ist, folgt auf diese Verben die *-ing*-Form.
Handelt es sich aber um eine **Ausnahmesituation**, dann verwendet man den **Infinitiv** (5).

advise, allow, encourage, forbid, permit, recommend
Handelt es sich um einen **konkreten Einzelfall**, wird mit diesen Verben ein **Objekt + Infinitiv** verwendet.
*I strongly **advise you to** be more polite to people.*
Wenn es sich aber um eine **allgemeine Situation** handelt, dann steht das nachfolgende Verb in der *-ing*-Form.
*Most firms don't **allow smoking** in their offices.*

forget/remember

Die Struktur *forget/remember* + *-ing*-Form bezieht sich auf die Vergangenheit. Sie drückt etwa die Idee „Ich werde nie vergessen ..." aus.

⚠ „Vergangenheit" bezieht sich hier nicht auf *forget/remember*, sondern auf das nachfolgende Verb.

*I still **remember getting** my first bicycle.*
*I'll never **forget going** to the Rock against Hunger concert last year.*

Die Struktur *forget/remember* + Infinitiv dagegen bezieht sich auf die Zukunft. Sie drückt etwa die Idee aus „Ich darf nicht vergessen, etwas zu tun" bzw. „ich habe noch etwas zu tun, weil ich es bis jetzt vergessen habe".

*Dad, please **remember/don't forget to pick me up** from the station.*
*Oh dear. I **forgot/didn't remember to pick Sally up** from the station.*

regret

Die Struktur *regret* + *-ing*-Form drückt Bedauern über eine vergangene Situation bzw. einen vergangenen Vorfall aus. Häufig geht es dabei um verpasste Chancen.

*I really **regret leaving** school without any qualifications.*
*I know they will **regret buying** such a big, expensive car.*

Die Struktur *regret* + Infinitiv – fast immer mit einem Verb des Mitteilens wie *inform, say, tell* kombiniert – drückt eine schlechte Nachricht aus.

*I **regret to say** that I can't attend the meeting tomorrow.*
*We **regret to inform** you that the vacancy has now been filled.*

stop

Bedeutet *stop* „aufhören, etwas zu tun", steht das nachfolgende Verb in der *-ing*-Form.
Bedeutet aber *stop* „kurz anhalten, um etwas anderes zu tun", folgt ein Verb im **Infinitiv**.

*For heaven's sake **stop shouting** at me.*
*I'm a little late because I **stopped to give** somebody a lift.*

try

Bedeutet *try* „etwas ausprobieren", steht das nachfolgende Verb in der *-ing*-Form. Bedeutet aber *try* „sich anstrengen, etwas zu tun", folgt ein Verb im **Infinitiv**.

*I **tried phoning** Ellie, but she wasn't at home.*
*We'll **try to repair** your computer by the weekend.*

ADJECTIVES AND ADVERBS

1 John has a **new** DVD player.
2 He always buys **expensive** equipment.
3 My computer has become **very slow**.
4 That CD sounds **terrible**.
5 We can make printouts **quickly** and **cheaply**.

> Um **Personen** oder **Sachen** näher zu beschreiben, benutzt man **Adjektive** (1–4).
> Adjektive stehen **unmittelbar** vor Substantiven oder **unmittelbar nach** einer Form von *be* (bzw. *become* oder *seem*, die *be* ersetzen können) (3).
> **Adjektive** können mit Verben wie *feel, look* (aussehen), *sound, smell* und *taste* eine **sinnliche Wahrnehmung** ausdrücken (4).
> Um einen **Tätigkeitsverb** näher zu beschreiben, setzt man ein Adverb **unmittelbar hinter das Verb** bzw. Verb + Objekt (5).

⚠ Im Englischen können ein Verb und sein Objekt – anders als im Deutschen – nicht durch ein Adverb getrennt werden. Also NICHT: ~~We can make quickly printouts~~. (siehe Word order unten)

> Adverbien werden auch benutzt, um **Adjektive, andere Adverbien** und **ganze Sätze** näher zu bestimmen:

*MP3 players have become **surprisingly cheap**.* (Adverb + Adjektiv)
*My fax machine prints out **terribly slowly**.* (Adverb + Adverb)
***Luckily** Gerd left a message on my mailbox.* (Satzadverb)

> Die meisten Adverbien werden durch Anhängen von *-ly* an das Adjektiv gebildet (5). Eine kleine Anzahl von Adverbien hat dieselbe Form wie Adjektive; die häufigsten sind *fast, hard, early late, long, daily*.

COMPARISON OF ADJECTIVES AND ADVERBS

1 A hundred years ago life was **slower** and people may have been **happier**.
2 Which technological innovation is the **most/least important**?
3 Today you can copy data **more easily than** ever before.

> **Einsilbige** und **zweisilbige Adjektive**, die auf *-y* enden – zum Beispiel *easy, happy* und *lucky* –, werden mit *-(i)er/-(i)est* gesteigert (1).

> **Mehrsilbige Adjektive** und **Adverbien**, die auf *-ly* enden, werden mit *more/most* gesteigert (2, 3).

⚠ Die Adverbien, die dieselbe Form wie das entsprechende Adjektiv haben (*fast, hard, early* usw.), werden mit *-er/-est* gesteigert.

> Um Personen oder Sachen im Satz miteinander zu vergleichen, gibt es folgende Möglichkeiten:

Kein Unterschied	*as good as*	genau so gut wie
Unterschied	*not as good as*	nicht so gut wie
Unterschied	*better than*	besser als

WORD ORDER
positions of adverbs of time, place and frequency

1 She goes shopping **every week**.
2 They play in a club **in Doherty Street**.
3 **Last year** we went to India for our holidays.
4 Paul and Emily went to **the USA last year**.
5 She **always finishes** school early on Fridays.
6 He **is never** at home when I call.
7 I like to stay at home **now and then**.
8 Gina acted **strangely at the party last night**.

> Zeitangaben (Wann?) und Ortsangaben (Wo?, Wohin?) stehen in der Regel am Satzende (1, 2).
> Um die Zeit eines bestimmten Ereignisses hervorheben, kann man die Zeitangabe an die erste Stelle setzen (3).
> Stehen eine Zeitangabe und eine Ortsangabe zusammen am Satzende, dann gilt die Reihenfolge Ort vor Zeit (alphabetisch merken: O vor Z!) (4).
> Besteht eine Häufigkeitsangabe aus einem Wort, z.B. *always, often, sometimes*, steht sie unmittelbar vor dem Vollverb (5).
> Lautet das Vollverb *to be*, steht das Adverb direkt dahinter (6).

> Besteht die Häufigkeitsangabe aus mehreren Wörtern, z.B. *every day, now and then*, steht sie wie eine Zeitangabe am Satzende (7).
> Adverbien der Art und Weise stehen in der Regel am Satzende. Kommen noch Zeit- oder Ortsadverbien hinzu, lautet die Reihenfolge: Art und Weise – Ort – Zeit (AOZ) (8).

RELATIVE CLAUSES AND CONTACT CLAUSES

1 Car manufacturers are designing cars **which/that** can use hydrogen fuel cells.
2 Wildernesses are being spoiled by tourists **who/that** want to go to 'unspoiled' places.
3 Tony filled in a Dateline questionnaire **(which/that)** he found on the internet.
4 Fred Foley is a paparazzo **whose** photos sell for huge sums of money.
5 Call centre employees, most **of whom** come from India, work long hours.
6 Some non-GM crops are attacked by pests **against which** they have no resistance.

> Relativsätze werden benutzt, um den Hauptsatz durch zusätzliche Informationen genauer zu bestimmen.
> Für **Sachen** benutzt man das Relativpronomen *which* bzw. *that* (1) und für Personen *who* bzw. *that* (2).
> Steht das Relativpronomen für das **Objekt des Hauptsatzes**, dann kann man es weglassen (3). Solche Relativsätze heißen **contact clauses**.
> Um **Besitz** bzw. **Zugehörigkeit** anzuzeigen, gebraucht man *whose* unmittelbar vor dem **Substantiv** bei Personen und Sachen (4).
> Steht eine **Präposition** vor dem **Relativpronomen**, wird *whom* für Personen und *which* für Sachen benutzt (5, 6). In solchen Fällen ist der Gebrauch von *that* nicht möglich.

DEFINING AND NON-DEFINING RELATIVE CLAUSES

1 The first Europeans **who** settled in Australia came from Britain.
2 Sydney, **which** is famous for its unusually designed opera house, is situated on the south-eastern coast of Australia.

> Im **ersten Beispielsatz** ist der Sinn des Hauptsatzes *The first Europeans came from Britain* ohne den Relativsatz *who settled in Australia* offensichtlich falsch bzw. unvollständig. Relativsätze dieser Art – die wesentlich für das Verständnis des gesamten Satzes sind – nennt man **defining relative clauses** (notwendige oder bestimmende Relativsätze).
> Im **zweiten Beispielsatz** ist die Aussage des Hauptsatzes *Sydney is situated on the south-eastern coast of Australia* ohne den Relativsatz völlig verständlich, weil der Relativsatz *which is famous for its unusually designed opera house* eine zusätzliche, also nebensächliche, Information enhält. Daher werden solche Relativsätze **non-*defining relative clauses*** (nicht notwendige oder nicht bestimmende Relativsätze) genannt.
> ⚠ Notwendige Relativsätze werden immer **ohne** trennende **Kommas** benutzt. Dies signalisiert, dass sie fester Bestandteil der Hauptaussage sind.

PARTICIPLE CONSTRUCTIONS

1 Malaria, preventable with a treated bed net **costing** less than one pound, is endemic.
2 Many men believe that any work **involved** with cooking is a woman's chore.
3 **Losing** more and more people to AIDS, Africa now needs effective help more urgently than ever before.

4 **Burdened** with declining life-expectancy, large parts of Africa are caught in a poverty trap.

5 **Having fetched** water from a river for many years, some women in developing countries are now happy to be able to use the Hippo Roller.

6 **Despite facing** extreme destitution, many rural residents haven't given up hope.

7 Donors should invest in projects that help local inhabitants become self-supporting, **thereby making** sure that the money isn't wasted.

8 Poor infrastructure is a key barrier to economic growth in Nepal, **thus causing** huge additional costs to the transport of commercial goods.

9 Life is becoming hard in the developing countries, **with** many small farmers **going** out of business.

10 AIDS represents a major challenge to sub-Saharan Africa, currently **killing** more than two million people every year.

Die englische Sprache ist geprägt durch häufige Verwendung von Partizipialkonstruktionen. Diese ermöglichen einen eleganteren Sprachfluss.

> Partizipialkonstruktionen verkürzen Relativsätze; dabei kann entweder das **present participle** (1) oder das **past participle** (2) verwendet werden.

> Sie werden auch verwendet, um adverbiale Nebensätze zu vekürzen. In diesen Fällen unterscheidet man zwischen Partizipialkonstruktionen ohne Konjunktion (3–5) und solchen mit Konjunktion (6–9). In Sätzen ohne Konjunktion ist der Inhalt des Satzes auch ohne eine solche klar. Dagegen sind Konjunktionen nötig, um zu verhindern, dass der logische Zusammenhang des Satzes verloren geht. Zum Beispiel wird der Inhalt von Satz 6 unklar, wenn die Konjunktion *despite* ausgelassen wird.

> Wie bei der Verkürzung von Relativsätzen kommen auch bei der Verkürzung von adverbialen Nebensätzen das **present participle** (3, 6–9) und das **past participle** (4) zur Anwendung. Darüber hinaus wird hier auch noch das **perfect participle** verwendet (5), und zwar um die Vorzeitigkeit der Handlung im Nebensatz auszudrücken. *(Nachdem sie jahrelang Wasser aus dem Fluss geholt hatten, ...)*

> Schließlich verknüpft man mit einer Partizipialkonstruktion zwei Hauptsätze zu einem einzigen Satz, und zwar ausnahmslos mittels **present participle** (10).

COUNTABLE AND UNCOUNTABLE NOUNS

1 Visit our website for more **information** on our firm.   NICHT ~~informations~~

2 Have you read the paper today? The political **news** is interesting.   NICHT ~~news are~~

3 Where can I get some **advice**?   NICHT ~~an advice~~

> Einige wichtige **Substantive** sind **zählbar im Deutschen, nicht jedoch im Englischen**. Diese Substantive können also nicht ohne weiteres mit dem unbestimmten Artikel *a/an* oder mit einem Zahlwort benutzt werden.
> Hier ist eine Liste solcher Wörter, die Sie auswendig lernen sollten:

> *advice, baggage, damage, data, equipment, evidence, furniture, information, knowledge, luck, luggage, machinery, news, progress, research, rubbish, work (housework, homework)*

> Um diese Substantive im Plural zu verwenden, muss *some, a bit of* bzw. *a piece of* hinzugefügt werden (3).

THE DEFINITE ARTICLE

1 **Sociologists** say that **violence** is increasing among young people.
2 Is **the current trend** partly caused by **the violent films** they watch?
3 **Most sentences** are not tough enough.
4 Nearly **half the prisoners** in **British prisons** are under 25.
5 **Spring** is my favourite season but **the spring** we're having this year is more like **winter**.
6 We had **breakfast** late this morning so we came to school **by car** instead of **by bus**.
7 They are thinking of legalizing soft drugs in **the Netherlands**.

> Hat ein Substantiv eine allgemeine, uneingeschränkte Bedeutung – also „alle ohne Ausnahme"
> – dann steht es ohne Artikel (1, 5).

> Ist die Bedeutung eines Substantives auf bestimmte Fälle eingeschränkt, benutzt man den Artikel
> (2, 5).

> Ferner wird der Artikel in den folgenden Fällen und Wendungen im Englischen – z. T. anders als
> im Deutschen – nicht gebraucht:
>   – bei *most* in der Bedeutung „die meisten" (3),
>   – bei öffentlichen Gebäuden im allgemeinen Sinn (4),
>   – bei Mahlzeiten (6),
>   – bei Verkehrsmitteln (6),
>   – bei Straßennamen,
>   – bei Tageszeiten, Wochentagen, Monaten und Jahreszeiten im allgemeinen Sinn (5).

> Der Artikel wird verwendet nach *all* und *half* (4) und mit den Pluralnamen von Staaten (7).
>   ⚠ Der bestimmte Artikel steht im Englischen (viel) seltener als im Deutschen. Daher: *When
>   in doubt, leave it out!*

Basic word list

Diese Liste enthält ca. 1000 Wörter und Ausdrücke, die in Focus on Success – The new edition: Ausgabe Wirtschaft als bekannt vorausgesetzt werden. Nicht aufgeführt, jedoch vorausgesetzt, sind einige elementare Wörter wie einfache Strukturwörter, Präpositionen, Zahlen, Wochentage usw. sowie internationale Wörter wie *email*, *hotel*, *cowboy* usw.

> **> TIP**
>
> Die folgende Grundwortschatzliste ist nach Themenbereichen angelegt. Auch innerhalb der Themenbereiche sind die Vokabeln nach sinnvollen Wortfeldern angeordnet. Dadurch eignet sich die Liste nicht nur zum Nachschlagen, sondern auch zum Lernen. Hierzu gibt es eine einfache, aber effektive Übung. Nehmen Sie sich einen Themenbereich vor und verdecken Sie ein paar Wörter in der linken Spalte. Schauen Sie nun auf die Übersetzungen in der rechten Spalte und bilden Sie englische Sätze, die so viele Übersetzungen der verdeckten deutschen Wörter wie möglich enthalten. Anschließend kontrollieren Sie Ihre Übersetzungen, indem Sie die linke Spalte aufdecken.

PEOPLE
(Menschen)

people *Personen*
population *Bevölkerung, Einwohner*
nationality *Staatsangehörigkeit*
race *Rasse*
racist *rassistisch; Rassist/in*
society *Gesellschaft*
social *sozial*
human *menschlich*
adult *Erwachsene/r*
child *Kind*
teenager *Teenager/in*
sex *Geschlecht*
lady *Dame*
man *Mann, Mensch*
men *Männer, Menschen*
woman *Frau*
women *Frauen*
male *männlich*
female *weiblich, Frauen-*
boy *Junge*
girl *Mädchen*
couple *Paar*
married *verheiratet*
to get married *heiraten*
Mr *Herr*
Mrs, Ms *Frau*
name *Name*
age *Alter*
born *geboren*
life *Leben*
death *Tod*
anybody *jemand, jede/r/s*
anyone *jemand, jede/r/s*
nobody *niemand*
some *einige, etwas*
somebody *jemand*

someone *jemand*
everybody *jede/r/s*
everyone *jede/r/s, alle*
friend *Freund/in*
guest *Gast*
host *Gastgeber/in*
leader *Leiter/in*
loser *Verlierer/in*
member *Mitglied*
group *Gruppe*
crowd *(Menschen-)Menge*
together *zusammen*

FAMILY
(Familie)

family *Familie*
parents *Eltern*
father *Vater*
mother *Mutter*
dad *Papa*
mum, mom *(AE) Mama*
stepfather *Stiefvater*
stepmother *Stiefmutter*
husband *(Ehe-)Mann*
wife *(Ehe-)Frau*
children *Kinder*
son *Sohn*
daughter *Tochter*
brother *Bruder*
sister *Schwester*
brothers and sisters *Geschwister*
cousin *Cousin/e*
grandparents *Großeltern*
grandfather *Großvater*
grandmother *Großmutter*
grandchildren *Enkel(kinder)*

EMOTIONS
(Gefühle)

to feel *(sich) fühlen*
feeling, emotion *Gefühl*
happy *glücklich, froh, zufrieden*
joy *Freude*
pleased *zufrieden*
(to) surprise *Überraschung; überraschen*
mad *verrückt, toll*
unhappy *unglücklich*
sad *traurig*
to cry *schreien, weinen*
angry *wütend, zornig*
crazy *verrückt*
afraid of *ängstlich*
to be frightened of *sich fürchten vor*
tired *müde*
care *Sorge*

BODY AND CLOTHING
(Körper und Kleidung)

body *Körper*
physical *physisch, körperlich*
leg *Bein*
arm *Arm*
hand *Hand*
shoulder *Schulter*
hair *Haar(e)*
to touch *anfassen, berühren*
head *Kopf*
face *Gesicht*
eye *Auge*
to look *(aus)sehen, blicken*
nose *Nase*

to smell *riechen*
mouth *Mund*
voice *Stimme*
to smile *lächeln*
to speak *sprechen, reden*
ear *Ohr*
to listen *zuhören*
to hear *hören*
to sound *klingen*
tooth *Zahn*
heart *Herz*
skin *Haut*
health *Gesundheit*
healthy *gesund*
well *gesund, gut*
able *fähig, in der Lage*
flexible *flexibel*
illness *Krankheit*
ill/sick *krank*
painful *schmerzhaft*
fat *dick*
thin *dünn*
short *kurz, klein*
small *klein*
tall/big *groß*
weak *schwach*
strong *stark, kräftig*
old *alt*
young *jung*
clothing *Bekleidung*
clothes *Kleidung, Kleider*
fashion *Mode*
design *Design*
(to) dress *Kleid; (be)kleiden*
to wear *tragen, anhaben*
to cover *(be)decken*
to wash *waschen*
to spray *(be)sprühen*
comfortable *bequem*
uncomfortable *unbequem*
elegant *elegant*
coat *Mantel*
shirt *Hemd*
shoes *Schuhe*
trainers *Turnschuhe*
boot *Stiefel*
bag *Tasche*
uniform *Uniform*

JOBS AND WORK
(Jobs und Arbeit)

to work *arbeiten, funktionieren*
worker *Arbeiter/in*
job *Arbeit, Stelle*
factory *Fabrik*
business *Geschäft, Firma*
company *Firma, Unternehmen*
firm *Firma*
office *Büro, Amt*
assistant *Assistent/in,
   Verkäufer/in*

director *Direktor/in, Geschäfts-
   führer/in*
boss *Chef/in*
customer *Kunde, Kundin*
meeting *Konferenz, Besprechung*
model *Modell, Model*
project *Projekt*
programme *Programm*
expert *Fachmann/frau*
doctor *Arzt, Ärztin*
police *Polizei*
politician *Politiker/in*
farmer *Bauer, Bäuerin*

SCHOOL
(Schule)

education *Erziehung, (Ausbildung)*
school *Schule*
to learn *lernen, erfahren*
college *Fachhochschule*
to train *trainieren, ausbilden*
university *Universität*
to study *lernen, studieren*
course *Kurs, Lehrgang,*
class *Klasse*
desk *(Schreib-)Tisch*
seat *Sitz(platz)*
teacher *Lehrer/in*
to teach *unterrichten, lehren*
pupil *Schüler/in*
student *Student/in, Lernende/r*
subject *(Schul-)Fach, Thema*
English *englisch*
German *deutsch*
history *Geschichte*
topic *Thema*
question *Frage*
exercise *Übung*
homework *Hausaufgaben*
rule *Vorschrift, Regel*
to match *zuordnen, (zusammen)
   passen*
correct *richtig*
true *richtig, wahr*
false *falsch*

HOUSES AND HOMES
(Haus und Einrichtung)

house *Haus*
home *Zuhause, Heim; nach Hause*
flat *Wohnung*
to live *wohnen, leben*
address *Adresse*
door *Tür*
key *Schlüssel*
roof *Dach*
window *Fenster*
stairs *Treppe*
room *Zimmer, Raum*

(to) clean *sauber; reinigen, säubern*
furniture *Möbel*
bed *Bett*
table *Tisch*
bath *Bad*
shower *Dusche*
kitchen *Küche*
floor *Etage, (Fuß-)Boden*
alarm *Alarm(anlage)*

HOBBIES AND SPORT
(Hobbys und Sport)

to like *mögen, gern tun*
to interest *interessieren*
to enjoy *genießen, gefallen*
to love *lieben, sehr gern mögen*
favourite *Lieblings-*
fun *Spaß*
sport *Sport*
active *aktiv, tätig, aktiviert*
to play *spielen*
match *Spiel, Wettkampf*
game *Spiel*
ball *Ball, Kugel*
to kick *treten*
score *Ergebnis, Punkt(estand)*
to win *gewinnen, siegen*
winner *Gewinner/in, Sieger/in*
to swim *schwimmen*
to fish *angeln*
cycling *Radfahren*
bike *Rad*
to ride *reiten, (Rad) fahren*
(to) dance *Tanz; tanzen*
dancer *Tänzer/in*
television *Fernsehen, Fernseher*
viewer *Zuschauer/in*
TV programme *Fernsehprogramm*
to smoke *rauchen*

SOCIETY AND SOCIAL PROBLEMS
(Gesellschaft und soziale Probleme)

religion *Religion*
politics *Politik*
political *politisch*
rights *Rechte*
vote *Stimme, Abstimmung*
to allow *erlauben, (zu)lassen*
to control *kontrollieren, regeln*
control *Kontrolle*
poor *arm, schlecht, mangelhaft*
rich *reich, wohlhabend*
protest *Protest*
crime *Verbrechen*
conflict *Konflikt*
problem *Problem*
crisis *Krise*

danger *Gefahr*
dangerous *gefährlich*
serious *schwer, ernst*
wrong *falsch*
to hurt *verletzen*
to hit *schlagen, treffen*
to break *brechen*
to burn *(ver)brennen*
to fight *(be)kämpfen*
to die *sterben*
dead *tot*
to kill *töten*
gun *Schusswaffe, Pistole*
to protect *(be)schützen*
to hide *verstecken, verbergen*
drug *Droge*
risk *Risiko*
mistake *Fehler, Irrtum*
to forbid *verbieten*
to forget *vergessen*
to ignore *ignorieren*
to steal *stehlen*
personal *persönlich*
chance *Chance, Gelegenheit*
responsible *verantwortlich*
law *Gesetz, Recht*
case *Fall*

INTERACTING WITH PEOPLE
(Umgehen mit Menschen)

to communicate *sich mit jdm verständigen*
to talk *sprechen, reden*
to say *sagen*
to tell *sagen, erzählen*
truth *Wahrheit*
to ask *fragen, bitten*
to answer *(be)antworten*
to reply *antworten*
to realize *bemerken, realisieren*
to understand *verstehen, begreifen*
to translate *übersetzen, -tragen*
to explain *erklären*
to repeat *wiederholen*
to agree *zustimmen, vereinbaren*
to express *ausdrücken*
to be sorry *leidtun*
to discuss *diskutieren (über), besprechen*
to argue *argumentieren, streiten*
argument *Argument; Streit*
to shout *schreien*
to order *befehlen, bestellen, ordnen*
to direct *leiten*
to shock *erschüttern, schockieren*
reaction *Reaktion*
to warn *warnen*
to disappoint *enttäuschen*
to promise *versprechen*
to help *helfen*

to share *(sich) teilen, gemeinsam (be)nutzen*
to show *zeigen*
to connect *verbinden*
to call *(an)rufen*
to phone *anrufen*
to ring *läuten, anrufen*
to chat *sich unterhalten, chatten (mit)*
dialogue *Dialog*
conversation *Unterhaltung*
to introduce *(sich) vorstellen*
to meet *(zusammen)treffen, begegnen*
to greet *(be)grüßen*
(to) kiss *Kuss; küssen*
to laugh *lachen*
(to) joke *Witz; scherzen*
(to) offer *Angebot; (an)bieten*
to invite *einladen*
party *Party, Partei*
to arrange *arrangieren, vereinbaren*
to inform *informieren*
to report *berichten*
to notice *bemerken*
to guess *raten, schätzen*

READING AND WRITING
(Lesen und Schreiben)

to read *lesen*
reader *Leser/in*
story *Erzählung, Geschichte*
mail *Post*
letter *Brief, Buchstabe*
to send *senden, schicken*
document *Dokument, Papier*
briefcase *Aktentasche*
key *Taste*
table *Tabelle*
diagram *Diagramm, Grafik*
content *Inhalt*
to write *schreiben*
paper *Papier, Zeitung*
pencil *Bleistift*
point *Punkt; Sinn*
word *Wort*
sentence *Satz*
message *Mitteilung, Nachricht*
slogan *Werbespruch*
form *Form, Formular*
summary *Zusammenfassung*
page *Seite*
title *Titel*
information *Auskunft, Information(en)*
dictionary *Wörterbuch*
to mean *bedeuten, meinen, heißen*
meaning *Bedeutung*
emphasis *Hervorhebung*
to copy *kopieren*
to list *auflisten, notieren*

to note *beachten, notieren*
to complete *vervollständigen*
to comment *kommentieren*
to describe *beschreiben*
description *Beschreibung, Schilderung*
detail *Detail*
stereotype *Klischee*
example *Beispiel*
language *Sprache*
grammar *Grammatik*
vocabulary *Wortschatz*
style *Stil*
clear *klar, deutlich*
formal *formell, förmlich*
dear *liebe/r*

BELIEFS AND ATTITUDES
(Glaube und Einstellungen)

to believe *glauben*
to consider *nachdenken über, halten für*
to think *denken, meinen, finden, glauben*
view *Ansicht, Aussicht*
opinion *Meinung, Einschätzung*
positive *positiv, bejahend*
opposite *Gegenteil; gegensätzlich*
to dislike *nicht mögen*
to hate *hassen, nicht mögen*
option *Option, Wahl, Alternative*
idea *Idee, Gedanke*
to hope *hoffen*
(to) dream *Traum; träumen*
to want *wollen*
to wish *wünschen*
to remember *sich erinnern, daran denken*
to suppose *vermuten*
to imagine *sich vorstellen*
to seem *(er)scheinen*
to prove *beweisen*
real *echt, wirklich*
to worry *sich Sorgen machen*
to know *kennen, wissen*
reason *Vernunft, Grund*
to need *brauchen, benötigen*
necessary *nötig, erforderlich*

MOVEMENT
(Bewegung)

to move *(sich) bewegen, umziehen*
fast *schnell*
slow *langsam*
to go *gehen, fahren*
to walk *(zu Fuß) gehen*
step *Schritt*
to run *laufen*
to jump *springen*

to climb *klettern, steigen*
to fall *fallen*
to sit *sitzen, sich hinsetzen*
to stand *stehen, aushalten*
to rise *steigen*
to turn *(sich) drehen*
to arrive *ankommen*
to come *kommen*
to enter *eintreten, eingeben*
to leave *(ver)lassen*
to bring *bringen, holen*
to carry *tragen*
to put *setzen, stellen, legen*
to press *drücken*
to push *drücken, schieben*
to pull *ziehen*
to lead *führen*
to follow *(be)folgen*
to pass *vorbeigehen, vergehen; bestehen*
to hurry *sich beeilen*
to rush *sich beeilen*
to reach *greifen, erreichen*
to catch *fangen*
to disappear *verschwinden*

TOWNS AND BUILDINGS
(Städte und Gebäude)

city *(Groß-)Stadt*
town *Stadt*
village *Dorf*
neighbourhood *Nachbarschaft*
street *Straße*
path *(Fuß-)Weg, Pfad*
road *(Land-)Straße*
sign *Zeichen, Schild*
corner *Ecke*
map *Karte*
local *örtlich, lokal*
building *Gebäude*
bank *Bank*
church *Kirche*
tower *Turm*
hospital *Krankenhaus*
supermarket *Supermarkt*
market *Markt*
entrance *Eingang, Einfahrt*
bridge *Brücke*
farm *Bauernhof*

TRAFFIC, TRAVEL AND HOLIDAYS
(Verkehr, Reisen und Urlaub)

holiday *Ferien, Urlaub, Feiertag*
abroad *im/ins Ausland*
foreign *fremd*
international *international*
national *national, staatlich*
country *Land, Staat*

European *europäisch*
American *amerikanisch*
tour *Tour, Rundgang*
trip *Ausflug, Reise, Besuch*
tourist *Tourist/in*
visitor *Besucher/in, Gast*
to travel *reisen, fahren*
to visit *besuchen, besichtigen*
to plan *planen*
boat *Boot, Schiff*
ship *Schiff*
bus *(Linien-)Bus*
truck *Laster, Lkw*
car *Auto*
vehicle *Fahrzeug, Wagen*
to drive *(Auto) fahren*
driver *Fahrer/in*
plane *Flugzeug*
helicopter *Hubschrauber*
flight *Flug*
to fly *fliegen*
airport *Flughafen*
train *Zug*
underground *unterirdisch; U-Bahn*
station *Bahnhof*
ticket *Fahrkarte, Eintrittskarte*
to miss *verpassen, vermissen*
to return *zurückkehren, -gehen*
hotel *Hotel*
beach *Strand*
to relax *sich erholen*
photo *Foto*

MONEY AND SHOPPING
(Geld und Einkaufen)

money *Geld*
to earn *verdienen*
to afford *es sich leisten können*
to spend *ausgeben, verbringen*
to buy *kaufen*
to pay *(be)zahlen*
to sell *(sich) verkaufen*
to charge *berechnen, verlangen, (auf)laden*
to cost *kosten*
price *(Kauf-)Preis*
worth *wert*
bill *Rechnung*
present *Geschenk*
prize *Preis*
free *kostenlos, frei*
cheap *billig, günstig*
expensive *teuer*
luxury *Luxus*
card *Karte*
cash *Bargeld*
to change *(aus)wechseln, (sich) ändern*
to borrow *borgen, leihen*
to belong *gehören zu*
to own *besitzen*

to prefer *vorziehen, bevorzugen*
to choose *(aus)wählen*
available *verfügbar*
product *Produkt, Erzeugnis*
to produce *produzieren, herstellen*
shop *Laden, Geschäft*
shopping *Einkaufen*
sale *Verkauf*
success *Erfolg*
to open *öffnen*
to close *schließen*
open *offen*
closed *geschlossen*

EATING AND DRINKING
(Essen und Trinken)

to eat *essen*
food *Essen, Nahrung*
to cook *kochen*
to prepare *(sich) vorbereiten*
meal *Essen, Mahlzeit*
breakfast *Frühstück*
lunch *Mittagessen*
dinner *(Abend-)Essen*
to taste *schmecken*
hunger *Hunger*
hungry *hungrig*
thirst *Durst*
thirsty *durstig*
meat *Fleisch*
potato *Kartoffel*
vegetable *Gemüse*
fruit *Obst, Frucht*
fresh *frisch*
salt *Salz*
burger *Hamburger*
chicken *Huhn, Hähnchen*
egg *Ei*
cheese *Käse*
chocolate *Schokolade, Praline*
cake *Kuchen, Torte*
sweet *süß; Süßigkeit*
to drink *trinken*
mineral water *Mineralwasser*
tea *Tee*
juice *Saft*
alcohol *Alkohol*
wine *Wein*
beer *Bier*
bar *Bar*
cup *Tasse*
glass *Glas*
bottle *Flasche*
knife *Messer*
fork *Gabel*
spoon *Löffel*
plate *Platte, Teller*
bowl *Schüssel*
box *Kiste, Kästchen, Schachtel*
packet *Schachtel, Packung*

NATURE AND WEATHER
(Natur und Wetter)

nature *Natur*
natural *natürlich*
planet *Planet*
world *Welt*
continent *Erdteil, Kontinent*
environment *Umwelt, Umfeld*
earth *Erde*
air *Luft*
water *Wasser*
ice *Eis*
fire *Feuer*
sky *Himmel*
mountain *(größerer) Berg*
river *Fluss*
wind *Wind*
rain *Regen*
sun *Sonne*
storm *Sturm*
heat *Hitze*
hot *heiß, warm*
warm *warm*
cold *kalt*
to dry *trocknen*
wet *nass*
light *Licht, hell, leicht*
to shine *scheinen*
dark *dunkel*
animal *Tier*
dog *Hund*
cat *Katze*
bird *Vogel*
fish *Fisch*
flower *Blume*
plant *Pflanze*
tree *Baum*
to recycle *wieder verwerten*
to waste *verschwenden*

SCIENCE AND TECHNOLOGY
(Wissenschaft und Technik)

science *Wissenschaft*
scientist *Wissenschaftler/in*
chemical *chemisch; Chemikalie*
technical *technisch*
to build *(auf)bauen*
tool *Werkzeug*
device *Gerät, Apparat*
machine *Maschine*
computer *Computer*
data *Daten*
image *Bild*
to switch on *an-, einschalten*
to click *klicken*
to print *drucken*
electric *elektrisch, Strom-*
electricity *Elektrizität, Strom*
power *Kraft, Strom*

instruction *Anleitung*
method *Methode, Verfahren*
system *System*
to repair *reparieren*
modern *modern*
new *neu*
safe *sicher*
automatic *automatisch*

ART AND CULTURE
(Kunst und Kultur)

art *Kunst*
picture *Bild*
symbol *Symbol, Zeichen*
to draw *zeichnen*
scene *Szene*
to represent *darstellen*
culture *Kultur*
to act *handeln*
movie *Film*
book *Buch*
author *Autor/in*
article *Artikel*
newspaper *Zeitung*
magazine *Zeitschrift*
news *Neuigkeit(en), Nachricht(en)*
media *Medien*
song *Lied*
singer *Sänger/in*
music *Musik*
band *Kapelle*

QUALITIES AND CHARACTERISTICS
(Eigenschaften und Besonderheiten)

character *Charakter*
kind *Art, Sorte*
similar *ähnlich*
different *anders, verschieden*
difference *Unterschied*
advantage *Vorteil*
disadvantage *Nachteil*
to be *sein*
to become *werden*

DESCRIBING PEOPLE AND SITUATIONS
(Menschen und Situationen beschreiben)

friendly *freund(schaft)lich*
kind *nett*
interesting *interessant*
individual *individuell*
boring *langweilig*
funny *komisch, merkwürdig*
busy *beschäftigt, besetzt*

lazy *faul*
helpful *hilfreich, nützlich*
careful *vorsichtig, sorgfältig*
creative *gestalterisch, kreativ*
romantic *romantisch*
smart *schick, clever*
stupid *dumm*
silly *albern*
nice *schön, nett*
tough *zäh*
strict *streng, strikt*
polite *höflich*
rude *unhöflich, rüde*
pretty *hübsch*
beautiful *schön*
ugly *hässlich*
positive *positiv*
negative *negativ, verneinend*
strange *fremd, seltsam*
normal *normal*
perfect *vollkommen, perfekt*
special *besondere*
well-known *sehr bekannt, berühmt*
famous *berühmt*
popular *beliebt, populär*
unknown *unbekannt*
good *gut*
better *besser*
best *beste/r/s, am besten*
great *groß(artig)*
amazing *erstaunlich*
excellent *ausgezeichnet*
wonderful *wunderbar, -voll*
fantastic *fantastisch, wunderbar*
bad *schlecht, schlimm*
worse *schlechter, schlimmer*
worst *schlechteste/r/s, schlimmste/r/s*
horrible, awful, terrible *furchtbar, schrecklich*
easy *leicht, einfach*
basic *elementar*
simple *einfach*
hard *schwer, schwierig, hart*
difficult *schwer, schwierig*
important *wichtig*
successful *erfolgreich*
exciting *aufregend, spannend*
useful *nützlich*
unfair *unfair*
poor *arm*
wealthy *reich*
loud *laut*
quiet, silent *ruhig, still*
wet *nass*
dry *trocken*
slow *langsam*
quick *schnell, rasch*

DESCRIBING OBJECTS
(Gegenstände beschreiben)

type *Typ, Art*
object *Gegenstand*
thing *Sache, Ding, Gegenstand*
piece *Stück, Teil*
unit *Unit, Einheit*
colour *Farbe*
this *dies, diese/r/s*
that *das*
these *diese*
those *jene*
their *ihr/e/r/s*

Size – shape – weight
(Größe – Form – Gewicht)
line *Linie*
circle *Kreis*
hole *Loch*
size *Größe*
little *klein, wenig*
to grow *wachsen*
big *groß*
large *groß, umfangreich*
weight *Gewicht*
heavy *stark, schwer*
light *leicht*
to fill *füllen*
full *voll, vollständig*
empty *leer*
wide *breit, weit*
narrow *eng*
metre *Meter*
long *lang*
short *kurz*
hard *fest*
soft *weich*

ACTIONS AND PROCESSES
(Handlungen und Prozesse)

action *Aktion, Handlung*
activity *Tätigkeit*
to do *tun, machen*
to happen *passieren, geschehen*
to start *anfangen, starten, beginnen*
to continue *fortsetzen*
to finish *beenden, erledigen*
to stop *(an)halten, aufhören (mit)*
to result from *folgen aus*
to let *erlauben, (zu)lassen*

Necessity, probability, possibility
(Notwendigkeit, Wahrschein-
lichkeit, Möglichkeit)
condition *Bedingung*
may *dürfen, können, mögen*
maybe *vielleicht*
possible *möglich, denkbar*
impossible *unmöglich*
probably *wahrscheinlich*

can *können, dürfen*
could *konnte/n, könnte/n*
would *würde/n*
will *werde(n), wollen*
should *soll/en, sollte/n*
must *müssen*
to have to *müssen*

Everyday actions
(Alltagshandlungen)
to take *nehmen, bringen, dauern*
to decide *(sich) entscheiden,
    beschließen*
decision *Entscheidung*
to make *machen*
to fix *festlegen, reparieren*
to check *(über)prüfen*
to organize *organisieren*
to get *holen, bekommen, werden*
to give *geben*
to hold *abhalten, veranstalten*
to keep *(be)halten*
to spare *übrig haben*
to set *setzen*
to mix *mischen*
to remove *entfernen*
to avoid *vermeiden*
to wait *warten*
to watch *beobachten*
to see *sehen*
to search *(durch)suchen*
to find *finden, suchen*
to use *benutzen, verwenden*
to try *versuchen, probieren*
to experience *erfahren, erleben*
to open *öffnen, beginnen*
to develop *entwickeln*
to save *retten, sichern*
to recover *sich erholen*
to sleep *schlafen*
to wake up *aufwachen, aufwecken*

TIME *(Zeit)*

period *Periode, Zeitraum*
date *Datum, Termin*
beginning *Anfang*
to begin *anfangen, beginnen*
(to) end *Ende, Schluss; (be)enden*
final *letzte/r/s*
first *erste/r/s, zuerst*
last *letzte/r/s, zuletzt*
time *Zeit, Mal*

Days, months, ...
(Tage, Monate, ...)
second *Sekunde*
minute *Minute*
hour *Stunde*
o'clock *... Uhr*
day *Tag*
morning *Morgen*

afternoon *Nachmittag*
evening *Abend*
night *Nacht*
tonight *heute Abend/Nacht*
today *heute*
yesterday *gestern*
tomorrow *morgen*
week *Woche*
weekend *Wochenende*
month *Monat*
year *Jahr*
season *Saison, Jahreszeit*
spring *Frühling*
summer *Sommer*
autumn *Herbst*
winter *Winter*
Christmas *Weihnachten*
Easter *Ostern*
birthday *Geburtstag*
age *Zeitalter*

Frequency
(Häufigkeit)
sometimes *manchmal*
often *oft, häufig*
usual *gewöhnlich, normal*
usually *normalerweise, gewöhnlich,
    meistens*
common *üblich, gemeinsam*
regular *regelmäßig, regulär*
daily *täglich*
always *immer*
never *nie(mals)*

Other words for talking about
time *(andere Zeitangaben)*
early *früh*
late *spät*
later *später*
until *bis*
now *nun, jetzt*
then *dann*
ago *vor*
as *wie, als, da*
yet *noch*
before *vor(her)*
after *nach*
past *vorbei, nach; Vergangenheit*
future *Zukunft; (zu)künftig*
soon *bald*
suddenly *plötzlich*
only *nur, einzig*
once *einmal, einst*
again *wieder*
next *nächste/r/s; danach*
already *schon, bereits*
recent *letzt, jüngst*
while *während*
at the moment *momentan,
    augenblicklich*
nowadays *heutzutage*
forever *für immer*
ever *je(mals)*

ready *fertig, bereit*

PLACE AND DIRECTION
(Orts- und Richtungsangaben)

space *(Zwischen-)Raum, Abstand, Platz, Weltall*
place *Stelle, Platz*
situation *Situation, Lage*
outside *außer(halb)*
outdoors *draußen, im Freien*
inside *innerhalb, drinnen*
far *weit (entfernt)*
near *bei, nahe*
around *herum*
away *weg, entfernt*
back *zurück*
forward *vorwärts*

Prepositions
(Präpositionen)
from *von*
across *(quer) über*
along *entlang*
over *(vor)über*
under *unter*
between *zwischen*
through *durch*
behind *hinter, hinten*

Other words for describing places
(andere Ortsangaben)
direct *direkt*
state *Zustand, Staat*
to stay *bleiben*
here *hier*
there *da, dort(hin)*
anywhere *irgendwo(hin)*
somewhere *irgendwo(hin)*
nowhere *nirgends*
front *Vorderseite*
side *Seite, Rand*
top *Spitze, Gipfel; Spitzen-*
bottom *Boden, Unterseite*
high *hoch*
low *tief, niedrig*
distance *Entfernung, Abstand*
kilometre *Kilometer*
north *Norden, Nord-*
east *Osten*
south *Süden, Süd-*
west *Westen*
middle *Mitte*
left *linke/r/s, links*
right *rechts*

QUANTITY *(Menge)*

number *Nummer, Zahl*
count *zählen*
to add *zusammenzählen, hinzufügen*
plus *plus*
kilo *Kilo(gramm)*
litre *Liter*
limit *Grenze*
all *alle(s)*
whole *ganz*
almost *fast, beinahe*
nearly *beinahe, fast*
very *sehr*
really *wirklich, eigentlich, tatsächlich*
a lot *viel, sehr*
lots of *viel, viele*
many *viele*
most *meist*
much *viel*
more *mehr*
extra *zusätzlich*
double *doppelt*
both *beide*
pair *Paar*
enough *ausreichend, genug*
half *Hälfte; halb*
part *Teil*
quite *ziemlich, ganz*
less *weniger, abzüglich*
few *ein paar, wenig/e/r/s*
a little *ein wenig, etwas*
alone *allein(e)*
minimum *Minimum; minimal*
none *kein/e/r/s*
nothing *nichts*
neither *auch nicht, keine/r/s*
any *irgendetwas, welche/r/s, jede/r/s*
anything *etwas, alles*
another *noch eine*
other *andere/r/s*
each *jede/r/s*
every *jede/r/s*
everything *alles*
exactly *exakt, genau*
specific *spezifisch*
just *einfach, nur, genau*
about *über, etwa*
to include *einschließen*

CONNECTORS
(Strukturwörter)

because *weil*
so *also, damit, deshalb, so (dass)*
simply *einfach*
certainly *sicherlich, bestimmt*
for example *zum Beispiel*
such as *wie zum Beispiel*

(in this) way *Weg, Methode, auf diese Art (und Weise)*
but *aber, sondern*
however *doch, jedoch*
except *außer*
else *andere/r/s*
than *als*
whether *ob*
if *wenn, falls, ob*
or *oder*
same *gleiche/r/s, der-, die-, dasselbe*
also *auch, außerdem*
too *zu, auch*
with *mit, bei*
without *ohne*
in case *falls*
perhaps *vielleicht, eventuell*
even *sogar (noch)*
anyway *jedenfalls, sowieso*

USEFUL WORDS AND PHRASES
(Nützliche Wörter und Ausdrücke)

to welcome *willkommen*
excuse me *Entschuldigung*
please *bitte*
of course *natürlich, selbstverständlich*
sure *freilich, sicher(lich)*
thanks *Dank; danke*
unfortunately *leider*
total *(End-)Summe; völlig, (ins) gesamt*
main *hauptsächlich, wichtigste/r/s*
something *etwas*
fact *Tatsache, Fakt*
tip *Vorschlag, Hinweis, Tipp*
pro *für*
con *wider*
against *gegen*

QUESTION WORDS
(Fragewörter)

what? *was?, welche/r/s?*
where? *wo(hin)?*
when? *wenn?, wann?*
who? *wer?, welche(r/s)?*
which? *welche/r/s?*
why? *warum?*
how? *wie?*

Unit word list

Dieses Wörterverzeichnis enthält alle Wörter in Focus on Success – The new edition: Ausgabe Soziales in der Reihenfolge ihres Erscheinens. Nicht aufgeführt sind die Wörter aus der *Basic word list* sowie internationale Wörter wie *hotel, email* usw.

Die Wörter der *Social Options*-Seiten werden in den darauf folgenden Units nicht vorausgesetzt. Wörter, die in den Hörverständnistexten vorkommen, sind mit einem CD-Symbol gekennzeichnet.

AE = American English	*inf* = informal (*informell, Umgangssprache*)
BE = British English	*phr* = phrase (*feststehende Wendung*)
abbrev = abbreviation (*Abkürzung*)	◇ = opposite (*Gegensatz*)
n = noun (*Substantiv*)	*fem* = feminine
v = verb	*pl* = plural
adj = adjective	*esp* = especially
adv = adverb	

REFRESHER COURSE

UNIT A

page 6

to chill out	[ˌtʃɪl 'aʊt]	*(inf)* to relax	*sich entspannen*
to hang around	[ˌhæŋ ə'raʊnd]	*(inf)* to spend a lot of time in a place	*rumhängen*
speech bubble	['spiːtʃ bʌbl]	circle with words to show what someone says	*Sprechblase*
text message	['tekst mesɪdʒ]	written message sent by phone	*SMS*
chatroom	['tʃætruːm]	internet site where you can communicate with other people online	*Chatroom, Diskussionsforum*
to discover	[dɪ'skʌvə]	*n* discovery	*entdecken*
movies	['muːviz]	*(AE) BE*: cinema	*Kino*
to go clubbing	[gəʊ 'klʌbɪŋ]	to go out to clubs	*in Discos gehen*
net	[net]	*(abbrev)* internet	*Internet*
to carry out	[ˌkæri 'aʊt]	to do (a task)	*ausführen*
survey	['sɜːveɪ]	set of questions used to find out people's opinions	*Umfrage*

page 7

according to	[ə'kɔːdɪŋ tə]	as reported by	*nach, gemäß*
Red Cross	[ˌred 'krɒs]	a community service that helps people in need	*Rotes Kreuz*
worthwhile	[ˌwɜːθ'waɪl]	important, worth doing	*der Mühe wert*
the box	[ðə 'bɒks]	*(inf)* television	*die Kiste*
the homeless	[ðə 'həʊmləs]	people who have no home	*die Obdachlosen*
to get a lot out of sth	[ˌget ə lɒt 'aʊt əv]	to benefit from sth	*viel davon haben*
Are you joking?	[ɑ: ju 'dʒəʊkɪŋ]	used to show surprise	*Ist das dein Ernst?*
schoolwork	['skuːlwɜːk]	homework	*Hausaufgaben*
to suffer	['sʌfə]	to become worse	*leiden*
to look round	[ˌlʊk 'raʊnd]	to visit a place and see what is there	*sich umsehen*
I'm afraid	[aɪm ə'freɪd]	unfortunately, sorry	*leider*
coach	[kəʊtʃ]	trainer	*Trainer/in*
to expect	[ɪk'spekt]	*phr* to expect sb to do sth	*erwarten*
violent	['vaɪələnt]	*n* violence	*gewalttätig*
stuff	[stʌf]	things	*Zeug*
to test	[test]	to examine	*prüfen*
skill	[skɪl]	thing you are good at	*Fähigkeit, Geschick*
to network	['netwɜːk]	to link up with	*vernetzen*
all over the place	[ɔːl ˌəʊvə ðə 'pleɪs]	everywhere	*überall*
voluntary	['vɒləntri]	*v* to volunteer	*freiwillig*

competitive	[kəm'petətɪv]	*phr* competitive sports	*Wettkampf-*
part-time job	[ˌpɑːt 'taɪm dʒɒb]	*v* to work part-time	*Teilzeitjob*
expression	[ɪk'spreʃn]	word or phrase	*Ausdruck*
definition	[ˌdefɪ'nɪʃn]	explanation of a word	*Definition*
valuable	['væljuəbl]	useful, important	*wertvoll*
permanent	['pɜːmənənt]	<> temporary	*ständig, dauerhaft*
certain	['sɜːtn]	definite	*gewiss, sicher*
ability	[ə'bɪləti]	skill	*Fähigkeit*

page 8

not necessarily	[nɒt ˌnesə'serəli]	*adj* necessary	*nicht unbedingt*
order	['ɔːdə]	sequence	*Reihenfolge*
employer	[ɪm'plɔɪə]	*v* to employ	*Unternehmer, Arbeitgeber*
qualification	[ˌkwɒlɪfɪ'keɪʃn]	*phr* job qualifications	*Qualifikation, Ausbildung*
cinema	['sɪnəmə]	*(BE) AE:* movie theater	*Kino*
instead of	[ɪn'sted əv]	rather than	*statt, anstatt (von)*
petrol	['petrəl]	*(BE) AE:* gas	*Benzin*
to refer to	[rɪ'fɜː tə]	to talk about sth specific	*sich beziehen auf*
to replace	[rɪ'pleɪs]	to put sth in the place of sth else	*ersetzen*
underlined	[ˌʌndə'laɪnd]	with a line underneath the word	*unterstrichen*
suitable	['suːtəbl]	appropriate	*passend, geeignet*
to score a goal	[skɔːr ə 'gəʊl]	e.g. Ronaldo scored three goals.	*ein Tor erzielen*
to be lucky	[bi 'lʌki]	not: ~~to have luck~~	*Glück haben*
times	[taɪmz]	*phr* many times	*mal*

page 9

rare	['reə]	not very often, unusual	*selten*
seldom	['seldəm]	not very often, rarely	*selten*
general	['dʒenrəl]	most of the time, basic	*allgemein*
weekday	['wiːkdeɪ]	*phr* on weekdays	*Wochentag*
drum	[drʌm]	*phr* to play the drums	*Trommel*
to surf	[sɜːf]	*phr* to surf the net	*surfen*
mark	[mɑːk]	result at school	*Note*
better	['betə]	<> worse	*besser*

page 10

below	[bɪ'ləʊ]	<> above	*unten*
pub	[pʌb]	*(BE) AE:* bar	*Kneipe*
mate	[meɪt]	*(inf)* friend	*Kumpel*
at present	[ət 'preznt]	at the moment	*gegenwärtig*
currently	['kʌrəntli]	at the moment	*zurzeit*

page 11

to serve	[sɜːv]	to give (a meal) to sb	*servieren*
ordinary	['ɔːdnri]	normal	*gewöhnlich, normal*
exercise bike	['eksəsaɪz baɪk]	bike which is used for keeping fit	*Heimtrainer*
to practise	['præktɪs]	*n* practice	*üben*
penalty	['penlti]	*phr* to take a penalty	*Strafstoß*
cash machine	['kæʃ məʃiːn]	machine which lets people take money from their bank accounts	*Geldautomat*
to manage	['mænɪdʒ]	to control sth, to deal with sth	*zurechtkommen, fertig werden (mit), (es) schaffen*
to try on	[ˌtraɪ 'ɒn]	to put on a piece of clothing to see whether you like it	*anprobieren*

UNIT B

page 12

to ban	[bæn]	to say that sth is not allowed	*verbieten*
discrimination	[dɪˌskrɪmɪ'neɪʃn]	*v* to discriminate against	*Diskriminierung*
public school	[ˌpʌblɪk 'skuːl]	*(AE) BE:* state school	*staatliche Schule*
requirement	[rɪ'kwaɪəmənt]	thing that is necessary	*Erfordernis*
to make up	[ˌmeɪk 'ʌp]	to form	*bilden*
awesome	['ɔːsəm]	very difficult or impressive	*überwältigend*
challenge	[tʃælɪndʒ]	a difficult task	*Herausforderung*
to wrestle	['resl]	to fight sb as a sport	*ringen*
mat	[mæt]	piece of material that people wrestle on	*Matte*

rival	['raɪvl]	person or team who plays against sb	Gegner/in, Rivale, -lin
unblinking	[ʌn'blɪŋkɪŋ]	to blink = blinzeln	unbewegt
shiver	['ʃɪvə]	phr a shiver of fear	Zittern
fear	[fɪə]	v to fear	Furcht
hulk	[hʌlk]	big strong man	Kerl wie ein Baum
stretcher	['stretʃə]	piece of equipment used to carry sb who has been hurt	Trage
hold	[həʊld]	v to hold	Griff
to twist	[twɪst]	to turn	(ver)drehen
muscle	['mʌsl]	⚠ Aussprache	Muskel
to injure	['ɪndʒə]	to hurt	verletzen
stereotype	['steriətaɪp]	e.g. racial stereotype	Klischee
to compete	[kəm'piːt]	to play against other people or teams	konkurrieren
teammate	['tiːmmeɪt]	person who is on the same team as you	Mannschaftskamerad/in
session	['seʃn]	time spent doing a particular activity	Treffen, Termin
nasty	['nɑːsti]	not nice	gemein
sweetie	['swiːti]	(inf) darling	Liebling, Schatz
next door	[ˌnekst 'dɔː]	in the next room or building	nebenan
to set to work	[set tə 'wɜːk]	to begin a task or project	ans Werk gehen
to impress	[ɪm'pres]	adj impressive	imponieren
to beat	[biːt]	to win against sb	schlagen
to back off	[ˌbæk 'ɒf]	to stop making things difficult for sb	zurücktreten
warrior	['wɒriə]	someone who fights in a war	Krieger
princess	[ˌprɪn'ses]	daughter of king or queen	Prinzessin
guy	[gaɪ]	(inf) boy, man	Kerl, Typ
equal	['iːkwəl]	person who is treated the same as others	Gleichberechtigte/r, Ebenbürtige/r

page 13

statement	['steɪtmənt]	v to state	Aussage
proud	[praʊd]	pleased with oneself	stolz
ice-hockey	['aɪs hɒki]	hockey played on ice	Eishockey
first aider	[ˌfɜːst 'eɪdə]	phr first aid	Sanitäter
opponent	[ə'pəʊnənt]	person or team who plays against sb	Gegner/in
feminine	['femənɪn]	connected with women	weiblich
to teach sb a lesson	[tiːtʃ ə 'lesn]	to show sb they were wrong by making sth bad happen to them	jdm eine Lektion erteilen
glad	[glæd]	pleased	froh
to accept	[ək'sept]	adj acceptable	akzeptieren
private	['praɪvət]	⟨⟩ public	privat, persönlich
precise	[prɪ'saɪs]	exactly	genau
frightening	['fraɪtnɪŋ]	scary	beängstigend, erschreckend
increasing	[ɪn'kriːsɪŋ]	getting bigger	zunehmend
pleasant	['pleznt]	nice	angenehm
to discriminate	[dɪ'skrɪmɪneɪt]	to contrast, but: to discriminate against sb	unterscheiden, diskriminieren
to require	[rɪ'kwaɪə]	n requirement	erfordern
injury	['ɪndʒəri]	v to injure	Verletzung
competition	[ˌkɒmpə'tɪʃn]	v to compete	Wettkampf
impression	[ɪm'preʃn]	a feeling or an idea about sth	Eindruck
to challenge	['tʃælɪndʒ]	to test sb's skills with a difficult task	herausfordern
to rival	['raɪvl]	to compete with	konkurrieren
wrestler	['reslə]	v to wrestle	Ringer/in
missing	['mɪsɪŋ]	absent	fehlend

page 14

EU	[ˌiː 'juː]	(abbrev) European Union	EU
football	['fʊtbɔːl]	AE: American football	American Football (BE: Fußball)
phenomenal	[fə'nɒmɪnl]	n phenomenon	phänomenal
talent	['tælənt]	special natural ability	Talent
although	[ɔːl'ðəʊ]	even though	obwohl
grade	[greɪd]	result in school	Note

page 15

planner	['plænə]	book in which people write their plans	(Termin-)Kalender

further	['fɜːðə]	additional	*weiter*
lunchtime	['lʌntʃtaɪm]	time when people eat their mid-day meal	*Mittagspause*
ironing	['aɪənɪŋ]	*v* to iron	*Bügeln*
hairdresser	['heədresə]	person who cuts and styles hair	*Friseur/in*
to record	[rɪ'kɔːd]	to store a film or TV programme on video/DVD	*aufzeichnen*
BBC	[ˌbiː biː 'siː]	*(abbrev)* British Broadcasting Corporation	*BBC*
to swap	[swɒp]	to switch	*tauschen*
role	[rəʊl]	role-play	*Rolle*
at least	[ət 'liːst]	at the minimum	*mindestens*
to go camping	[gəʊ 'kæmpɪŋ]	to go on holiday in a tent or caravan	*campen*
leisure centre	['leʒə sentə]	place where people go to keep fit	*Freizeitzentrum*
to go on a date	[gəʊ ɒn ə 'deɪt]	to meet a (possible) boyfriend or girlfriend	*eine Verabredung haben*

UNIT C

page 16

case study	['keɪs stʌdi]	detailed description of a particular person/situation	*Fallstudie*
double life	['dʌbl laɪf]	*phr* to lead a double life	*Doppelleben*
genuine	['dʒenjuɪn]	real	*echt*
eating disorder	[ˌiːtɪŋ dɪs'ɔːdə]	e.g. anorexia, bulimia	*Essstörung*
anorexia	[ˌænə'reksiə]	illness where people don't eat because they want to be very thin	*Magersucht*
bulimia	[bjuː'lɪmiə]	illness where people eat and make themselves sick to stay thin	*Bulimie, Ess-Brech-Sucht*
charming	['tʃɑːmɪŋ]	*n* charm	*charmant*
attractive	[ə'træktɪv]	*v* to attract	*attraktiv*
community	[kə'mjuːnəti]	people who live together in an area/ a society	*Gemeinde*
secret	['siːkrɪt]	*phr* to keep sth secret	*geheim*
double-decker	[ˌdʌbl 'dekə]	*phr* double-decker bus	*Doppeldecker*
packet	['pækɪt]	small paper or plastic container	*Schachtel, Packung, Tüte*
tub	[tʌb]	small round plastic container	*Becher*
to scream	[skriːm]	here: to attract attention with big writing and bright colours	*schreien*
familiar	[fə'mɪliə]	*n* familiarity	*bekannt*
tingling	['tɪŋglɪŋ]	*v* to tingle	*kribbelnd, prickelnd*
to lose control over	[luːz kən'trəʊl əʊvə]	to no longer be able to control sth	*die Beherrschung verlieren*
to stuff	[stʌf]	to push sth into a space	*stopfen*
greedy	['griːdi]	*n* greed	*gierig*
in no time	[ɪn 'nəʊ taɪm]	very quickly	*im Handumdrehen*
counter	['kaʊntə]	*phr* over the counter	*Tresen, Ladentisch*
dessert	[dɪ'zɜːt]	sweet food eaten at the end of a meal	*Nachspeise, -tisch*
caramel	['kærəmel]	sweet sauce made by melting sugar	*Karamel*
donut	['dəʊnʌt]	*(AE) BE:* doughnut	*Pfannkuchen, Krapfen*
cheeky	['tʃiːki]	a bit rude but in a funny way	*frech, kess*
to grin	[grɪn]	smile	*lächeln, grinsen*
to sink	[sɪŋk]	to go down	*sinken*
dirty	['dɜːti]	◇ clean	*schmutzig*
guilty	['gɪlti]	◇ innocent	*schuldig*
cubicle	['kjuːbɪkl]	e.g. shower/toilet cubicle	*Kabine*
to bend	[bend]	*phr* to bend over	*(sich) beugen*
toilet pan	['tɔɪlət pæn]	*(AE) BE:* toilet bowl	*Kloschüssel*
to throw up	[ˌθrəʊ 'ʌp]	to be sick	*(sich) erbrechen*
to not be able to help	[nɒt bi ˌeɪbl tə 'help]	to not be able to avoid sth	*nicht umhin können*
association	[əˌsəʊsi'eɪʃn]	group of people with a common goal or interest	*Verband, Verein*
to go down a road	[gəʊ ˌdaʊn ə 'rəʊd]	to experience sth	*etwas erleben*
to refuse	[rɪ'fjuːz]	to reject, turn down	*ablehnen, sich weigern, widerstehen*
to put on weight	[ˌpʊt ɒn 'weɪt]	◇ to lose weight	*zunehmen*
addiction	[ə'dɪkʃn]	*v* to be addicted	*Sucht, Abhängigkeit*

to vomit	['vɒmɪt]	to throw up	erbrechen

task	[tɑːsk]	work, assignment	Aufgabe
to compare	[kəm'peə]	n comparison	vergleichen
evidence	['evɪdəns]	proof	Beweis, Beleg
embarrassed	[ɪm'bærəst]	n embarrassment	verlegen
ashamed	[ə'ʃeɪmd]	n shame	beschämt
attitude	['ætɪtjuːd]	phr attitude towards sth	Haltung, Einstellung
to disagree (with)	[,dɪsə'griː wɪð]	<> agree	widersprechen, nicht zustimmen
choice	[tʃɔɪs]	v to choose	Wahl
to starve yourself	[stɑːv]	to not allow yourself to eat	hungern
otherwise	['ʌðəwaɪz]	if not	sonst, ansonsten
to get real	[get 'riːəl]	to accept the truth	die Realität anerkennen
to pull oneself together	[,pʊl wʌnself tə'geðə]	to take control of your feelings	sich zusammenreißen
mental	['mentl]	n mentality	mental
treatment	['triːtmənt]	v to treat	Behandlung
sufferer	['sʌfərə]	sb who suffers from an illness	Leidende/r
sympathetic	[,sɪmpə'θetɪk]	n sympathy	mitfühlend, verständnisvoll
medical	['medɪkl]	connected with illnesses and treatments	medizinisch
criticism	['krɪtɪsɪzəm]	negative feedback	Kritik
phrase	[freɪz]	expression	Wendung, Ausdruck
waiter	['weɪtə]	fem waitress	Kellner, Ober

to attract	[ə'trækt]	to draw attention to	anziehen, anlocken
special offer	[,speʃl 'ɒfə]	phr on special offer	Sonderangebot
to get drunk	[get 'drʌŋk]	to drink so much alcohol that you can no longer think clearly	sich betrinken
good-looking	[,gʊd 'lʊkɪŋ]	attractive	gut aussehend
ad	[æd]	(inf) advertisement	Anzeige
disgusting	[dɪs'gʌstɪŋ]	n disgust	ekelhaft
to overcome	[,əʊvə'kʌm]	to beat or deal with (a problem or illness)	überwinden
capital	['kæpɪtl]	main city in a country	Hauptstadt
equivalent (of)	[ɪ'kwɪvələnt əv]	sth that is equal in size/importance, etc. to sth else	Entsprechung
curable	['kjʊərəbl]	v to cure	heilbar
fatty	['fæti]	containing a large amount of fat	fetthaltig, fettig
What's the matter with ...?	[,wɒts ðə 'mætə wɪð]	What's wrong with ...?	Was ist los mit ...?

countable	['kaʊntəbl]	which can be counted	zählbar
uncountable	[,ʌn'kaʊntəbl]	which cannot be counted	nicht zählbar
ham	[hæm]	type of meat from a pig	Schinken
research	[rɪ'sɜːtʃ]	study to find out more about a subject	Forschung
advice	[əd'vaɪs]	suggestion	Rat(schlag)
luggage	['lʌgɪdʒ]	suitcases	Gepäck
hardware	['hɑːdweə]	parts of a computer	Hardware, Geräte
software	['sɒftweə]	computer programs	Software, Programme
knowledge	['nɒlɪdʒ]	what sb knows	Wissen
police officer	[pə'liːs ɒfɪsə]	policeman/-woman	Polizeibeamter/-beamtin
column	['kɒləm]	vertical sections which separate a page	Spalte
mustard	['mʌstəd]	yellow-brown sauce usually served with meat	Senf
paint	[peɪnt]	v to paint	Farbe
can	[kæn]	e.g. a can of beans	Dose
queue	[kjuː]	v to queue up for sth	(Warte-)Schlange
loaf	[ləʊf]	e.g. a loaf of bread	(Laib) Brot
tube	[tjuːb]	e.g. a tube of toothpaste	Tube
jar	[dʒɑː]	e.g. a jam jar	(Einmach)Glas

unspecified	[,ʌn'spesɪfaɪd]	unclear	unbestimmt
quantity	['kwɒntəti]	amount	Menge, Quantität

cookbook	['kʊkbʊk]	book that shows how to cook different meals	*Kochbuch*
to have room	[həv 'ru:m]	to have enough space for	*Platz haben*
barbecue	['bɑ:bɪkju:]	outdoor party where food is cooked on a metal frame over a fire	*Grillparty*
plenty of	['plenti əv]	many of	*viel(e)*
freezer	['fri:zə]	cupboard where food can be stored at a very low temperature	*Gefrierschrank*

page 21

to panic	['pænɪk]	<> to stay calm	*in Panik geraten*
Why on earth?	[ˌwaɪ ɒn 'ɜ:θ]	phrase used to emphasize the question 'why?'	*Warum um Himmels willen?*
not ... either	[nɒt 'aɪðə]	e.g. Pete can't go and I can't either.	*auch nicht*
carrot	['kærət]	long orange vegetable	*Karotte*
fridge	[frɪdʒ]	cupboard where food can be stored at a low temperature	*Kühlschrank*
understandable	[ˌʌndə'stændəbl]	which can be understood	*verständlich*
time off	[ˌtaɪm 'ɒf]	*phr* to take time off	*Freizeit*

UNIT D

page 22

time out	[ˌtaɪm 'aʊt]	*phr* to take time out	*Freizeit*
financial	[faɪ'nænʃə]	connected with money	*finanziell*
exotic	[ɪg'zɒtɪk]	exciting because it is strange or unusual	*exotisch*
destination	[ˌdestɪ'neɪʃn]	place to which people travel, the end of a journey	*(Fahrt-)Ziel*
proper	['prɒpə]	real, full, correct	*richtig, geeignet, korrekt, ordentlich*
bright	[braɪt]	clever	*hell; glänzend, schlau*
to pick fruit	[pik 'fru:t]	to take fruit from trees or plants	*Obst pflücken*
absolutely	['æbsəlu:tli]	definitely	*absolut*
especially	[ɪ'speʃəli]	particularly	*besonders, insbesondere*
uncool	[ˌʌn'ku:l]	⚠ Betonung	*uncool*
come on	[ˌkʌm 'ɒn]	used to show that you think sb is wrong	*komm (schon)*
living expenses	[ˌlɪvɪŋ ɪk'spensɪz]	money spent on everyday things	*Lebenshaltungskosten*

page 23

to break into	['breɪk ɪntə]	to enter by force	*einbrechen*

page 24

to give a lift	[gɪv ə 'lɪft]	to give sb a ride	*mit dem Auto mitnehmen*
weatherman	['weðəmæn]	man on TV who predicts the weather	*Meteorologe*
to watch out	[ˌwɒtʃ 'aʊt]	to be careful	*aufpassen*
visa	['vi:zə]	mark in a passport which allows you to enter a country	*Visum*
to take off	[ˌteɪk 'ɒf]	(of an aeroplane) to leave the ground	*starten*

page 25

several	['sevrəl]	a few more than one	*mehrere, einige*
school-leaver	[ˌsku:l 'li:və]	person who has just left school	*Schulabgänger/in*
farewell	[ˌfeə'wel]	saying goodbye to sb	*Abschied*
definitely	['defɪnətli]	certainly	*bestimmt, definitiv*

UNIT E

page 26

pushy	['pʊʃi]	trying to persuade sb to do sth	*aufdringlich*
sales	[seɪlz]	selling goods	*Verkaufs-*
staff	[stɑ:f]	a group of workers or employees	*Personal, Angestellte, Mitarbeiter/innen*
virtual	['vɜ:tʃuəl]	existing only on a computer screen	*virtuell*
mail-order catalogue	[meɪl 'ɔ:də kætəlɒg]	book with a list of goods that will be sent to customers by post	*Versandhauskatalog*
bargain	['bɑ:gɪn]	special offer	*Sonderangebot*
department store	[dɪ'pɑ:tmənt stɔ:]	large shop selling clothes, food, etc.	*Kauf-, Warenhaus*
purchase	['pɜ:tʃəs]	*v* to purchase	*(Ein-) Kauf*

fabulous	['fæbjələs]	great, wonderful	*fabelhaft*
blouse	[blauz]	piece of clothing like a shirt for women	*Bluse*
quality	['kwɒləti]	◇ quantity	*Qualität*
fashion-conscious	['fæʃn kɒnʃəs]	very interested in fashionable clothes	*modebewusst*
exclusive	[ɪk'sklu:sɪv]	good quality and expensive and only bought by a small number of people	*exklusiv*
label	['leɪbl]	*phr* brand label	*Label, Marke*
wardrobe	['wɔːdrəʊb]	large cupboard for clothes	*Kleiderschrank, Garderobe*
thrill	[θrɪl]	*adj* thrilling	*Spannung*
lovely	['lʌvli]	nice, pleasant	*hübsch*
pure	[pjʊə]	*n* purity	*rein*
silk	[sɪlk]	a soft shiny material	*Seide*
site	[saɪt]	*(inf)* website	*Website*
shopping trolley	['ʃɒpɪn trɒli]	AE: shopping cart	*Einkaufswagen*
in the meantime	[ɪn ðə 'miːntaɪm]	in the time between two events	*inzwischen*
to run up debts	[ˌrʌn ˈʌp dets]	to spend more money than you have	*sich verschulden, Schulden anhäufen*

page 27

second-hand	[ˌsekənd 'hænd]	which used to belong to somebody else	*gebraucht*
auction	['ɔːkʃn]	*phr* to put sth up for auction	*Auktion*
to link	[lɪŋk]	to connect, to join	*verbinden*

page 28

sceptical	['skeptɪkl]	having doubts	*skeptisch*
to keep in touch with	[ˌkiːp ɪn 'tʌtʃ wɪð]	to stay in contact with	*in Verbindung bleiben*
creditor	['kredɪtə]	person who gives money to people who must pay it back later	*Gläubiger/in*
to repay	[rɪ'peɪ]	*n* repayment	*zurückzahlen*
convenient	[kən'viːniənt]	*n* convenience	*bequem*
honest	['ɒnɪst]	*n* honesty	*ehrlich*
display	[dɪ'spleɪ]	⚠ Betonung	*Ausstellung*
row	[rəʊ]	line	*Reihe*
occasional	[ə'keɪʒənl]	now and then, sometimes	*gelegentlich*
fixed	[fɪkst]	set in place	*befestigt*
anti-theft pad	['ænti θeft pæd]	piece of material designed to stop people stealing goods	*Diebstahlsicherung*
to glow	[gləʊ]	to produce light	*leuchten*
reliable	[rɪ'laɪəbl]	which can be trusted	*zuverlässig*
value	['vælju:]	how much sth is worth	*Wert*
feature	['fiːtʃə]	aspect of a product	*Eigenschaft*
to switch off	[ˌswɪtʃ 'ɒf]	to turn off	*abschalten*

page 29

position	[pə'zɪʃn]	arrangement	*Stellung*
fortunately	['fɔːtʃənətli]	luckily	*glücklicherweise*
actually	['æktʃuəli]	in fact	*tatsächlich, eigentlich*
unluckily	[ʌn'lʌkɪli]	unfortunately	*unglücklicherweise*
obviously	['ɒbviəsli]	clearly	*offensichtlich*
irresponsible	[ˌɪrɪ'spɒnsəbl]	◇ responsible	*unverantwortlich*
from time to time	[frəm ˌtaɪm tə 'taɪm]	sometimes	*von Zeit zu Zeit*
now and then	[naʊ ənd 'ðen]	sometimes	*ab und zu*
frequency	['friːkwənsi]	*adj* frequent	*Häufigkeit*
retailer	['riːteɪlə]	person or company that sells products	*Einzelhändler/in*
shoplifting	['ʃɒplɪftɪŋ]	stealing from a shop	*Ladendiebstahl*
punishment	['pʌnɪʃmənt]	*v* to punish	*Strafe, Bestrafung*
shoplifter	['ʃɒplɪftə]	person who steals things from a shop	*Ladendieb/in*
sale	[seɪl]	event where goods are sold at a cheaper price	*Schlussverkauf*
to buy sth on credit	[baɪ ɒn 'kredɪt]	to buy sth using borrowed money	*etw auf Kredit kaufen*
congratulations	[kənˌgrætʃu'leɪʃnz]	*v* to congratulate	*Glückwunsch*

UNIT F

page 30

questionnaire	[ˌkwestʃə'neə]	list of questions	*Fragebogen*
to fit	[fɪt]	to be suitable	*passen*
to stay up	[ˌsteɪ 'ʌp]	to not go to bed	*aufbleiben*
to text	[tekst]	to write a text message	*SMS schicken, simsen*
loads	[ləʊdz]	*(inf)* a lot	*eine Menge*
to depend	[dɪ'pend]	to be dependent upon	*abhängen von*
social life	[ˌsəʊʃl 'laɪf]	time spent meeting friends	*Sozialkontakte*
to hand in	[ˌhænd 'ɪn]	to give in (e.g. your homework)	*abgeben*
to sit back	[ˌsɪt 'bæk]	to relax and not play an active role in sth	*sich zurückhalten, sich zurücklehnen*

page 31

sensible	['sensəbl]	<> silly	*vernünftig*
careers adviser	[kə'rɪəz ədvaɪzə]	person whose job is to give people advice about different jobs	*Berufsberater/in*
to interview	['ɪntəvju:]	to have a conversation with questions and answers	*interviewen*
theme	[θi:m]	a topic or subject	*Thema*
don't mention it	['menʃn]	you're welcome	*gern geschehen*
to concentrate	['kɒnsntreɪt]	to focus on sth	*sich konzentrieren*
to get by	[ˌget 'baɪ]	to have just enough money to live	*durchkommen*
to increase	[ɪn'kri:s]	to grow	*ansteigen, zunehmen*
since	[sɪns]	before the present time	*seit*
generation	[ˌdʒenə'reɪʃn]	people born around the same time	*Generation*
at a disadvantage	[ət ə ˌdɪsəd'vɑ:ntɪdʒ]	having more problems than other people	*benachteiligt*
job-related	['dʒɒb rɪleɪtɪd]	having to do with the job	*beruflich*
shelf	[ʃelf]	flat surface on a wall or in a cupboard where things can be placed	*Regal*

page 32

objection to	[əb'dʒekʃn tə]	*v* to object to	*Ablehnung gegenüber*
misunderstanding	[ˌmɪsʌndə'stændɪŋ]	*v* to misunderstand	*Missverständnis*
cartoon	[kɑ:'tu:n]	a humorous drawing	*Karikatur*
brochure	['brəʊʃə]	e.g. advertising brochure	*Broschüre, Prospekt*
careless	['keələs]	<> careful	*sorglos, nachlässig*
travel agency	['trævl eɪdʒənsi]	company that helps to organize holidays	*Reisebüro*
rack	[ræk]	object used to hold things or hang things from	*Ständer*
to sort	[sɔ:t]	to organize	*sortieren*
to deal with	['di:l wɪð]	to work with	*sich beschäftigen mit, mit jdm zu tun haben*
to complain	[kəm'pleɪn]	*n* complaint	*reklamieren, sich beklagen, beschweren*

page 33

to take it in turns	[ˌteɪk ɪt ɪn 'tɜ:nz]	to alternate	*sich abwechseln*
bartender	['bɑ:tendə]	*(AE) BE:* barman, barmaid	*Barmann, -frau*
cashier	[kæ'ʃɪə]	person who takes money from and gives money to customers in a shop or bank	*Kassierer/in*
shelf-stacker	['ʃelf stækə]	person who works in a supermarket putting products on shelves	*Regalauffüller/in*
tuition	[tju'ɪʃn]	*v* to tutor	*Unterricht*
old people's home	[ˌəʊld 'pi:plz həʊm]	place where old people live together and are cared for	*Seniorenheim*
filling station	['fɪlɪŋ steɪʃn]	petrol station	*Tankstelle*
recently	['ri:sntli]	lately, not long ago	*kürzlich, neulich*

page 34

day off	[ˌdeɪ 'ɒf]	*phr* to take a day off	*freier Tag*
part-timer	[ˌpɑ:t 'taɪmə]	person who works part-time	*Teilzeitarbeiter/in*
arrival	[ə'raɪvl]	*v* to arrive	*Ankunft*

MAIN COURSE

UNIT 1

page 35

focus	['fəʊkəs]	theme	Blickpunkt
quotation	[kwəʊ'teɪʃn]	v to quote	Zitat
to set foot in	[set 'fʊt ɪn]	to enter	betreten
to feature	['fiːtʃə]	to appear	eine Rolle spielen
sequence	['siːkwəns]	part of a film	Episode, Sequenz

page 36

perspective	[pə'spektɪv]	view point	Perspektive, Ansicht
to contrast	[kən'trɑːst]	to compare differences	gegenüberstellen
to scan	[skæn]	read sth quickly to find a piece of information	überfliegen, absuchen
roughly	['rʌfli]	◇ exactly	ungefähr
event	[ɪ'vent]	sth that is happening	Ereignis, Veranstaltung
particularly	[pə'tɪkjələli]	specific, especially	bestimmt, speziell, besonders
urban	['ɜːbən]	◇ rural	städtisch
rural	['rʊərəl]	◇ urban	ländlich
calm	[kɑːm]	quiet	ruhig
enjoyable	[ɪn'dʒɔɪəbl]	v to enjoy	angenehm
gentle	['dʒentl]	kind	freundlich
intense	[ɪn'tens]	n intensity	intensiv

page 37

to check out	[ˌtʃek 'aʊt]	to find out about	herausfinden
pretty soon	[ˌprɪti 'suːn]	very soon	sehr bald
to get used to	[get 'juːst tə]	to become familiar with sth	sich gewöhnen an
to yell	[jel]	to shout	schreien
really something	['riːəli sʌmθɪŋ]	something impressive	toll, beeindruckend
downtown	['daʊntaʊn]	(esp AE) in the city centre	im Stadtzentrum
skyline	['skaɪlaɪn]	buildings, etc. that can be seen against the background of the sky	Silhouette
to blow sb away	[ˌbləʊ ə'weɪ]	to really impress sb	jdn überwältigen
scary	['skeəri]	frightening	unheimlich, beängstigend
elevator	['elɪveɪtə]	(AE) BE: lift	Lift
senior	['siːniə]	student in the last year of high school in the US	Schüler/in im letzten Schuljahr
skyscraper	['skaɪskreɪpə]	very tall building	Wolkenkratzer
huge	[hjuːdʒ]	very big	gewaltig
forest	['fɒrɪst]	woods	Wald
waterfall	['wɔːtəfɔːl]		Wasserfall
to be stuck	[bi 'stʌk]	to be unable to get away	feststecken
nightmare	['naɪtmeə]	adj nightmarish	Albtraum

page 38

context	['kɒntekst]	circumstances	Kontext, Zusammenhang
shopping mall	['ʃɒpɪŋ mɔːl]	a large building with many shops inside	Einkaufszentrum
exhibition	[ˌeksɪ'bɪʃn]	v to exhibit	Ausstellung
tourist guide	['tʊərɪst gaɪd]	person whose job is to show tourists around	Reiseführer/in
presenter	[prɪ'zentə]	v to present	Moderator/in
to cross out	[ˌkrɒs 'aʊt]	to draw a line through	durchstreichen
suggestion	[sə'dʒestʃən]	recommendation	Vorschlag
ferry	['feri]	a large boat used to transport people	Fähre
geography	[dʒi'ɒgrəfi]	layout	Lage, Geographie
gateway	['geɪtweɪ]	entrance	Tor, Pforte
to rent	[rent]	to hire	mieten
lake	[leɪk]	area of water surrounded by land	(Binnen-)See
ride	[raɪd]	phr to go for a ride	Tour, Fahrt, Flug
tight	[taɪt]	phr a tight fit	knapp, eng
budget	['bʌdʒɪt]	amount of money you plan to spend	Budget, Etat

security check	[sɪ'kjʊərəti tʃek]	a measure to stop dangerous items/ people entering a building/country, etc.	Sicherheitskontrolle
greeting	['griːtɪŋ]	v to greet	Begrüßung
to receive	[rɪ'siːv]	to get	empfangen
relationship	[rɪ'leɪʃnʃɪp]	a connection between two or more people	Verhältnis

page 39

immigrant	['ɪmɪɡrənt]	v to immigrate	Einwanderer/Einwanderin
bite	[baɪt]	phr to take a bite of sth	Bissen, Happen
sub-heading	[ˌsʌb 'hedɪŋ]	title that comes under the main title	Untertitel
encyclopedia	[ɪnˌsaɪklə'piːdiə]	book that gives information about many different subjects	Lexikon, Enzyklopädie
entry	['entri]	piece of written information in a book	Eintrag
novel	['nɒvl]	book containing a story	Roman
guidebook	['ɡaɪdbʊk]	book which gives information on a particular place	Reiseführer

page 40

distant	['dɪstənt]	n distance	fern
to shine	[ʃaɪn]	adj shiny	glänzen
magical	['mædʒɪkl]	wonderful	magisch
to take sb's breath away	[teɪk 'breθ əweɪ]	to surprise sb by being very impressive	jdm den Atem rauben
to explore	[ɪk'splɔː]	to travel around and see different areas	erkunden
borough	['bʌrə]	area, quarter in a city	(Stadt-)Bezirk
shore	[ʃɔː]	place where land meets water	Ufer
island	['aɪlənd]	land which is surrounded by water	Insel
within	[wɪ'ðɪn]	inside	innerhalb
characteristic	[ˌkærəktə'rɪstɪk]	quality	Eigenschaft, Merkmal
sense	[sens]	a feeling	Sinn, Gefühl
melting pot	['meltɪŋ pɒt]	place where people from different cultures live together	Schmelztiegel
variety	[və'raɪəti]	adj various	Vielfalt
cultural	['kʌltʃərəl]	connected with culture	kulturell
ethnic	['eθnɪk]	connected with origin or race	ethnisch
tradition	[trə'dɪʃn]	adj traditional	Tradition
wave	[weɪv]	large number of people moving somewhere	Welle
effect	[ɪ'fekt]	result	Auswirkung
dish	[dɪʃ]	plate or shallow bowl	Gericht
crowded	['kraʊdɪd]	filled with people	überfüllt
energy	['enədʒi]	force	Energie
newly	['njuːli]	recently	kürzlich
to invent	[ɪn'vent]	n invention	erfinden
steel-frame	['stiːl freɪm]	with a frame of steel (strong metal)	Stahlträger
construction	[kən'strʌkʃn]	building	Bau, Bauweise
area	['eəriə]	a space	Gebiet, Bereich
including	[ɪn'kluːdɪŋ]	abbrev: incl.	einschließlich, inbegriffen, darunter
finance	['faɪnæns]	adj financial	Finanzen
advertising	['ædvətaɪzɪŋ]	industry connected with producing adverts	Werbung
to take over	[ˌteɪk 'əʊvə]	to start to have control over people or things	übernehmen
taxpayer	['tækspeɪə]	person who pays taxes	Steuerzahler/in
bankrupt	['bæŋkrʌpt]	n bankruptcy	bankrott, pleite
terrorist	['terərɪst]	person who takes part in political attacks	Terrorist/in
attack	[ə'tæk]	assault	Angriff
failure	['feɪljə]	<> success	Versagen
unemployment	[ˌʌnɪm'plɔɪmənt]	adj unemployed	Arbeitslosigkeit
former	['fɔːmə]	from an earlier time	früher
recovery	[rɪ'kʌvəri]	v to recover	Erholung

page 41

structure	['strʌktʃə]	something that has been built, a foundation and organized system	Gebäude, Struktur, Aufbau

man-made	['mæn meɪd]	◇ natural	*von Menschenhand*
industry	['ɪndəstri]		*Industrie*
birth	[bɜ:θ]	*v* to be born	*Geburt*
aspect	['æspekt]	area, part	*Aspekt, Seite*
to collect	[kə'lekt]	to bring together	*sammeln*
to differ	['dɪfə]	to be different	*sich unterscheiden*
to immigrate	['ɪmɪgreɪt]	to come to live in a new country	*einwandern*
attraction	[ə'trækʃn]	feeling of being attracted to sth/sb	*Anziehung*
sleepy	['sli:pi]	tired	*müde*
informative	[ɪn'fɔ:mətɪv]	*v* to inform	*informativ*
to strengthen	['streŋθn]	to make stronger	*stärken*

page 42

comprehension	[ˌkɒmprɪ'henʃn]	*v* to comprehend	*Verständnis*
large-scale	['lɑ:dʒ skeɪl]	in large numbers	*in großer Zahl*
timetable	['taɪmteɪbl]	e.g. train timetable	*Zeitplan, Fahrplan*
rather	['rɑ:ðə]	*phr* rather you than me	*lieber, eher*

page 43

gang	[gæŋ]	a group of people who behave badly	*(Straßen-)Bande*
adolescent	[ˌædə'lesnt]	a teenager	*Jugendliche/r*
contact	['kɒntækt]	meeting	*Kontakt*
to monitor	['mɒnɪtə]	to supervise sb	*überwachen, kontrollieren*
to lack	[læk]	to not have sth	*fehlen*
factual	['fæktʃuəl]	*n* fact	*sachlich*
involved with	[ɪn'vɒlvd wɪð]	*phr* to be a part of	*beteiligt an*
bandana	[bæn'dænə]	cloth worn around the head	*Kopftuch*
bead	[bi:d]	e.g. a necklace of beads	*Perle*
belt	[belt]	worn around the waist to hold up trousers	*Gürtel*
shoelace	['ʃu:leɪs]	string used to tie shoes	*Schnürsenkel*
headband	['hedbænd]	a band of material worn on the head	*Stirnband*
jewellery	['dʒu:əlri]	e.g. ring, bracelet, necklace, etc.	*Schmuck*
to mark	[mɑ:k]	to leave an impression	*markieren, kennzeichnen*
territory	['terətri]	area of land	*Revier, Gebiet*
to threaten	['θretn]	to be a danger to sb or sth	*(be)drohen*
tattoo	[tə'tu:]	permanent mark or design on the skin	*Tätowierung*
loyalty	['lɔɪəlti]		*Loyalität*
initials	[ɪ'nɪʃlz]	first letters of a name	*Anfangsbuchstaben*
membership	['membəʃɪp]	being a member of a group	*Mitgliedschaft*
gangsta rap	[ˌgæŋstə 'ræp]	type of rap	*Gangsta Rap*
lyrics	['lɪrɪks]	e.g. song lyrics	*(Lied-)Text(e)*
to glorify	['glɔ:rɪfaɪ]	to praise	*verherrlichen*
fascination	[ˌfæsɪ'neɪʃn]	attraction	*Faszination*
juvenile	['dʒu:vənaɪl]	young	*jugendlich, Jugend-*
justice	['dʒʌstɪs]	fairness	*Recht, Justiz*
delinquency	[dɪ'lɪŋkwənsi]	wrong or illegal behaviour	*Kriminalität*
prevention	[prɪ'venʃn]	stopping sth from happening	*Vorbeugung*
department	[dɪ'pɑ:tmənt]	a section of an organisation	*Ministerium*
to motivate	['məʊtɪveɪt]	to cause	*motivieren*
council	['kaʊnsl]	an assembly of people who make decisions	*Gemeinderat*

page 44

comparison	[kəm'pærɪsn]	comparing things	*Vergleich, Steigerung*
approx.	[ə'prɒksɪmətli]	*(abbrev)* approximately	*ungefähr, etwa, zirka*
clue	[klu:]	something which helps solve a puzzle	*Schlüssel*
farther	['fɑ:ðə]	= further	*weiter*
to guess	[ges]	to try to answer	*raten*
junior	['dʒu:niə]	low-ranking	*untergeordnet*
comment	['kɒment]	*v* to comment	*Kommentar*
length	[leŋθ]	measurement of time, distance, etc.	*Länge, Dauer*
departure	[dɪ'pɑ:tʃə]	*v* to depart	*Abfahrt*
frequent	['fri:kwənt]	*n* frequency	*häufig*
service	['sɜ:vɪs]	assistance	*(Bus-/Zug-)Verbindung*

UNIT 2

page 45

advertisement	[əd'vɜːtɪsmənt]	*abbrev:* ad, advert	*Anzeige, Werbespot*
classified	['klæsɪfaɪd]	arranged by subject	*nach Rubriken geordnet*
panel	['pænl]	section of a page	*hier: Spalte, Fläche*
leaflet	['liːflət]	flyer	*Broschüre, Flugblatt*
pop-up ad	['pɒp ʌp æd]	advert that appears on the screen when you are online	*Internet-Anzeige*
banner ad	['bænər æd]	advert that covers the top/bottom/side of an internet page	*Bannerwerbung*
product placement	['prɒdʌkt pleɪsmənt]	advertising products by showing them in films or on TV shows	*Schleichwerbung*
commercial	[kə'mɜːʃl]	advertisement	*Anzeige, Werbespot*
sponsorship	['spɒnsəʃɪp]	giving financial support to a group/event, etc.	*finanzielle Unterstützung*
annoying	[ə'nɔɪɪŋ]	irritating	*lästig, ärgerlich*
glamorous	['glæmərəs]	*n* glamour	*glamourös*
aim	[eɪm]	goal	*Ziel*
to vary	['veəri]	*n* variety	*variieren*
to promote	[prə'məʊt]	to advertise	*fördern*
brand	[brænd]	*phr* brand name	*Marke*

page 46

agency	['eɪdʒənsi]	e.g. advertising agency	*Agentur*
to design	[dɪ'zaɪn]	to create	*entwerfen*
sponsor	['spɒnsə]	*v* to sponsor	*Sponsor/in*
freelance	['friːlɑːns]	e.g. freelance journalist	*freiberuflich*
developer	[dɪ'veləpə]	person whose job is to create new products	*Entwickler/in*
to expand	[ɪk'spænd]	to get bigger	*expandieren, (sich) ausdehnen*
potential	[pə'tenʃl]	possible	*potentiell*
client	['klaɪənt]	customer	*Kunde/Kundin*
campaign	[kæm'peɪn]	*phr* advertising campaign	*(Werbe-)Feldzug, Kampagne*
to pitch	[pɪtʃ]	to present an idea or a product to persuade people to use or buy it	*anbieten, anpreisen*
contract	['kɒntrækt]	a formal document or agreement	*(Arbeits-)Vertrag*
account manager	[ə'kaʊnt mænɪdʒə]	person who looks after regular customers	*Kundenbetreuer/in*
to get the green light	[get ðə ˌgriːn 'laɪt]	to be allowed to begin	*grünes Licht erhalten*
to launch	[lɔːntʃ]	to start	*einführen, starten*
journey	['dʒɜːni]	trip	*Reise, Fahrt*

page 47

innovative	['ɪnəveɪtɪv]	*n* innovation	*innovativ*
to decline	[dɪ'klaɪn]	to decrease	*abnehmen, sinken, zurückgehen*
fairly	['feəli]	quite	*ziemlich*
slight	['slaɪt]	a little, small	*leicht*
stable	['steɪbl]	*n* stability	*fest*
flow chart	['fləʊ tʃɑːt]	diagram showing the order in which a process happens	*Flussdiagramm*
to set up	[ˌset 'ʌp]	to found	*begründen*
booker	['bʊkə]	person whose job is to book appointments	*Besteller/in*
slot	[slɒt]	appointment	*Termin*
PA	[ˌpiː 'eɪ]	*(abbrev)* personal assistant	*persönliche/r Assistent/in*
to be due to	[bi 'djuː tə]	due to = because of	*darauf zurückzuführen sein*
stressful	['stresfl]	*n* stress	*stressig, anstrengend*
process	['prəʊses]	systematic action	*Prozess, Vorgang*

page 48

to sponsor	['spɒnsə]	*n* sponsor, sponsorship	*finanziell unterstützen*
to supply	[sə'plaɪ]	to provide	*liefern*
supply	[sə'plaɪ]	giving people what they want or need	*Lieferung; Stoff, Material*
urgent	['ɜːdʒənt]	*n* urgency	*dringend, eilig*
application	[ˌæplɪ'keɪʃn] (fɔːm)]	*v* to apply to/for	*Bewerbung*

Human Resources	[ˌhjuːmən rɪˈsɔːsɪz]	abbrev: HR	Personal(abteilung)
candidate	[ˈkændɪdət]	person who has applied for a job	Kandidat/in, Bewerber/in
shortlisted	[ˈʃɔːtlɪstɪd]	chosen to go on a list of possible candidates	in der engeren Wahl
to confirm	[kənˈfɜːm]	n confirmation	bestätigen
to attend	[əˈtend]	to be present at	teilnehmen (an)
correspondence	[ˌkɒrɪˈspɒndəns]	letters sent and received by people	Korrespondenz
to suggest	[səˈdʒest]	n suggestion	vorschlagen, andeuten
closeness	[ˈkləʊsnəs]	adj close	Vertrautheit

page 49

heading	[ˈhedɪŋ]	title	Überschrift
forum	[ˈfɔːrəm]	discussion	Forum
discussion	[dɪˈskʌʃn]	v to discuss sth	Diskussion
to drown in	[ˈdraʊn ɪn]	to be surrounded by	ertränken in
terrible	[ˈterəbl]	awful	schrecklich, furchtbar
commercial break	[kəˌmɜːʃl ˈbreɪk]	pause between TV programmes when adverts are shown	Werbepause
to cut	[kʌt]	to get rid of sth	ausblenden
lively	[ˈlaɪvli]	fun	lebhaft
to lighten up	[ˌlaɪtn ˈʌp]	to feel less worried	aufheitern
to escape	[ɪˈskeɪp]	to get away from	flüchten
advertiser	[ˈædvətaɪzə]	person or company that advertises	Werbefirma
branded	[ˈbrændɪd]	showing the name of a company	Marken-
entertainment	[ˌentəˈteɪnmənt]	amusement	Unterhaltung
placement	[ˈpleɪsmənt]	v to place	(Produkt-)Werbung
extended	[ɪkˈstendɪd]	n extension	verlängert
competing	[kəmˈpiːtɪŋ]	v to compete	konkurrierend
viral	[ˈvaɪrəl]	like a virus	viral, Virus-
to pass	[pɑːs]	to move, go by	weitergegeben werden
to spread	[spred]	n spread	(sich) verbreiten
word of mouth	[ˌwɜːd əv ˈmaʊθ]	phr to spread by word of mouth	Mundpropaganda
to recognize	[ˈrekəgnaɪz]	to see sth or sb familiar	erkennen
channel	[ˈtʃænl]	phr to change channels	Kanal
to admit	[ədˈmɪt]	to confess	zugeben, gestehen
wasteful	[ˈweɪstfə]	v to waste	verschwenderisch
to drop	[drɒp]	to fall	fallen
to collapse	[kəˈlæps]	to fail suddenly	zusammenbrechen
to fail	[feɪl]	to not succeed	versagen, scheitern
Middle Ages	[ˌmɪdl ˈeɪdʒɪz]	period from about 600 AD to 1450 AD	Mittelalter

page 50

to mention	[ˈmenʃn]	to be mentioned = to appear in a text	erwähnen
hard sell	[ˌhɑːd ˈsel]	selling technique that puts a lot of pressure on the customer	aggressive Verkaufstechnik
soft sell	[ˌsɒft ˈsel]	selling technique that persuades customers without putting pressure on them	zurückhaltende Verkaufstechnik
to influence	[ˈɪnfluəns]	n influence	beinflussen
raw material	[ˌrɔː məˈtɪəriəl]	material that is used to make a product	Rohstoff
disagreement	[ˌdɪsəˈgriːmənt]	v to disagree	Widerspruch, Uneinigkeit
to exaggerate	[ɪgˈzædʒəreɪt]	n exaggeration	übertreiben
one-sided	[ˌwʌn ˈsaɪdɪd]	showing only one aspect of a situation	einseitig

page 51

leading	[ˈliːdɪŋ]	v to lead	führend
technique	[tekˈniːk]	method	Methode, (Arbeits-)Technik
college of further education	[ˌkɒlɪdʒ əv ˌfɜːðər ˌedʒuˈkeɪʃn]	vocational school	Fachoberschule, Weiterbildungskolleg
to stand for sth	[ˈstænd fə]	to mean	für etw stehen
formula	[ˈfɔːmjələ]	method	Formel
immediate	[ɪˈmiːdiət]	happening without delay, straight away	umgehend, sofort
acronym	[ˈækrənɪm]	an abbreviation pronounced as a word	Akronym, Initialwort
attention	[əˈtenʃn]	phr to pay attention to	Aufmerksamkeit

to raise	[reɪz]	to build up	wecken
to create	[kri'eɪt]	adj creative	hervorrufen, erzeugen, wecken
desire	[dɪ'zaɪə]	adj desirable	Begehren, Verlangen
to encourage	[ɪn'kʌrɪdʒ]	to promote	anregen
to analyze	['ænəlaɪz]	to study in detail	analysieren
aimed at	['eɪmd ət]	v to aim sth at	abgezielt auf, gerichtet an
play on words	[pleɪ ɒn 'wɜːdz]	pun	Wortspiel
to work out	[ˌwɜːk 'aʊt]	to train	trainieren
membership	['membəʃɪp]	phr gym membership	Mitgliedschaft
to join	[dʒɔɪn]	to sign up	beitreten, sich anmelden
statistical	[stə'tɪstɪkl]	n statistic	statistisch
presentation	[ˌprezn'teɪʃn]	a business talk	Vorstellung, Präsentation
to decrease	[dɪ'kriːs]	to go down	fallen, sinken
rapid	['ræpɪd]	happening in a short period	rapide, schnell
sharp	['ʃɑːp]	sudden(ly) and by a large amount	rasch, schnell, stark
steady	['stedi, -li]	even(ly), stable	stetig, fest, regelmäßig
gradual	['grædʒuə]	happening slowly over a period of time	allmählich, nach und nach
decline	[dɪ'klaɪn]	decrease	Rückgang
to remain	[rɪ'meɪn]	to stay the same	bleiben

page 52

trend	[trend]	general way in which things are changing, fashion	Trend
timeline	['taɪmlaɪn]	diagram showing the order in which events happened	Zeitachse, -leiste
abbreviation	[əˌbriːvi'eɪʃn]	short form of a word or phrase	Abkürzung
crash	[kræʃ]	phr a market crash	Zusammenbruch
to go bankrupt	[gəʊ 'bæŋkrʌpt]	to no longer have enough money to pay off your debts	in Konkurs gehen, Pleite gehen
to hire sb/sth	['haɪə]	(esp AE) to give sb a job, to pay to borrow sth	ein-/anstellen, mieten, anheuern
award	[ə'wɔːd]	prize	Auszeichnung
expansion	[ɪk'spænʃn]	act of making sth bigger	Erweiterung

page 53

ethical	['eθɪkl]	moral	ethisch
consumer	[kən'sjuːmə]	a person who uses goods or services	Verbraucher/in
trainers	['treɪnəz]	(BE) AE: sneakers	Turnschuhe
standard	['stændəd]		Maßstab
jacket	['dʒækɪt]		Jacke, Jackett
best-known	[ˌbest 'nəʊn]	very well-known	bekannteste
employee	[ɪm'plɔiiː]	worker	Angestellte/r
worker	['wɜːkə]		Arbeiter/in
to earn	[ɜːn]	phr to earn money	verdienen
celebrity	[sə'lebrəti]	famous person	Prominente/r
environment	[ɪn'vaɪrənmənt]	surroundings	Umwelt
to reuse	[ˌriː'juːz]	to use again	wieder verwenden
to recycle	[ˌriː'saɪkl]	to make into sth else	wieder verwerten
solution	[sə'luːʃn]	answer	Lösung
heated	['hiːtɪd]	warmed up	geheizt
greenhouse	['griːnhaʊs]	a house where plants are grown	Treib-, Gewächshaus
outdoors	['aʊtdɔːz]	outside	im Freien
issue	['ɪʃuː]	problem	Frage, Problem
classmate	['klɑːsmeɪt]	person who is in the same class as you	Klassenkamerad/in

page 54

sales figures	['seɪlz fɪgəz]	the amount of things that have been sold	Verkaufszahlen
account executive	[əˌkaʊnt ɪg'zekjətɪv]	manager for regular customers or clients	Kundenberater/in, -betreuer/in
microwave	['maɪkrəweɪv]	oven which heats food quickly using electromagnetic waves	Mikrowelle
to not break the bank	[nɒt ˌbreɪk ðə 'bæŋk]	to not cost too much	nicht die Welt kosten

UNIT 3

page 55

madness	['mædnəs]	*adj* mad	*Wahnsinn*
contact	['kɒntækt]	*phr* to stay in contact	*Kontakt, Verbindung*
celebrity	[sə'lebrəti]	sb famous	*Promi(nente/r)*
interactive	[ˌɪntər'æktɪv]	*v* to interact with sb	*interaktiv*
newsletter	['njuːzletə]	printed report of news	*Rundschreiben, (Info-)Blatt*
blog	[blɒg]	an online journal	*Blog*
to react	[ri'ækt]	*n* reaction	*reagieren*
hurricane	['hʌrɪkən]	severe storm	*Orkan, Wirbelsturm*
latest	['leɪtɪst]	newest	*neueste, letzte*
public	['pʌblɪk]	in front of other people	*öffentlich*
to raise	[reɪz]	*phr* to raise money for sth	*sammeln*
charity	['tʃærəti]	*phr* an act of charity	*wohltätiger Verein*
in need	[ɪn 'niːd]	needing help	*bedürftig*
communication	[kəˌmjuːnɪ'keɪʃn]	*v* to communicate	*Kommunikation, Mitteilung, Benachrichtigung*
refugee	[ˌrefju'dʒiː]	sb fleeing their country	*Flüchtling*
background	['bækgraʊnd]	origin	*Hintergrund, Herkunft*
library	['laɪbrəri]	place where books can be borrowed	*Bücherei, Bibliothek*

page 56

reality TV	[riˌæləti tiː 'viː]	shows using real people, not actors	*Reality TV*
bother	['bɒðə]	difficulty, trouble	*Ärger*
long-running	['lɒŋrʌnɪŋ]	having been on TV for a long time	*mit langer Laufzeit*
to screen	['skriːnɪŋ]	to show a programme on TV	*ausstrahlen*
series	['sɪəriːz]	programme in episodes	*Serie*
producer	[prə'djuːsə]	film-maker, manufacturer	*Produzent/in, Erzeuger*
action	['ækʃn]	*phr* to take action	*Aktion, Handlung*
entertaining	[ˌentə'teɪnɪŋ]	*n* entertainment	*unterhaltsam*
audience	['ɔːdiəns]	viewers	*Zuschauer*
to vote	[vəʊt]	*phr* to vote in favour of/against	*abstimmen, wählen*
to throw out	[ˌθrəʊ 'aʊt]	to force sb to leave	*hinauswerfen*
trouble	['trʌbl]	problem	*Schwierigkeiten, Ärger*
actress	['æktrəs]	female actor	*Schauspielerin*
popular press	[ˌpɒpjələ 'pres]	media that aims to reach a wide audience	*Boulevardpresse*
to exploit	[ɪk'splɔɪt]	*n* exploitation	*be-, ausnutzen*
abuse	[ə'bjuːs]	*v* to abuse sb	*Anpöbelung, Beschimpfung(en)*
to blame sb	[bleɪm]	to think that sb is responsible for sth	*die Schuld geben, verantwortlich machen*
psychological	[ˌsaɪkə'lɒdʒɪkl]	mental	*psychologisch*
profile	['prəʊfaɪl]	description	*Profil, Ansicht, Herkunft, Berufsbild, Porträt*
personality	[ˌpɜːsə'næləti]	a person's character	*Persönlichkeit*
clash	[klæʃ]	conflict	*Konflikt, Zusammenstoß*
profit	['prɒfɪt]	*adj* profitable	*Profit, Gewinn*
to survive	[sə'vaɪv]	*n* survival	*überleben*
addicted	[ə'dɪktɪd tə]	*n* addiction	*süchtig nach*
to appear	[ə'pɪə]	*n* appearance	*erscheinen*
embarrassing	[ɪm'bærəsɪŋ]	*v* to embarrass	*peinlich*
fame	[feɪm]	*adj* famous	*Ruhm*
to wonder	['wʌndə]	to think about	*sich fragen, sich wundern*
psychology	[saɪ'kɒlədʒi]	*adj* psychological	*Psychologie*
to behave	[bɪ'heɪv]	to act in a certain way	*sich benehmen, sich verhalten*
contestant	[kən'testənt]	sb taking part in a contest	*Kandidat/in*
grotesque	[grəʊ'tesk]	terrible	*grotesk*
Roman	['rəʊmən]	inhabitant of the ancient Roman empire	*Römer/in*

page 57

to force	[fɔːs]	to make sb do sth that they don't want to do	*zwingen*
housemate	['haʊsmeɪt]	person that you share a house with	*Mitbewohner/in*
remark	[rɪ'mɑːk]	*phr* to make a remark about sth	*Bemerkung*
abusive	[ə'bjuːsɪv]	*n* abuse	*beleidigend, ausfallend*

accurate	['ækjərət]	correct, precise	genau
legal	['li:gl]	v to legalize	legal
legible	['ledʒəbl]	clear enough to read	leserlich
logical	['lɒdʒɪkl]	sensible or reasonable	logisch
moral	['mɒrəl]	n morality	moralisch
perfect	['pɜ:fɪkt]	n perfection	vollkommen
relevant	['reləvənt]	phr to be relevant to sth/sb	relevant, wichtig
behaviour	[bɪ'heɪvjə]	phr good/bad behaviour	Verhalten, Benehmen

page 58

brave	[breɪv]	n bravery	tapfer
to be up for	[bi ʌp fə]	to be keen to do	bereit sein für, Lust haben auf
to pick up	[,pɪk 'ʌp]	to collect	abholen
either	['aɪðə]	phr either one or the other	hier: beides
genre	['ʒɑ:nrə]	type or style	Genre
comedy	['kɒmədi]	funny film	Komödie, Comedy
documentary	[,dɒkju'mentri]	programme about sth real	Dokumentarbericht, -film
satire	['sætaɪə]	adj satirical	Satire
sci-fi	['saɪ faɪ]	(abbrev) science fiction	Science-Fiction, wissenschaftlich-utopisch
spy	[spaɪ]	person who tries to find out secret information	Spion/in, Spionage-
pirate	['paɪrət]	phr pirate DVDs	Pirat
all-star	['ɔ:l stɑ:]	full of celebrities	Star-, mit vielen Stars
to put forward	[,pʊt 'fɔ:wəd]	to suggest or present	vorbringen, zur Diskussion stellen
point of view	[,pɔɪnt əv 'vju:]	opinion	Standpunkt, Ansicht
ought to	['ɔ:t tə]	should	sollte/n
it's a pity	[ɪts ə 'pɪti]	it's a shame	es ist schade
whatever	[wɒt'evə]	no matter what	was (auch) immer

page 59

medium	['mi:diəm]	way of communicating	Medium
butterfly	['bʌtəflaɪ]	type of winged insect	Schmetterling
altogether	[,ɔ:ltə'geðə]	in total	alles in allem
stranger	['streɪndʒə]	person you don't know	Fremde/r
unusual	[ʌn'ju:ʒuəl]	strange	ungewöhnlich
applicant	['æplɪkənt]	person who applies for a job, etc.	Bewerber/in
offline	['ɒflaɪn]	◇ online	offline, nicht im Internet
to make no sense	[meɪk nəʊ 'sens]	to be hard to understand	nicht sinnvoll sein
freely	['fri:li]	willingly and honestly	freimütig
provider	[prə'vaɪdə]	v to provide	Anbieter
user	['ju:zə]	person who uses sth	Anwender/in, Benutzer/in
at risk	[ət 'rɪsk]	in danger of	gefährdet
to be worried	[bi 'wʌrid]	to be afraid	befürchten
identity	[aɪ'dentəti]	who sb is	Identität
thief	[θi:f]	pl: thieves	Dieb/in
researcher	[rɪ'sɜ:tʃə]	v to research sth	Forscher/in
reunion	[ri:'ju:niən]	v to reunite	Treffen, Wiedersehen
to abridge	[ə'brɪdʒ]	to make (a text) shorter	(ab)kürzen
to adapt	[ə'dæpt]	to change	adaptieren

page 60

to lie	[laɪ]	◇ to tell the truth	lügen
circle	['sɜ:kl]	phr circle of friends	Kreis
to pay attention to	[peɪ ə'tenʃn tə]	to be careful with	beachten, achten auf

page 61

to reduce	[rɪ'dju:s]	n reduction	reduzieren, verringern
component	[kəm'pəʊnənt]	part	Bestandteil
to shorten	['ʃɔ:tn]	to make sth shorter	(ver)kürzen
keyboard	['ki:bɔ:d]	set of keys for controlling a computer	Tastatur
over the top	[,əʊvə ðə 'tɒp]	too much	übertrieben
to bet	[bet]	to be sure that	wetten

experience	[ɪkˈspɪərɪəns]	*phr* to have experience of sth	*Erfahrung*

page 62

netiquette	[ˈnetɪket]	*(inf)* rules for behaving correctly online	*Netiquette, Umgangsformen (im Internet)*
range	[reɪndʒ]	*phr* a wide range of	*Reihe, Spektrum*
polite	[pəˈlaɪt]	*n* politeness	*höflich*
capital (letter)	[ˈkæpɪtl]	e.g. A, B, C	*Groß(buchstabe)*
to be considered	[bɪ kənˈsɪdəd]	to be thought of as	*berücksichtigt werden*
to emphasize	[ˈemfəsaɪz]	*n* emphasis	*betonen, hervorheben*
bold	[bəʊld]	in a thick dark print	*fett*
to underline	[ˌʌndəˈlaɪn]	to draw a line under a word	*unterstreichen*
spelling	[ˈspelɪŋ]	*phr* a spelling mistake	*Rechtschreibung*
to avoid	[əˈvɔɪd]	to try not to do sth	*(ver)meiden*
punctuation	[ˌpʌŋktʃuˈeɪʃn]	marks used to separate phrases/ sentences	*Zeichensetzung, Interpunktion*
unnecessary	[ʌnˈnesəsəri]	⬦ necessary	*unnötig*
to shut up	[ˌʃʌt ˈʌp]	*(inf)* to be quiet	*den Mund halten*
kid	[kɪd]	*(inf)* child	*Kind*

page 63

sword	[sɔːd]	a very large knife used as a weapon	*Schwert*
deadly	[ˈdedli]	*adj* dead	*tödlich, Todes-*
dozen	[ˈdʌzn]	twelve	*Dutzend*
phase	[feɪz]	a stage in development	*Phase, Abschnitt*
unfortunate	[ʌnˈfɔːtʃənət]	less than ideal	*unglücklich, bedauerlich*
criticism	[ˈkrɪtɪsɪzəm]	negative feedback	*Kritik*
health	[helθ]	*phr* to be in good/poor health	*Gesundheit*
to twist	[twɪst]		*verdrehen*
mind	[maɪnd]	the part of our body that thinks and feels	*Verstand, Kopf*
campaigner	[kæmˈpeɪnə]	person set to achieve a certain goal	*Kämpfer/in*
psychologist	[saɪˈkɒlədʒɪst]	person who studies the thoughts and feelings of the human mind	*Psychologe/Psychologin*
recovery	[rɪˈkʌvəri]	getting better after an illness	*Heilung*
TV panel	[ˌtiː ˈviː pænl]	public group discussion on television	*Fernsehrunde, Talkshow*
harmless	[ˈhaːmləs]	sth which does not cause harm	*harmlos, ungefährlich*
banned	[bænd]	prohibited or forbidden	*verboten*
to educate	[ˈedʒukeɪt]	*n* education	*unterrichten*
to underestimate	[ˌʌndərˈestɪmeɪt]	to think sth is less than it really is	*unterschätzen*

page 64

fundraising	[ˈfʌndreɪzɪŋ]	raising money for a charity/organization	*Wohltätigkeitsveranstaltung, Spendensammeln*
bouncy castle	[ˈbaʊnsi kaːsl]	plastic castle filled with air for children to play on	*Hüpfburg*
soft drink	[ˌsɒft ˈdrɪŋk]	cold drink containing no alcohol	*alkoholfreies Getränk*
exchange	[ɪksˈtʃeɪndʒ]	conversation	*(Kurz-)Dialog*
exam results	[ɪgˌzæm rɪˈzʌlts]	grades or marks	*Examensnoten*
secure	[sɪˈkjuə]	*n* security, safe	*sicher*

UNIT 4

page 65

on the move	[ɒn ðə ˈmuːv]	travelling	*unterwegs*
various	[ˈveərɪəs]	a range of	*verschieden*
transport	[ˈtrænspɔːt]	*phr* means of transport	*Verkehr(smittel)*
salesman	[ˈseɪlzmən]	man whose job is to sell goods	*Verkäufer*
ideal	[aɪˈdiːəl]	perfect	*ideal*
budget	[ˈbʌdʒɪt]	cheap	*hier: Billig-*
extent	[ɪkˈstent]	*phr* to a certain extent	*(Aus-)Maß, Umfang, Grad*
reality	[riˈæləti]	*adj* real	*Wirklichkeit*
amazed	[əˈmeɪzd]	*n* amazement	*erstaunt*
annoyed	[əˈnɔɪd]	*v* to annoy sb	*verärgert*
anxious	[ˈæŋkʃəs]	*n* anxiety	*besorgt, beunruhigt*
delighted	[dɪˈlaɪtɪd]	happy	*(sehr) erfreut, entzückt*
depressed	[dɪˈprest]	*n* depression	*deprimiert, niedergeschlagen*

disappointed	[ˌdɪsə'pɔɪntɪd]	n disappointment	enttäuscht
excited	[ɪk'saɪtɪd]	n excitement	aufgeregt, erregt
exhausted	[ɪg'zɔːstɪd]	n exhaustion	erschöpft
frustrated	[frʌ'streɪtɪd]	n frustration	frustriert
nervous	['nɜːvəs]	n nervousness	nervös
relaxed	[rɪ'lækst]	n relaxation	entspannt, locker
shocked	[ʃɒkt]	n shock	schockiert
surprised	[sə'praɪzd]	n surprise	überrascht, erstaunt
terrified	['terɪfaɪd]	very scared	erschrocken
upset	[ˌʌp'set]	unhappy	bestürzt, entsetzt

page 66

traffic jam	['træfɪk dʒæm]	phr to be stuck in a traffic jam	(Verkehrs-)Stau
nursery	['nɜːsəri]	phr day nursery, nursery school	Kindertagesstätte, Kita,
dry cleaner's	[ˌdraɪ 'kliːnəz]	shop where clothes are cleaned using chemicals	chemische Reinigung
fortune	['fɔːtʃuːn]	phr to cost a fortune	Vermögen
surely	['ʃʊəli]	almost certainly	sicherlich
government	['gʌvənmənt]	v to govern	Regierung
fuel	['fjuːəl]	e.g. petrol, coal, gas	Kraftstoff
tax	[tæks]	phr tax increases/cuts	Steuer
tailback	['teɪlbæk]	long line of still or slow-moving traffic	Autoschlange
freedom	['friːdəm]	adj free	Freiheit
flexibility	[ˌfleksə'bɪləti]	adj flexible	Flexibilität
privacy	['prɪvəsi]	adj private	Privatsphäre
campaigner	[kæm'peɪnə]	a person who campaigns for/against sth	Aktivist/in, Kämpfer/in
pollution	[pə'luːʃn]	v to pollute	(Umwelt)Verschmutzung
environmental	[ɪnˌvaɪrən'mentl]	n environment	Umwelt-
damage	['dæmɪdʒ]	physical harm	Schaden, Schäden
exhaust	[ɪg'zɔːst]	pipe in a car through which waste gases pass	Auspuff(rohr)
fumes	[fjuːmz]	smoke or gas	Abgase
to choke	[tʃəʊk]	to be unable to breathe	ersticken
gridlock	['grɪdlɒk]	situation where there are so many cars that none can move	Verkehrskollaps
to contain	[kən'teɪn]	to hold, include	enthalten
passenger	['pæsɪndʒə]	person in a car who is not the driver	Fahrgast
minister	['mɪnɪstə]	government official	Minister/in
congestion	[kən'dʒestʃən]	adj congested	Verkehrsstau, Verstopfung
congested	[kən'dʒestɪd]	full of traffic	verstopft
chaos	['keɪɒs]	adj chaotic	Chaos
to improve	[ɪm'pruːv]	to get better, ◇ to worsen	verbessern, besser werden
balance	['bæləns]	of equal weight	Gleichgewicht
efficient	[ɪ'fɪʃnt]	n efficiency	effizient, leistungsfähig
emission	[ɪ'mɪʃn]	v to emit	Emission, Ausstoß
suburb	['sʌbɜːb]	adj suburban	Vorort, Außenbezirk
saving	['seɪvɪŋ]	v to save (money)	Einsparung, Ersparnis
impact	['ɪmpækt]	phr to have an impact on sth	(Aus-)Wirkung, Einfluss
colleague	['kɒliːg]	person you work with	Kollege/Kollegin
car sharing	['kɑː ʃeərɪŋ]	sharing a ride to reduce costs/pollution, etc.	gemeinsame Pkw-Nutzung

page 67

idiomatic	[ˌɪdiə'mætɪk]	n idiom	idiomatisch
illegal	[ɪ'liːgl]	◇ legal	verboten, illegal
idiom	['ɪdiəm]	adj idiomatic	Idiom, Redewendung
accident	['æksɪdənt]	phr car accident	Unfall
mile	[maɪl]	= 1609 metres	Meile
motorway	['məʊtəweɪ]	wide road where cars travel long distances	Autobahn
to brainstorm	['breɪnstɔːm]	to write down or think of different ideas quickly	(Ideen) sammeln
route	[ruːt]	(in US road names) main road	Route, Strecke, Weg
state	[steɪt]	e.g. California, Kentucky	(Bundes-)Staat
direction	[də'rekʃn]	phr to change direction	Richtung

commuter	[kə'mju:tə]	person who travels a long way to get to work every day	Pendler/in

page 68

visual	['vɪʒuəl]	*n* vision	visuell, optisch
to deliver	[dɪ'lɪvə]	to give or provide	vermitteln, überbringen
message	['mesɪdʒ]	written or spoken information	Botschaft
memorable	['memərəbl]	easy to remember	unvergesslich, einprägsam
vertical	['vɜːtɪkl]	◇ horizontal	senkrecht, vertikal
cliff	[klɪf]	steep edge of a high area of rock	Klippe, Felsen
gas	[gæs]	(AE) BE: petrol	Benzin, Treibstoff
SUV	[ˌes juː 'viː]	(abbrev) sport utility vehicle	Geländewagen (mit Vierradantrieb)
cartoonist	[kɑː'tuːnɪst]	person who draws cartoons	Karikaturist/in
appendix	[ə'pendɪks]	section at the end of a book	Anhang

page 69

satellite	['sætəlaɪt]	*phr* satellite television	Satellit
zone	[zəʊn]	area	Zone, Bereich
rush hour	['rʌʃaʊə]	time when roads are busy	Hauptverkehrszeit, Berufsverkehr
unless	[ən'les]	if not	wenn nicht
satnav	['sætnæv]	(abbrev) satellite navigation	Satellitennavigation, Navi
location	[ləʊ'keɪʃn]	*v* to locate	(Stand-)Ort, Position
monthly	['mʌnθli]	every month	monatlich
haulier	['hɔːliə]	person who transports goods by road	Spediteur, Fuhrunternehmen
to destroy	[dɪ'strɔɪ]	*n* destruction	zerstören, vernichten
to estimate	['estɪmeɪt]	*n* estimation	schätzen
zero	['zɪərəʊ]	the number 0	Null
owner	['əʊnə]	person who owns sth	Besitzer/in
environmentalist	[ɪnˌvaɪrən'mentəlɪst]	person who wants to protect the environment	Umweltschützer/in
engineer	[ˌendʒɪ'nɪə]	person who designs/builds roads/machines, etc.	Ingenieur/in, Techniker/in
to race	[reɪs]	to compete to be the first to do sth	sich ein Wettrennen liefern
dweller	['dwelə]	inhabitant	Bewohner/in
electricity	[ɪˌlek'trɪsəti]	*adj* electric, electrical	Elektrizität, Strom
traditional	[trə'dɪʃənl]	*n* tradition	traditionell
power station	['paʊə steɪʃn]	building where electricity is produced	Kraftwerk
hybrid	['haɪbrɪd]	using a mixture of fuels	hybrid
cleverly	['klevəli]	in a clever way	klug, intelligent
movement	['muːvmənt]	*v* to move	Bewegung
motor	['məʊtə]	device that uses fuel to produce movement	Motor
to support	[sə'pɔːt]	to help, back up	unterstützen
engine	['endʒɪn]	part of vehicle that produces power to move	Motor
hill	[hɪl]	*adj* hilly	Hügel, Berg
complicated	['kɒmplɪkeɪtɪd]	complex, intricate	kompliziert
development	[dɪ'veləpmənt]	progress	Entwicklung
production	[prə'dʌkʃn]	creation, manufacture	Produktion, Herstellung
to combine	[kəm'baɪn]	*n* combination	(sich) verbinden
hydrogen	['haɪdrədʒən]	chemical element H	Wasserstoff
oxygen	['ɒksɪdʒən]	chemical element O	Sauerstoff
waste	[weɪst]	*phr* waste product	Abfall
to manufacture	[ˌmænju'fæktʃə]	to produce	herstellen, produzieren
renewable	[rɪ'njuːəbl]	*phr* renewable energy	erneuerbar
source	[sɔːs]	*phr* energy source	Quelle
environmentally friendly	[ɪnˌvaɪrənˌmentəli 'frendli]	not harmful to the environment	umweltfreundlich

page 70

to calculate	['kælkjuleɪt]	*n* calculation	kalkulieren, berechnen
charge	[tʃɑːdʒ]	*phr* free of charge	Kosten
in common	[ɪn 'kɒmən]	*phr* to have sth in common	gemeinsam
eventually	[ɪ'ventʃuəli]	at the end of a period of time	schließlich, zum Schluss
to power	['paʊə]	to supply a machine/vehicle with energy	antreiben, betreiben

| solution | [sə'luːʃn] | v to solve | Lösung, Ausweg |
| income | ['ɪnkʌm] | money earned | Einkommen |

page 71

congestion charging	[kən'dʒestʃən tʃɑːdʒɪŋ]	money you have to pay for driving your car in the city centre	Staugebühr
to enter	['entə]	to go into	hineingehen, -fahren
result	[rɪ'zʌlt]	phr as a result of	Resultat, Ergebnis
reduction	[rɪ'dʌkʃn]	v to reduce	Verringerung, Senkung
central	['sentrəl]	in the centre	zentral
anger	['æŋgə]	v to anger sb	Zorn, Ärger
to affect	[ə'fekt]	to have an effect on	betreffen
to benefit from	['benɪfɪt frəm]	to be in a better position because of sth	Nutzen ziehen aus, profitieren von
businessperson	['bɪznəspɜːsn]	businessman, businesswoman	Geschäftsmann/-frau
official	[ə'fɪʃl]	person in a position of authority	Beamter/Beamtin
councillor	['kaʊnsələ]	member of a council	Ratsmitglied
to persuade	[pə'sweɪd]	n persuasion	überzeugen, überreden

page 72

appropriate	[ə'prəʊpriət]	suitable	angemessen, passend, entsprechend
old-fashioned	[ˌəʊld 'fæʃənd]	no longer modern or fashionable	altmodisch, veraltet
major	['meɪdʒə]	large or important	groß, größer
complete	[kəm'pliːt]	total	völlig
unavailable	[ˌʌnə'veɪləbl]	<> available	nicht verfügbar
extremely	[ɪk'striːmli]	very	äußerst, außerordentlich
personally	['pɜːsənəli]	individually	persönlich

page 73

walkable	['wɔːkəbl]	suitable for walking	zu Fuß erreichbar
fitness	['fɪtnəs]	health and physical condition	Fitness, Kondition
path	[pɑːθ]	walkway	(Fuß-)Weg
cracked	[krækt]	with small breakes	rissig
blocked	[blɒkt]	closed off	versperrt
pole	[pəʊl]	n telephone pole	Pfahl
bush	[bʊʃ]	a small tree	Busch, Strauch
vehicle	['viːəkl]	e.g. car, bus, motorbike, etc.	Fahrzeug
pavement	['peɪvmənt]	AE: sidewalk	Bürgersteig
to cross	[krɒs]	phr to cross the street	überqueren
traffic signals	['træfɪk sɪgnəlz]	e.g. traffic light	Verkehrsampel
pedestrian	[pɪ'destriən]	person who is walking	Fußgänger/in
motorist	['məʊtərɪst]	person driving a vehicle	Autofahrer/in
cyclist	['saɪklɪst]	person riding a bicycle	Radfahrer/in
driveway	['draɪvweɪ]	a private street for vehicles, often leading to a house	Ein-, Ausfahrt
offensive	[ə'fensɪv]	insulting	beleidigend
litter (BE)	['lɪtə]	AE: garbage	Abfall, Müll
abridged	[ə'brɪdʒd]	shortened	gekürzt
adapted	[ə'dæptɪd]	adjusted	adaptiert
to evaluate	[ɪ'væljueɪt]	to examine	bewerten
to identify	[aɪ'dentɪfaɪ]	to find	feststellen
disability	[ˌdɪsə'bɪləti]		Behinderung
wheelchair	['wiːltʃeə]	chair with wheels for people who cannot walk	Rollstuhl
pram (BE)	[præm]	AE: baby stroller	Kinderwagen
pushchair (BE)	['pʊʃtʃeə]	AE: baby stroller	Kinderwagen, Buggy

page 74

| return | [rɪ'tɜːn] | ticket to go to a place and back again | (hin und) zurück |
| election | [ɪ'lekʃn] | a political vote | (politische) Wahl |

UNIT 5

page 75

| disaster | [dɪ'zɑːstə] | a very bad situation or event | Katastrophe, Unglück |
| mixture | ['mɪkstʃə] | combination | Mischung |

brief	['bri:f]	quick, for a short time	*kurz*
asteroid	['æstərɔɪd]	a small planet which revolves around the sun	*Asteroid*
catastrophe	[kə'tæstrəfi]	disaster	*Katastrophe*
destruction	[dɪ'strʌkʃn]	*v* to destroy	*Zerstörung, Vernichtung*
epidemic	[ˌepɪ'demɪk]	outbreak of a disease or illness	*Epidemie*
flood	[flʌd]	a place that is filled or covered with water	*Flut, Überschwemmung*
to be set in	[bi 'set ɪn]	the film is set in ..., NOT: ~~the film plays in ...~~	*spielen in*

page 76

report	[rɪ'pɔ:t]	*v* to report	*Bericht, Reportage*
fitted	['fɪtɪd]	*v* to fit in place	*eingebaut*
low-energy	[ˌləʊ 'enədʒi]	small or little amount of power	*Niedrigenergie-, Spar-*
bulb	[bʌlb]	*phr* light bulb	*Glühbirne, -lampe*
matter	['mætə]	situation, problem	*Sache, Ding, Angelegenheit*
journalist	['dʒɜːnəlɪst]	a person who collects and writes news stories	*Journalist / in*
progress	['prəʊgres]	⚠ Betonung	*Fortschritt / e*
to turn down	[ˌtɜːn 'daʊn]	*phr* to turn down the temperature	*herunterregeln*
sweater	['swetə]	a piece of clothing for the upper body	*Pullover*
alternative	[ɔ:l'tɜːnətɪv]	different option	*alternativ*
turbine	['tɜːbaɪn]	⚠ Aussprache	*Turbine, Rad*
strength	[strenθ]	*adj* strong	*Kraft, Stärke*
unreliable	[ˌʌnrɪ'laɪəbl]	◇ reliable	*unzuverlässig*
solar	['səʊlə]	using the sun's energy to create power	*Sonnen-, Solar-*
to meet needs	[mi:t 'ni:dz]	to get sth done	*Bedürfnisse decken*
insulation	[ˌɪnsjʊ'leɪʃn]	*phr* wall insulation	*Isolierung*
to face	[feɪs]	*phr* to face a decision	*sich gegenübersehen, vor sich haben*
cycle	['saɪkl]	*n* bicycle	*radfahren*
double-glazing	[ˌdʌbl 'gleɪzɪŋ]	*phr* double-glazed windows	*mit Isolierverglasung versehen*
previous	['pri:viəs]	before	*vorher(gehend)*
to run out of	[ˌrʌn 'aʊt əv]	*phr* to run out of money	*ausgehen*
tonne	[tʌn]	1000 kilograms	*Tonne*
amount	[ə'maʊnt]	quantity	*Menge*
average	['ævərɪdʒ]	typical, normal	*durchschnittlich*
lifestyle	['laɪfstaɪl]	how a person lives and works	*Lebensstil*
somehow	['sʌmhaʊ]	in a way which is not clear	*irgendwie*

page 77

benefit	['benɪfɪt]	advantage	*Nutzen, Vorteil*

page 78

to rewrite	[ˌri:'raɪt]	to write again	*umschreiben, neu schreiben*
original	[ə'rɪdʒənl]	*phr* the original words from the text	*original, ursprünglich*
to advise	[əd'vaɪz]	to suggest, offer an opinion	*raten, beraten*
to request	[rɪ'kwest]	to ask for	*anfordern, bitten (um)*
junction	['dʒʌŋkʃn]	a place or point where two things come together	*Kreuzung*
bored	[bɔ:d]	uninterested	*gelangweilt*
switch	[swɪtʃ]	a device for turning off and on an electrical current	*Schalter*
machinery	[mə'ʃi:nəri]	*n* machine	*Maschine(n), Gerät*
appliance	[ə'plaɪəns]	electronic device	*Gerät*
worried	['wʌrɪd]	*v* to worry	*besorgt*
cloudy	['klaʊdi]	*n* cloud	*bewölkt*
valley	['væli]	the lowest point between two mountains	*Tal*
path	[pɑ:θ]	a walkway	*Pfad, Weg*

page 79

version	['vɜːʃn]	*phr* different versions of the same picture	*Version, Fassung*

page 80

global	['gləʊbl]	worldwide	*global, weltweit*
desperate	['despərət]	urgent	*verzweifelt*

airwaves	['eəweɪvz]	radio waves used to broadcast radio and TV	Äther
atmosphere	['ætməsfɪə]	the mixture of gases that surround the earth	Atmosphäre
twice	[twaɪs]	once, twice, three times	zweimal, doppelt
level	['levl]	amount	Niveau, Stand
industrial	[ɪn'dʌstrɪəl]	n industry	industriell
revolution	[ˌrevə'lu:ʃn]	radical change	Revolution
climate	['klaɪmət]	weather	Klima
eastern	['i:stən]	◇ western, northern, southern	östlich
cyclone	['saɪkləʊn]	bad storm with wind and rain	Zyklon
desert	['dezət]	dry empty land	Wüste
moreover	[mɔ:r'əʊvə]	also	außerdem, zudem
sheet	[ʃi:t]	phr sheet of ice	Platte, Decke
to melt	[melt]	◇ freeze	schmelzen
centimetre	['sentɪmi:tə]	unit for measuring length	Zentimeter
low-lying	[ˌləʊ 'laɪɪŋ]	located at a low level	tief gelegen
coastal	['kəʊstl]	on the coast	Küsten-
to prevent	[prɪ'vent]	to stop sth from happening	verhindern, verhüten
champagne	[ʃæm'peɪn]	French sparkling white wine	Champagner
to celebrate	['selɪbreɪt]	phr to celebrate a birthday	feiern
atmospheric	[ˌætməs'ferɪk]	in the atmosphere	atmosphärisch
ppm	[ˌpi: pi: 'em]	(abbrev) parts per million	Teile pro Million
economy	[ɪ'kɒnəmi]	phr the world economy	Wirtschaft
stabilization	[ˌsteɪbəlaɪ'zeɪʃn]	adj stable	Stabilisierung
coal	[kəʊl]	type of fuel	Kohle
fossil fuel	['fɒsl fju:əl]	type of fuel	fossiler Brennstoff
tidal	['taɪdl]	n tides	Gezeiten-
hydroelectric	[ˌhaɪdrəʊɪ'lektrɪk]	using the power of water to make electricity	hydroelektrisch
nuclear	['nju:klɪə]	phr nuclear weapons	Atom-
fusion	['fju:ʒn]	joining things together to make one	Fusion, Verschmelzung
thanks to	['θæŋks tə]	because of	dank
vision	['vɪʒn]	goal	Vision, Vorausschau
to delay	[dɪ'leɪ]	n delay	aufschieben, hinauszögern
warming	['wɔ:mɪŋ]	adj warm	Erwärmung
severe	[sɪ'vɪə]	very bad	ernst, schwer, stark
wise	[waɪz]	smart	weise, klug
leader	['li:də]	phr leader of the group	Führer/in
to owe	[əʊ]	phr to owe money	verdanken, schulden
to emerge	[ɪ'mɜ:dʒ]	to come out of some place	heraustreten, hervorkommen
carbon	['kɑ:bən]	a chemical element	Kohlenstoff

page 81

century	['sentʃəri]	100 years	Jahrhundert
beyond	[bɪ'jɒnd]	further	darüber hinaus, danach
fraction	['frækʃn]	a part of a whole	Bruch(teil)
percentage	[pə'sentɪdʒ]	%	Prozentsatz
a fifth	[fɪfθ]	a third, a fourth, a fifth	Fünftel
guest	[gest]	visitor	Gast
possibility	[ˌpɒsə'bɪləti]	adj possible	Möglichkeit
climate change	['klaɪmət tʃeɪndʒ]	alteration of the world's weather patterns	Klimawandel
rise	[raɪz]	increase	Anstieg
carbon dioxide	[ˌkɑ:bən daɪ'ɒksaɪd]	the gas CO_2	Kohlendioxid
though	[ðəʊ]	however	doch, jedoch
poverty	['pɒvəti]	adj poor	Armut
standard of living	[ˌstændəd əv 'lɪvɪŋ]	quality of life	Lebensstandard
to make up for	[ˌmeɪk 'ʌp fə]	to compensate for	ausgleichen
increase	['ɪŋkri:s]	adj increasing	Anstieg
to hold down	[ˌhəʊld 'daʊn]	to prevent from increasing	niedrig halten
cut	[kʌt]	reduction	Kürzung, Senkung
figure	['fɪgə]	number or amount	Zahl
target	['tɑ:gɪt]	goal	Ziel(vorgaben), Soll(zahlen)

chart	[tʃɑːt]	diagram	*Diagramm, Tabelle*
required	[rɪ'kwaɪəd]	necessary	*erforderlich*
per capita	[pə 'kæpɪtə]	average per person	*pro Kopf*
to rephrase	[ˌriː'freɪz]	to say again using different words	*anders ausdrücken, umformulieren*
essential	[ɪ'senʃl]	vital, necessary, important	*notwendig, wesentlich*
anecdote	['ænɪkdəʊt]	a short story	*Anekdote*
simile	['sɪməli]	comparing two things using 'like' or 'as'	*Vergleich*
rhetorical	[rɪ'tɒrɪkl]	*phr* to ask a rhetorical question	*rhetorisch*
repetition	[ˌrepə'tɪʃn]	*adj* repetitive	*Wiederholung*
stormy	['stɔːmi]	*n* storm	*stürmisch*
to respond to	[rɪ'spɒnd tə]	to give an answer	*reagieren auf*
warning	['wɔːnɪŋ]	*v* to warn	*Warnung*

oasis	[əʊ'eɪsɪs]	a green spot in a desert	*Oase*
organic	[ɔː'gænɪk]	grown without chemicals	*organisch, Bio-*
chemical	['kemɪkl]	e.g. *n* chemical fertilizer	*Chemikalie*
vegetable	['vedʒtəbl]	a type plant you can eat	*Gemüse*
curving	['kɜːvɪŋ]	slightly bending	*geschwungen*
sculpture	['skʌlptʃə]		*Plastik, Skulptur*
drawn to sth	['drɔːn tə]	attracted to sth	*zu etw hingezogen*
experienced	[ɪk'spɪərɪənst]	having experience in sth	*mit Erfahrung*
multicultural	[ˌmʌlti'kʌltʃərəl]	including many cultures	*multikulturell*
to be reflected	[bi rɪ'flektɪd]	shown	*sich widerspiegeln*
plot	[plɒt]	e.g. garden plot	*Stück Land, Beet*
slice	[slaɪs]	e.g. slice of pizza	*Stück*
native	['neɪtɪv]	coming from a certain country	*gebürtig, ursprünglich*
herb	[hɜːb]	plant used to improve flavour	*(Gewürz-)Kraut*
crop	[krɒp]	plants and vegetables grown	*Anbau*
egg plant *(AE)*	[eg plɑːnt]	*BE:* aubergine	*Aubergine*
flat *(BE)*	[flæt]	*AE:* apartment	*Wohnung*
balcony	['bælkəni]	e.g. hotel room with balcony	*Balkon*
exercise	['eksəsaɪz]	e.g. running, jogging, swimming, etc.	*(körperliche) Bewegung*
pleasure	['pleʒə]	enjoyment	*Vergnügen, Freude*
to appeal to	[ə'piːl tə]	to seem attractive, pleasing or enjoyable	*ansprechen, gefallen*
single mum	['sɪŋgl]		*allein erziehende Mutter*
cucumber	['kjuːkʌmbə]	green vegetable often used for sandwiches	*Gurke*
to emphasize	['emfəsaɪz]	something that is given extra importance	*betonen*
beneficial	[ˌbenɪ'fɪʃl]	positive, helpful	*nützlich, vorteilhaft*
elderly	['eldəli]	old people	*älter, Senioren*
obesity	[əʊ'biːsəti]	condition of being overweight	*Fettleibigkeit*
junk food	['dʒʌŋk fuːd]	food with lots of fat and sugar	*minderwertiges Essen*
diet	['daɪət]	*phr* to be on a diet	*ErnährungDiät(kost)*
allotment	[ə'lɒtmənt]	plot of land rented to a gardener	*Schrebergarten*
resources	[rɪ'sɔːsɪz]	money, time, people, equipment, etc.	*Mittel*
arrangement	[ə'reɪndʒmənt]	to prepare or plan sth	*Vorkehrung*

dramatic	[drə'mætɪ]	*adv.* dramatically	*dramatisch, drastisch*
issue	['ɪʃuː]	problem	*Frage, Thema, Anliegen*

UNIT 6

to operate	['ɒpəreɪt]	to run	*betreiben*
seaside	['siːsaɪd]	along the ocean	*Bade-, Strand-, See-*
resort	[rɪ'zɔːt]	a place where people go to on holiday to relax	*Erholungsort*
accountant	[ə'kaʊntənt]	person who looks after and checks financial accounts	*Buchhalter/in*
booking	['bʊkɪŋ]	*v* to book	*Buchung*
clerk	[klɑːk]	a worker in charge of accounts and records, etc.	*(Bank-)Angestellte/r*

customer relations officer	[ˌkʌstəmə rɪ'leɪʃnz ɒfɪsə]	person who deals with customers	Kundendienstmitarbeiter/in, Kundenbetreuer/in
IT technician	[ˌaɪ 'tiː tek'nɪʃn]	person who is skilled with information technology	Informationstechniker/in
receptionist	[rɪ'sepʃənɪst]	works in a reception	Empfangsdame, -chef
publicity	[pʌb'lɪsəti]	n public	Öffentlichkeitsarbeit
activities officer	[æk'tɪvətiz ɒfɪsə]	person who is in charge of organizing events	Verantwortliche/r für Aktivitäten und Veranstaltungen
salesperson	['seɪlzpɜːsn]	salesman, saleswoman	Verkaufsmitarbeiter/in, Verkäufer/in
instructor	[ɪn'strʌktə]	person who gives instructions	Lehrer/in, Ausbilder/in
temporary	['temprəri]	<> permanent	zeitlich befristet
seasonal	['siːzənl]	n season	Saison-
paid	[peɪd]	phr to get paid money	bezahlt
irregular	[ɪ'regjələ]	<> regular	unregelmäßig
outdoors	[ˌaʊt'dɔːz]	outside	draußen, im Freien
independent	[ˌɪndɪ'pendənt]	self-reliant	unabhängig
office-based	['ɒfɪs beɪst]	to be working within an office	im Büro, bürogebunden
routine	[ruː'tiːn]	a regular fixed way of doing things	Routine, Ablauf
challenging	['tʃælɪndʒɪŋ]	difficult	herausfordernd, anstrengend
reasonable	['riːznəbl]	okay	vernünftig
salary	['sæləri]	amount of money earned	Gehalt, Lohn
fringe benefits	['frɪndʒ benəfɪts]	extra things that an employer gives you as well as your salary	zusätzliche Leistungen, freiwillige Sozialleistungen

page 86

workplace	['wɜːkpleɪs]	area where one works	Arbeitsplatz
complex	['kɒmpleks]	complicated	komplex, kompliziert
diploma	[dɪ'pləʊmə]	graduation certificate	Diplom
secretarial course	[ˌsekrə'teəriəl kɔːs]	course on how to become a secretary	Sekretariatskurs
CV	[ˌsiː 'viː]	(abbrev) Curriculum Vitae	Lebenslauf
to drift	[drɪft]	to move slowly and casually	treiben, zufällig kommen
stock control	['stɒk kəntrəʊl]	control of supplies	Lagersteuerung, Lagerkontrolle
dead-end	[ˌded 'end]	phr a dead-end job	ohne Perspektiven
redundant	[rɪ'dʌndənt]	made unemployed	arbeitslos
to upgrade	[ˌʌp'greɪd]	to make better or to improve	erweitern, verbessern
to apply for	[ə'plaɪ fə]	n application	sich bewerben um

page 87

vocational	[vəʊ'keɪʃənl]	preparing sb for a specific occupation or trade	in der beruflichen Ausbildung, beruflich, Berufs-
to outline	['aʊtlaɪn]	to summarize	umreißen, skizzieren
to matter	['mætə]	to be of importance	von Bedeutung sein
backwards	['bækwədz]	<> forward(s)	rückwärts
oral	['ɔːrəl]	verbal	mündlich

page 88

employment	[ɪm'plɔɪmənt]	job	Arbeit, Beschäftigung, Beruf
wages	['weɪdʒɪz]	amount of money earned by or paid to sb	Lohn, Löhne
pressure	['preʃə]	stress	Druck
responsibility	[rɪˌspɒnsə'bɪləti]	adj responsible	Verantwortung, Verantwortlichkeit
export sales	['ekspɔːt seɪlz]	things that are being sold to other countries	Exportverkäufe, Auslandsverkäufe
IT	[ˌaɪ 'tiː]	(abbrev) information technology	Informationstechnologie
to mess up	[ˌmes 'ʌp]	(inf) to do badly	es verderben, es verpeilen
skint	[skɪnt]	(inf) having no money	pleite
to put down	[ˌpʊt 'daʊn]	to pay up front	anzahlen
solar heating	[ˌsəʊlə 'hiːtɪŋ]	system which uses the sun's energy to heat a house	Solarheizung
to push up	[ˌpʊʃ 'ʌp]	to increase	ausbauen, hochtreiben
to hire	[haɪə]	to recruit, look for new employees	anstellen
IT officer	[ˌaɪ 'tiː ɒfɪsə]	= IT technician	EDV-Techniker/in
support	[sə'pɔːt]	help	Hilfe, Unterstützung
pen	[pen]	phr ballpoint pen	Stift
car seat	['kɑː siːt]	seat in a car	Autositz

page 89

beyond	[bɪˈjɒnd]	apart/aside from	*abgesehen von*
aptitude	[ˈæptɪtjuːd]	ability	*Fähigkeit, Eignung*
prospect	[ˈprɒspekt]	a probable future	*Aussicht*
commitment	[kəˈmɪtmənt]	*v* to commit	*Einsatz, Engagement*
retired	[rɪˈtaɪəd]	having finished working, usually late in life	*pensioniert, im Ruhestand*
grandad	[ˈɡrændæd]	grandfather	*Opa*
hardly	[ˈhɑːdli]	barely	*kaum*
terms	[tɜːmz]	conditions	*Bedingungen, Konditionen*
generous	[ˈdʒenərəs]	*n* generosity	*großzügig*
subsidized	[ˈsʌbsɪdaɪzd]	supported financially	*subventioniert*
healthcare	[ˈhelθkeə]	service of providing medical care	*medizinische Versorgung*
travel insurance	[ˌtrævl ɪnˈʃʊərəns]	*phr* to take out travel insurance	*Reiseversicherung*
maternity leave	[məˈtɜːnəti liːv]	the amount of paid time soon-to-be mothers have off from work	*Mutterschaftsurlaub*
paternity leave	[pəˈtɜːnəti liːv]	the amount of paid time soon-to-be fathers have off from work	*Vaterschaftsurlaub*
creche facilities	[ˌkreʃ fəˈsɪlətiz]	a place where babies and small children are taken care of	*Krippeneinrichtungen*
employee	[ɪmˈplɔiːiː]	worker	*Arbeitnehmer/in, Beschäftigte/r*
union	[ˈjuːniən]	group of working people	*Gewerkschaft*
to invest	[ɪnˈvest]	to put money into a business	*investieren*
workforce	[ˈwɜːkfɔːs]	the workers	*Belegschaft*
resource	[rɪˈsɔːs]	reserves	*Reserve, Ressource*
white-collar	[ˌwaɪt ˈkɒlə]	working in an office	*Schreibtisch-, Büro-*
clerical	[ˈklerɪkl]	connected with office work	*Schreib-, Büro-*
low-cost	[ˌləʊˈkɒst]	inexpensive	*Niedriglohn-*

page 90

to illustrate	[ˈɪləstreɪt]	to visually show	*illustrieren, veranschaulichen*
conclusion	[kənˈkluːʒn]	summary	*(Schluss-)Folgerung*

page 91

marketing	[ˈmɑːkɪtɪŋ]		*Marketing, Vertrieb*
ID	[ˌaɪ ˈdiː]	*(abbrev)* (proof of) identity	*Ausweis*
letter of appointment	[ˌletər əv əˈpɔintmənt]	letter sent to a new employee	*Bewerbungsschreiben*
as a matter of fact	[əz ə ˌmætər əv ˈfækt]	actually	*um genau zu sein*
to be off to	[bi ˈɒf tə]	to be about to go to	*losgehen*

page 92

indirectness	[ˌɪndəˈrektnəs]	to be indirect	*Indirektheit*
absurd	[əbˈsɜːd]	ridiculous	*absurd*
reply	[rɪˈplaɪ]	*v* to reply	*Antwort, Erwiderung, Reaktion*
freezing	[ˈfriːzɪŋ]	very cold	*eiskalt, sehr kalt*
elderly	[ˈeldəli]	older	*älter*
parcel	[ˈpɑːsl]	package	*Paket*
to guide	[ɡaɪd]	to lead	*führen, leiten*

page 93

profession	[prəˈfeʃn]	occupation	*Beruf*
nurse	[nɜːs]	person who takes care of the sick	*Krankenschwester, Kranken-pfleger/in*
despite	[dɪˈspaɪt]	*phr* in spite of	*trotz*
recruitment	[rɪˈkruːtmənt]		*(Neu-)Einstellung*
shortage	[ˈʃɔːtɪdʒ]	short supply of sth	*Fehlen, Mangel*
to anticipate	[ænˈtɪsɪpeɪt]	to expect	*voraussehen, erwarten*
critical	[ˈkrɪtɪkl]	in a state of crisis or emergency	*kritisch*
nationwide	[ˈneɪʃnwaɪd]	throughout the nation	*landesweit*
non-existence	[ˌnɒn ɪɡˈzɪstəns]	not existing	*Fehlen*
comprehensive	[ˌkɒmprɪˈhensɪv]	thorough, wide-ranging	*umfassend*
social worker	[ˈsəʊʃl wɜːkə]	community worker	*Sozialarbeiter/in*
vulnerable	[ˈvʌlnərəbl]	weak	*wehrlos, verletzlich,*

| to be aware of sth | [bi ə'weər əv] | to know about sth | (sich) einer Sache bewusst sein |
| responsibility | [rɪˌspɒnsə'bɪləti] | adj responsible | Verantwortung, Verantwortlichkeit |

page 94

for ages	[fər 'eɪdʒɪz]	for a very long time	eine Ewigkeit
How have you been keeping?	[ˌhaʊ həv ju biːn 'kiːpɪŋ]	How are you doing?	Wie geht es dir?
revision	[rɪ'vɪʒn]	review	Wiederholung

UNIT 7

page 95

directed at	[də'rektɪd ət]	aimed at	gerichtet auf, abzielend auf
microchip	['maɪkrəʊtʃɪp]	a chip used in computers	Mikrochip
studio	['stjuːdɪəʊ]	the place where art, films or music is created	Studio
checklist	['tʃeklɪst]	a list of items	Checkliste
equipment	[ɪ'kwɪpmənt]	the things necessary for a particular kind of job	Ausrüstung

page 96

globalization	[ˌɡləʊbəlaɪ'zeɪʃn]	the expansion of the economy, industry, market or culture	Globalisierung
transmission	[træns'mɪʃn]	transfer	Übertragung
opportunity	[ˌɒpə'tjuːnəti]	a good chance to advance oneself	Chance, Möglichkeit
textile	['tekstaɪl]	e.g. weaving, knitting, etc.	Textil-
to be required to	[bi rɪ'kwaɪəd tə]	to have to	müssen
overtime	['əʊvətaɪm]	working more hours	Überstunden
to sack	[sæk]	to fire	entlassen, feuern
slave	[sleɪv]	person who is forced to work for no money	Sklave / Sklavin
offshore	[ˌɒf'ʃɔː]	to be relocated in a new country	ins / im Ausland
paycheck	['peɪtʃek]	(AE) BE: wages, salary, income	Gehalt(sscheck)
to rescue	['reskjuː]	to save	retten
to redevelop	[ˌriːdɪ'veləp]	to restore	erneuern, neu entwickeln
reborn	[ˌriː'bɔːn]	new	wiedergeboren
competitive advantage	[kəm'petətɪv ədvɑːntɪdʒ]	e.g. lower price, better quality, etc.	Wettbewerbsvorteil
cutting-edge	[ˌkʌtɪŋ 'edʒ]	modern	Spitzen-, Hightech-, modern

page 97

goods	[ɡʊdz]	merchandise	Ware(n), Güter
explanation	[ˌeksplə'neɪʃn]	v to explain	Erklärung
disease	[dɪ'ziːz]	illness	Krankheit, Erkrankung
infrastructure	['ɪnfrəstrʌktʃə]	the structure of a system or an organization	Infrastruktur

page 98

body language	['bɒdi læŋgwɪdʒ]	the signs and gestures we make with our body	Körpersprache
personal space	['pɜːsənl speɪs]	the space around us	Distanzzone, Abstand zwischen Personen
acceptable	[ək'septəbl]	approved	annehmbar, akzeptabel
sensitive	['sensətɪv]	being easily affected by sth	empfindlich
to dominate	['dɒmɪneɪt]	to have command or influence over	dominieren
listener	['lɪsnə]	v to listen	Zuhörer / in
dishonest	[dɪs'ɒnɪst]	<> honest	unehrlich
to trust	[trʌst]	to believe or have confidence in sth or sb	vertrauen
warmth	[wɔːmθ]	adj warm	Wärme
to shake	[ʃeɪk]	phr to shake hands	schütteln
activist	['æktɪvɪst]	sb who actively stands up for a cause / belief	Aktivist / in

page 99

| to rely on | [rɪ'laɪ ɒn] | to depend on | angewiesen sein auf, sich verlassen auf |
| supply chain | [sə'plaɪ tʃeɪn] | the chain through which products are distributed from producer to retailer | Versorgungskette |

casual	['kæʒuəl]	occasional	Gelegenheits-
picker	['pɪkə]	v to pick	Pflücker/in
to despair	[dɪ'speə]	to lose hope	verzweifeln
to bury	['berɪ]	phr to bury your feelings/hopes/dreams	begraben
concern	[kən'sɜːn]	worry	Sorge, Interesse, Anliegen
coordinator	[kəʊ'ɔːdɪneɪtə]	organizer	Koordinator/in
weakness	['wiːknəs]	adj weak	Schwäche
guaranteed	[ˌgærən'tiːd]	secured	garantiert
craft	[krɑːft]	handmade art pieces	(Kunst-)Handwerk
middlemen	['mɪdlmən]	people in the middle of the supply chain	Zwischenhändler
precarious	[prɪ'keərɪəs]	risky	unsicher, prekär
shareholder	['ʃeəhəʊldə]	sb who owns stocks in a company	Aktionär/in
to offload	[ˌɒf'ləʊd]	unload	weitergeben
to seek	[siːk]	to look for	suchen
sub-contractor	[ˌsʌbkən'træktə]		Subunternehmer

page 100

to identify	[aɪ'dentɪfaɪ]	to find	herausfinden
to relate to	[rɪ'leɪt tə]	to connect	sich beziehen auf

page 101

hectare	['hekteə]	= 10,000 square metres	Hektar
co-operative	[kəʊ 'ɒpərətɪv]	workers' group	Kooperative
coffee mill	['kɒfi mɪl]	where coffee is produced	Kaffeemühle
to install	[ɪn'stɔːl]	to set up	installieren
earnings	['ɜːnɪŋz]	money made	Einkünfte

page 102

security	[sɪ'kjʊərəti]	stability	Sicherheit
instability	[ˌɪnstə'bɪləti]	◇ stability	Instabilität
draft	[drɑːft]	a preliminary sketch or idea	Entwurf
restatement	[ˌriː'steɪtmənt]	saying sth again	Neuformulierung
to weigh up	[ˌweɪ 'ʌp]	to consider everything	abwägen
neat	[niːt]	tidy	ordentlich, sauber

page 103

to minimize	['mɪnɪmaɪz]	to reduce	minimieren, gering halten
carbon footprint	[ˌkɑːbən 'fʊtprɪnt]	the amount of carbon dioxide a person produces	O_2-Bilanz/Ökobilanz
respect	[rɪ'spekt]	regard, consideration	Respekt, Achtung
operator	['ɒpəreɪtə]	v to operate	Veranstalter/in
conservation	[ˌkɒnsə'veɪʃn]	v to conserve	Schutz
in preference to sth	[ɪn 'prefrəns tə]	as a priority over sth	vorzugsweise
imported	[ɪm'pɔːtɪd]	◇ exported	importiert
endangered	[ɪn'deɪndʒəd]	in danger of becoming extinct	(vom Aussterben) bedroht, gefährdet
holy	['həʊli]	sacred or religious	heilig
doubt	[daʊt]		Zweifel
sparingly	['speərɪŋli]	using only a small amount of sth	sparsam
precious	['preʃəs]	very special	kostbar
to tend to do sth	['tend tə du]	to be inclined to be sth	dazu neigen, etw zu tun
feedback	['fiːdbæk]	response	Rückmeldung
to promise	['prɒmɪs]		versprechen, zusagen
memory	['meməri]	sth remembered from the past	Erinnerung
to reflect on	[rɪ'flekt ɒn]	to think back on sth	nachdenken über
globalized	['gləʊbəlaɪzd]	n globalization	globalisiert
to fund	[fʌnd]	to support sb or sth financially	finanzieren
eco-tourism	[ˌiːkəʊ 'tʊərɪzəm]	tourism intended to help preserve nature	Ökotourismus
resort	[rɪ'zɔːt]	a ski resort	Ferien-, Urlaubsort
to harm	[hɑːm]	to hurt	schaden, schädigen
aid worker	['eɪd wɜːkə]	person who offers help and support in developing countries	Entwicklungshelfer/in

page 104

dryer	['draɪə]	a machine that dries	Trockner

dried	[draɪd]	when sth lacks water	Trocken-
basket	['bɑːskɪt]	an object used to hold things	Korb
specialist	['speʃəlɪst]	expert	speziell, Fach-
payment	['peɪmənt]	v to pay (for)	Bezahlung
receipt	[rɪ'siːt]	written statement that money has been received	Eingang, Erhalt

UNIT 8

page 105

treaty	['triːti]	an agreement between countries	Vertrag
headquarters	[ˌhed'kwɔːtəz]	main office	Hauptsitz, Zentrale
commission	[kə'mɪʃn]	an official group of people who control sth	Kommission
voter	['vəʊtə]	v to vote	Wähler/in
to reject	[rɪ'dʒekt]	to refuse	ablehnen
constitution	[ˌkɒnstɪ'tjuːʃn]	an established arrangement	Verfassung
anthem	['ænθəm]	phr national anthem	Hymne
peace	[piːs]	a state of mutual harmony	Frieden
prosperity	[prɒ'sperəti]	success	Wohlstand

page 106

internship	['ɪntɜːnʃɪp]	work providing experience in firm	Volontariat
to involve	[ɪn'vɒlv]	to include	einschließen, beinhalten
tourism	['tʊərɪzəm]	n tourist	Tourismus, Fremdenverkehr
practical	['præktɪkl]	basic	praktisch
intern	['ɪntɜːn]	person doing an internship	Praktikant/in, Volontär/in
to contact	['kɒntækt]	to get in touch with sb	Kontakt aufnehmen zu, sich wenden an
to specialize in	['speʃəlaɪz ɪn]	to be good at sth specific	sich spezialisieren auf
sector	['sektə]	section	Sektor, Bereich
duty	['djuːti]	task	Pflicht, Aufgabe
enquiry	[ɪn'kwaɪəri]	question	Anfrage
accommodation	[əˌkɒmə'deɪʃn]	food and lodging	Unterkunft
fluent	['fluːənt]	phr to be fluent in a language	fließend, gewandt, flüssig
licence	['laɪsns]	phr driving licence	Führerschein
outgoing	['aʊtɡəʊɪŋ]	confident and friendly	kontaktfreudig
contribution	[ˌkɒntrɪ'bjuːʃn]	v to contribute	Beitrag, Beihilfe
expenses	[ɪk'spensɪz]	costs	Kosten, Ausgaben
negotiation	[nɪˌɡəʊʃi'eɪʃn]	discussion	Verhandlung
attachment	[ə'tætʃmənt]	v to attach	Anlage
reference	['refrəns]	written statement about character and skills	Zeugnis
to provide	[prə'vaɪd]	to supply	(an)bieten, sorgen für, zur Verfügung stellen
fee	[fiː]	phr admission fee	Gebühr
council	['kaʊnsl]	an assembly of people	Rat, Gemeinderat
to gain	[ɡeɪn]	to receive	sammeln, erlangen
to attach	[ə'tætʃ]	to join onto sth	beilegen, -fügen
query	['kwɪəri]	question	Frage, Rückfrage
Yours faithfully	[jɔːz 'feɪθfʊli]	phrase used to end formal letters	Mit freundlichen Grüßen

page 107

unpaid	[ˌʌn'peɪd]	◇ paid	unbezahlt
enthusiasm	[ɪn'θjuːziæzəm]	excitement	Begeisterung (-sfähigkeit)
agreement	[ə'ɡriːmənt]	v to agree	Vertrag, Abkommen, Zusage
department	[dɪ'pɑːtmənt]	a section of a business	Abteilung
theoretical	[ˌθɪə'retɪkl]	◇ practical	theoretisch
request	[rɪ'kwest]	v to request	Bitte, Aufforderung, Wunsch

page 108

referee	[ˌrefə'riː]	person who writes a job reference	Referenzgeber/in
regarding	[rɪ'ɡɑːdɪŋ]	concerning	bezüglich, betreffend
marital status	[ˌmærɪtl 'steɪtəs]	whether or not you are married	Familienstand
operator	['ɒpəreɪtə]	v to operate	Veranstalter/in

page 109

landline	['lændlaɪn]	home phone	*Festnetz(leitung)*
Do you mind if ...?	[də ju 'maɪnd ɪf]	Is it all right if ...?	*Haben Sie etwas dagegen, wenn ...?*
cyclist	['saɪklɪst]	bike rider	*Fahrradfahrer/in*
outdoor clothing	['aʊtdɔ: kləʊðɪŋ]	clothes for hiking, camping, etc.	*Wanderbekleidung*
prompt	['prɒmpt]	immediate	*unverzüglich, zügig*
typical	['tɪpɪkl]	ordinary	*typisch*

page 110

corruption	[kə'rʌpʃn]	*v* to corrupt	*Korruption*
bureaucracy	[bjʊə'rɒkrəsi]		*Bürokratie*
interference	[ˌɪntə'fɪərəns]	*v* to interfere	*Einmischung*
affair	[ə'feə]	event or happening	*Angelegenheit*
undemocratic	[ˌʌndemə'krætɪk]	not practising social equality	*undemokratisch*
bunch	[bʌntʃ]	a lot of	*Gruppe, Haufen*
unelected	[ˌʌnɪ'lektɪd]	people who were not chosen	*nicht gewählt*
bang	[bæŋ]	expression used when sth starts dramatically	*Paukenschlag*
misleading	[ˌmɪs'li:dɪŋ]	leading in the wrong direction	*irreführend*
frank	['fræŋk]	honest	*offen, ehrlich*
legislative	['ledʒɪslətɪv]	legal	*gesetzgebend*
to recommend	[ˌrekə'mend]	to suggest	*empfehlen*
to defend	[dɪ'fend]	to ward off attack from sb or sth	*verteidigen*
take on	['teɪk ɒn]	opinion on	*Einstellung zu*
relatively	['relətɪvli]	quite, somewhat	*verhältnismäßig*
wrongdoing	['rɒŋdu:ɪŋ]	to do sth wrong	*Fehlverhalten*
frontier	['frʌntɪə]	boundary	*Grenze*

page 111

currency	['kʌrənsi]	system of money that a country uses	*Währung*
stability	[stə'bɪləti]	*adj* stable	*Stabilität*
sovereignty	['sɒvrənti]	independent power/authority	*Souveränität, Unabhängigkeit*
anyhow	['enihaʊ]	in any case	*sowieso*
threat	[θret]	sth that is a source of danger	*Bedrohung, Drohung*
scarcity	['skeəsəti]	*adj* scarce	*Knappheit*
migration	[maɪ'greɪʃn]	to move from one part of the world to another	*Wanderung(sbewegung)*
border	['bɔ:də]	boundary	*Grenze, Grenz-*
to integrate	['ɪntɪgreɪt]	to become part of sth	*sich integrieren*
recommendation		*v* to recommend	*Empfehlung*
widening	['waɪdnɪŋ]	increase in size	*Erweiterung*

page 112

lawyer	['lɔ:jə]	person who has studied law	*(Rechts-)Anwalt/Anwältin*
to evaluate	[ɪ'væljueɪt]	to assess	*einschätzen, bewerten*
federal	['fedərəl]	*phr* federal government of the USA	*föderal(istisch)*
to unite	[ju'naɪt]	to bring together	*vereinigen*
diverse	[daɪ'vɜ:s]	differing from one another	*verschieden, unterschiedlich*

page 113

overstretched	[ˌəʊvə'stretʃt]	finding it hard to cope	*überfordert*
approximately	[ə'prɒksɪmətli]	about	*ungefähr, etwa, zirka*
household	['haʊshəʊld]	members of a family living in a house	*Haushalt*
cooking	['kʊkɪŋ]	*v* to cook	*das Kochen*
medication	[ˌmedɪ'keɪʃn]	medicine	*medizinische Versorgung, Medikamente*
to point out	[ˌpɔɪnt 'aʊt]	to make sb aware of sth	*hinweisen auf*
shortage	['ʃɔ:tɪdʒ]	not enough of sth	*Mangel*
hypocritical	[ˌhɪpə'krɪtɪkl]	*n* hypocrite	*heuchlerisch, scheinheilig*
addition	[ə'dɪʃn]	sth added	*Zugabe, Ergänzung*
relative	['relətɪv]	family member	*Verwandte/r*
affordable	[ə'fɔ:dəbl]	not too expensive	*erschwinglich*

page 114

pound	[paʊnd]	currency of the United Kingdom	*Pfund (Sterling)*
to adopt	[ə'dɒpt]	to vote to accept	*einführen*

to opt out	[ˌɒpt ˈaʊt]	to choose not to participate in sth	austreten, aussteigen
isolated	[ˈaɪsəleɪtɪd]	being separated from	isoliert
referendum	[ˌrefəˈrendəm]	when everyone in a country votes on an important issue	Volksentscheid
gigantic	[dʒaɪˈgæntɪk]	huge	gigantisch, riesig
office block	[ˈɒfɪs blɒk]	tall building containing offices	Bürogebäude, -hochhaus
nonsense	[ˈnɒnsns]	not making sense	Unsinn
luck	[lʌk]	adj lucky	Glück

UNIT 9

page 115

heritage	[ˈherɪtɪdʒ]	sth that is passed on through generations	Erbe, Herkunft
musician	[mjuˈzɪʃn]	a person who writes or performs music	Musiker/in
peer group	[ˈpɪə gruːp]	people who have equal standing in age, class or rank	Gleichaltrige, Clique
role model	[ˈrəʊl mɒdl]	sb whose actions other people follow	Vorbild

page 116

to bring up	[ˌbrɪŋ ˈʌp]	to raise	großziehen
washing powder	[ˈwɒʃɪŋ paʊdə]	clothes detergent	Waschpulver
to polish	[ˈpɒlɪʃ]	to make clean	polieren, putzen
emotional	[ɪˈməʊʃənl]	sad, happy, in love, angry, fearful, etc.	emotional
childcare	[ˈtʃaɪldkeə]	taking care of children	(Kinder-)Erziehung
abandoned	[əˈbændənd]	deserted	verlassen
rejected	[rɪˈdʒektɪd]	v to reject	abgelehnt
to care for sb	[ˈkeə fə]	to raise or nurture sb	jdn pflegen, sich um jdn kümmern

page 117

upbringing	[ˈʌpbrɪŋɪŋ]	v to bring up	Erziehung
childminder	[ˈtʃaɪldmaɪndə]	babysitter	Kinderbetreuer/in, Tagesmutter/-vater
nervous breakdown	[ˌnɜːvəs ˈbreɪkdaʊn]	illness when you are mentally not be able to deal with life	Nervenzusammenbruch
social services	[ˌsəʊʃl ˈsɜːvɪsɪz]	a service that ensures child safety within the household	Sozialamt, Sozialdienste
to retire	[rɪˈtaɪə]	to go into retirement	in Rente/Pension gehen

page 118

custom	[ˈkʌstəm]	practices, habits, norms, traditions	Brauch
psychiatric	[ˌsaɪkiˈætrɪk]	n psychiatrist	psychiatrisch
to come to terms with	[kʌm tə ˈtɜːmz]	to accept	zurechtkommen mit
board game	[ˈbɔːd geɪm]	e.g. monopoly, backgammon, etc.	Brettspiel
to catch sb off guard	[kætʃ ɒf ˈgɑːd]	to surprise	jdn überraschen, ertappen
braid	[breɪd]	small tight plait	(geflochtener) Zopf
input	[ˈɪnpʊt]	contribution	hier: Aufwendung, Hingabe
schoolyard	[ˈskuːljɑːd]	(AE) BE: (school) playground	Schulhof
myth	[mɪθ]	rumour	Legende
literally	[ˈlɪtərəli]	honestly	buchstäblich
to fail sb	[feɪl]	to not give sb what they need	jdn enttäuschen, jdm etw nicht geben können
ultimate	[ˈʌltɪmət]	definitive example of	ultimativ
baggage	[ˈbægɪdʒ]	phr emotional baggage	Gepäck, Last
to miss out on	[ˌmɪs ˈaʊt ɒn]	to not get to do	verpassen
nail polish	[ˈneɪl pɒlɪʃ]	paint for fingernails	Nagellack
to lean on	[ˈliːn ɒn]	to support oneself against	sich lehnen an
once in a while	[ˌwʌns ɪn ə ˈwaɪl]	now and then, from time to time	dann und wann
overly	[ˈəʊvəli]	excessively	übermäßig
minor	[ˈmaɪnə]	very small	geringfügig
wound	[wuːnd]	injury	Wunde
to rub	[rʌb]	phr to rub salt into the wound	reiben
to carry on	[ˌkæri ˈɒn]	to keep going	weitermachen
motherly	[ˈmʌðəli]	maternal	mütterlich
you bet	[ju ˈbet]	of course	ganz bestimmt, und ob

doll	[dɒl]	phr Barbie doll	Puppe
hairstyle	['heəstaɪl]	the way hair is styled	Frisur
inability	[ˌɪnə'bɪləti]	◇ ability	Unfähigkeit
effort	['efət]	attempt	Bemühung, Anstrengung
depressing	[dɪ'presɪŋ]	very sad	bedrückend, deprimierend
tiring	['taɪərɪŋ]	exhausting	anstrengend, ermüdend

page 119

nurse	[nɜːs]	sb who looks after sick people	Krankenschwester, -pfleger/in
priest	[priːst]	a minister of any religion	Priester/in, Geistliche/r
solicitor	[sə'lɪsɪtə]	legal advisor	(Rechts-)Anwalt/Anwältin
powerful	['paʊəfl]	n power	mächtig, stark
shade	[ʃeɪd]		Schattierung
march	[mɑːtʃ]	phr peace march	(Protest-)Marsch
disobedience	[ˌdɪsə'biːdiəns]	misbehaving, breaking rules	Ungehorsam
demonstration	[ˌdemən'streɪʃn]	a public display of discontent	Demonstration
arrest	[ə'rest]	v to arrest	Verhaftung, Festnahme
violence	['vaɪələns]	physical fighting	Gewalt
sympathy	['sɪmpəθi]	feeling sorry for	Mitgefühl, Mitleid
suffragette	[ˌsʌfrə'dʒet]	female supporter of votes for women	Frauenrechtlerin
battle	['bætl]	a conflict or struggle	Kampf
logging	['lɒgɪŋ]	cutting down and removing trees	Abholzung
rope	[rəʊp]	cord	Seil, Tau
mainstream	['meɪnstriːm]	dominant, popular	vorherrschend(e Meinung)

page 120

to achieve	[ə'tʃiːv]	to accomplish sth	erreichen
demo	['deməʊ]	(abbrev) demonstration	Demo(nstration)
foot	[fʊt]	measurement: 30.48cm	Fuß
height	[haɪt]	distance from ground upwards	Höhe, Größe
to be concerned with	[bi kən'sɜːnd wɪð]	to be worried about	sich befassen mit, sich kümmern um

page 121

broad	[brɔːd]	wide	breit
proportion	[prə'pɔːʃn]	dimensions or size	Teil, Verhältnis
registered	['redʒɪstəd]	v to register	registriert, eingetragen
runner-up	[ˌrʌnər 'ʌp]	person or team that finished second	Zweite/r
to extend	[ɪk'stend]	to make bigger	ausweiten, ausbauen
extension	[ɪk'stenʃn]	development	Ausbau
to recap	['riːkæp]	to repeat the main facts	rekapitulieren, zusammenfassen
runway	['rʌnweɪ]	landing strip	Landebahn
to knock down	[ˌnɒk 'daʊn]	to demolish	abreißen
to crash	[kræʃ]	to have an accident	(ab)stürzen
air pollution	[eə pə'luːʃn]	v to pollute	Luftverschmutzung
to go ahead	[ˌgəʊ ə'hed]	to continue as planned	vorangehen, vonstatten gehen
to summarize	['sʌməraɪz]	n summary	zusammenfassen
estuary	['estʃuəri]	where a river meets the sea	Mündung

page 122

delivery	[dɪ'lɪvəri]	v to deliver	Darbietung
inclusion	[in'kluːʒn]	v to include	Einbeziehung
single-issue	[ˌsɪŋgl 'ɪʃuː]	phr a single-issue campaign	Ein-Themen-, auf ein Thema beschränkt
agenda	[ə,dʒendə]		Tagesordnung

page 123

rebel	['rebl]	person who resists authority	Rebell/in
ain't	[eɪnt]		= is not, are not
the rage	[ðə 'reɪdʒ]		der letzte Schrei
polyester	[ˌpɒli'estə]	type of fabric	Polyester
shmolitics	['ʃmɒlətɪks]		Frei erfundenes Wort = shmo (Schwachkopf) + politics (Politik)
vicious circle	[ˌvɪʃəs 'sɜːkl]		Teufelskreis
linear	['lɪniə]	straight	linear, ersten Grades
equation	[ɪ'kweɪʒn]	n mathematical equation	Gleichung

corporation	[ˌkɔːpəˈreɪʃn]	a large business or company	Konzern
permission	[pəˈmɪʃn]	being allowed to do sth	Erlaubnis, Genehmigung
theme park	[ˈθiːm pɑːk]	amusement park (e.g. Disneyland)	Freizeitpark
woodland	[ˈwʊdlənd]	area with many trees	Wald(gebiet)
to drain	[dreɪn]	to empty	entwässern, trockenlegen
debate	[dɪˈbeɪt]	discussion involving opposing viewpoints	diskutieren über, debattieren
radical	[ˈrædɪkl]	extreme	radikal
to chain	[tʃeɪn]		anketten
lawful	[ˈlɔːfl]	legal	rechtmäßig
peaceful	[ˈpiːsfl]	n peace	friedlich
songwriter	[ˈsɒŋraɪtə]	person who writes songs	Texter
verse	[vɜːs]	e.g. the second verse in the poem	Vers, Strophe

page 124

high	[haɪ]	effect experienced when taking drugs	high, auf Drogen
to snort	[snɔːt]	to inhale power through the nose	sniffen, schnupfen
needle	[ˈniːdl]	medical instrument used to insert liquid into the body	Nadel
to break	[breɪk]	to give up addiction to sth	abbrechen
overdose	[ˈəʊvədəʊs]	consuming too much of sth	Überdosis
to get clear of	[get ˈklɪər əv]	phr to get clear of sth bad	wegkommen von
enemy	[ˈenəmi]	sb you hate	Feind
experienced	[ɪkˈspɪəriənst]	having a lot of experience	erfahren
social worker	[ˈsəʊʃl wɜːkə]	sb whose job is social work	Sozialarbeiter/in
broken	[ˈbrəʊkən]	used for a family where the parents are divorced or separated	getrennt, kaputt
foster family	[ˌfɒstə ˈfæməli]	foster mother/father, foster parents	Pflegefamilie

UNIT 10

page 125

multiculturalism	[ˌmʌltiˈkʌltʃərəlɪzəm]	different cultures coexisting in a society	Multikulturalismus
Afro-Caribbean	[ˌæfrəʊ ˌkærəˈbiːən]	African and Caribbean	afro-karibisch
headscarf	[ˈhedskɑːf]	worn by Muslim women to cover their heads	Kopftuch
sari	[ˈsɑːri]	a garment worn by Hindu women	Sari (Kleidungsstück)

page 126

fanatic	[fəˈnætɪk]	n fanatic, fanaticism	Fanatiker/in
to tremble	[ˈtrembl]	to shake with fear, nerves or cold	zittern
to loosen	[ˈluːsn]	to make less tight	lockern
tie	[taɪ]	garment worn around the neck	Krawatte, Schlips
harsh	[hɑːʃ]	unpleasant	scharf, harsch
forbidden	[fəˈbɪdn]	not allowed	verboten
gambling	[ˈgæmblɪŋ]	betting money in a game	Glücksspiel
accompaniment	[əˈkʌmpənimənt]	v to accompany	Begleitung
disgust	[dɪsˈgʌst]	repulsion, horror	Ekel
censure	[ˈsenʃə]	disapproval	Tadel, Missbilligung
temper	[ˈtempə]	phr to lose one's temper	Beherrschung
to stare	[steə]	to look directly and fixedly at sth	starren
conscience	[ˈkɒnʃəns]	inner sense of what is right and wrong	Gewissen
monotonous	[məˈnɒtənəs]	to speak using one tone of voice	monoton
countless	[ˈkaʊntləs]	so many that they cannot be counted	zahllos
for instance	[fəˈrɪnstəns]	for example	zum Beispiel
to demand	[dɪˈmɑːnd]	to ask in a bold, authoritative way	(nach)fragen

page 127

to deny	[dɪˈnaɪ]	to state that sth is not true	bestreiten
mushroom	[ˈmʌʃrʊm]	phr fried mushrooms	Pilz
fried	[fraɪd]	cooked in oil	gebraten, geröstet
perplexed	[pəˈplekst]	confused	perplex, verblüfft
civilisation	[ˌsɪvəlaɪˈzeɪʃn]	an advanced state of human society	Zivilisation
materialist	[məˈtɪəriəlɪst]	person only concerned with material things	Materialist/in
miserable	[ˈmɪzrəbl]	unhappy	kläglich

rowdy	['raʊdi]	disorderly	laut, randalierend
to convince	[kən'vɪns]	to persuade	überzeugen
homosexual	[ˌhəʊmə'sekʃʊəl]	person sexually attracted to people of the same sex	Homosexuelle/r
prostitute	['prɒstɪtjuːt]	person who engages in sexual acts for money	Prostituierte/r
paradise	['pærədaɪs]	a state of supreme happiness	Paradies
to swallow	['swɒləʊ]	muscle movement used when eating and drinking	(ver)schlucken

page 128

setting	['setɪŋ]	scene	Szenerie, Schauplatz
incident	['ɪnsɪdənt]	event	Vorfall, Ereignis
conflicting	[kɒn'flɪktɪŋ]	different	gegensätzlich
gesture	['dʒestʃə]	body movement	Geste(n), Gestik
to mediate	['miːdieɪt]	to settle an argument	vermitteln
to work oneself up	[ˌwɜːk 'ʌp]	to get excited	sich aufregen
rage	[reɪdʒ]	extreme anger	Wut, Zorn

page 129

cheekbones	['tʃiːkbəʊnz]	bones at the top of the cheeks, below the eyes	Wangenknochen
jet-colored	[ˌdʒet 'kʌləd]	(AE) BE: jet-coloured	pechschwarz
ancestry	['ænsestri]	lineage, parentage	Abstammung, Herkunft
to define	[dɪ'faɪn]	to describe sth accurately	(sich) definieren
to apply to	[ə'plaɪ tə]	to count for	gelten für, zutreffen auf
neutral	['njuːtrəl]	indifferent	neutral
unclear	[ˌʌn'klɪə]	◇ clear	unklar
tremendous	[trɪ'mendəs]	huge	gewaltig
appeal	[ə'piːl]	attraction	Anziehungskraft, Anreiz
census	['sensəs]	periodic count of population	(Volks-)Zählung
to tick	[tɪk]	to mark an option with a tick	ankreuzen
multiracial	[ˌmʌlti'reɪʃl]	of many races, mixed-race	ethnisch gemischt
demographer	[dɪ'mɒgrəfi]	person who studies population data	Demograph
intermarriage	[ˌɪntə'mærɪdʒ]	the marriage of two people of different races	Mischehe
segregation	[ˌsegrɪ'geɪʃn]	the separation of different races	Rassentrennung
casting agent	['kɑːstɪŋ eɪdʒənt]	person who chooses models and actors for events/films	Besetzungsagent/in
Nordic	['nɔːdɪk]	connected with the countries of Scandinavia	nordisch
asset	['æset]	a valuable thing to own or have	Wert, Vorteil
to enable	[ɪ'neɪbl]	to help to make possible	(es) ermöglichen, in die Lage versetzen
ethnicity	[eθ'nɪsəti]	race	ethnische Zugehörigkeit
to pose	[pəʊz]	to take on the role of sb	posieren, darstellen
to reflect	[rɪ'flekt]	to show	widerspiegeln
fascination	[ˌfæsɪ'neɪʃn]	strong interest	Faszination
uniformity	[juːnɪ'fɔːməti]	quality or state of being alike	Gleichmäßigkeit
badge	[bædʒ]	trademark	Abzeichen

page 130

respondent	[rɪ'spɒndənt]	person who responds	Befragte/r
out-dated	[ˌaʊt 'deɪtɪd]	old-fashioned	überholt, veraltet
minority	[maɪ'nɒrəti]	◇ majority	Minderheit
to outnumber	[ˌaʊt'nʌmbə]	to exceed in amount	übertreffen
to shrink	[ʃrɪŋk]	to get smaller	schrumpfen, zurückgehen

page 131

Caucasian	[kɔː'keɪziən]	person of European descent	Weiße/r, Hellhäutige/r
Native American	[ˌneɪtɪv ə'merɪkən]	person descended from the original inhabitants of America	Indianer/in, indianisch
to tolerate	['tɒləreɪt]	adj tolerant	tolerieren, ertragen
entire	[ɪn'taɪə]	complete	vollkommen, gänzlich
selfish	['selfɪʃ]	only interested in oneself	egoistisch

limitless	['lɪmɪtləs]	boundless	grenzenlos, uneingeschränkt
cooperative	[kəʊ'ɒpərətɪv]	willing to help	kooperativ
to be to blame	[bi tə 'bleɪm]	he's to blame = it's his fault	an etwas schuld sein
law-abiding	['lɔː əbaɪdɪŋ]	non-criminal	gesetzestreu
domestic	[də'mestɪk]	in the household	in der Familie, häuslich
nanny	['næni]	child-minder	Kindermädchen
citizenship	['sɪtɪznʃɪp]	membership of a country	Staatsbürgerschaft
humane	[hjuː'meɪn]	kind to humans and animals	human
civil rights	[ˌsɪvl 'raɪts]	democratic rights	bürgerliche Rechte
to reward	[rɪ'wɔːd]	to give a prize to	belohnen
to break a law	[breɪk ə 'lɔː]	to commit a crime	das Gesetz brechen / übertreten
to deport	[dɪ'pɔːt]	to remove sb from a country	ausweisen, abschieben
to ship	[ʃɪp]	to send by boat	verschiffen, transportieren
for sb's sake	[fə 'seɪk]	for the good of sb (used as an exclamation of annoyance)	um jds willen
wage	[weɪdʒ]	salary	Lohn
to flood	[flʌd]	to fill to overflowing	überschwemmen
to claim	[kleɪm]	to state sth as true	behaupten, erklären
humanitarian	[hjuːˌmænɪ'teəriən]	having concern for the welfare of other people	humanitär
domestic service	[dəˌmestɪk 'sɜːvɪs]	paid help with household chores	Hausangestellte
to be willing	[bi 'wɪlɪŋ]	to be inclined / open to	bereit / gewillt sein

page 132

foreground	['fɔːgraʊnd]	front	Vordergrund
to cart sth away	[ˌkɑːt ə'weɪ]	to transport sth in a cart	wegkarren
barbed wire	[ˌbɑːbd 'waɪə]	twisted strands of wire with sharp points	Stacheldraht(zaun)
fence	[fens]	barrier to confine or prevent entrance	Zaun
spade	[speɪd]	tool used for digging	Spaten
contradictory	[ˌkɒntrə'dɪktəri]	opposite	widersprüchlich
canyon	['kænjən]	a deep valley with steep sides	Canyon, tiefes / enges Tal
to wander	['wɒndə]	to walk aimlessly	(ziellos) herumlaufen
to crawl	[krɔːl]	to move on your hands and knees	kriechen, krabbeln
wreck	[rek]	mess left after car crash	(Auto-)Wrack
confused	[kən'fjuːzd]	unclear, difficult to understand	verwirrt
temperature	['temprətʃə]	e.g. Fahrenheit, Celsius	Temperatur
hunter	['hʌntə]	person who hunts animals	Jäger / in
to light	[laɪt]	phr to light a fire	anzünden
unhurt	[ʌn'hɜːt]	◇ hurt	unverletzt

page 133

diversity	[daɪ'vɜːsəti]		Mannigfaltigkeit, Vielfalt
correctness	[kə'rektnəs]	adj correct	Korrektheit
row	[raʊ]	(BE) AE: fight	Streit
to erupt	[ɪ'rʌpt]	to explode suddenly	ausbrechen
infant school	['ɪnfənt skuːl]	school for children aged approx. 4–8 years	Grundschule (für ca. 4–8-Jährige)
festival	['festɪvl]	celebration	Fest
curriculum	[kə'rɪkjələm]	the courses of study at a school or university	Lehrplan
pupil (BE)	['pjuːpl]	AE: students	Schüler / in
first school	['fɜːst skuːl]	school for children aged approx. 4–8 years	Grundschule (für ca. 4–8-Jährige)
outrage	['aʊtreɪdʒ]	the feeling of being offended or insulted	Schock, Entrüstung
among	[ə'mʌŋ]	in the group of	unter
to cancel	['kænsl]	to call sth off	streichen, absagen
nativity play	[nə'tɪvəti pleɪ]		Krippenspiel
in favour of	[ɪn 'feɪvər əv]	in preference of	zugunsten von
to showcase	['ʃəʊkeɪs]	to perform	zur Schau stellen
to opt to do sth	['ɒpt tə du]	to choose	sich entscheiden, etw. zu tun
to stage	[steɪdʒ]	to perform	veranstalten
reflection	[rɪ'flekʃn]	v to reflect	Spiegelbild
secular	['sekjələ]	◇ religious	weltlich
sensitivity	[ˌsensə'tɪvəti]	adj sensitive	Sensibilität

to take offence at	[teɪk əˈfens ət]	to be offended	Anstoß nehmen an
majority	[məˈdʒɒrəti]	most	Mehrheit
festivity	[feˈstɪvəti]	celebration	Feierlichkeit
linked	[lɪŋkt]	connected	verbunden
faith	[feɪθ]	here: religion	Glaube

page 134

governor	[ˈgʌvənə]	the executive head of a state in the US	Gouverneur/in
crossing point	[ˈkrɒsɪŋ pɔɪnt]	place where people cross a border	Übergang(sstelle)
guard	[gɑːd]	person who protects a place or people	Wache
valid	[ˈvælɪd]	relevant	gültig
to inquire	[ɪnˈkwaɪə]	to ask	fragen, sich erkundigen
vehicle papers	[ˈviːəkl peɪpəz]	car registration documents	Wagenpapiere
to seal off	[ˌsiːl ˈɒf]	to close	absperren, abriegeln
virtually	[ˈvɜːtʃuəli]	entirely	praktisch, nahezu
feasible	[ˈfiːzəbl]	capable of being done	(praktisch) durchführbar, machbar
amnesty	[ˈæmnəsti]	a general pardon for offences	Amnestie
quota system	[ˈkwəʊtə sɪstəm]	a proportional share assigned to each person	Quotensystem
to go bust	[gəʊ ˈbʌst]	to fall apart or lose money	Pleite gehen

UNIT 11

page 135

patience	[ˈpeɪʃns]	adj patient	Geduld
ransom	[ˈrænsəm]	money paid to kidnappers	Lösegeld
diet	[ˈdaɪət]	phr to be on a strict diet	Ernährung, Diät
to deceive	[dɪˈsiːv]	to lie to, trick	betrügen
to trick	[trɪk]	to deceive or create an illusion	betrügen, hereinlegen
victim	[ˈvɪktɪm]	someone who suffers injury, loss or death	Opfer
burglary	[ˈbɜːgləri]	breaking into a building with the intention of stealing something	Einbruch
prison	[ˈprɪzn]	a place where criminals are locked up	Gefängnis
drink driving	[ˈdrɪŋk draɪvɪŋ]	driving after drinking too much alcohol	Trunkenheit am Steuer
fraud	[frɔːd]	using lies and deceit to get access to money	Betrug, Unterschlagung
armed robbery	[ˌɑːmd ˈrɒbəri]	a robbery with weapons involved	bewaffneter Raubüberfall
trivial	[ˈtrɪviəl]	not important	trivial, geringfügig
property	[ˈprɒpəti]	what sb owns	Eigentum

page 136

cruel	[kruːəl]	unfeeling and harsh	grausam
Supreme Court	[suˌpriːm ˈkɔːt]	highest judicial body in the US	Oberster Gerichtshof
to rule	[ruːl]	to decide (legally)	entscheiden
death penalty	[ˈdeθ penlti]	execution of a person by the state as punishment for a crime	Todesstrafe
constitutional	[ˌkɒnstɪˈtjuːʃənl]	acceptable to the US Constitution	verfassungsgemäß
execution	[ˌeksɪˈkjuːʃn]	the act of killing by law as a punishment	Hinrichtung
murder	[ˈmɜːdə]	the crime of killing sb	Mord
convention	[kənˈvenʃn]	socially accepted way of doing sth	Konvention
lethal	[ˈliːθl]	deadly	tödlich
injection	[ɪnˈdʒekʃn]	fluid introduced into body using a needle	Spritze, Injektion
painless	[ˈpeɪnləs]	without pain	schmerzlos
massive	[ˈmæsɪv]	very large	massiv, enorm
dose	[dəʊs]	amount	Dosis
fast-acting	[ˌfɑːst ˈæktɪŋ]	taking effect quickly	schnell wirkend
anaesthetic	[ˌænəsˈθetɪk]	a substance that causes no physical pain and in large amounts is deadly	Narkosemittel
routinely	[ruːˈtiːnli]	n routine	routinemäßig
to be troubled	[bi ˈtrʌbld]	to be concerned	beunruhigt sein
to subject	[səbˈdʒekt]	to force sb to suffer sth	unterwerfen, aussetzen
attempt	[əˈtempt]	try	Versuch
feminist	[ˈfemənɪst]	person who supports women's rights	Feministin
awkward	[ˈɔːkwəd]	uncomfortable	unangenehm, lästig, peinlich

victory	['vɪktəri]	win	*Sieg*
capital punishment	[ˌkæpɪtl 'pʌnɪʃmənt]	execution as punishment	*Todesstrafe*
corporal punishment	[ˌkɔːpərəl 'pʌnɪʃmənt]	physical injury as punishment	*körperliche Züchtigung*
alliance	[ə'laɪəns]	union, agreement	*Allianz, Bündnis*
fundamentalist	[ˌfʌndə-'mentəlɪst]	believing strongly in one idea	*fundamentalistisch*
conservative	[kən'sɜːvətɪv]	favouring traditional views and values	*Konservative/r*
to be opposed to sth	[bi ə'pəʊzd tə]	to be against sth	*gegen etw sein*
principle	['prɪnsəpl]	personal rule for correct conduct	*Prinzip*
hence	[hens]	therefore	*daher*
apparent	[ə'pærənt]	visible	*offensichtlich, deutlich*
bias	['baɪəs]	supporting sth more due to external factors	*Vorurteil*
repugnant	[rɪ'pʌgnənt]	offensive, unpleasant	*widerlich*

page 137

remorse	[rɪ'mɔːs]	regret	*Reue*
devout	[dɪ'vaʊt]	committed (religious)	*fromm*
clemency	['klemənsi]	mercy	*Milde, Nachsicht*
insane	[ɪn'seɪn]	mentally ill, crazy	*geisteskrank*
liberal	['lɪbərəl]	sb who supports progress and change	*Liberale/r*
passion	['pæʃn]	powerful emotion	*Leidenschaft, Emotion*
reformed	[rɪ'fɔːmd]	made better, altered	*gebessert*
repentant	[rɪ'pentənt]	feeling guilty for committing a sin	*reuig, reumütig*
uncanny	[ʌn'kæni]	extraordinary, strange	*ungeheuer, unheimlich*
bedfellow	['bedfeləʊ]	companion	*Bettgenosse, Schlafkamerad*
to strap	[stræp]	to tie down	*anschnallen, festbinden*
to deserve	[dɪ'zɜːv]	to be worthy of receiving sth	*verdienen*
axe	[æks]	tool used to chop wood	*Axt*
microphone	['maɪkrəfəʊn]	device used to record/emit sound	*Mikrophon*

page 138

to abolish	[ə'bɒlɪʃ]	to get rid off	*abschaffen*
to reintroduce	[ˌriːˌɪntrə'djuːs]	to introduce again	*wieder einführen*
abolition	[ˌæbə'lɪʃn]	*v* to abolish	*Abschaffung*
even	['iːvn]	smooth	*gleichmäßig*
imprisonment	[ɪm'prɪznmənt]	being kept in prison	*Haft, Gefängnis(strafe)*
retribution	[ˌretrɪ'bjuːʃn]	punishment which was deserved	*Vergeltung*
deterrent	[dɪ'terənt]	making people not want to do sth	*abschreckend*
rehabilitation	[ˌriːəˌbɪlɪ'teɪʃn]	sth giving people a fresh start in life	*Rehabilitation*

page 139

to associate	[ə'səʊʃieɪt]	to connect with, be in the company of	*assoziieren, verbinden*
justice	['dʒʌstɪs]	fair outcome	*Gerechtigkeit*
stitch	[stɪtʃ]	A stitch in time saves nine = *Vorsicht ist besser als Nachsicht*	*Stich*
to slide	[slaɪd]	to glide smoothly downwards	*(ab)rutschen, (ab)sacken*
heavily-armed	[ˌhevɪli 'ɑːmd]	protected using weapons	*schwer bewaffnet*
to register	['redʒɪstə]	to record	*registrieren*
rape	[reɪp]	unwanted sexual assault	*Vergewaltigung*
robbery	['rɒbəri]	*v* to rob	*Raub, Überfall*
to dare	[deə]	to try sth risky	*(es) wagen*
turnaround	['tɜːnəraʊnd]	big change/improvement	*Kehrtwendung, Umschwung*
decent	['diːsnt]	respectable	*anständig*
tolerant	['tɒlərənt]	able to endure/accept sth	*tolerant*
rotten	['rɒtn]	corrupt	*korrupt*
drug abuse	[ˌdrʌg ə'bjuːs]	excessive use of drugs	*Drogenmissbrauch*
bribery	['braɪbəri]	*v* to bribe	*Bestechung*
nepotism	['nepətɪzəm]	when people hire relatives	*Vetternwirtschaft*
merciless	['mɜːsiləs]	*n* mercy	*unbarmherzig*
to weed out	[ˌwiːd 'aʊt]	weed = *Unkraut*	*aussondern, -merzen*
tolerance	['tɒlərəns]	*adj* tolerant	*Toleranz*

pension	['penʃn]	payment made by the government to those not in work due to age/illness	*Rente, Pension*
to prosecute	['prɒsɪkju:t]	to accuse sb of a crime and question them	*anklagen, strafrechtlich verfolgen*
policy	['pɒləsi]	rule	*Politik, Linie*
seed	[si:d]	thing from which a plant grows, starting point	*Samen(korn)*
to focus on	['fəʊkəs ɒn]	to concentrate on sth	*sich konzentrieren auf*
dealing	['di:lɪŋ]	*phr* drug dealing	*Handel*
incidence	['ɪnsɪdəns]	recorded number of sth	*Vorkommen, Häufigkeitsrate*

page 140

radical	['rædɪkl]	extreme	*radikal*
diametrically opposed	[ˌdaɪə'metrɪkli əpəʊzd]	completely different	*diametral entgegengesetzt*
nickname	['nɪkneɪm]	an informal name for a person	*Spitzname*
offence	[ə'fens]	sth done against the law	*Delikt, Straftat*
warehouse	['weəhaʊs]	a building that stores supplies	*Lager(halle)*
flick knife	['flɪk naɪf]	a folding pocket knife	*Springmesser*
to resist	[rɪˌzɪst]	to refuse	*Widerstand leisten gegen, sich etw widersetzen*
appointment	[ə'pɔɪntmənt]	an arranged meeting	*Termin, Verabredung*

page 141

verdict	['vɜ:dɪkt]	a decision (legal)	*Urteil, Beurteilung*
probation	[prə'beɪʃn]	test period to monitor good behaviour	*Bewährung*
suspended sentence	[sə,spendɪd 'sentəns]	a possible punishment used as a threat	*(Freiheits-)Strafe auf Bewährung*
to impose	[ɪm'pəʊz]	to force	*auferlegen, erlassen*
nationwide	['neɪʃnwaɪd]	across the country	*landesweit*
to speculate	['spekjuleɪt]	to think about, wonder	*spekulieren, Vermutungen anstellen*
policing	[pə'li:sɪŋ]	police control/surveillance	*Kontrolle, Überwachung*
homicide	['hɒmɪsaɪd]	murder	*Tötung, Mord*
involvement	[ɪn'vɒlvmənt]	being involved in sth	*Beteiligung*

page 142

speeding	['spi:dɪŋ]	driving above the speed limit	*Geschwindigkeitsüberschreitung*
deputy	['depjuti]	officer ranked just below the head of a police department	*Hilfs-, Vertretungs-*
drunk driving	['drʌŋk draɪvɪŋ]	*(AE) BE:* drink driving	*Trunkenheit am Steuer*
registration papers	[ˌredʒɪ'streɪʃn peɪpəz]	official documents (for a car)	*Papiere, Zulassung*
to hack up	[ˌhæk 'ʌp]	to roughly cut up into pieces	*zerstückeln*
trunk	[trʌŋk]	*(AE) BE:* boot (of car)	*Kofferraum*
to back away	['bæk ə'weɪ]	to retreat	*zurückgehen*
backup	['bækʌp]	help	*Hilfe, Unterstützung*
to approach	[ə'prəʊtʃ]	to go towards	*sich nähern, zugehen auf*
to dig into	['dɪg ɪntə]	to rummage in	*wühlen in*
puzzled	['pʌzld]	confused	*verdutzt*
liar	['laɪə]	*v* to lie	*Lügner/in*
to arrest	[ə'rest]	to hold sb by law as a potential criminal	*festnehmen, verhaften*
punch line	['pʌntʃ laɪn]	funny conclusion of a joke	*Pointe*

page 143

cyberbullying	[ˌsaɪbə'bʊliɪŋ]	verbal and emotional abuse on the internet or using mobile phones	*Mobbing im Netz oder per Handy*
black eye	[blæk 'aɪ]	bruise around the eye, common after being punched in the eye	*blaues Auge*
playground	['pleɪgraʊnd]	an area for children to play	*Spielplatz*
bully	['bʊli]	a person who is mean to other people	*Mobber/in, jemand, der/die Schwächere schikaniert*
instant messaging	[ˌɪnstənt 'mesɪdʒɪŋ]	electronic conversation messages via a computer	*Nachrichtensofortversand*
prime	[praɪm]		*hauptsächlich*

breeding ground	['briːdɪŋ graʊnd]	a place or set of circumstances that encourages the development of certain ideas or conditions	*Brutplatz*
exclusion	[ɪk'skluːʒn]	*v* to exclude	*Ausgrenzung*
to ridicule	['rɪdɪkjuːl]	to make fun of sb	*verspotten*
to engage with	[ɪn'geɪdʒ wɪð]	to become involved in	*sich einlassen auf*
to prove	[pruːv]	to show the truth with evidence	*nachweisen*
fault	[fɔːlt]	an error or mistake	*Fehler, Schuld*
innocent	['ɪnəsnt]	<> guilty	*unschuldig*
to upload	[ˌʌp'ləʊd]	to transfer data, often onto the internet	*(ins Internet) stellen*
press	[pres]	media, journalism	*Presse*
debate	[dɪ'beɪt]	discussion involving opposing viewpoints	*Debatte, Diskussion*
involved in	[ɪn'vɒlvd ɪn]	*phr* to be a part of	*beteiligt an, verwickelt in*
to regret	[rɪ'gret]	wishing that one had not done the things one did	*bedauern, bereuen*
offender	[ə'fendə]	someone who breaks the law	*Straftäter/in*
to contribute	[kən'trɪbjuːt]	to give sth	*beisteuern*
seriousness	['sɪəriəsnəs]	*adj* serious	*Ernst(haftigkeit)*

page 144

cell	[sel]	room in a prison where inmates live	*(Gefängnis-)Zelle*
scandalous	['skændələs]	socially inappropriate, shocking	*skandalös*

UNIT 12

page 145

hereditary	[hə'redɪtri]	sth that passes from parent to offspring	*erblich*
cloning	['kləʊnɪŋ]	to make a genetic replica of sth	*Klonen*
conservation	[ˌkɒnsə'veɪʃn]	preservation, protection	*Schutz, Erhaltung*

page 146

boycott	['bɔɪkɒt]	refusing to buy or use a product	*Boykott*
genetically modified	[dʒə,netɪkli 'mɒdɪfaɪd]	when genes have been altered in food	*genmanipuliert*
to announce	[ə'naʊns]	to declare	*ankündigen*
offspring	['ɒfsprɪŋ]	children	*Nachkommen*
revelation	[ˌrevə'leɪʃn]	to reveal information	*Enthüllung*
separate	['seprət]	<> together	*getrennt*
loophole	['luːphəʊl]	when a law can be disobeyed due to ambiguous word use	*Schlupfloch*
to stock	[stɒk]	to have sth in a shop, warehouse, etc.	*führen, anbieten*
to derive	[dɪ'raɪv]	to come from, originate	*abstammen*
ban	[bæn]	an official rule that says sth is not allowed	*Verbot*
ingredient	[ɪn'griːdiənt]	one of the foods that make up a dish	*Zutat, Bestandteil*
astonishing	[ə'stɒnɪʃɪŋ]	unexpected or amazing	*erstaunlich*

page 147

nucleus	['njuːkliəs]	the centre of a cell where DNA is located	*Kern*
dairy	['deəri]	e.g. the dairy industry	*hier: Milchvieh*
herd	[hɜːd]	a group of grazing animals	*Herde*
to be capable of	[bi 'keɪpəbl əv]	to be able to	*können, fähig sein*
vast	[vɑːst]	immense	*riesig, ungeheuer*
mammal	['mæml]	animal that gives birth to live young and feeds them on milk	*Säugetier*
premature	['premətʃə]	unexpectedly early	*vorzeitig, frühzeitig*
lung	[lʌŋ]	organ used to breathe	*Lunge*
infection	[ɪn'fekʃn]	*adj* infectious	*Entzündung*
to diagnose	['daɪəgnəʊz]	to identify a disease or an illness	*diagnostizieren*
arthritis	[ɑː'θraɪtɪs]	painful inflammation of the joints	*Arthritis, Gelenkentzündung*
miscarriage	[ˌmɪs'kærɪdʒ]	failed pregnancy	*Fehlgeburt*
abnormal	[æb'nɔːml]	<> normal	*abnorm, anomal, ungewöhnlich*
organ	['ɔːgən]	body part with specific function	*Organ*
labelling	['leɪblɪŋ]	system of labels on products	*Kennzeichnung*
omission	[ə'mɪʃn]	leaving sth out	*Lücke*
doubt	[daʊt]	uncertainty	*Zweifel*

alteration	[ˌɔːltəˈreɪʃn]	change	*Veränderung*
exceptional	[ɪkˈsepʃənl]	unusually (positive)	*außergewöhnlich*
supervision	[ˌsuːpəˈvɪʒn]	watching/observing sb	*Überwachung*

page 148

supporter	[səˈpɔːtə(r)]	*v* to support	*Anhänger/in*
to introduce	[ˌɪntrəˈdjuːs]	to make sth available for use	*einführen*
outline	[ˈaʊtlaɪn]	*v* to outline	*Umriss*

page 149

gene	[dʒiːn]	*adj* genetic	*Gen*
to maintain	[meɪnˈteɪn]	to support	*aufrechterhalten*
to alter	[ˈɔːltə]	to change	*(ver)ändern*
organism	[ˈɔːɡənɪzəm]	a living thing	*Organismus*
yield	[jiːld]	e.g. crop yield, milk yield	*Ertrag*
tendency	[ˈtendənsi]	inclination, trend	*Tendenz*
dementia	[dɪˈmenʃə]	mental illness	*Demenz*
diabetes	[ˌdaɪəˈbiːtiːz]	metabolic disorder	*Zuckerkrankheit, Diabetes*
transplant	[ˈtrænsplɑːnt]	operation to replace damaged organ	*Transplantation*
breeding	[ˈbriːdɪŋ]	producing offspring	*Zucht, Züchtung*
crop	[krɒp]	agricultural plant	*(Anbau)Pflanze*
to cross-breed	[ˈkrɒs briːd]	to breed from two different species	*kreuzen*
species	[ˈspiːʃiːz]	animal type, e.g. monkeys, dogs, birds, etc.	*Art(en)*
mule	[mjuːl]	male donkey used for farm labour	*Maultier, -esel*
time-consuming	[ˈtaɪm kənsjuːmɪŋ]	taking up a lot of time	*zeitraubend*
predictable	[prɪˈdɪktəbl]	*n* prediction	*voraussagbar*
to interact	[ˌɪntərˈækt]	to work with one another	*sich gegenseitig beeinflussen*
manipulation	[məˌnɪpjuˈleɪʃn]	*v* to manipulate	*Manipulation, Veränderung*
accidental	[ˌæksɪˈdentə]	unintentional	*zufällig, versehentlich*
substance	[ˈsʌbstəns]	matter	*Substanz, Stoff*
poisonous	[ˈpɔɪzənəs]	toxic	*giftig*
to trigger	[ˈtrɪɡə]	to make sth active	*auslösen*
allergy	[ˈælədʒi]	*adj* allergic	*Allergie*
antibiotic-resistant	[ˌæntibaɪˌɒtɪk rɪˈzɪstənt]	not affected by antibiotic drugs	*resistent gegen Antibiotika*
micro-organism	[ˌmaɪkrəʊ ˈɔːɡənɪzəm]	very small organism	*Mikroorganismus*
flavour	[ˈfleɪvə]	taste	*Geschmack*
shelf life	[ˈʃelf laɪf]	date when a product expires	*Haltbarkeit*
nutritional	[njuˈtrɪʃənl]	to do with food and health	*Nähr-*

page 150

consumption	[kənˈsʌmpʃn]	when sb uses/eats sth	*Verzehr*
to obey	[əˈbeɪ]	to follow a rule	*befolgen*
to store	[stɔː]	to keep sth somewhere	*lagern, aufbewahren*
lobby	[ˈlɒbi]	e.g. gun lobby	*Lobby, Interessengruppe*
harmful	[ˈhɑːmfl]	bad, dangerous	*schädlich*
herbicide	[ˈhɜːbɪsaɪd]	chemical substance used to inhibit the growth of unwanted plants	*Unkrautvernichtungsmittel*
contaminated	[kənˈtæmɪneɪtɪd]	polluted	*verunreinigt, verseucht*
to play havoc	[pleɪ ˈhævək]	to ruin, to mess sth up	*verheerende Schäden anrichten*
contrary	[ˈkɒntrəri]	*phr* on the contrary	*Gegenteil*
bioengineer	[ˌbaɪəʊ-ˌendʒɪˈnɪə]	a person who has studied genetic engineering	*Gentechniker/in*
fertilizer	[ˈfɜːtəlaɪzə]	a substance added to soil which improves plant growth	*Dünger*
pesticide	[ˈpestɪsaɪd]	chemical used to kill pests on plants	*Schädlingsbekämpfungsmittel*
uncultivated	[ʌnˈkʌltɪveɪtɪd]	untidy, not looked after carefully	*brachliegend*
habitat	[ˈhæbɪtæt]	the natural home and environment of an organism	*Lebensraum*
convincing	[kənˈvɪnsɪŋ]	persuasive	*überzeugend*
toxic	[ˈtɒksɪk]	poisonous	*giftig, toxisch*

page 151

blueprint	[ˈbluːprɪnt]	prototype, plan	*Blaupause, Bauplan*

to imply	[ɪmˈplaɪ]	to suggest	andeuten, implizieren
unintentional	[ˌʌnɪnˈtenʃənl]	not on purpose	unabsichtlich
to halve	[hɑːv]	to split sth into two, make half of a whole	(sich) halbieren
by-product	[ˈbaɪ prɒdʌkt]	side effect, unintentional outcome	Nebenprodukt
pollination	[ˌpɒləˈneɪʃn]	fertilization of plants causing production of seeds	Bestäubung
radiation	[ˌreɪdiˈeɪʃn]	energy transmitted as electromagnetic waves	Strahlung
mast	[mɑːst]	pole, tower	Mast

page 152

spare part	[ˌspeə ˈpɑːt]	replacement	Ersatzteil
potential	[pəˈtenʃl]	possibilities	Potenzial
cure	[kjʊə]	remedy	Heilung, Heilmittel
downside	[ˈdaʊnsaɪd]	disadvantage	Nachteil
to abuse	[əˈbjuːz]	to use for a bad purpose	missbrauchen
clone	[kləʊn]	exact genetic copy	Klon
media hype	[ˈmiːdiə haɪp]	over-the-top journalism	Medienrummel
to feed	[fiːd]	n food	ernähren
conventional	[kənˈvenʃənl]	traditional	konventionell, herkömmlich
field trial	[ˈfiːld traɪəl]	test in natural conditions	Freilandversuch
superweed	[ˈsuːpəwiːd]	weed which is hard to kill	hoch resistentes Unkraut
bee	[biː]		Biene
cross-breeding	[ˈkrɒsbriːdɪŋ]	v to cross-breed	Kreuzung
shortage	[ˈʃɔːtɪdʒ]	not having enough of sth	Knappheit, Mangel

page 153

to get to grips with sth	[get tə ˈɡrɪps wɪð]	to deal with sth	mit etw klarkommen, etw in den Griff bekommen
gadget	[ˈɡædʒɪt]	a small mechanical device	Vorrichtung, Gerät
designer	[dɪˈzaɪnə]		Konstrukteur/in, Designer/in
can opener	[ˈkæn əʊpnə]	a device that opens cans	Büchsen-, Dosenöffner
to count	[kaʊnt]	here: to be important	zählen
to pour	[pɔː]	phr to pour milk	gießen
mug	[mʌɡ]	e.g. coffee mug	Becher(tasse)
to scald	[skɔːld]	burning	(sich) verbrühen
bathing	[ˈbeɪðɪŋ]	taking a bath	Baden
to cope	[kəʊp]	to deal with	zurechtkommen, fertig werden
case	[keɪs]	situation	Fall
disability	[ˌdɪsəˈbɪləti]	physical or mental handicap	Behinderung
assistive	[əˈsɪstɪv]	helpful	unterstützend
exciting	[ɪkˈsaɪtɪŋ]		aufregend, spannend
to recognize	[ˈrekəɡnaɪz]	to identify	erkennen
to consult	[kənˈsʌlt]	to get advice	konsultieren
input	[ˈɪnpʊt]	opinion	Beitrag, Einfluss
bath plug	[ˈbɑːθ plʌɡ]	device used to keep water in the bath	Badewannenstöpsel
pressure-sensitive	[ˈsensətɪv]	designed to recognize small changes in pressure	druckempfindlich
plate	[pleɪt]		Platte
excess	[ˈekses]	more than usual	überschüssig
energetic	[ˌenəˈdʒetɪk]	n energy	voller Energie
myth	[mɪθ]	a fictitious story	Mythos
to exist	[ɪɡˈzɪst]	to be real	existieren
to struggle	[ˈstrʌɡl]	to have difficulty with sth	kämpfen
retirement	[rɪˈtaɪəmənt]	v to retire	(Eintritt in den) Ruhestand, Pensionierung

page 154

to publish	[ˈpʌblɪʃ]	to make e.g. a book public	veröffentlichen, herausgeben
stamp	[stæmp]	mark of payment on an envelope	Briefmarke

SOCIAL TOPICS

TOPIC 1

page 156

to relax [rɪ'læks]	(sich) entspannen, ausruhen
pressure ['preʃə]	Druck
brain [breɪn]	Gehirn
stress-free ['stres friː]	stressfrei
willing ['wɪlɪŋ]	gewillt, bereit(willig)
volunteer [ˌvɒlən'tɪə]	Ehrenamtliche/r,
local government	Gemeindeverwaltung,
['gʌvənmənt]	Kommunalverwaltung
benefit ['benɪfɪt]	Vorteil
to run sth [rʌn]	etw leiten, führen
committee [kə'mɪti]	Ausschuss, Komitee
snack bar ['snæk bɑː]	Imbissstube
to raise [reɪz]	auftreiben, aufbringen
funds [fʌndz]	Geldmittel, Kapital
to provide [prə'vaɪd]	zur Verfügung stellen, (an)
	bieten
to improve [ɪm'pruːv]	verbessern
facility [fə'sɪləti]	Einrichtung
Youth Council ['kaʊnsl]	Jugendkomitee
questionnaire	Fragebogen
[ˌkwestʃə'neə]	
to recall [rɪ'kɔːl]	sich erinnern
showcase ['ʃəʊkeɪs]	Vorstellung

page 158

potential [pə'tenʃl]	möglich

TOPIC 2

page 159

childcare ['tʃaɪldkeə]	(Kinder-)Erziehung
consumer [kən'sjuːmə]	Verbraucher/in
to pester ['pestə]	löchern, quengeln
power ['paʊə]	Kraft
to ban [bæn]	verbieten
to nag [næg]	in den Ohren liegen
particularly [pə'tɪkjələli]	besonders
run-up ['rʌn ʌp]	Vorfeld
in the ~ to ['rʌn ʌp]	im Vorfeld von
treat [triːt]	Vergnügen, Leckerbissen
majority [mə'dʒɒrəti]	Mehrheit
useful ['juːsfl]	nützlich
tool [tuːl]	Instrument, Mittel
desirable [dɪ'zaɪərəbl]	wünschenswert
necessary ['nesəsəri]	notwendig
to ensure [ɪn'ʃʊə]	sicherstellen
available [ə'veɪləbl]	verfügbar
to remark [rɪ'mɑːk]	bemerken
disappointment	Enttäuschung
[ˌdɪsə'pɔɪntmənt]	
balance ['bæləns]	Gleichgewicht
spoiled [spɔɪld]	verdorben
psychologist	Psychologe/Psychologin
[saɪ'kɒlədʒɪst]	
inevitable [ɪn'evɪtəbl]	unvermeidlich
media ['miːdiə]	Medien
~ -awareness	Bewusstsein, die Medien richtig
	einzuschätzen
~ -literate ['lɪtərət]	medienkundig, sich mit Medien
	auskennen

to encourage [ɪn'kʌrɪdʒ]	auffordern
to associate [ə'səʊʃieɪt]	verbinden

page 160

healthy ['helθi]	gesund
fizzy ['fɪzi]	sprudelnd, spritzig
to persuade [pə'sweɪd]	überzeugen, überreden

page 161

retail ['riːteɪl]	Einzelhandel
merchandise	Waren(angebot), Produkte
['mɜːtʃəndaɪs]	
communication	Kommunikation
[kəˌmjuːnɪ'keɪʃn]	
education [ˌedʒu'keɪʃn]	Erziehung, (Schul-)Bildung
toy [tɔɪ]	Spielzeug
alarming [ə'lɑːmɪŋ]	alarmierend, beunruhigend
obesity [əʊ'biːsəti]	Fettleibigkeit
debt [det]	Schuld(en)

TOPIC 3

page 162

education [ˌedʒu'keɪʃn]	Erziehung, (Schul-)Bildung
well-lit [ˌwel 'lɪt]	hell erleuchtet
robber ['rɒbə]	Räuber/in
donkey ['dɒŋki]	Esel
cockerel ['kɒkərəl]	junger Hahn
sort [sɔːt]	Art
to drive away	vertreiben
[ˌdraɪv ə'weɪ]	
forefeet ['fɔːfiːt]	Vorderfüße
window ledge	Fensterbank, -brett
['wɪndəʊ ledʒ]	
to jump [dʒʌmp]	springen
to climb [klaɪm]	klettern
adapted [ə'dæptɪd]	adaptiert
extract ['ekstrækt]	Auszug
wicked ['wɪkɪd]	bösartig
heart [hɑːt]	Herz
poor [pʊə]	arm
stupid ['stjuːpɪd]	dumm
goose [guːs]	Gans
servant ['sɜːvənt]	Dienstmädchen
wooden ['wʊdn]	hölzern, Holz-
dressed [drest]	angezogen, gekleidet
daybreak ['deɪbreɪk]	Tagesanbruch
besides [bɪ'saɪdz]	außerdem
to upset [ˌʌp'set]	verwirren, ärgern
to empty ['empti]	schütten
pea [piː]	Erbse
lentil ['lentl]	Linse
ashes ['æʃɪz]	Asche
to force so to sth [fɔːs]	jmd zu etwas zwingen
to pick out [ˌpɪk 'aʊt]	heraussuchen
brick [brɪk]	Ziegel(stein), Backstein
wolf [wʊlf]	Wolf
huff [hʌf]	schnauben
puff [pʌf]	keuchen
to blow down	umblasen
[ˌbləʊ 'daʊn]	
Cinderella [ˌsɪndə'relə]	Aschenputtel
Little Red Riding Hood	Rotkäppchen
[ˌlɪtl red raɪdɪŋ 'hʊd]	

cruel ['kruːəl] — grausam
stepmother ['stepmʌðə] — Stiefmutter
death [deθ] — Tod
patient ['peɪʃnt] — geduldig
bunch [bʌntʃ] — Gruppe
misfit ['mɪsfɪt] — Außenseiter
core [kɔː] — Kern
literacy ['lɪtərəsi] development [dɪ'veləpmənt] — Entwicklung der Lese- und Schreibfertig- keiten
repetitive [rɪ'petətɪv] — (sich) wiederholend
element ['elɪmənt] — Element
to memorize ['meməraɪz] — auswendig lernen
vivid ['vɪvɪd] — lebhaft
exciting [ɪk'saɪtɪŋ] — aufregend, spannend
opportunity [ˌɒpə'tjuːnəti] — Gelegenheit, Möglichkeit
old-fashioned [ˌəʊld 'fæʃənd] — altmodisch, veraltet
irrelevant [ɪ'reləvənt] — unbedeutend
relevance ['reləvəns] — Bedeutung, Wert
gender ['dʒendə] — Geschlecht
stereotyping ['steriətaɪpɪŋ] — Vorurteile gegenüber anderen beruhend auf Vorstellungs- klischees
aboriginal [ˌæbə'rɪdʒənl] — (austral.) Ureinwohner/in
universal [ˌjuːnɪ'vɜːsl] — allgemein, universell
canoe [kə'nuː] — Kanu
juicy ['dʒuːsi] — saftig
edge [edʒ] — Rand
tired ['taɪəd] — müde
voice [vɔɪs] — Stimme

camp [kæmp] — Lager
to taste [teɪst] — kosten, probieren
to choke [tʃəʊk] — würgen
bony ['bəʊni] — voller Gräten
slightly ['slaɪtli] — leicht
alternatively [ɔːl'tɜːnətɪvli] — alternativ, als weitere Möglichkeit
to outline ['aʊtlaɪn] — umreißen, skizzieren
plot [plɒt] — Handlung(sverlauf)

TOPIC 4

caring ['keərɪŋ] — Pflege
blind [blaɪnd] — blind,
impaired [ɪm'peəd] — behindert
to take for granted [ˌteɪk fə 'grɑːntɪd] — als selbstverständlich betrachten
partially ['pɑːʃəli] — teilweise
to require [rɪ'kwaɪə] — erfordern
pedestrian [pɪ'destriən] — Fußgänger/in
edge [edʒ] — Rand, Kante
tactile ['tæktaɪl] — tastbar
cane [keɪn] — (Blinden-)Stock
auditory ['ɔːdətri] — hörbar, auditiv
unfamiliar [ˌʌnfə'mɪliə] — unbekannt
intersection [ˌɪntə'sekʃn] — Kreuzung

map [mæp] — (Stadt-)Plan
to keep track of sth [kiːp 'træk əv] — verfolgen
unsure [ˌʌn'ʃʊə] — unsicher, ungewiss
laid out [ˌleɪd 'aʊt] — angelegt
sighted ['saɪtɪd] — sehend
to identify [aɪ'dentɪfaɪ] — erkennen
button ['bʌtn] — Taste, Knopf
to press [pres] — drücken
interval ['ɪntəvl] — Zeit, Phase
to gather ['gæðərɪŋ] — Sammeln
to include [ɪn'kluːd] — umfassen, einschließen
pavement ['peɪvmənt] — Bürgersteig
pole [pəʊl] — Mast, Stange
pushbutton ['pʊʃbʌtn] — Drucktaste
layout ['leɪaʊt] — Anordnung
signal ['sɪgnəl] — Ampel
walkability [ˌwɔːkə'bɪləti] — Benutzbarkeit zu Fuß
straight [streɪt] — gerade
raised [reɪzd] — erhöht
aggressive [ə'gresɪv] — aggressiv
slightly ['slaɪtli] — leicht

tolerant ['tɒlərənt] — tolerant
curb [kɜːb] — Bordkante, -stein

to prepare [prɪ'peə] — vorbereiten
to approach [ə'prəʊtʃ] — sich nähern
to pause [pɔːz] — kurz innehalten
to step [step] — treten
to assume [ə'sjuːm] — annehmen, davon ausgehen
roadside ['rəʊdsaɪd] — Straßenrand
angle ['æŋgl] — Winkel
to part company [pɑːt 'kʌmpəni] — sich trennen
to alert [ə'lɜːt] — aufmerksam machen

TOPIC 5

overweight [ˌəʊvə'weɪt] — übergewichtig
to intervene [ˌɪntə'viːn] — eingreifen
slim [slɪm] — schlank
toddler ['tɒdlə] — Krabbel-, Kleinkind
vegetable ['vedʒtəbl] — Gemüse
to overeat [ˌəʊvər'iːt] — zu viel essen
diet ['daɪət] — Ernährung, Nahrung
to consist of [kən'sɪst əv] — bestehen aus
carbohydrate [ˌkɑːbəʊ'haɪdreɪt] — Kohle(n)hydrat
biscuit ['bɪskɪt] — Keks
gym [dʒɪm] — Fitnessstudio
membership ['membəʃɪp] — Mitgliedschaft
to bear [beə] — etwas ertragen
body frame ['bɒdi freɪm] — Konstitution
metabolic rate [ˌmetə'bɒlɪk reɪt] — Stoffwechsel
to perceive [pə'siːv] — wahrnehmen
alone [ə'ləʊn] — allein(e)

assumption [ə'sʌmpʃn]	Annahme, Voraussetzung
concern [kən'sɜːn]	Sorge, Bedenken
to arrange [ə'reɪndʒ]	vereinbaren

page 169

appearance [ə'pɪərəns]	Aussehen, Äußeres
self-esteem [ˌself ɪ'stiːm]	Selbstachtung, -wertgefühl
constantly ['kɒnstəntli]	ständig

page 170

obesity [əʊ'biːsəti]	Fettleibigkeit
factor ['fæktə]	Faktor
peers [pɪəz]	Gleichaltrige, Altersgruppe
explanation [ˌeksplə'neɪʃn]	Erklärung

TOPIC 6

page 171

childcare ['tʃaɪldkeə]	(Kinder-)Erziehung
training ['treɪnɪŋ]	Ausbildung, Training
disability [ˌdɪsə'bɪləti]	Behinderung
temperature ['temprətʃə]	(erhöhte) Temperatur
to involve [ɪn'vɒlv]	einschließen, umfassen
to educate ['edʒukeɪt]	erziehen
diploma [dɪ'pləʊmə]	Abschlusszeugnis, Diplom
degree [dɪ'griː]	(akademischer) Abschluss
full-time [ˌfʊl 'taɪm]	Ganztags-, Vollzeit(stelle)
paediatrics [ˌpiːdi'ætrɪks]	Kinderheilkunde, Pädiatrie
trainee [treɪ'niː]	Auszubildende/r, Praktikant/in
vocational [vəʊ'keɪʃənl]	beruflich
competence ['kɒmpɪtəns]	Kompetenz
evidence ['evɪdəns]	Beweis(e)
assessor [ə'sesə]	Prüfer/in
to observe [əb'zɜːv]	beobachten
to pass [pɑːs]	bestehen

page 172

assessment [ə'sesmənt]	Beurteilung, Prüfung
to gain [geɪn]	erlangen
ladder ['lædə]	Leiter
day release [ˌdeɪ rɪ'liːs]	tageweise Freistellung (zur praktischen Ausbildung)
deputy ['depjəti]	stellvertretend
determined [dɪ'tɜːmɪnd]	(fest) entschlossen

page 173

to insert [ɪn'sɜːt]	einfügen
staff [stɑːf]	Mitarbeiter, Personal

TOPIC 7

page 174

adventurous [əd'ventʃərəs]	abenteuerlich
nationality [ˌnæʃə'næləti]	Staatsangehörigkeit, Nationalität
involved [ɪn'vɒlvd]	beteiligt
unique [ju'niːk]	einzigartig, einmalig
venturer ['ventʃərə]	Abenteurer/in
phase [feɪz]	Phase
lack [læk]	Mangel

infrastructure ['ɪnfrəstrʌktʃə]	Infrastruktur
alongside [əˌlɒŋ'saɪd]	neben
renovating ['renəveɪtɪŋ]	Renovieren
ranger ['reɪndʒə]	Aufseher/in, Wildhüter/in
trail [treɪl]	(Wander-)Weg
conservation [ˌkɒnsə'veɪʃn]	Schutz, Erhaltung
eco-system ['iːkəʊ sɪstəm]	Ökosystem
biodiversity [ˌbaɪəʊdaɪ'vɜːsəti]	Artenvielfalt
trekking ['trekɪŋ]	Wanderreiten, Trekking
canoeing [kə'nuːɪŋ]	Kanufahren
scenery ['siːnəri]	Landschaft
to get in with [ˌget 'ɪn wɪð]	geraten an
to get caught up [ˌget ˌkɔːt 'ʌp]	verwickelt werden
crime [kraɪm]	Verbrechen, Kriminalität
theft [θeft]	Diebstahl
assault [ə'sɔːlt]	(tätlicher) Angriff
robbery ['rɒbəri]	Raub(überfall)
sentenced ['sentənst]	verurteilt
offender [ə'fendə]	Straftäter/in
institute ['ɪnstɪtjuːt]	Institut, Anstalt
accommodation [əˌkɒmə'deɪʃn]	Unterkunft
jail [dʒeɪl]	Gefängnis
anxiety [æŋ'zaɪəti]	Angst(zustand)
to pursue [pə'sjuː]	verfolgen, nachgehen
sector ['sektə]	Sektor, Bereich
motivation [ˌməʊtɪ'veɪʃn]	Motivation
to teach [tɔːt]	lehren, unterrichten
overseas [ˌəʊvə'siːz]	Auslands-

page 175

rough [rʌf]	rau, uneben

page 176

to afford [ə'fɔːd]	(es) sich leisten (können)

TOPIC 8

page 177

outdoor ['aʊtdɔː]	im Freien
aimless ['eɪmləs]	ziellos
to prepare [prɪ'peə]	(sich) vorbereiten
afterthought ['ɑːftəθɔːt]	(nachträglicher) Einfall
fellow ['feləʊ]	Mit-
trainee [treɪ'niː]	Auszubildende/r, Praktikant/in
wooden ['wʊdn]	aus Holz, Holz-, hölzern
to appeal to [ə'piːl tə]	ansprechen
academic [ˌækə'demɪk]	Schul-
subject ['sʌbdʒɪkt]	(Schul-)Fach
mainstream ['meɪnstriːm]	vorherrschend
abstract ['æbstrækt]	abstrakt
concept ['kɒnsept]	Begriff, Konzept, Idee
basis ['beɪsɪs]	Grundlage
enthusiasm [ɪn'θjuːziæzəm]	Begeisterung(sfähigkeit)
to dust [dʌst]	Staub wischen

to polish ['pɒlɪʃ]	putzen	
to repair [rɪ'peə]	reparieren	
toy [tɔɪ]	Spielzeug	
to fold [fəʊld]	zusammenlegen	
laundry ['lɔːndri]	Wäsche	
the dishes [ðə 'dɪʃɪz]	das Geschirr	
to sew [səʊ]	nähen	
to mend [mend]	flicken, ausbessern	
to accomplish [ə'kʌmplɪʃ]	schaffen, leisten	
mechanized ['mekənaɪzd]	mechanisiert	
formerly ['fɔːməli]	früher	
to throw away [θrəʊn]	wegwerfen	
engaged [ɪn'geɪdʒd]	beschäftigt, engagiert	
to boost [buːst]	erhöhen, steigern	
to undertake sth [ˌʌndə'teɪk]	(sich) vornehmen	
perseverance [ˌpɜːsɪ'vɪərəns]	Ausdauer, Beharrlichkeit	
to carve [kɑːv]	schnitzen,	
branch [brɑːntʃ]	Ast, Zweig	
outcome ['aʊtkʌm]	Resultat, Ergebnis	
paddle ['pædl]	Paddel	
sword [sɔːd]	Schwert	
walking stick ['wɔːkɪŋ stɪk]	Spazierstock	
response [rɪ'spɒns]	Reaktion, Antwort	
eager ['iːgə]	eifrig bestrebt	
porridge ['pɒrɪdʒ]	Hafer(flocken)brei	
purpose ['pɜːpəs]	Zweck, Sinn	

page 178

dissatisfied [dɪs'sætɪsfaɪd]	unzufrieden	
supervision [ˌsuːpə'vɪʒn]	Aufsicht	
harvest ['hɑːvɪst]	ernten	
herb [hɜːb]	(Heil-, Gewürz-)Kraut	
flower ['flaʊə]	Blume	
dye [daɪ]	Färbemittel	
fabric ['fæbrɪk]	Stoff	
to sweep [swiːp]	fegen, kehren	
leaves [liːvz]	Laub, Blätter	
seed [siːd]	Same, Kern	
necklace ['nekləs]	(Hals-)Kette	
to weed [wiːd]	(Unkraut) jäten	
to water ['wɔːtə]	wässern, gießen	
to maintain [meɪn'teɪn]	aufrechterhalten	
bird feeder ['bɜːd fiːdə]	Futterhäuschen (für Vögel)	
peanut ['piːnʌt]	Erdnuss	
slice [slaɪs]	Scheibe, Stück	
string [strɪŋ]	Schnur, Bindfaden	
to shovel ['ʃʌvl]	schaufeln, schippen	
snow [snəʊ]	Schnee	
path [pɑːθ]	(Fuß-)Weg	
to nail [neɪl]	nageln	
plank [plæŋk]	Bohle	
log [lɒg]	Baumstamm	
bench [bentʃ]	Sitzbank	
to saw [sɔː]	sägen	
fence [fens]	Zaun	
ladder ['lædə]	Leiter	

TOPIC 9

page 180

tale [teɪl]	Geschichte, Erzählung	
unexpected [ˌʌnɪk'spektɪd]	unerwartet	
to reveal [rɪ'viːl]	zum Vorschein bringen, zeigen	
rich [rɪtʃ]	reich(haltig)	
diversity [daɪ'vɜːsəti]	Vielfalt	
dozen ['dʌzn]	Dutzend	
file [faɪl]	(Akten-)Ordner	
printout ['prɪntaʊt]	(Computer-)Ausdruck	
handwritten [ˌhænd'rɪtn]	handgeschrieben	
memory ['meməri]	Erinnerung	
childhood ['tʃaɪldhʊd]	Kindheit	
camp [kæmp]	Lager	
unique [ju'niːk]	einzigartig	
collection [kə'lekʃn]	Sammlung	
autobiographical [ˌɔːtəˌbaɪə'græfɪkl]	autobiographisch	
hardship ['hɑːdʃɪp]	Not, Mühsal	
workshop ['wɜːkʃɒp]	Workshop	
unwaged [ˌʌn'weɪdʒd]	ohne Einkommen	
fellow ['feləʊ]	Mit-	
contributor [kən'trɪbjuːtə]	Mitwirkende / r	
lonely ['ləʊnli]	einsam	
lifeline ['laɪflaɪn]	Rettungsleine	
to recall [rɪ'kɔːl]	sich erinnern (an)	
sorrow ['sɒrəʊ]	Trauer, Kummer, Sorge(n)	
dyslexic [dɪs'leksɪk]	legasthenisch	
marriage ['mærɪdʒ]	Ehe	
to break down [ˌbreɪk 'daʊn]	in die Brüche gehen	
insomnia [ɪn'sɒmniə]	Schlaflosigkeit	
alcoholism ['ælkəhɒlɪzəm]	Alkoholismus	
complicated ['kɒmplɪkeɪtɪd]	kompliziert	
clarity ['klærəti]	Klarheit, Reinheit	
to envy ['envi]	beneiden	
door frame ['dɔː freɪm]	Türrahmen	
confident ['kɒnfɪdənt]	selbstsicher, -bewusst	
streetwise ['striːtwaɪz]	gerissen, gewieft	
abortion [ə'bɔːʃn]	Abtreibung	
adapted [ə'dæptɪd]	adaptiert	
abridged [ə'brɪdʒd]	gekürzt	

page 181

extraordinary [ɪk'strɔːdnri]	außergewöhnlich	
participant [pɑː'tɪsɪpənt]	Teilnehmer / in	
necessity [nə'sesəti]	Bedürfnis	
therapy ['θerəpi]	Therapie, Behandlung	
to argue ['ɑːgjuː]	(sich) streiten	
divorce [dɪ'vɔːs]	Scheidung	
to quarrel ['kwɒrəl]	(sich) streiten	

page 182

authority [ɔː'θɒrəti]	Behörde	
recreation [ˌrekri'eɪʃn]	Erholung	
claimant ['kleɪmənt]	Anspruchsberechtigte / r	
crèche [kreʃ]	(Kinder-)Krippe, Kinderhort	

refreshment [rɪˈfreʃmənt]   Erfrischung
welfare [ˈwelfeə]   Fürsorge-, Sozial-
pensioner [ˈpenʃənə]   Rentner/in
traveller [ˈtrævələ]   Person ohne festen Wohnsitz
advance [ədˈvɑːns]   (im) Voraus
exception [ɪkˈsepʃn]   Ausnahme

TOPIC 10

page 183
bilingual [ˌbaɪˈlɪŋgwəl]   zweisprachig
headteacher [ˌhedˈtiːtʃə]   Schulleiter/in
represented [ˌreprɪˈzentɪd]   vertreten
reflection [rɪˈflekʃn]   Spiegelbild
linguistic [lɪnˈgwɪstɪk]   linguistisch
to inspire [ɪnˈspaɪə]   inspirieren, begeistern
multilingual [ˌmʌltiˈlɪŋgwəl]   mehrsprachig
factor [ˈfæktə]   Faktor
thirst [θɜːst]   Durst
monolingual [ˌmɒnəˈlɪŋgwəl]   einsprachig
firmly [ˈfɜːmli]   entschlossen, kräftig
to squash [skwɒʃ]   zunichtemachen
myth [mɪθ]   Mythos
to achieve [əˈtʃiːv]   leisten
buzz [bʌz]   Gemurmel, Stimmengewirr
culturally-inclusive [ɪnˈkluːsɪv]   die Kultur mit einbeziehend
curriculum [kəˈrɪkjələm]   Lehrplan
equality [ɪˈkwɒləti]   Gleichberechtigung
access [ˈækses]   Zugang
supportive [səˈpɔːtɪv]   verständnisvoll
keen [kiːn]   (sehr) interessiert
well-trodden path [ˌwel ˈtrɒdn pɑːθ]   viel beschrittener Weg
economic [ˌiːkəˈnɒmɪk]   wirtschaftlich
political [pəˈlɪtɪkl]   politisch
migrant [ˈmaɪgrənt]   Migrant/in
funding [ˈfʌndɪŋ]   finanzielle Unterstützung
adapted [əˈdæptɪd]   adaptiert
abridged [əˈbrɪdʒd]   gekürzt

page 184
prejudice [ˈpredʒudɪs]   Vorurteil

TOPIC 11

page 186
foster [ˈfɒstə]   Pflege
to argue [ˈɑːgjuː]   (sich) streiten
to kick out [ˌkɪk ˈaʊt]   hinauswerfen
social worker [ˈsəʊʃl wɜːkə]   Sozialarbeiter/in
group home [ˈgruːp həʊm]   betreutes Wohnprojekt
still [stɪl]   trotzdem, (immer) noch
staff [stɑːf]   Mitarbeiter/innen
shift [ʃɪft]   Schicht
roommate [ˈruːmmeɪt]   Zimmerkollege/-kollegin
chores [tʃɔːz]   regelmäßige Haushaltsarbeiten

therapist [ˈθerəpɪst]   Therapeut/in
respectful [rɪˈspektfl]   respektvoll
permission [pəˈmɪʃn]   Erlaubnis
backyard [ˌbækˈjɑːd]   (Hinter-)Hof
schedule [ˈʃedjuːl]   Zeitplan
allowance [əˈlaʊəns]   Vergütung, Zuschuss
to interview [ˈɪntəvjuː]   interviewen
to minimize [ˈmɪnɪmaɪz]   verringern
restriction [rɪˈstrɪkʃn]   Einschränkung
jail [dʒeɪl]   Gefängnis

page 187
to regret [rɪˈgret]   bedauern, bereuen

page 188
to maintain [meɪnˈteɪn]   einhalten
discipline [ˈdɪsəplɪn]   Disziplin
to ensure [ɪnˈʃʊə]   sicherstellen, gewährleisten
complaint [kəmˈpleɪnt]   Beschwerde
compromise [ˈkɒmprəmaɪz]   Kompromiss
recommendation [ˌrekəmenˈdeɪʃn]   Empfehlung

TOPIC 12

page 189
hall of fame [hɔːl əv ˈfeɪm]   Ruhmeshalle
founder [ˈfaʊndə]   Gründer/in
organization [ˌɔːgənaɪˈzeɪʃn]   Organisation
volunteer [ˌvɒlənˈtɪə]   Ehrenamtliche/r
to distribute [dɪˈstrɪbjuːt]   verteilen
shelter [ˈʃeltə]   Heim, Unterkunft
facility [fəˈsɪləti]   Einrichtung
to afford [əˈfɔːd]   (es) sich leisten (können)
dyslexia [dɪsˈleksɪə]   Legasthenie
drive (AE) [draɪv]   Sammelaktion
to prompt [prɒmpt]   veranlassen
recruiting [rɪˈkruːtɪŋ]   Anwerbung
to sort [sɔːt]   sortieren
donated [dəʊˈneɪtɪd]   gespendet
underprivileged [ˌʌndəˈprɪvəlɪdʒd]   unterprivilegiert
daycare center [ˈdeɪkeə sentə]   Tagesstätte
tornado [tɔːˈneɪdəʊ]   Tornado
rough [rʌf]   rau, hart
ultimately [ˈʌltɪmətli]   schließlich, letzten Endes
counselor [ˈkaʊnsələ]   Berater/in, Betreuer/in
mentor [ˈmentɔː]   Mentor/in
to conduct [kənˈdʌkt]   abhalten, (durch)führen
tutoring [ˈtjuːtərɪŋ]   Nachhilfe
recreation [ˌrekriˈeɪʃn]   Erholung
activity [ækˈtɪvəti]   Aktivität
foundation [faʊnˈdeɪʃn]   Stiftung
scholarship [ˈskɒləʃɪp]   Stipendium

page 190
eager [ˈiːgə]   eifrig, bestrebt

page 191
caption [ˈkæpʃn]   Bildunterschrift

A–Z word list

Dieses Wörterverzeichnis enthält alle Wörter aus Focus on Success – The new edition: Ausgabe Soziales in alphabetischer Reihenfolge. Nicht aufgeführt sind die Wörter aus der *Basic word list* sowie internationale Wörter wie *hotel, email* usw.

Wörter, die in den Hörverständnistexten vorkommen, sind mit einem *t* hinter der Seitenzahl gekennzeichnet.

A

abandoned *116* verlassen
abbreviation *52* Abkürzung
ability *7* Fähigkeit
abnormal *147* abnorm, anomal, ungewöhnlich
to abolish *138* abschaffen
abolition *138* Abschaffung
aboriginal *163* (austral.) Ureinwohner/in
abortion *180* Abtreibung
to abridge *59* (ab)kürzen
absolutely *22* absolut
abstract *177* abstrakt
absurd *92* absurd
abuse *56* Anpöbelung, Beschimpfung(en)
to abuse *152t* missbrauchen
abusive *57* beleidigend, ausfallend
academic *177* Schul-
to accept *13* akzeptieren
acceptable *98* annehmbar, akzeptabel
access *183* Zugang
accessory *95* Zubehör, Accessoire
accident *67* Unfall
accidental *149* zufällig, versehentlich
accommodation *106* Unterkunft
accompaniment *126* Begleitung
to accomplish *177* schaffen, leisten
according to *7* nach, gemäß
account executive *54* Kunden-berater/in, -betreuer/in
account manager *46* Kunden-betreuer/in
accountant *85* Buchhalter/in
accurate *57* genau
to achieve *120, 183* erreichen, leisten
acronym *51t* Akronym, Initialwort
action *56* Aktion, Handlung
activist *98* Aktivist/in
activities officer *85* Verantwortliche/r für Aktivitäten und Veranstaltungen
activity *189* Aktivität
actress *56* Schauspielerin
actually *29* tatsächlich, eigentlich

ad *18* Anzeige
to adapt *59* adaptieren
adapted *73* adaptiert
addicted *56* süchtig nach
addiction *16* Sucht, Abhängigkeit
addition *113* Zugabe, Ergänzung
to admit *49* zugeben, gestehen
adolescent *43* Jugendliche/r
to adopt *114* einführen
advance *182* (im) Voraus
adventurous *174* abenteuerlich
advertisement *45* Anzeige, Werbespot
advertiser *49* Werbefirma
advertising *40* Werbung
advice *19* Rat(schlag)
to advise *78* raten, beraten
affair *110* Angelegenheit
to affect *71* betreffen
to afford *176, 189* (es) sich leisten (können)
affordable *113* erschwinglich
afraid: I'm afraid *7* leider
Afro-Caribbean *125* afro-karibisch
afterthought *177* (nachträglicher) Einfall
agency *46* Agentur
ages: for ages *94* eine Ewigkeit
aggressive *165* aggressiv
agreement *107* Vertrag, Abkommen, Zusage
ahead *73* voraus, kommend
ahead: to go ahead *121t* voran-gehen, vonstatten gehen
aid worker *103* Entwicklungs-helfer/in
aim *45* Ziel
aimed at *51t* abgezielt auf, gerichtet an
aimless *177* ziellos
ain't *123* = is not, are not
air pollution *121t* Luftverschmutzung
airwaves *80* Äther
alarming *161* alarmierend, beunruhigend
alcoholism *180* Alkoholismus
to alert *167* aufmerksam machen
all over the place *7* überall
allergy *149* Allergie
alliance *136* Allianz, Bündnis

allotment *83* Schrebergarten
allowance *186* Vergütung, Zuschuss
all-star *58t* Star-, mit vielen Stars
alone *168* allein(e)
alongside *174* neben
to alter *149* (ver)ändern
alteration *147* Veränderung
alternative *76* alternativ
alternatively *164* alternativ, als weitere Möglichkeit
although *14* obwohl
altogether *59* alles in allem
amazed *65* erstaunt
amnesty *134* Amnestie
among *133* unter
amount *76* Menge
anaesthetics *136* Narkosemittel
to analyze *51t* analysieren
ancestry *129* Abstammung, Herkunft
anecdote *82* Anekdote
anger *71* Zorn, Ärger
angle *167* Winkel
to announce *146* ankündigen
annoyed *65* verärgert
annoying *45* lästig, ärgerlich
anorexia *16* Magersucht
anthem *105* Hymne
antibiotic-resistant *149* resistent gegen Antibiotika
to anticipate *93* voraussehen, erwarten
anti-theft pad *28* Diebstahl-sicherung
anxiety *174* Angst(zustand)
anxious *65* besorgt, beunruhigt
anyhow *111* sowieso
apparent *136* offensichtlich, deutlich
appeal *129* Anziehungskraft, Anreiz
to appeal to *177* ansprechen, gefallen
to appear *56* erscheinen
appearance *169* Aussehen, Äußeres
appendix *68* Anhang
appliance *78* Gerät
applicant *59* Bewerber/in
application *48* Bewerbung
to apply for *86* sich bewerben um

to apply to *129* gelten für, zutreffen auf

appointment *140* Termin, Verabredung

to approach *142t, 167* sich nähern, zugehen auf

appropriate *72* angemessen, passend, entsprechend

approx. *44* ungefähr, etwa, zirka

approximately *113* ungefähr, etwa, zirka

aptitude *89* Fähigkeit, Eignung

area *40* Gebiet, Bereich

to argue *181, 186* (sich) streiten

armed robbery *135* bewaffneter Raubüberfall

to arrange *168* vereinbaren

arrangement *83* Anordnung, Vorkehrung

arrest *119* Verhaftung, Festnahme

to arrest *142* festnehmen, verhaften

arrival *34* Ankunft

arthritis *147* Arthritis, Gelenkentzündung

ashamed *17* beschämt

ashes *162* Asche

aspect *41* Aspekt, Seite

assault *174* (tätlicher) Angriff

assessment *172* Beurteilung, Prüfung

assessor *171* Prüfer/in

asset *129* Wert, Vorteil

assistive *153* unterstützend

to associate *139, 159* assoziieren, verbinden

association *16* Verband, Verein

to assume *167* annehmen, davon ausgehen

assumption *168* Annahme, Voraussetzung

asteroid *75* Asteroid

astonishing *146* erstaunlich

at a disadvantage *31* benachteiligt

atmosphere *80* Atmosphäre

atmospheric *80* atmosphärisch

to attach *106* beilegen, -fügen

attachment *106* Anlage

attack *40* Angriff

attempt *136* Versuch

to attend *48* teilnehmen (an)

attention *51t* Aufmerksamkeit

attention: to pay attention to *60* beachten, achten auf

attitude *17* Haltung, Einstellung

to attract *18* anziehen, anlocken

attraction *41* Anziehung

attractive *16* attraktiv

auction *27* Auktion

audience *56* Zuschauer

auditory *165* hörbar, auditiv

authority *182* Behörde

autobiographical *180* autobiographisch

available *159* verfügbar

average *76* durchschnittlich

to avoid *62* (ver)meiden

award *52* Auszeichnung

awesome *12* überwältigend

awkward *136* unangenehm, lästig, peinlich

axe *137* Axt

B

to back away *142t* zurückgehen

to back off *12* zurücktreten

background *55* Hintergrund, Herkunft

backup *142t* Hilfe, Unterstützung

backwards *87* rückwärts

backyard *186* (Hinter-)Hof

badge *129* Abzeichen

baggage *118t* Gepäck, Last

balance *66, 159* Gleichgewicht

balcony *83* Balkon

to ban *12* verbieten

ban *146* Verbot

bandana *43* Kopftuch

bang *110* Paukenschlag

bank: to not break the bank *54* nicht die Welt kosten

bankrupt *40* bankrott, pleite

bankrupt: to go bankrupt *52* in Konkurs gehen, Pleite gehen

banned *63* verboten

banner ad *45* Bannerwerbung

barbecue *20* Grillparty

barbed wire *132* Stacheldraht(zaun)

bargain *26* Sonderangebot

bartender *33* Barmann, -frau

basis *177* Grundlage

basket *104* Korb

bath plug *153* Badewannenstöpsel

battle *119* Kampf

to be aware of sth *93* (sich) einer Sache bewusst sein

to be capable of *147* können, fähig sein

to be due to *47* darauf zurückzuführen sein

bead *43* Perle

to bear *168* etwas ertragen

to beat *12* schlagen

bedfellow *137* Bettgenosse, Schlafkamerad

bee *152t* Biene

to behave *56* sich benehmen, sich verhalten

behaviour *57* Verhalten, Benehmen

below *10* unten

belt *43* Gürtel

bench *178* Sitzbank

to bend *16* (sich) beugen

beneficial *83* nützlich, vorteilhaft

benefit *77, 156* Nutzen, Vorteil

to benefit from *71* Nutzen ziehen aus, profitieren von

besides *162* außerdem

best-known *53* bekannteste

to bet *61* wetten

bet: you bet *118t* ganz bestimmt, und ob

beyond *81, 89* darüber hinaus, danach, abgesehen von

bias *136* Vorurteil

bilingual *183* zweisprachig

biodiversity *174* Artenvielfalt

bioengineer *150* Gentechniker/in

bird feeder *178* Futterhäuschen (für Vögel)

birth *41* Geburt

biscuit *168* Keks

bite *39* Bissen, Happen

black eye *143* blaues Auge

to blame sb *56* die Schuld geben, verantwortlich machen

blame: to be to blame *131t* an etwas schuld sein

blind *165* blind,

blind spot *73* blinder Fleck

blocked *73* versperrt

blog *55* Blog

blouse *26* Bluse

to blow down *162* umblasen

to blow sb away *37* jdn überwältigen

blueprint *151* Blaupause, Bauplan

board game *118t* Brettspiel

body frame *168* Konstitution

body language *98* Körpersprache

bold *62* fett

bony *164* voller Gräten

booker *47* Besteller/in

booking *85* Buchung

to boost *177* erhöhen, steigern

border *111* Grenze, Grenz-

bored *78* gelangweilt

borough *40* (Stadt-)Bezirk

bother *56* Ärger

bouncycastle *64* Hüpfburg

box: the box *7* die Kiste

boycott *146* Boykott

braid *118t* (geflochtener) Zopf

brain *156* Gehirn

to brainstorm *67* (Ideen) sammeln

branch *177* Ast, Zweig

brand *45* Marke

branded *49* Marken-

brave *58t* tapfer

to break *124* abbrechen

to break a law *131t* das Gesetz brechen/übertreten

to break down *180* in die Brüche gehen

to break into *23* einbrechen
breath: to take sb's breath
   away *40* jdm den Atem rauben
breeding *149* Zucht, Züchtung
breeding ground *143* Brutplatz
bribery *139* Bestechung
brick *162* Ziegel(stein), Backstein
brief *75* kurz
bright *22* hell; glänzend, schlau
to bring up *116* großziehen
broad *121* breit
brochure *32* Broschüre, Prospekt
broken *124* getrennt, kaputt
to brush *83* bürsten, putzen
budget *38t, 65* Budget, Etat; Billig-
bulb *76* Glühbirne, -lampe
bulimia *16* Bulimie, Ess-Brech-
   Sucht
bully *143* Mobber/in, jemand, der/
   die Schwächere schikaniert
bunch *110, 163* Gruppe, Haufen
bureaucracy *110* Bürokratie
burglary *135* Einbruch
to bury *99* begraben
bush *73* Busch, Strauch
business per-
   son *71* Geschäftsmann/-frau
bust: to go bust *134* Pleite gehen
butterfly *59* Schmetterling
button *165* Taste, Knopf
to buy sth on credit *29* etw auf
   Kredit kaufen
buzz *183* Gemurmel, Stimmengewirr
by-product *151* Nebenprodukt

C

to calculate *70* kalkulieren,
   berechnen
calm *36* ruhig
camp *164, 180* Lager
campaign *46* (Werbe-)Feldzug,
   Kampagne
campaigner *63, 66* Kämpfer/in,
   Aktivist/in
camping: to go camping *15*
   campen
can *19* Dose
can opener *153* Büchsen-, Dosen-
   öffner
to cancel *133* streichen, absagen
candidate *48* Kandidat/in,
   Bewerber/in
cane *165* (Blinden-)Stock
canoe *163* Kanu
canoeing *174* Kanufahren
canyon *132* Canyon, tiefes/enges
   Tal
capital *18* Hauptstadt
capital (letter) *62* Groß(buchstabe)
capital punishment *136*
   Todesstrafe

caption *191* Bildunterschrift
car seat *88t* Autositz
car sharing *66* gemeinsame Pkw-
   Nutzung
caramel *16* Karamel
carbohydrate *168* Kohle(n)hydrat
carbon *80* Kohlenstoff
carbon dioxide *81t* Kohlendioxid
carbon footprint *103* O_2-Bilanz/
   Ökobilanz
to care for sb *116* jdn pflegen, sich
   um jdn kümmern
careers adviser *31* Berufs-
   berater/in
careless *32* sorglos, nachlässig
caring *165* Pflege
carrot *21* Karotte
to carry on *118t* weitermachen
to carry out *6* ausführen
to cart sth away *132* wegkarren
cartoon *32* Karikatur
cartoonist *68* Karikaturist/in
to carve *177* schnitzen
case study *16* Fallstudie
cash machine *11* Geldautomat
cashier *33* Kassierer/in
casting agent *129* Besetzungs-
   agent/in
casual *99* Gelegenheits-
catastrophe *75* Katastrophe
to catch sb off guard *118t*
   jemanden überraschen, ertappen
Caucasian *131* Weiße/r,
   Hellhäutige/r
to celebrate *80* feiern
celebrity *53, 55* Promi(nente/r)
cell *144* (Gefängnis-)Zelle
censure *126* Tadel, Missbilligung
census *129* (Volks-)Zählung
centimetre *80* Zentimeter
central *71* zentral
century *81* Jahrhundert
certain *7* gewiss, sicher
to chain *123* anketten
challenge *12* Herausforderung
to challenge *13* herausfordern
challenging *85* herausfordernd,
   anstrengend
champagne *80* Champagner
channel *49* Kanal
chaos *66* Chaos
characteristic *40* Eigenschaft,
   Merkmal
charge *70* Kosten
charity *55* wohltätiger Verein
charming *16* charmant
chart *82* Diagramm, Tabelle
chatroom *6* Chatroom,
   Diskussionsforum
to check out *37* herausfinden
checklist *95* Checkliste
cheekbones *129* Wangenknochen
cheeky *16* frech, kess

chemical *83* Chemikalie
childcare *116* (Kinder-)Erziehung
childhood *180* Kindheit
childminder *117* Kinderbetreuer/
   in, Tagesmutter/-vater
to chill out *6* sich entspannen
choice *17* Wahl
to choke *66, 164* ersticken, würgen
chores *186* regelmäßige Haushaltsarbeiten
Cinderella *162* Aschenputtel
cinema *8* Kino
circle *60* Kreis
citizenship *131t* Staatsbürger-
   schaft
civil rights *131t* bürgerliche Rechte
civilisation *127* Zivilisation
to claim *131* behaupten, erklären
claim-
   ant *182* Anspruchsberechtigte/r
clarity *180* Klarheit, Reinheit
clash *56* Konflikt, Zusammenstoß
classified *45* nach Rubriken
   geordnet
classmate *53* Klassenkamerad/in
clemency *137* Milde, Nachsicht
clerical *89* Schreib-, Büro-
clerk *85* (Bank-)Angestellte/r
cleverly *69* klug, intelligent
client *46* Kunde/Kundin
cliff *68* Klippe, Felsen
climate *80* Klima
climate change *81t* Klimawandel
to climb *162* klettern
clone *152t* Klon
cloning *145* Klonen
closeness *48* Vertrautheit
cloudy *78* bewölkt
clubbing: to go clubbing *6* in
   Discos gehen
clue *44* Schlüssel
coach *7* Trainer/in
coal *80* Kohle
coastal *80* Küsten-
cockerel *162* junger Hahn
coffee mill *101t* Kaffeemühle
to collapse *49* zusammenbrechen
colleague *66* Kollege/Kollegin
to collect *41* sammeln
collection *180* Sammlung
college of further educa-
   tion *51t* Fachoberschule,
   Weiterbildungskolleg
column *19* Spalte
to combine *69* (sich) verbinden
come on *22* komm (schon)
comedy *58* Komödie,comedy
comment *44* Kommentar
commercial *45* Anzeige, Werbespot
commercial break *49* Werbepause
commission *105* Provision,
   Gebühr; Kommission

to commit *83* (sich) verpflichten
commitment *89* (Selbst-)Verpflich-
   tung, Einsatz, Engagement
committee *156* Ausschuss,
   Komitee
common: in common *70*
   gemeinsam
communication *55*
   Kommunikation, Mitteilung,
   Benachrichtigung
community *16* Gemeinde
commuter *67* Pendler/in
to compare *17* vergleichen
comparison *44* Vergleich,
   Steigerung
to compete *12* konkurrieren
competence *171* Kompetenz
competing *49* konkurrierend
competition *13* Wettkampf
competitive *7* Wettkampf-
competitive advantage *96*
   Wettbewerbsvorteil
to complain *32* reklamieren, sich
   beklagen, beschweren
complaint *187* Beschwerde
complete *72* völlig
complex *86* komplex, kompliziert
complicated *69, 180* kompliziert
component *61* Bestandteil
comprehension *42* Verständnis
comprehensive *93* umfassend
compromise *187* Kompromiss
to concentrate *31* sich
   konzentrieren
concept *177* Begriff, Konzept, Idee
concern *99, 168* Sorge, Interesse,
   Anliegen, Bedenken
concern: to be concerned
   with *120* sich befassen mit, sich
   kümmern um
conclusion *90* (Schluss-)Folgerung
to conduct *189* abhalten, (durch)
   führen
confident *180* selbstsicher,
   -bewusst
to confirm *48* bestätigen
conflicting *128* gegensätzlich
confused *132* verwirrt
congested *66* verstopft
congestion *66* Verkehrsstau,
   Verstopfung
congestion charging *71*
   Staugebühr
congratulations *29* Glückwunsch
conscience *126* Gewissen
conservation *103, 145, 174* Schutz,
   Erhaltung
conservative *136* Konservative/r
considered: to be consid-
   ered *62* berücksichtigt werden
to consist of *168* bestehen aus
constantly *169* ständig
constitution *105* Verfassung

constitutional *136* verfassungs-
   gemäß
construction *40* Bau, Bauweise
to consult *153* konsultieren
consumer *53, 159* Verbraucher/in
consumption *150* Verzehr
contact *43, 55* Kontakt,
   Verbindung
to contact *106* Kontakt aufnehmen
   zu, sich wenden an
to contain *66* enthalten
contaminated *150* verunreinigt,
   verseucht
contestant *56* Kandidat/in
context *38* Kontext, Zusammenhang
contract *46* (Arbeits-) Vertrag
contradictory *132* widersprüchlich
contrary *150* Gegenteil
to contrast *36* gegenüberstellen
to contribute *143* beisteuern
contribution *106* Beitrag, Beihilfe
contributor *180* Mitwirkende/r
convenient *28* bequem
convention *136* Konvention
conventional *152t* konventionel,
   herkömmlich
to convince *127* überzeugen
convincing *150* überzeugend
cookbook *20* Kochbuch
cooking *113* das Kochen
cooperative *131t* kooperativ
co-operative *101t* Kooperative
coordinator *99* Koordinator/in
to cope *153* zurechtkommen, fertig
   werden
core *163* Kern
corporal punishment *136*
   körperliche Züchtigung
corporation *123* Konzern
correctness *133* Korrektheit
correspondence *48*
   Korrespondenz
corruption *110* Korruption
council *43, 106* Rat, Gemeinderat
councillor *71* Ratsmitglied
counselor *189* Berater/in,
   Betreuer/in
to count *153* zählen
countable *19* zählbar
counter *16* Tresen, Ladentisch
countless *126* zahllos
cracked *73* rissig
craft *99* (Kunst-)Handwerk
crash *52* Zusammenbruch
to crash *121t* (ab)stürzen
to crawl *132* kriechen, krabbeln
to create *51t* hervorrufen,
   erzeugen, wecken
crèche *182* (Kinder-)Krippe,
   Kinderhort
crèche facilities *89*
   Krippeneinrichtungen

creditor *28* Gläubiger/in
crime *174* Verbrechen, Kriminalität
critical *93* kritisch
criticism *17, 63* Kritik
crop *83, 149* Anbau,
   (Anbau)Pflanze
to cross *73* überqueren
to cross out *38* durchstreichen
to cross-breed *149* kreuzen
cross-breeding *152t* Kreuzung
crossing
   point *134* Übergang(sstelle)
crowded *40* überfüllt
cruel *136, 163* grausam
cubicle *16* Kabine
cucumber *83* Gurke
cultural *40* kulturell
culturally-inclusive *183* die Kultur
   mit einbeziehend
curable *18* heilbar
curb *166* Bordkante, -stein
cure *152t* Heilung, Heilmittel
currency *111* Währung
currently *10* zurzeit
curriculum *133, 183* Lehrplan
curving *83* geschwungen
custom *118* Brauch
customer relations officer *85*
   Kundendienstmitarbeiter/in,
   Kundenbetreuer/in
customs *154* Zoll
to cut *49* ausblenden
cut *81t* Kürzung, Senkung
cutting-edge *96* Spitzen-,
   Hightech-, modern
CV *86* Lebenslauf
cyberbullying *143* Mobbing im
   Netz oder per Handy
to cycle *76* radfahren
cyclist *73, 109t* Fahrradfahrer/in
cyclone *80* Zyklon

D

dairy *147* hier: Milchvieh
damage *66* Schaden, Schäden
to dare *139* (es) wagen
date: to go on a date *15* eine
   Verabredung haben
day off *34* freier Tag
day release *172* tageweise Freistel-
   lung (zur praktischen Ausbildung)
daybreak *162* Tagesanbruch
daycare center *189* Tagesstätte
dead-end *86* ohne Perspektiven
deadly *63* tödlich, Todes-
to deal with *32* sich beschäftigen
   mit, mit jdm zu tun haben
dealing *139* Handel
death *163* Tod
death penalty *136* Todesstrafe
to debate *123* diskutieren über,
   debattieren

debate *143* Debatte, Diskussion

debt *161* Schuld(en)

to deceive *135* betrügen

decent *139* anständig

to decline *47* abnehmen, sinken, zurückgehen

decline *51* Rückgang

to decrease *51* fallen, sinken

to defend *110* verteidigen

to define *129* (sich) definieren

definitely *25* bestimmt, definitiv

definition *7* Definition

degree *171* (akademischer) Abschluss

to delay *80* aufschieben, hinauszögern

delighted *65* (sehr) erfreut, entzückt

delinquency *43* Kriminalität

to deliver *68* vermitteln, überbringen

delivery *122* Darbietung

to demand *126* (nach)fragen

dementia *149* Demenz

demo *120* Demo(nstration)

demographer *129* Demograph

demonstration *119* Demonstration

to deny *127* bestreiten

department *43* Ministerium

department *107* Abteilung

department store *26* Kauf-, Warenhaus

departure *44* Abfahrt

to depend on *30* abhängen von

to deport *131t* ausweisen, abschieben

depressed *65* deprimiert, niedergeschlagen

depressing *118* bedrückend, deprimierend

deputy *142t* Hilfs-, Vertretungs-

deputy *172* stellvertretend

to derive *146* abstammen

desert *80* Wüste

to deserve *137* verdienen

to design *46* entwerfen

designer *153* Konstrukteur/in, Designer/in

desirable *159* wünschenswert

desire *51t* Begehren, Verlangen

to despair *99* verzweifeln

desperate *80* verzweifelt

despite *93* trotz

dessert *16* Nachspeise, -tisch

destination *22* (Fahrt-)Ziel

destination *103* Ziel(hafen), Entladehafen

to destroy *69* zerstören, vernichten

destruction *75* Zerstörung, Vernichtung

determined *172* (fest) entschlossen

deterrent *138* abschreckend

developer *46* Entwickler/in

development *69, 163* Entwicklung

devout *137* fromm

diabetes *149* Zuckerkrankheit, Diabetes

to diagnose *147* diagnostizieren

diametrically opposed *140* diametral entgegengesetzt

diet *83, 168* Ernährung, Diät(kost), Nahrung

to differ *41* sich unterscheiden

to dig into *142t* wühlen in

diploma *86, 171* Diplom, Abschlusszeugnis

directed at *95* gerichtet auf, abzielend auf

direction *67* Richtung

dirty *16* schmutzig

disability *73, 171* Behinderung

to disagree (with) *17* widersprechen, nicht zustimmen

disagreement *50* Widerspruch, Uneinigkeit

disappointed *65* enttäuscht

disappointment *159* Enttäuschung

disaster *75* Katastrophe, Unglück

discipline *187* Disziplin

to discover *6* entdecken

to discriminate *13* unterscheiden, diskriminieren

discrimination *12* Diskriminierung

discussion *49* Diskussion

disease *97* Krankheit, Erkrankung

disgust *126* Ekel

disgusting *18* ekelhaft

dish *40* Gericht

dishes: the dishes *177* das Geschirr

dishonest *98* unehrlich

disobedience *119* Ungehorsam

display *28* Ausstellung

dissatisfied *178* unzufrieden

distant *40* fern

to distribute *189* verteilen

diverse *112* verschieden, unterschiedlich

diversity *133, 180* Mannigfaltigkeit, Vielfalt

divorce *181* Scheidung

documentary *58* Dokumentarbericht, -film

doll *118* Puppe

domestic *131t* in der Familie, häuslich

domestic service *131* Hausangestellte

to dominate *98* dominieren

donated *189* gespendet

donkey *162* Esel

donut *16* Pfannkuchen, Krapfen

door frame *180* Türrahmen

dose *136* Dosis

double life *16* Doppelleben

double-decker *16* Doppeldecker

double-glazing *76* mit Isolierverglasung versehen

doubt *103, 147* Zweifel

downside *152t* Nachteil

downtown *37* im Stadtzentrum

dozen *63, 180* Dutzend

draft *102* Entwurf

to drain *123* entwässern, trockenlegen

dramatic *84* dramatisch, drastisch

drawn to sth *83* zu etw hingezogen

dreaming *163* Traumbild

dressed *162* angezogen, gekleidet

dried *104* Trocken-

to drift *86* treiben, zufällig kommen

drink driving *135* Trunkenheit am Steuer

drive (AE) *189* Sammelaktion

to drive away *162* vertreiben

driveway *73* Ein-, Ausfahrt

to drop *49* fallen

to drown in *49* ertränken in

drug abuse *139* Drogenmissbrauch

drum *9* Trommel

drunk driving (AE) *142t* Trunkenheit am Steuer

drycleaner's *66* chemische Reinigung

dryer *104* Trockner

to dust *177* Staub wischen

duty *106* Pflicht, Aufgabe

dweller *69* Bewohner/in

dye *178* Färbemittel

dyslexia *189* Legasthenie

dyslexic *180* legasthenisch

E

eager *177, 190* eifrig bestrebt

to earn *53* verdienen

earth: Why on earth? *21* Warum um Himmels willen?

eastern *80* östlich

eating disorder *16* Essstörung

economic *183* wirtschaftlich

economy *80* Wirtschaft

eco-system *174* Ökosystem

eco-tourism *103* Ökotourismus

edge *163, 165* Rand, Kante

to educate *63* unterrichten

to educate *171* erziehen

education *161, 162* Erziehung, (Schul-)Bildung

effect *40* Auswirkung

efficient *66* effizient, leistungsfähig

effort *118* Bemühung, Anstrengung

egg plant *83* Aubergine

either *58t* hier: beides;

either: not ... either *21* auch nicht

elderly *83, 92* älter, Senioren

election *74* (politische) Wahl

electricity *69* Elektrizität, Strom

element *163* Element

elevator *37* Lift
embarrassed *17* verlegen
embarrassing *56* peinlich
to emerge *80* heraustreten,
hervorkommen
emission *66* Emission, Ausstoß
emotional *116* emotional
to emphasize *83* betonen,
hervorheben
employee *53, 89* Angestellte/r,
Arbeitnehmer/in, Beschäftigte/r
employer *8* Unternehmer,
Arbeitgeber
employment *88* Arbeit,
Beschäftigung, Beruf
to empty *162* schütten
to enable *129* (es) ermöglichen, in
die Lage versetzen
to encourage *51t, 159* anregen,
auffordern, verleiten
encyclopedia *39* Lexikon,
Enzyklopädie
endangered *103* (vom Aussterben)
bedroht, gefährdet
enemy *124* Feind
energetic *153* voller Energie
energy *40* Energie
to engage with *143* sich einlassen
auf
engaged *177* beschäftigt, engagiert
engine *69* Motor
engineer *69* Ingenieur/in,
Techniker/in
enjoyable *36* angenehm
enquiry *106* Anfrage
to ensure *159, 187* sicherstellen,
gewährleisten
to enter *71* hineingehen, -fahren
entertaining *56* unterhaltsam
entertainment *49* Unterhaltung
enthusiasm *107, 177* Begeisterung
(-sfähigkeit)
entire *131t* vollkommen, gänzlich
entry *39* Eintrag
environment *53* Umwelt
environmental *66* Umwelt-
environmentalist *69*
Umweltschützer/in
environmentally friendly *69*
umweltfreundlich
to envy *180* beneiden
epidemic *75* Epidemie
equal *12* Gleichberechtigte/r,
Ebenbürtige/r
equality *183* Gleichberechtigung
equation *123* Gleichung
equipment *95* Ausrüstung
equivalent (of) *18* Entsprechung
to erupt *133* ausbrechen
to escape *49* flüchten
especially *22* besonders,
insbesondere
essential *82* notwendig, wesentlich

to estimate *69* schätzen
estuary *121t* Mündung
ethical *53* ethisch
ethnic *40* ethnisch
ethnicity *129* ethnische
Zugehörigkeit
to evaluate *73* bewerten,
einschätzen
even *138* gleichmäßig
event *36* Ereignis, Veranstaltung
eventually *70* schließlich, zum
Schluss
evidence *17, 171* Beweis(e), Beleg
to exaggerate *50* übertreiben
exam results *64* Examensnoten
exception *182* Ausnahme
exceptional *64* (Kurz-)Dialog
exceptional *147* außergewöhnlich
excess *153* überschüssig
excited *65* aufgeregt, erregt
exciting *153, 163* aufregend,
spannend
exclusion *143* Ausgrenzung
exclusive *26* exklusiv
execution *136* Hinrichtung
exercise *83* (körperliche)
Bewegung
exercise bike *11* Heimtrainer
exhaust *66* Auspuff(rohr)
exhausted *65* erschöpft
exhibition *38* Ausstellung
to exist *153* existieren
exotic *22* exotisch
to expand *46* expandieren, (sich)
ausdehnen
expansion *52* Erweiterung
to expect *7* erwarten
expenses *106* Kosten, Ausgaben
experience *61* Erfahrung
experienced *83, 124* mit Berufserfahrung, erfahren
explanation *97, 170* Erklärung
to exploit *56* be-, ausnutzen
to explore *40* erkunden
export sales *88* Exportverkäufe,
Auslandsverkäufe
expression *7* Ausdruck
to extend *121t* ausweiten,
ausbauen
extended *49* verlängert
extension *121t* Ausbau
extent *65* (Aus-)Maß, Umfang, Grad
extract *109, 162, 189* Auszug,
Extrakt
extraordinary *181*
außergewöhnlich
extremely *72* äußerst,
außerordentlich

F

fabric *178* Stoff
fabulous *26* fabelhaft

to face *76* sich gegenübersehen,
vor sich haben
facility *156, 189* Einrichtung
factor *170, 183* Faktor
factual *43* sachlich
to fail *49* versagen, scheitern
to fail sb *118t* jdn enttäuschen, jdn
etwas nicht geben können
failure *40* Versagen
fairly *47* ziemlich
faith *133* Glaube
fame *56* Ruhm
familiar *16* bekannt
fanatic *126* Fanatiker/in
farewell *25* Abschied
farther *44* weiter
fascination *43, 129* Faszination
fashion-conscious *26*
modebewusst
fast-acting *136* schnell wirkend
fatty *18* fetthaltig, fettig
fault *143* Fehler, Schuld
fear *12* Furcht
feasible *134* (praktisch)
durchführbar, machbar
feature *28* Eigenschaft
to feature *35* eine Rolle spielen
federal *112* föderal(istisch)
fee *106* Gebühr
to feed *152t* ernähren
fellow *177, 180* Mit-
feminine *13* weiblich
feminist *136* Feministin
fence *132, 178* Zaun
ferry *38* Fähre
fertilizer *150* Dünger
festival *133* Fest
festivity *133* Feierlichkeit
fictional *63* erfunden
field trial *152t* Experimente in der
freien Natur
fifth; a fifth *81* Fünftel
figure *81t* Zahl
file *180* (Akten-)Ordner
filling station *33* Tankstelle
finance *40* Finanzen
financial *22* finanziell
firmly *183* entschlossen, kräftig
first aider *13* Ersthelfer/in
first school *133* Grundschule
(für ca. 4–9-Jährige)
to fit *30* passen
fitness *73* Fitness, Kondition
fitted *76* eingebaut
fixed *28* befestigt
fizzy *160* sprudelnd, spritzig
flat (BE) *83* Wohnung
flavour *149* Geschmack
flexibility *66* Flexibilität
flick knife *140* Springmesser
flood *75* Flut, Überschwemmung
to flood *131t* überschwemmen
flowchart *47* Flussdiagramm

flower *178* Blume
fluent *106* fließend, gewandt, flüssig
focus *35* Blickpunkt
to focus on *139* sich konzentrieren auf
to fold *177* verschränken, falten, zusammenlegen
foot *120* Fuß
foot: to set foot in *35* betreten
football *14* American Football (*BE:* Fußball)
forbidden *126* verboten
to force *57* zwingen
to force so to sth *162* jmd zu etwas zwingen
forefeet *162* Vorderfüße
foreground *132* Vordergrund
forest *37* Wald
former *40* früher
formerly *177* früher
formula *51t* Formel
fortunately *29* glücklicherweise
fortune *66* Vermögen
forum *49* Forum
fossil fuel *80* fossiler Brennstoff
foster *186* Pflege
foster family *124* Pflegefamilie
foundation *189* Stiftung
founder *189* Gründer/in
fraction *81* Bruch(teil)
frank *110* offen, ehrlich
fraud *135* Betrug, Unterschlagung
freedom *66* Freiheit
freelance *46* freiberuflich
freely *59* freimütig
freezer *20* Gefrierschrank
freezing *92* eiskalt, sehr kalt
frequency *29* Häufigkeit
frequent *44* häufig
fridge *21* Kühlschrank
fried *127* gebraten, geröstet
frightening *13* beängstigend, erschreckend
fringe benefits *85* zusätzliche Leistungen, freiwillige Sozialleistungen
frontier *110* Grenze
frustrated *65* frustriert
fuel *66* Kraftstoff
full-time *171* Ganztags-, Vollzeit(stelle)
fumes *66* Abgase
to fund *103* finanzieren
fundamentalist *136* fundamentalistisch
funding *183* finanzielle Unterstützung
fundraising *64* Wohltätigkeitsveranstaltung, Spendensammeln
funds *156* Geldmittel, Kapital
further *15* weiter
fusion *80* Fusion, Verschmelzung

G

gadget *153* Vorrichtung, Gerät
to gain *106, 172* sammeln, erlangen
gambling *126* Glücksspiel
gang *43* (Straßen-)Bande
gangsta rap *43* Gangsta Rap
gas *68* Benzin, Treibstoff
gateway *38t* Tor, Pforte
to gather *165* Sammeln
gender *163* Geschlecht
gene *149* Gen
general *9* allgemein
generation *31* Generation
generous *89* großzügig
genetically-modified *146* genmanipuliert
genre *58* Genre
gentle *36* freundlich
genuine *16* echt
geography *38t* Lage, Geographie
gesture *128* Geste(n), Gestik
to get a lot out of sth *7* viel davon haben
to get by *31* durchkommen
to get caught up *174* verwickelt werden
to get clear of *124* wegkommen von
to get drunk *18* sich betrinken
to get in with *174* geraten an
to get real *17* die Realität anerkennen
to get the green light *46* grünes Licht erhalten
to get to grips with sth *153* mit etw klarkommen, etw in den Griff bekommen
to get used to *37* sich gewöhnen an
gigantic *114* gigantisch, riesig
glad *13* froh
glamorous *45* glamourös
global *80* global, weltweit
globalization *96* Globalisierung
globalized *103* globalisiert
to glorify *43* verherrlichen
to glow *28* leuchten
good-looking *18* gut aussehend
goods *97* Ware(n), Güter
goose *162* Gans
government *66* Regierung
governor *134* Gouverneur/in
grade *14* Note
gradual *51* allmählich, nach und nach
grandad *89* Opa
greedy *16* gierig
greenhouse *53* Treib-, Gewächshaus
greeting *38* Begrüßung
gridlock *66* Verkehrskollaps

to grin *16* lächeln, grinsen
grotesque *56* grotesk
group home *186* betreutes Wohnprojekt
guaranteed *99* garantiert
guard *134* Wache
to guess *44* raten
guest *81* Gast
to guide *92* führen, leiten
guidebook *39* Reiseführer
guilty *16* schuldig
guy *12* Kerl, Typ
gym *168* Fitnessstudio

H

habitat *150* Lebensraum
to hack up *142t* zerstückeln
hairdresser *15* Friseur/in
hairstyle *118* Frisur
hall of fame *189* Ruhmeshalle
to halve *151* (sich) halbieren
ham *19* Schinken
to hand in *30* abgeben
handwritten *180* handgeschrieben
to hang around *6* rumhängen
hard sell *50* aggressive Verkaufstechnik
hardly *89* kaum
hardship *180* Not, Mühsal
hardware *19* Hardware, Geräte
to harm *103* schaden, schädigen
harmful *150* schädlich
harmless *63* harmlos, ungefährlich
harsh *126* scharf, harsch
harvest *178* ernten
haulier *69* Spediteur, Fuhrunternehmen
havoc: to play havoc *150* verheerende Schäden anrichten
headband *43* Stirnband
heading *49* Überschrift
headquarters *105* Hauptsitz, Zentrale
headscarf *125* Kopftuch
headteacher *183* Schulleiter/in
health *63* Gesundheit
healthcare *89* medizinische Versorgung
healthy *160* gesund
heated *53* geheizt
heating *78* Heizung
heavily-armed *139* schwer bewaffnet
hectare *101t* Hektar
height *120* Höhe, Größe
hence *136* daher
herb *83, 178* (Gewürz-, Heil-) Kraut
herbicide *150* Unkrautvernichtungsmittel
herd *147* Herde
hereditary *145* erblich
heritage *115* Erbe, Herkunft

high *124* high, auf Drogen
hill *69* Hügel, Berg
to hire sb/sth *52* ein-/anstellen, mieten, anheuern
hold *12* Griff
to hold down *81t* niedrig halten
holy *103* heilig
home grown *83* selbst angebaut
homeless: the homeless *7* die Obdachlosen
homicide *141* Tötung, Mord
homosexual *127* Homosexuelle/r
honest *28* ehrlich
household *83, 113* Haushalt
housemate *57* Mitbewohner/in
huff *162* schnauben
huge *37* gewaltig
hulk *12* Kerl wie ein Baum
Human Resources *48* Personal(abteilung)
humane *131t* human
humanitarian *131* humanitär
hunter *132* Jäger/in
hurricane *55* Orkan, Wirbelsturm
hybrid *69* hybrid
hydroelectric *80* hydroelektrisch
hydrogen *69* Wasserstoff
hypocritical *113* heuchlerisch, scheinheilig

I

ice-hockey *13* Eishockey
ID *91t* Ausweis
ideal *65* ideal
to identify *73, 100, 165* feststellen, herausfinden, erkennen
identity *59* Identität
idiom *67* Idiom, Redewendung
idiomatic *67* idiomatisch
illegal *67* verboten, illegal
to illustrate *90* illustrieren, veranschaulichen
immediate *51t* umgehend, sofort
immigrant *39* Einwanderer/ Einwanderin
to immigrate *41* einwandern
impact *66* (Aus-)Wirkung, Einfluss
impaired *165* behindert
to imply *151* andeuten, implizieren
imported *103* importiert
to impose *141* auferlegen, erlassen
to impress *12* imponieren
impression *13* Eindruck
imprisonment *138* Haft, Gefängnis(strafe)
to improve *66, 156* verbessern, besser werden
in favour of *133* zugunsten von
in preference to sth *103* vorzugsweise
inability *118* Unfähigkeit

incidence *139* Vorkommen, Häufigkeitsrate
incident *128* Vorfall, Ereignis
to include *43, 165* einschließen, einbeziehen, umfassen
including *40* einschließlich, inbegriffen, darunter
inclusion *122* Einbeziehung
income *70* Einkommen
to increase *31* ansteigen, zunehmen
increase *81t* Anstieg
increasing *13* zunehmend
independent *85* unabhängig
indirectness *92* Indirektheit
industrial *80* industriell
industry *41* Industrie
inevitable *159* unvermeidlich
infant school *133* Grundschule (für ca. 4–7-Jährige)
infection *147* Entzündung
to influence *50* beinflussen
informative *41* informativ
infrastructure *97, 174* Infrastruktur
ingredient *146* Zutat, Bestandteil
initials *43* Anfangsbuchstaben
injection *136* Spritze, Injektion
to injure *12* verletzen
injury *13* Verletzung
innocent *143* unschuldig
innovative *47* innovativ
input *118t* hier: Aufwendung, Hingabe
input *153* Beitrag, Einfluss
to inquire *134* fragen, sich erkundigen
insane *137* geisteskrank
to insert *173* einfügen
insomnia *180* Schlaflosigkeit
to inspire *183* inspirieren, begeistern
instability *102* Instabilität
to install *101t* installieren
instance: for instance *126* zum Beispiel
instant messaging *143* Nachrichtensofortversand
instead of *8* statt, anstatt (von)
institute *174* Institut, Anstalt
instructor *85* Lehrer/in, Ausbilder/in
insulation *76* Isolierung
to integrate *111* sich integrieren
intense *36* intensiv
to interact *149* sich gegenseitig beeinflussen
interactive *55* interaktiv
interference *110* Einmischung
intermarriage *129* Mischehe
intern *106* Praktikant/in, Volontär/in
internship *106* Volontariat
intersection *165* Kreuzung

interval *165* Zeit, Phase
to intervene *168* eingreifen
to interview *31, 186* interviewen
to introduce *148* einführen
to invent *40* erfinden
to invest *89* investieren
to involve *106, 171* einschließen, beinhalten, umfassen
involved *174* beteiligt
involved in *143* beteiligt an, verwickelt in
involved with *43* beteiligt an
involvement *141* Beteiligung
ironing *15* Bügeln
irregular *85* unregelmäßig
irrelevant *163* unbedeutend
irresponsible *29* unverantwortlich
island *40* Insel
isolated *114* isoliert
issue *53, 84* Frage, Problem, Thema, Anliegen
IT *88t* Informationstechnologie
IT officer *88t* EDV-Techniker/in
IT technician *85* Informationstechniker/in

J

jacket *53* Jacke, Jackett
jail *174, 186* Gefängnis
jar *19* (Einmach)Glas
jet-colored *129* pechschwarz
jewellery *43* Schmuck
job-related *31* beruflich
to join *51t* beitreten, sich anmelden
to joke: Are you joking? *7* Ist das dein Ernst?
journalist *76* Journalist/in
journey *46* Reise, Fahrt
juicy *163* saftig
to jump *162* springen
junction *78* Kreuzung
junior *44* untergeordnet
junk food *83* minderwertiges Essen
justice *43* Recht, Justiz
justice *139* Gerechtigkeit
juvenile *43* jugendlich, Jugend

K

keen *183* (sehr) interessiert
to keep in touch with *28* in Verbindung bleiben
to keep track of sth *165* verfolgen
to keep: How have you been keeping? *94* Wie geht es dir?
keyboard *61* Tastatur
to kick out *186* hinauswerfen
kid *62* Kind
to knock down *121t* abreißen
knowledge *19* Wissen

L

label *26* Label, Marke
labelling *147* Kennzeichnung
to *43* fehlen
lack *174* Mangel
ladder *172, 178* Leiter
laid out *165* angelegt
lake *38t* (Binnen-)See
landline *109* Festnetz(leitung)
lane *73* (Fahr-)Spur
large-scale *42* in großer Zahl
latest *55* neueste, letzte
to launch *46* einführen, starten
laundry *177* Wäsche
law-abiding *131t* gesetzestreu
lawful *123* rechtmäßig
lawyer *112* (Rechts-)Anwalt/
   Anwältin
layout *165* Anordnung
leader *80* Führer/in
leading *51t* führend
leaflet *45* Broschüre, Flugblatt
to lean on *118t* sich lehnen an
least: at least *15* mindestens
leaves *178* Laub, Blätter
legal *57* legal
legible *57* leserlich
legislative *110* gesetzgebend
leisure centre *15* Freizeitzentrum
length *44* Länge, Dauer
lentil *162* Linse
lesson: to teach sb a lesson *13* jdm eine Lektion erteilen
lethal *136* tödlich
letter of appointment *91t*
   Bewerbungsschreiben
level *80* Niveau, Stand
liar *142t* Lügner/in
liberal *137* Liberale/r
library *55* Bücherei, Bibliothek
licence *106* Führerschein
to lie *60* lügen
lifeline *180* Rettungsleine
lifestyle *76* Lebensstil
lift: to give a lift *24* mit dem Auto
   mitnehmen
to light *132* anzünden
to lighten up *49* aufheitern
limitless *131t* grenzenlos,
   uneingeschränkt
linear *123* linear, ersten Grades
linguistic *183* linguistisch
to link *27* verbinden
linked *133* verbunden
listener *98* Zuhörer/in
literacy *163* Lese- und Schreib-
   fertigkeiten
literally *118t* buchstäblich
litter (BE) *73* Abfall, Müll
Little Red Riding Hood *162*
   Rotkäppchen
lively *49* lebhaft

living expenses *22*
   Lebenshaltungskosten
loads *30* eine Menge
loaf *19* (Laib) Brot
lobby *150* Lobby, Interessengruppe
local government *156* Gemeinde-
   verwaltung, Kommunalverwaltung
location *69* (Stand-)Ort, Position
log *178* Baumstamm
logging *119* Abholzung
logical *57* logisch
lonely *180* einsam
long-running *56* mit langer Laufzeit
to look round *7* sich umsehen
loophole *146* Schlupfloch
to loosen *126* lockern
to lose control over *16* die
   Beherrschung verlieren
lovely *26* hübsch
low-cost *89* Niedriglohn-
low-energy *76* Niedrigenergie-,
   Spar-
low-lying *80* tief gelegen
loyalty *43* Loyalität
luck *114* Glück
lucky: to be lucky *8* Glück haben
luggage *19* Gepäck
lunchtime *15* Mittagspause
lung *147* Lunge
lyrics *43* (Lied-)Text(e)

M

machinery *78* Maschine(n), Gerät
madness *55* Wahnsinn
magical *40* magisch
mail-order catalogue *26* Versandhauskatalog
mainstream *119,*
   177 vorherrschend(e Meinung)
to maintain *149, 178, 187* aufrecht-
   erhalten, einhalten
major *72* groß, größer
majority *133, 159* Mehrheit
to make up *12* bilden
to make up for *81t* ausgleichen
mammal *147* Säugetier
to manage *11* zurechtkommen,
   fertig werden (mit), (es) schaffen
manipulation *149* Manipulation,
   Veränderung
man-made *41* von Menschenhand
to manufacture *69* herstellen,
   produzieren
map *165* (Stadt-)Plan
march *119* (Protest-)Marsch
marital status *108* Familienstand
mark *9* Note
to mark *43* markieren,
   kennzeichnen
marketing *91* Marketing, Vertrieb
marriage *180* Ehe

massive *136* massiv, enorm
mast *151* Mast
mat *12* Matte
mate *10* Kumpel
materialist *127* Materialist/in
maternity leave *89*
   Mutterschaftsurlaub
matter *76* Sache, Ding,
   Angelegenheit;
to matter *87* von Bedeutung sein
matter: as a matter of fact *91t* um
   genau zu sein
matter: What's the matter with ...?
   18 Was ist los mit ...?
meantime: in the meantime *26* Inzwischen
mechanized *177* mechanisiert
media *159* Medien
media hype *152t* Medienrummel
media-awareness *159*
   Bewusstsein, die Medien richtig
   einzuschätzen
media-literate *159* medienkundig,
   sich mit Medien auskennen
to mediate *128* vermitteln
medical *17* medizinisch
medication *113* medizinische
   Versorgung, Medikamente
medium *59* Medium
to melt *80* schmelzen
melting pot *40* Schmelztiegel
membership *43, 51t, 168*
   Mitgliedschaft
memorable *68* unvergesslich,
   einprägsam
to memorize *163* auswendig lernen
memory *103, 180* Erinnerung
to mend *177* flicken, ausbessern
mental *17* mental
to mention *50* erwähnen
to mention: Don't mention
   it. *31* Gern geschehen.
mentor *189* Mentor/in
merchandise *161* Waren(angebot),
   Produkte
merciless *139* unbarmherzig
to mess up *88t* es verderben, es
   verpeilen
message *68* Botschaft
metabolic rate *168* Stoffwechsel
microchip *95* Mikrochip
micro-organism *149*
   Mikroorganismus
microphone *137* Mikrophon
microwave *54* Mikrowelle
Middle Ages *49* Mittelalter
middlemen *99* Zwischenhändler
migrant *183* Migrant/in
migration *111*
   Wanderung(sbewegung)
mile *67* Meile
mind *63* Verstand, Kopf

to mind: Do you mind if ...?
109t Haben Sie etwas dagegen, wenn ...?

to minimize *103, 186* minimieren, gering halten, verringern

minister *66* Minister/in

minor *118t* geringfügig

minority *130* Minderheit

miscarriage *147* Fehlgeburt

miserable *127* kläglich

misfit *163* Außenseiter

misleading *110* irreführend

to miss out on *118t* verpassen

missing *13* fehlend

misunderstanding *32* Missverständnis

mixture *75* Mischung

to monitor *43* überwachen, kontrollieren

monolingual *183* einsprachig

monotonous *126* monoton

monthly *69* monatlich

moral *57* moralisch

moreover *80* außerdem, zudem

motherly *118t* mütterlich

to motivate *43* motivieren

motivation *174* Motivation

motor *69* Motor

motorist *73* Autofahrer/in

motorway *67* Autobahn

move: on the move *65* unterwegs

movement *69* Bewegung

movies *6* Kino

mug *153* Becher(tasse)

mule *149* Maultier, -esel

multicultural *83* multikulturell

multiculturalism *125* Multikulturalismus

multilingual *183* mehrsprachig

multiracial *129* ethnisch gemischt

murder *136* Mord

muscle *12* Muskel

mushroom *127* Pilz

musician *115* Musiker/in

mustard *19* Senf

myth *118t, 153, 183* Legende, Mythos

N

to nag *159* in den Ohren liegen

to nail *178* nageln

nail polish *118t* Nagellack

nanny *131t* Kindermädchen

nasty *12* gemein

nationality *174* Staatsangehörig- keit, Nationalität

nationwide *93, 141* landesweit

native *83* gebürtig, ursprünglich

Native American *131* Indianer/in, indianisch

nativity play *133* Krippenspiel

neat *102* ordentlich, sauber

necessarily: not necessarily *8* nicht unbedingt

necessary *159* notwendig

necessity *181* Bedürfnis

necklace *178* (Hals-)Kette

need: in need *55* bedürftig

need: to meet needs *76* Bedürfnisse decken

needle *124* Nadel

negotiation *106* Verhandlung

nepotism *139* Vetternwirtschaft

nervous *65* nervös

nervous breakdown *117* Nervenzusammenbruch

net *6* Internet

netiquette *62* Netiquette, Umgangsformen (im Internet)

to network *7* vernetzen

neutral *129* neutral

newly *40* kürzlich

newsletter *55* Rundschreiben, (Info-)Blatt

next door *12* nebenan

nickname *140* Spitzname

nightmare *37* Albtraum

non-existence *93* Fehlen

nonsense *114* Unsinn

Nordic *129* nordisch

to not be able to help *16* nicht umhin können

now and then *29* ab und zu

nuclear *80* Atom-

nucleus *147* Kern

nurse *93, 119* Krankenschwester, -pfleger/in

nursery *66* Kindertagesstätte, Kita,

nutritional *149* Nähr-

O

oasis *83* Oase

obesity *83, 161, 170* Fettleibigkeit

to obey *150* befolgen

objection to *32* Ablehnung gegen- über

to observe *171* beobachten

obviously *29* offensichtlich

occasional *28* gelegentlich

off: to be off *91t* losgehen

offence *140* Straftat, Vergehen, Delikt

offender *143, 174* Straftäter/in

offensive *73* beleidigend

office block *114* Bürogebäude, -hochhaus

office-based *85* im Büro, büroge- bunden

official *71* Beamter/Beamtin

offline *59* offline, nicht im Internet

to offload *99* weitergeben

offshore *96* ins/im Ausland

offspring *146* Nachkommen

old people's home *33* Seniorenheim

old-fashioned *72, 163* altmodisch, veraltet

omission *147* Lücke

once in a while *118t* dann und wann

one-sided *50* einseitig

to operate *85* betreiben

operator *103, 108* Veranstalter/in

opponent *13* Gegner/in

opportunity *96, 163* Chance, Möglichkeit, Gelegenheit

opposed: to be opposed to sth *136* gegen etw sein

to opt out *114* austreten, aussteigen

to opt to do sth *133* sich entscheiden, etw. zu tun

oral *87* mündlich

order *8* Reihenfolge

ordinary *11* gewöhnlich, normal

organ *147* Organ

organic *83* organisch, Bio-

organism *149* Organismus

organization *189* Organisation

original *78* original, ursprünglich

otherwise *17* sonst, ansonsten

ought to *58* sollte/n

outcome *177* Resultat, Ergebnis

out-dated *130* überholt, veraltet

outdoor *177* im Freien

outdoor clothing *109t* Wanderbekleidung

outdoors *53, 85* im Freien, draußen

outgoing *106* kontaktfreudig

to outline *87, 148, 164* umreißen, skizzieren; Umriss

to outnumber *130* übertreffen

outrage *133* Schock, Entrüstung

to overcome *18* überwinden

overdose *124* Überdosis

to overeat *168* zu viel essen

overly *118t* übermäßig

overseas *174* Auslands-

overstretched *113* überfordert

overtime *96* Überstunden

overweight *168* übergewichtig

to owe *80* verdanken, schulden

owner *69* Besitzer/in

oxygen *69* Sauerstoff

P

PA *47* persönliche/r Assistent/in

packet *16* Schachtel, Packung, Tüte

paddle *177* Paddel

paediatrics *171* Kinderheilkunde, Pädiatrie

paid *85* bezahlt

painless *136* schmerzlos
paint *19* Farbe
panel *45* hier: Spalte, Fläche
to panic *21* in Panik geraten
paradise *127* Paradies
parcel *92* Paket
parking space *73* Parkplatz,
  Parklücke
to part company *167* sich trennen
partially *165* teilweise
participant *181* Teilnehmer/in
particular *36* bestimmt, speziell,
  besonders
particularly *159* besonders
part-time job *7* Teilzeitjob
part-timer *34* Teilzeitarbeiter/in
to pass *49, 171* weitergegeben
  werden; bestehen
passenger *66* Fahrgast
passion *137* Leidenschaft, Emotion
paternity leave *89*
  Vaterschaftsurlaub
path *73, 78, 178* (Fuß-)Weg, Pfad
patience *135* Geduld
patient *163* geduldig
to pause *167* kurz innehalten
pavement *73, 165* Bürgersteig
paycheck *96* Gehalt(sscheck)
payment *104* Bezahlung
pea *162* Erbse
peace *105* Frieden
peaceful *123* friedlich
peanut *178* Erdnuss
pedestrian *73, 165* Fußgänger/in
peer group *115* Gleichaltrige,clique
peers *170* Gleichaltrige,
  Altersgruppe
pen *88t* Stift
penalty *11* Strafstoß
pension *139* Rente, Pension
pensioner *182* Rentner/in
percapita *82* pro Kopf
to perceive *168* wahrnehmen
percentage *81* Prozentsatz
perfect *57* vollkommen
permanent *7* ständig, dauerhaft
permission *123, 186* Erlaubnis,
  Genehmigung
perpetrator *143* Täter/in
perplexed *127* perplex, verblüfft
perseverance *177* Ausdauer,
  Beharrlichkeit
personal space *98* Distanzzone,
  Abstand zwischen Personen
personality *56* Persönlichkeit
personally *72* persönlich
perspective *36* Perspektive,
  Ansicht
to persuade *71, 160* überzeugen,
  überreden
to pester *159* löchern, quengeln
pesticide *150*
  Schädlingsbekämpfungsmittel

petrol *8* Benzin
phase *63, 174* Phase, Abschnitt
phenomenal *14* phänomenal
phrase *17* Wendung, Ausdruck
to pick fruit *22* Obst pflücken
to pick out *162* heraussuchen
to pick up *58t* abholen
picker *99* Pflücker/in
pirate *58* Pirat
to pitch *46* anbieten, anpreisen
pity: it's a pity *58* es ist schade
placement *49* (Produkt-)Werbung
plank *178* Bohle
planner *15* (Termin-)Kalender
plate *153* Platte
play on words *51t* Wortspiel
playground *143* Spielplatz
pleasant *13* angenehm
pleasure *83* Vergnügen, Freude
plenty of *20* viel(e)
plot *83* Stück Land, Beet
plot *164* Handlung(sverlauf)
point of view *58* Standpunkt,
  Ansicht
to point out *113* hinweisen auf
poisonous *149* giftig
pole *73, 165* Pfahl, Mast, Stange
police officer *19* Polizeibeamter/
  beamtin
policing *141* Kontrolle,
  Überwachung
policy *139* Politik, Linie
to polish *116, 177* polieren, putzen
polite *62* höflich
political *183* politisch
pollination *151* Bestäubung
pollution *66*
  (Umwelt)Verschmutzung
polyester *123* Polyester
popular press *56* Boulevardpresse
pop-up ad *45* Internet-Anzeige
porridge *177* Hafer(flocken)brei
to pose *129* posieren, darstellen
position *29* Stellung
possibility *81* Möglichkeit
to post *143* veröffentlichen, bekannt geben
potential *157* möglich
potential *46, 152t* potentiell; Po-
  tenzial
pound *114* Pfund (Sterling)
pour *153* gießen
poverty *81t* Armut
to power *70* antreiben, betreiben
power *159* Kraft
power station *69* Kraftwerk
powerful *119* mächtig, stark
ppm *80* Teile pro Million
practical *106* praktisch
to practise *11* üben
pram (BE) *73* Kinderwagen
precarious *99* unsicher, prekär
precious *103* kostbar

precisely *13* genau
predictable *149* voraussagbar
prejudice *184* Vorurteil
premature *147* vorzeitig, frühzeitig
to prepare *167, 177* (sich)
  vorbereiten
present: at present *10*
  gegenwärtig
presentation *51* Vorstellung,
  Präsentation
presenter *38* Moderator/in
to press *165* drücken
pressure *88, 156* Druck
pressure-sensitive *153*
  druckempfindlich
pretty soon *37* sehr bald
to prevent *43, 80* verhindern,
  verhüten
prevention *43* Vorbeugung
previous *76* vorher(gehend)
priest *119* Priester/in, Geistliche/r
prime *143* hauptsächlich
princess *12* Prinzessin
principle *136* Prinzip
printout *180* (Computer-)Ausdruck
prison *135* Gefängnis
privacy *66* Privatsphäre
private *13* privat, persönlich
probation *141* Bewährung
process *47* Prozess, Vorgang
producer *56* Produzent/in,
  Erzeuger
product placement *45*
  Schleichwerbung
production *69* Produktion,
  Herstellung
egg plant *83* Aubergine
profession *93* Beruf
profile *56* Profil, Ansicht, Herkunft,
  Berufsbild, Porträt
profit *56* Profit, Gewinn
progress *76* Fortschritt/e
to promise *103* versprechen,
  zusagen
to promote *45* fördern
prompt *109* unverzüglich, zügig
to prompt *189* veranlassen
proper *22* richtig, geeignet,
  korrekt, ordentlich
property *135* Eigentum
proportion *121* Teil, Verhältnis
to prosecute *139* anklagen,
  strafrechtlich verfolgen
prospect *89* Aussicht
prosperity *105* Wohlstand
prostitute *127* Prostituierte/r
proud *13* stolz
to prove *143* nachweisen
to provide *106, 156* (an)bieten,
  sorgen für, zur Verfügung stellen
provider *59* Anbieter
psychiatric *118* psychiatrisch
psychological *56* psychologisch

psychologist *63, 159* Psychologe/
Psychologin
psychology *56* Psychologie
pub *10* Kneipe
public *55* öffentlich
public school *12* staatliche Schule
publicity *85* Öffentlichkeitsarbeit
to publish *154* veröffentlichen,
herausgeben
puff *162* keuchen
to pull oneself together *17* sich
zusammenreißen
punch line *142* Pointe
punctuation *62* Zeichensetzung,
Interpunktion
punishment *29* Strafe, Bestrafung
pupil (BE) *133* Schüler/in
purchase *26* (Ein-) Kauf
pure *26* rein
purpose *177* Zweck, Ziel, Sinn
to pursue *174* verfolgen,
nachgehen
to push up *88t* ausbauen,
hochtreiben
pushbutton *165* Drucktaste
pushchair (BE) *73* Kinderwagen,
Buggy
pushy *26* aufdringlich
to put down *88t* anzahlen
to put forward *58* vorbringen, zur
Diskussion stellen
to put on weight *16* zunehmen
puzzled *142t* verdutzt

Q

qualification *8* Qualifikation,
Ausbildung
quality *26* Qualität
quantity *20* Menge, Quantität
to quarrel *181* (sich) streiten
query *106* Frage, Rückfrage
questionnaire *30, 156* Fragebogen
queue *19* (Warte-)Schlange
quota system *134* Quotensystem
quotation *35* Zitat

R

to race *69* sich ein Wettrennen
liefern
rack *32* Ständer
radiation *151* Strahlung
radical *123, 140* radikal
rage *128* Wut, Zorn
rage: the rage *123* der letzte
Schrei
to raise *51t, 55* wecken; sammeln
to raise *156* auftreiben, aufbringen
raised *165* erhöht
range *62* Reihe, Spektrum
ranger *174* Aufseher/in,
Wildhüter/in

ransom *135* Lösegeld
rape *139* Vergewaltigung
rapid *51* rapide, schnell
rare *9* selten
rather *42* lieber, eher
raw material *50* Rohstoff
to react *55* reagieren
reality *65* Wirklichkeit
reality TV *56* Reality TV
really something *37* toll,
beeindruckend
reasonable *85* vernünftig
rebel *123* Rebell/in
reborn *96* wiedergeboren
to recall *156, 180* sich erinnern
(an)
to recap *121t* rekapitulieren,
zusammenfassen
receipt *104* Eingang, Erhalt
to receive *38* empfangen
recently *33* kürzlich, neulich
receptionist *85* Empfangsdame,
-chef
to recognize *49* erkennen
to recommend *110* empfehlen
recommendation *111, 187*
Empfehlung
to record *15* aufzeichnen
recovery *40, 63* Erholung; Heilung
recreation *182, 189* Erholung
recruiting *189* Anwerbung
recruitment *93* (Neu-)Einstellung
to recycle *53* wieder verwerten
Red Cross *7* Rotes Kreuz
to redevelop *96* erneuern, neu
entwickeln
to reduce *61* reduzieren, verringern
reduction *71* Verringerung,
Senkung
redundant *86* arbeitslos
to refer to *8* sich beziehen auf
referee *108* Referenzgeber/in
reference *106* Zeugnis
referendum *114* Volksentscheid
to reflect *129* widerspiegeln
to reflect on *103* nachdenken über
reflection *133* Spiegelbild
reformed *137* gebessert
refreshment *182* Erfrischung
refugee *55* Flüchtling
to refuse *16* ablehnen, sich
weigern, widerstehen
regarding *108* bezüglich,
betreffend
to register *139* registrieren
registered *121* registriert,
eingetragen
registration papers *142t* Papiere,
Zulassung
to regret *143, 187* bedauern,
bereuen
rehabilitation *138* Rehabilitation

to reintroduce *138* wieder
einführen
to reject *105* ablehnen
rejected *116* abgelehnt
to relate to *100* sich beziehen auf
relationship *38* Verhältnis
relative *113* Verwandte/r
relatively *110* verhältnismäßig
to relax *156* (sich) entspannen,
ausruhen
relaxed *65* entspannt, locker
relevance *163* Bedeutung, Wert
relevant *57* relevant, wichtig
reliable *28* zuverlässig
to rely on *99* angewiesen sein auf,
sich verlassen auf
to remain *51* bleiben
remark *57* Bemerkung
to remark *159* bemerken
remorse *137* Reue
renewable *69* erneuerbar
renovating *174* Renovieren
to rent *38t* mieten
to repair *177* reparieren
to repay *28* zurückzahlen
repentant *137* reuig, reumütig
repetition *82* Wiederholung
repetitive *163* (sich) wiederholend
to rephrase *82* anders ausdrücken,
umformulieren
to replace *8* ersetzen
reply *92* Antwort, Erwiderung,
Reaktion
report *76* Bericht, Reportage
represented *183* vertreten
repugnant *136* widerlich
to request *78* anfordern, bitten
(um)
request *107* Bitte, Aufforderung,
Wunsch
to require *13, 165* erfordern
required *82* erforderlich
required: to be required
to *96* müssen
requirement *12* Erfordernis
to rescue *96* retten
research *19* Forschung
researcher *59* Forscher/in
to resist *140* Widerstand leisten
gegen, sich etw widersetzen
resort *85, 103* Ferien-, Erholungs-,
Urlaubsort
resource *89* Reserve, Ressource
resources *83* Mittel
respect *103* Respekt, Achtung
respectful *186* respektvoll
to respond to *82* reagieren auf
respondent *130* Befragte/r
response *177* Reaktion, Antwort
responsibility *88, 93* Verantwor-
tung, Verantwortlichkeit
restatement *102* Neuformulierung
restriction *186* Einschränkung

result 71 Resultat, Ergebnis
retail 161 Einzelhandel
retailer 29 Einzelhändler/in
to retire 117 in Rente/Pension gehen
retired 89 pensioniert, im Ruhestand
retirement 153 (Eintritt in den) Ruhestand, Pensionierung
retribution 138 Vergeltung
return 74 (hin und) zurück
reunion 59 Treffen, Wiedersehen
to reuse 53 wieder verwenden
to reveal 180 enthüllen, zeigen, zum Vorschein bringen
revelation 146 Enthüllung
revision 94 Wiederholung
revolution 80 Revolution
to reward 131t belohnen
to rewrite 78 umschreiben, neu schreiben
rhetorical 82 rhetorisch
rich 180 reich(haltig)
ride 38t Tour, Fahrt, Flug
to ridicule 143 verspotten
rise 81t Anstieg
risk: at risk 59 gefährdet
rival 12 Gegner/in, Rivale, -lin
to rival 13 konkurrieren
road: to have been down that road 16 etwas schon erlebt haben
roadside 73, 167 (am) Straßenrand
robber 162 Räuber/in
robbery 139, 174 Raub, Überfall
role 15 Rolle
role model 115 Vorbild
Roman 56 Römer/in
room: to have room 20 Platz haben
roommate 186 Zimmerkollege/-kollegin
rope 119 Seil, Tau
rotten 139 korrupt
rough 175, 189 rau, uneben, hart
roughly 36 ungefähr
route 67 Route, Strecke, Weg
routine 85 Routine, Ablauf
routinely 136 routinemäßig
row 28 Reihe
row 133 Streit
rowdy 127 laut, randalierend
to rub 118t reiben
to rule 136 entscheiden
to run out of 76 ausgehen
to run sth 156 etw leiten, führen
to run up debts 26 sich verschulden, Schulden anhäufen
runner-up 121 Zweite/r
run-up 159 Vorfeld
runway 121t Landebahn
rural 36 ländlich
rush hour 69 Hauptverkehrszeit, Berufsverkehr

S

to sack 96 entlassen, feuern
safety 73 Sicherheit
sake: for sb's sake 131t um jds willen
salary 85 Gehalt, Lohn
sale 29 Schlussverkauf
sales 26 Verkaufs-
sales figures 54 Verkaufszahlen
salesman 65 Verkäufer
salesperson 85 Verkaufsmitarbeiter/in, Verkäufer/in
sari 125 Sari (Kleidungsstück)
satellite 69 Satellit
satire 58 Satire
satnav 69 Satellitennavigation, Navi
saving 66 Einsparung, Ersparnis
to saw 178 sägen
to scald 153 (sich) verbrühen
to scan 36 überfliegen, absuchen
scandalous 144 skandalös
scarcity 111 Knappheit
scary 37 unheimlich, beängstigend
scenery 174 Landschaft
sceptical 28 skeptisch
schedule 186 Zeitplan
scholarship 189 Stipendium
school-leaver 25 Schulabgänger/in
schoolwork 7 Hausaufgaben
schoolyard 118t Schulhof
sci-fi 58 Science-Fiction, wissenschaftlich-utopisch
to score a goal 8 ein Tor erzielen
to scream 16 schreien
to screen 56 ausstrahlen
sculpture 83 Plastik, Skulptur
to seal off 134 absperren, abriegeln
seaside 85 Bade-, Strand-, See-
seasonal 85 Saison-
second-hand 27 gebraucht
secret 16 geheim
secretarial course 86 Sekretariatskurs
sector 106, 174 Sektor, Bereich
secular 133 weltlich
secure 64 sicher
security 102 Sicherheit
security check 38t Sicherheitskontrolle
seed 139, 178 Samen(korn), Kern
to seek 99 suchen
segregation 129 Rassentrennung
seldom 9 selten
to select 93 auswählen
self-esteem 169 Selbstachtung, -wertgefühl
selfish 131t egoistisch
senior 37 Schüler/in im letzten Schuljahr
sense 40 Sinn, Gefühl

sense: to make no sense 59 nicht sinnvoll sein
sensible 31 vernünftig
sensitive 98 empfindlich
sensitivity 133 Sensibilität
sentenced 174 verurteilt
separate 146 getrennt
sequence 35 Episode, Sequenz
series 56 Serie
seriousness 143 Ernst(haftigkeit)
servant 162 Dienstmädchen
to serve 11 servieren
service 44 (Bus-/Zug-)Verbindung
session 12 Treffen, Termin
to set to work 12 ans Werk gehen
to set up 47 begründen
set: to be set in 75 spielen in
setting 128 Szenerie, Schauplatz
several 25 mehrere, einige
severe 80 ernst, schwer, stark
to sew 177 nähen
shade 119 Schattierung
to shake 98 schütteln
shareholder 99 Aktionär/in
sharp 51 rasch, schnell, stark
sheet 80 Platte, Decke
shelf 31 Regal
shelf life 149 Haltbarkeit
shelf-stacker 33 Regalauffüller/in
shelter 189 Heim, Unterkunft
shift 186 Schicht
shine 40 glänzen
ship 131t verschiffen, transportieren
shiver 12 Zittern
shmolitics 123 Frei erfundenes Wort = shmo (Schwachkopf) + politics (Politik)
shocked 65 schockiert
shoelace 43 Schnürsenkel
shoplifter 29 Ladendieb/in
shoplifting 29 Ladendiebstahl
shopping mall 38 Einkaufszentrum
shopping trolley 26 Einkaufswagen
shore 40 Ufer
shortage 93, 113, 152 Fehlen, Mangel, Knappheit
to shorten 61 (ver)kürzen
shortlisted 48 in der engeren Wahl
to shovel 178 schaufeln, schippen
to showcase 133 zur Schau stellen
showcase 156 Vorstellung
to shrink 130 schrumpfen, zurückgehen
to shut up 62 den Mund halten
sighted 165 sehend
signal 73 Signal
signal 165 Ampel
silk 26 Seide
simile 82 Vergleich
since 31 seit
single mum 83 allein erziehende Mutter

single-issue agenda *122* Ein-Themen-, auf ein Thema beschränkte Tagesordnung
to sink *16* sinken
to sit back *30* sich zurückhalten, sich zurücklehnen
site *26* Website
skill *7* Fähigkeit, Geschick
skint *88t* pleite
skyline *37* Silhouette
skyscraper *37* Wolkenkratzer
slave *96* Sklave/Sklavin
sleepy *41* müde
slice *83, 178* Stück, Scheibe
to slide *139* (ab)rutschen, (ab)sacken
slight *47* leicht
slightly *164, 165* leicht
slim *168* schlank
slot *47* Termin
snack bar *156* Imbissstube
to snort *124* sniffen, schnupfen
snow *178* Schnee
social life *30* Sozialkontakte
social services *117* Sozialamt, Sozialdienste
social worker *93, 124, 186* Sozialarbeiter/in
soft drink *64* alkoholfreies Getränk
soft sell *50* zurückhaltende Verkaufstechnik
software *19* Software, Programme
solar *76* Sonnen-, Solar-
solar heating *88t* Solarheizung
solicitor *119* (Rechts-)Anwalt/Anwältin
solution *53, 70* Lösung, Ausweg
somehow *76* irgendwie
songwriter *123* Texter
sorrow *180* Trauer, Kummer, Sorge(n)
to sort *32, 162, 189* sortieren; Art
source *69* Quelle
sovereignty *111* Souveränität, Unabhängigkeit
spade *132* Spaten
spare part *152t* Ersatzteil
sparingly *103* sparsam
special offer *18* Sonderangebot
specialist *104* speziell, Fach-
to specialize in *106* sich spezialisieren auf
species *149* Art(en)
to speculate *141* spekulieren, Vermutungen anstellen
speech bubble *6* Sprechblase
speeding *142* Geschwindigkeits-überschreitung
spelling *62* Rechtschreibung
spoiled *159* verdorben
sponsor *46* Sponsor/in
to sponsor *48* finanziell unterstützen

sponsorship *45* finanzielle Unterstützung
to spread *49* (sich) verbreiten
spy *58* Spion/in, Spionage-
to squash *183* zunichtemachen
stability *111* Stabilität
stabilization *80* Stabilisierung
stable *47* fest
staff *26, 173, 186* Personal, Angestellte, Mitarbeiter/innen
to stage *133* veranstalten
stamp *154* Briefmarke
to stand for sth *51* für etw stehen
standard of living *81t* Lebensstandard
to stare *126* starren
to starve yourself *17* hungern
state *67* (Bundes-)Staat
statement *13* Aussage
statistical *51* statistisch
to stay up *30* aufbleiben
steady *51* stetig, fest, regelmäßig
steel-frame *40* Stahlträger
to step *167* treten
stepmother *163* Stiefmutter
stereotype *12* Klischee
stereotyping *163* Vorurteile gegen-über anderen beruhend auf Vorstellungsklischees
still *186* trotzdem, (immer) noch
stitch *139* Stich
to stock *146* führen, anbieten
stock control *86* Lagersteuerung, Lagerkontrolle
to store *150* lagern, aufbewahren
stormy *82* stürmisch
straight *165* gerade
stranger *59* Fremde/r
to strap *137* anschnallen, festbinden
streetwise *180* gerissen, gewieft
strength *76* Kraft, Stärke
to strengthen *41* stärken
stress-free *156* stressfrei
stressful *47* stressig, anstrengend
stretcher *12* Trage
string *178* Schnur, Bindfaden
structure *41* Gebäude, Struktur, Aufbau
to struggle *153* kämpfen
stuck: to be stuck *37* feststecken
studio *95* Studio
stuff *7* Zeug
to stuff *16* stopfen
sub-contractor *99* Subunternehmer
sub-heading *39* Untertitel
to subject *136* unterwerfen, aussetzen
subject *177* (Schul-)Fach
subsidized *89* subventioniert
substance *149* Substanz, Stoff
suburb *66* Vorort, Außenbezirk

to suffer *7* leiden
sufferer *17* Leidende/r
suffragette *119* Frauenrechtlerin
to suggest *48* vorschlagen, andeuten
suggestion *38* Vorschlag
suitable *8* passend, geeignet
to summarize *121t* zusammenfassen
supervision *147, 178* Überwachung, Aufsicht
superweed *152t* hoch resistentes Unkraut
to supply *48* liefern
supply *48* Lieferung
supply chain *99* Versorgungskette
to support *69* unterstützen
support *88t* Hilfe, Unterstützung
supporter *148* Anhänger/in
supportive *183* verständnisvoll
Supreme Court *136* Oberster Gerichtshof
surely *66* sicherlich
to surf *9* surfen
surprised *65* überrascht, erstaunt
surveillance *134* Überwachung
survey *6* Umfrage
to survive *56* überleben
suspended sentence *141* (Freiheits-)Strafe auf Bewährung
SUV *68* Geländewagen (mit Vierradantrieb)
to swallow *127* (ver)schlucken
to swap *15* tauschen
sweater *76* Pullover
to sweep *178* fegen, kehren
sweetie *12* Liebling, Schatz
switch *78* Schalter
to switch off *28* abschalten
sword *63, 177* Schwert
sympathetic *17* mitfühlend, verständnisvoll
sympathy *119* Mitgefühl, Mitleid

T

tactile *165* tastbar
tailback *66* Autoschlange
to take for granted *165* als selbstverständlich betrachten
to take off *24* starten
to take offence at *133* Anstoß nehmen an
take on *110* Einstellung zu
to take over *40* übernehmen
tale *180* Geschichte, Erzählung
talent *14* Talent
target *81t* Ziel(vorgaben), Soll(zahlen)
task *17* Aufgabe
to taste *164* kosten, probieren
tattoo *43* Tätowierung
tax *66* Steuer

taxpayer *40* Steuerzahler/in
to teach *174* lehren, unterrichten
teammate *12*
    Mannschaftskamerad/in
technique *51t* Methode, (Arbeits-)
    Technik
temper *126* Beherrschung
temperature *132* Temperatur
temperature *171* (erhöhte)
    Temperatur, Fieber
temporary *85* zeitlich befristet
to tend to do sth *103* dazu neigen,
    etw zu tun
tendency *149* Tendenz
terms *89* Bedingungen,
    Konditionen
terms: to come to terms
    with *118t* zurechtkommen mit
terrible *49* schrecklich, furchtbar
terrified *65* erschrocken
territory *43* Revier, Gebiet
terrorist *40* Terrorist/in
to test *7* prüfen
to text *30* SMS schicken, simsen
text message *6* SMS
textile *96* Textil-
thanks to *80* dank
theft *174* Diebstahl
theme *31* Thema
theme park *123* Freizeitpark
theoretical *107* theoretisch
therapist *186* Therapeut/in
therapy *181* Therapie, Behandlung
thief *59* Dieb/in
thirst *183* Durst
though *81t* doch, jedoch
threat *111* Bedrohung, Drohung
threaten *43* (be)drohen
thrill *26* Spannung
to throw away *177* wegwerfen
to throw out *56* hinauswerfen
to throw up *16* (sich) erbrechen
to tick *129* ankreuzen
tidal *80* Gezeiten-
tie *126* Krawatte, Schlips
tight *38t* knapp, eng
time off *21* Freizeit
time out *22* Freizeit
time: from time to time *29* von
    Zeit zu Zeit
time: in no time *16* im
    Handumdrehen
time-consuming *149* zeitraubend
timeline *52* Zeitachse
times *8* mal
timetable *42* Zeitplan, Fahrplan
tingling *16* kribbelnd, prickelnd
tired *163* müde
tiring *118* anstrengend, ermüdend
toddler *168* Krabbel-, Kleinkind
toilet pan *16* Kloschüssel
tolerance *139* Toleranz
tolerant *139, 166* tolerant

to tolerate *131t* tolerieren
tonne *76* Tonne
tool *159* Instrument, Mittel
top: over the top *61* übertrieben
tornado *189* Tornado
tourism *106* Tourismus,
    Fremdenverkehr
tourist guide *38* Reiseführer/in
toxic *150* giftig, toxisch
toy *161, 177* Spielzeug
tradition *40* Tradition
traditional *69* traditionell
traffic jam *66* (Verkehrs-)Stau
traffic signals *73* Verkehrsampel
trail *174* (Wander-)Weg
trainee *171, 177* Auszubildende/r,
    Praktikant/in
trainers *53* Turnschuhe
training *171* Ausbildung, Training
transmission *96* Übertragung
transplant *149* Transplantation
transport *65* Verkehr(smittel)
travel agency *32* Reisebüro
travel insurance *89*
    Reiseversicherung
traveller *182* Person ohne festen
    Wohnsitz
treat *159* Vergnügen, Leckerbissen
treatment *17* Behandlung
treaty *105* Vertrag
trekking *174* Wanderreiten,
    Trekking
to tremble *126* zittern
tremendous *129* gewaltig
trend *52* Trend
to trick *135* betrügen, hereinlegen
to trigger *149* auslösen
trivial *135* trivial, geringfügig
trouble *56* Schwierigkeiten, Ärger
troubled: to be troubled *136*
    beunruhigt sein
trunk *142t* Kofferraum
to trust *98* vertrauen
to try on *11* anprobieren
tub *16* Becher
tube *19* Tube
tuition *33* Unterricht
turbine *76* Turbine, Rad
turn: to take it in turns *33* sich
    abwechseln
turn: to turn down *76*
    herunterregeln
turnaround *139* Kehrtwendung,
    Umschwung
tutoring *189* Nachhilfe
TV panel *63* Fernsehrunde,
    Talkshow
twice *80* zweimal, doppelt
to twist *12* (ver)drehen
to twist *63* verdrehen
typical *109* typisch

U

ultimate *118t* ultimativ
ultimately *189* schließlich, letzten
    Endes
unavailable *72* nicht verfügbar
unblinking *12* unbewegt
uncanny *137* ungeheuer,
    unheimlich
unclear *129* unklar
uncool *22* uncool
uncountable *19* nicht zählbar
uncultivated *150* brachliegend
undemocratic *110* undemokratisch
to underestimate *63*
    unterschätzen
to underline *62* unterstreichen
underlined *8* unterstrichen
underprivileged *189*
    unterprivilegiert
understandable *21* verständlich
to undertake sth *177* (sich)
    vornehmen
unelected *110* nicht gewählt
unemployment *40* Arbeitslosigkeit
unexpected *180* unerwartet
unfamiliar *165* unbekannt
unfortunate *63* unglücklich,
    bedauerlich
unhurt *132* unverletzt
uniformity *129* Gleichmäßigkeit
unintentional *151* unabsichtlich
union *89* Gewerkschaft
unique *174, 180* einzigartig,
    einmalig
to unite *112* vereinigen
universal *163* allgemein, universell
unless *69* wenn nicht
unluckily *29* unglücklicherweise
unnecessary *62* unnötig
unpaid *107* unbezahlt
unreliable *76* unzuverlässig
unspecified *20* unbestimmt
unsure *165* unsicher, ungewiss
unusual *59* ungewöhnlich
unwaged *180* ohne Einkommen
up: to be up for *58t* bereit sein für,
    Lust haben auf
upbringing *117* Erziehung
to upgrade *86* erweitern,
    verbessern
to upload *143* (ins Internet) stellen
upset *65* bestürzt, entsetzt
to upset *162* verwirren, ärgern
urban *36* städtisch
urgent *48* dringend, eilig
useful *159* nützlich
user *59* Anwender/in, Benutzer/in

V

valid *134* gültig
valley *78* Tal

valuable *7* wertvoll
value *28* Wert
variety *40* Vielfalt
various *65* verschieden
to vary *45* variieren
vast *147* riesig, ungeheuer
vegetable *83, 168* Gemüse
vehicle *73* Fahrzeug
vehicle papers *134* Wagenpapiere
venturer *174* Abenteurer/in
verdict *141* Urteil, Beurteilung
verse *123* Vers, Strophe
version *79* Version, Fassung
vertical *68* senkrecht, vertikal
vicious circle *123* Teufelskreis
victim *135* Opfer
victory *136* Sieg
violence *119* Gewalt
violent *7* gewalttätig
viral *49* viral, Virus-
virtual *26* virtuell
virtually *134* praktisch, nahezu
visa *24* Visum
vision *80* Vision, Vorausschau
visual *68* visuell, optisch
vivid *163* lebhaft
vocational *87, 171* in der beruf-
   lichen Ausbildung, beruflich,
   Berufs-
voice *163* Stimme
voluntary *7* freiwillig
volunteer *156, 189*
   Ehrenamtliche/r
to vomit *16* erbrechen
to vote *56* abstimmen, wählen
voter *105* Wähler/in
vulnerable *93* wehrlos, verletzlich

W

wage *131t* Lohn
wages *88* Lohn, Löhne
waiter *17* Kellner, Ober
walkability *73, 165* Benutzbarkeit
   zu Fuß
walkable *73* zu Fuß erreichbar
walking stick *177* Spazierstock
to wander *132* (ziellos)
   herumlaufen
wardrobe *26* Kleiderschrank,
   Garderobe
warehouse *140* Lager(halle)
warming *80* Erwärmung
warmth *98* Wärme
warning *82* Warnung
warrior *12* Krieger
washing powder *116* Waschpulver
waste *69* Abfall
wasteful *49* verschwenderisch
to watch out *24* aufpassen
to water *178* wässern, gießen
waterfall *37* Wasserfall
wave *40* Welle
weakness *99* Schwäche
weatherman *24* Meteorologe
to weed *178* (Unkraut) jäten
to weed out *139* aussondern,
   -merzen
weekday *9* Wochentag
to weigh up *102* abwägen
welfare *182* Fürsorge, Soziales;
   Fürsorge-, Sozial-
well-lit *162* hell erleuchtet
well-trodden path *183* viel
   beschrittener Weg
whatever *58* was (auch) immer
wheelchair *73* Rollstuhl
white-collar *89* Schreibtisch-, Büro-

wicked *162* bösartig
widening *111* Erweiterung
willing *156, 131* gewillt,
   bereit(willig)
window ledge *162* Fensterbank,
   -brett
wise *80* weise, klug
within *40* innerhalb
wolf *162* Wolf
to wonder *56* sich fragen, sich
   wundern
wooden *162, 177* hölzern, Holz-
woodland *123* Wald(gebiet)
word of mouth *49*
   Mundpropaganda
to work oneself up *128* sich
   aufregen
to work out *51t* trainieren
workforce *89* Belegschaft
workplace *86* Arbeitsplatz
worried *78* besorgt
worried: to be worried *59*
   befürchten
worthwhile *7* der Mühe wert
wound *118t* Wunde
wreck *132* (Auto-)Wrack
to wrestle *12* ringen
wrestler *13* Ringer/in
wrongdoing *110* Fehlverhalten

XYZ

to yell *37* schreien
yield *149* Ertrag
Yours faithfully *106* Mit
   freundlichen Grüßen
Youth council *156* Jugendkomitee
zero *69* Null
zone *69* Zone, Bereich

Geographical names

Abilene ['æbəli:n] — Abilene

Africa ['afrɪkə] — Afrika

Alexandria [ˌælɪg'zɑːndrɪə] — Alexandria

America [ə'merɪkə] — Amerika

Antarctic [ænt'ɑːktɪk] — die Antarktis

Arizona [ærɪ'zəʊnə] — Arizona

Asia ['eɪʃə] — Asien

Atlanta [ət'læntə] — Atlanta

Austin [ˌtɪm 'ɒstɪn] — Austin

Australia [ɒ'streɪlɪə] — Australien

Austria ['ɒstrɪə] — Österreich

Bangalore [ˌbæŋgə'lɔː] — Bangalore

Belgium ['beldʒəm] — Belgien

Bengal [ˌben'gɔːl] — Bengalen

Big Apple [ˌbɪd 'æpl] — Spitzname für New York

Brazil [brə'zɪl] — Brasilien

Bristol ['brɪstl] — Bristol

Britain ['brɪtn] — Großbritannien

Broadway ['brɔːdweɪ] — Broadway (Straßenname)

Bronx [brɒŋks] — Bronx

Brooklyn ['brʊklɪn] — Brooklyn

Brussels ['brʌslz] — Brüssel

Bulgaria [bʌl'geərɪə] — Bulgarien

California [ˌkælə'fɔːnɪə] — Kalifornien

Canada ['kænədə] — Kanada

Cape Town ['keɪptaʊn] — Kapstadt

(the) Caribbean [ðə ˌkærə'biːən] — (die) Karibik

Central America [ˌsentrəl ə'merɪkə] — Mittelamerika

Chicago [ʃɪ'kɑːgəʊ] — Chicago

China ['tʃaɪnə] — China

Cologne [kə'ləʊn] — Köln

Colorado [ˌkɒlə'rɑːdəʊ] — Colorado

Dublin ['dʌblɪn] — Dublin

East Asia [ˌiːst 'eɪʃə] — Ostasien

East River [ˌiːst 'rɪvə] — East River

eastern Europe [ˌiːstən 'jʊərəp] — Osteuropa

Eighth Ave [ˌeɪtθ 'ævənjuː] — Eighth Ave (Straßenname)

England ['ɪŋglənd] — England

Europe ['jʊərəp] — Europa

Finland ['fɪnlənd] — Finnland

Florida ['flɒrɪdə] — Florida

France [frɑːns] — Frankreich

Galax ['gæləks] — Galax

Georgia ['dʒɔːdʒə] — Georgia

Germany ['dʒɜːməni] — Deutschland

Greenland ['griːnlənd] — Grönland

Guatemala [ˌgwɑːtə'mɑːlə] — Guatemala

Harlem ['hɑːləm] — Harlem

Holland ['hɒlənd] — Holland

Houston ['hjuːstən] — Houston

Hudson River [ˌhʌdsn 'rɪvə] — Hudson River

Hull [hʌl] — Hull

Illinois [ˌɪlə'nɔɪ] — Illinois

India ['ɪndɪə] — Indien

Indonesia [ˌɪndəʊ'niːzɪə] — Indonesien

Iran [ɪ'rɑːn] — Iran

Ireland ['aɪələnd] — Irland

Italy ['ɪtəli] — Italien

Kings Street [ˌkɪŋz 'striːt] — Kings Street (Straßenname)

Latin America [ˌlætɪn ə'merɪkə] — Lateinamerika

Littleton ['lɪtltən] — Littleton

London ['lʌndən] — London

Los Angeles [lɒs 'ændʒəliːz] — Los Angeles

Luxemburg ['lʌksəmbɜːg] — Luxemburg

Manchester ['mæntʃɪstə] — Manchester

Manhattan [mæn'hætn] — Manhattan

(the) Mediterranean [ðə ˌmedɪtə'reɪnɪən] — Mittelmeer

Miami [maɪ'æmi] — Miami

Morocco [mə'rɒkəʊ] — Marokko

(the) Netherlands [ðə 'neðələndz] — die Niederlande

New Orleans [ˌnjuː ɔː'liːəns] — New Orleans

New York (NY) [ˌnjuː 'jɔːk] — New York

New York Bay [ˌnjuː jɔːk 'beɪ] — New Yorker Bucht

New York City [ˌnjuː jɔːk 'sɪti] — New York City

New Zealand [ˌnjuː 'ziːlənd] — Neuseeland

Norfolk ['nɔːfək] — Norfolk

North America [ˌnɔːθ ə'merɪkə] — Nordamerika

Norway ['nɔːweɪ] — Norwegen

Norwich ['nɒrɪdʒ] — Norwich

Oak Street [ˌəʊk 'striːt] — Oak Street (Straßenname)

Oregon ['ɒrɪgən] — Oregon

Oxford ['ɒksfəd] — Oxford

Paris ['pærɪs] — Paris

Perryton ['perɪtən] — Perryton

(the) Philippines [ðə 'fɪləpiːnz] — die Philippinen

Phoenix ['fiːnɪks] — Phoenix

Queens [kwiːnz] — Queens

Richmond ['rɪtʃmənd] — Richmond

Rio Grande [ˌriːəʊ 'grænd] — Rio Grande

Rome [rəʊm] — Rom

Route 66 [ˌruːt ˌsɪksti 'sɪks] — Route 66 (Straßenverbindung zur US-amerikanischen Westküste)

Russia ['rʌʃə] — Russland

San Bernando   *San Bernando*
  [sæn bə'næ014ndəʊ]

San Diego [ˌsæn di'eɪɡəʊ]   *San Diego*

San Francisco   *San Francisco*
  [ˌsæn frən'sɪskəʊ]

Seattle [si'ætl]   *Seattle*

Shanghai [ˌʃæŋ'haɪ]   *Shanghai*

Shropshire ['ʃrɒpʃə]   *Shropshire*

Silver Creek [ˌsɪlvə 'kriːk]   *Silver Creek*

South Africa [saʊθ 'æfrɪkə] *Südafrika*

South America   *Südamerika*
  [ˌsaʊθ ə'merɪkə]

Stafford ['stæfəd]   *Stafford*

Staten Island   *Staten Island*
  [ˌstætn 'aɪlənd]

Strasbourg ['stræzbɜːɡ]   *Straßburg*

Sweden ['swiːdn]   *Schweden*

Swindon ['swɪndən]   *Swindon*

Texas ['teksəs]   *Texas*

Tokyo ['təʊkiəʊ]   *Tokio*

Tucson ['tuːsɒn]   *Tucson*

Turkey ['tɜːki]   *Türkei*

Tuusula ['tuːsulɑ]   *Tuusula*

(the) UK [ðə ˌjuː 'keɪ]   *(das) Vereinigte Königreich*

(the) USA [ðə ˌjuː es 'eɪ] *(die) Vereinigten Staaten
                      von Amerika*

Vermont [və'mɒnt]   *Vermont*

Virginia [və'dʒɪniə]   *Virginia*

Wales [weɪlz]   *Wales*

Washington D.C.   *Washington D.C.*
  ['wɒʃɪŋtən ˌdiː 'siː]

Irregular verbs

be	was/were	been	*sein*		hurt	hurt	hurt	*verletzen*
beat	beat	beaten	*schlagen, besiegen*		keep	kept	kept	*behalten*
					know	knew	known	*kennen, wissen*
become	became	become	*werden*		lay	laid	laid	*legen*
begin	began	begun	*anfangen, beginnen*		lead	led	led	*führen*
					lean	leant/ leaned	leant/ leaned	*sich lehnen, sich beugen*
bend	bent	bent	*(sich) beugen*					
blow	blew	blown	*wehen, blasen, ziehen*		learn	learnt/ learned	learnt/ learned	*lernen*
break	broke	broken	*brechen*		leave	left	left	*abfahren, verlassen, weggehen*
breed	bred	bred	*sich vermehren, sich ausbreiten*					
					let	let	let	*lassen*
bring	brought	brought	*(mit)bringen*		lie	lay	lain	*liegen*
build	built	built	*bauen*		light	lit	lit	*anzünden, beleuchten*
burn	burnt/ burned	burnt/ burned	*(ver)brennen*					
					lose	lost	lost	*verlieren*
buy	bought	bought	*kaufen*		make	made	made	*machen*
catch	caught	caught	*fangen, fassen, erreichen*		mean	meant	meant	*meinen, bedeuten*
					meet	met	met	*treffen*
choose	chose	chosen	*(aus)wählen*		overcome	overcame	overcome	*überwinden, überwältigen*
come	came	come	*kommen*					
cost	cost	cost	*kosten*		override	overrode	overridden	*sich hinwegsetzen über*
cross-breed	cross-bred	cross-bred	*kreuzen*					
					panic	panicked	panicked	*in Panik geraten*
cut	cut	cut	*schneiden*		pay	paid	paid	*bezahlen*
deal	dealt	dealt	*versetzen, verteilen*		put	put	put	*setzen, stellen, legen*
dig	dug	dug	*graben*		quit	quit/ quitted	quit/ quitted	*verlassen, aufhören*
do	did	done	*tun, machen*					
draw	drew	drawn	*zeichnen*		read	read	read	*lesen*
dream	dreamt/ dreamed	dreamt/ dreamed	*träumen*		repay	repaid	repaid	*zurückzahlen*
					rewrite	rewrote	rewritten	*umschreiben*
drink	drank	drunk	*trinken*		ride	rode	ridden	*reiten, fahren*
drive	drove	driven	*fahren*		ring	rang	rung	*anrufen, läuten*
eat	ate	eaten	*essen*		rise	rose	risen	*(an)steigen*
fall	fell	fallen	*fallen*		run	ran	run	*laufen, rennen*
feed	fed	fed	*füttern, ernähren*		say	said	said	*sagen*
feel	felt	felt	*(sich) fühlen, empfinden*		see	saw	seen	*sehen*
					seek	sought	sought	*suchen*
fight	fought	fought	*kämpfen*		sell	sold	sold	*verkaufen*
find	found	found	*finden*		send	sent	sent	*senden, schicken*
fit	fit/fitted	fit/fitted	*passen, entsprechen, anbringen*		set	set	set	*setzen, stellen*
					shake	shook	shaken	*schütteln*
					shine	shone	shone	*scheinen, glänzen*
fly	flew	flown	*fliegen*		show	showed	shown	*zeigen*
forbid	forbade	forbidden	*verbieten*		shrink	shrank	shrunk	*schrumpfen, zurückgehen*
forget	forgot	forgotten	*vergessen*					
get	got	got (*AE* gotten)	*bekommen*		shut	shut	shut	*schließen*
					sing	sang	sung	*singen*
give	gave	given	*geben*		sink	sank	sunk	*sinken*
go	went	gone	*gehen, fahren*		sit	sat	sat	*sitzen*
grow	grew	grown	*wachsen*		sleep	slept	slept	*schlafen*
hang	hung	hung	*hängen*		slide	slid	slid	*(ab)rutschen, (ab)sacken*
have	had	had	*haben*					
hear	heard	heard	*hören*		smell	smelt/ smelled	smelt/ smelled	*riechen*
hide	hid	hidden	*(sich) verstecken*					
hit	hit	hit	*schlagen*		speak	spoke	spoken	*sprechen*
hold	held	held	*halten, festhalten*					

spell	spelt/ spelled	spelt/ spelled	*buchstabieren*
spend	spent	spent	*ausgeben, verbringen*
spread	spread	spread	*(sich) verbreiten*
stand	stood	stood	*stehen*
steal	stole	stolen	*stehlen*
swim	swam	swum	*schwimmen*
take	took	taken	*nehmen*
teach	taught	taught	*unterrichten, beibringen*

tell	told	told	*sagen, erzählen*
think	thought	thought	*denken*
throw	threw	thrown	*werfen*
under- stand	under- stood	under- stood	*verstehen*
wake	woke	woken	*aufwachen, aufwecken*
wear	wore	worn	*tragen*
win	won	won	*gewinnen*
write	wrote	written	*schreiben*

Quellenverzeichnis

Titel: GettyRF (2), Corbis RF, istockphoto

RF photos:
Alamy: S. 6/2/E. Audras, S. /3/Itani, S. 7/4/IS503; S. 16/T. Kroeger, S. 46/moodboard, S. 52/
K. Brofsky, S. 77/2/J. Pelaez, S. 85/2/BananaStock, S. 85/4/EV107, S. 85/5/R. McVay, S. 85/6/
IS147, S. 89/2/J. Hollingsworth, S. 89/3/Bananastock, S. 95/3/WidStock, S. 105/3/BigCheese
Special, S. 96/1/J. Woodhouse, S. 96/5/SomosGroup1, S. 106/Niehoff, S. 110/K. Glubish, S. 111/1/
IS945, S. 111/2/rubberball, S. 111/3Radius images, S. 111/4/J. Hollingsworth, S. 116/2/BananaStock,
S. 116/3/IS732, S. 120/1/Shoosh, S. 123/indykb, S. 140/2/Photodisc, S. 140/3/S. Marcus, S. 183/
BananaStock; Corbis: S. 14/moodboard, S. 17/1, S. 93/2/T. Grill, S. 113, S. 141/5/R. Meinychuk;
Comstock: S.17/2; Istock: S. 6/1/3; S. 7/1/2, S. 37/2, S. 159/1; Maly, V.: S. 43/2, S. 95/2, S. 99/
1/2; Masterfile: S. 72/1/2, S. 114; Shutterstock: S. 22/1/2, S. 26/1/2, S. 30/1, S. 35/3/4/6,
S. 43/4/6, S. 50/1–5, S. 58, S. 66/1/3/4/5, S. 73, S. 76/3/4, S. 77/1, S. 95/1, S. 96/1/3, S. 99/3,
S. 103, S. 105/1, S. 115/2–8, S. 124, S. 140/1, S. 141/4, S. 143, S. 145/2/4/6, S. 172, S. 181

RM photos:
Actionpress: S. 145/7; Advertising Archives: S. 45/1/2/3/5, S. 53; Alamy: S. 30/2/J. West, S. 35/5/
BLimages, S. 37/1/D. Frates, S. 40/P. Bennett, S. 43/1/S. Hoogerhuis, S. 43/3/S. Sprague, S. 66/2/
Travelshots, S. 71/Kiedrowski, S. 76/1/G. Williams, S. 76/3/J. Moers, S. 89/4/zoonar.com, S. 94/
Pixland0907, S. 116/1/ClassicStock, S. 123/P. Corr, S. 127/1/dbtravel, S. 139/1/H. Threlfall,
S. 139/2/D. Grossman, S. 146/A. Segre, S. 150/R. Rivett; S. 156/A. Sherratt; Condé Nast Publications:
S. 129 Allure Cover; Corbis: S. 12/1/Emely, S. 12/2/Duomo, S. 89/1, S. 93/1/J. hollingsworth,
S. 96/3/E. Jansson; Content Mine International: S. 43/5/KPA; Fotofinder: S. 16/2/Andreas Buck,
S. 26/Fotoagtur Magics/P. Schatz, S. 30/Weisflog, S. 35/2/S. Frances; S. 73/Bildmaschine.de/
M. Begsteiger, S. 76/2/ImageSource, S. 83/plainpicture, S. 85/1/A1Pix, S. 85/3/Matthias Stolt,
S. 86/Mediacolors, S. 93/4/image.de, S. 105/2/F1online; S. 115/tranistArchiv/T. Roetting, S. 120/2/
Caro/Teschner, S. 165/Bilderbox, S. 168/Keystone/N. Schulz, S. 177/P. Sudermann, S. 186/
photothek, S. 189/1/A. Hess, S. 189/2/S. Schupfner; PictureAlliance: S. 35/7, S. 56/1/GMTV, S. 53/
dpa-Zentralbild, S. 56/2/J. Ryan, S. 75/2/3/4, S. 93/3/B0508_Polfoto, S. 105/4/R. Hirschberger,
S. 105/5/dpa, S. 119/1/PA, S. 119/2/L. Ruymen, S. 121/EPA, S. 127/2, S. 129/2/A. Teich,
S. 129/3/I. West, S. 131/1/L. Stringer, S. 131/2/G. Caddick, S. 136/P. Buck, S. 143/1/AFP, S. 143/3/
DB Thüringer Allgemeine, S. 143/3/PA-5322625, S. 145/1/EPA, S. 145/5/P. Kneffel, S. 153/KPA;
S. 156/6PA/MAXPPP; Mondolithic Studios: S. 79/Kenn Brown; Ullstein-Bild: S. 137; S. 75 akg-images/
Album/TOUCHSTONE PICTURES

Cartoons: cartoonStock.com: S. 62, S. 65, S. 68, S. 122; Martyn Ford, LGP, Brighton: S. 92; Julie Brown,
Tribune Media Service Inc.: S. 132; The Cartoonist Group: S. 132; Punch Ltd: S. 135

Texte: S. 59: Adapted and abridged from *Things you wouldn't tell your mother* by Alison George,
New Scientist 16/09/06, p. 50; S. 63: www.theage.com.au/news; S. 73: *www.walkinginfo.org*,
S. 83: *www.abc.net.au/gardening*, S. 93: *www.migrationcommission.org*, *www.cbsnews.com*,
www.smh.com, *www.guardian.co.uk*, S. 103: *www.responsibletravel.com*, S. 113: *www.dw-world.de*,
S. 126/127: Hanif Kureishi, *Love in a Blue Time*, Faber and Faber, 1997, S. 133: news.bbc.co.uk;
S. 136: Based on *http://en.wikipedia.org/wiki/Karla_Faye_Tucker*, S. 143: *www.theage.com.au*;
S. 146: abridged from *British supermarkets call for a boycott of 'cloned' meat and milk*, Daily Mail
10.01.07, S. 153: *www.theage.com.au*, www.magiplug.com; S. 156:www.princes-trust.org.uk,
S. 159: *www.raisingkids.co.uk*, S. 162: *www.mainlesson.com*, S. 165: *www.walkinginfo.org*, S. 168:
lifeandhealth.guardian.co.uk, S. 172: *www.ndna.org.uk*, S. 174: *www.raleighinternational.org*, S. 177:
The role of purposeful work in a Waldorf Kindergarten by Karen Smith, S. 180: *www.guardian.co.uk*,
S. 183: guardian.co.uk, S. 186: *www.layouth.com*; S. 189: *www.thekidshalloffame.com*

European Union